KNIGHTS OF THE SKIES

ARMOUR PROTECTION FOR
BRITISH FIGHTING AEROPLANES

"In the war of 1914–18 air power was still too much in its infancy to have a decisive influence in its own right. And this, I think, is important to remember, because it means that the war of 1939–45 was really the first air war. And so when we look back on our errors of judgement and the shortcomings in our planning in those later days before the outbreak of World War II ..., do not let us forget that we had, to all practical intents and purposes, no experience on which to base our judgements. We, in the Air Staff in London in those days, made many mistakes. ... . But, in view of our almost total lack of relevant experience, we may perhaps claim that what is really surprising is not how wrong we turned out to be, but – once we got the weapons of the necessary quality in adequate numbers – how right!"

Marshal of the Royal Air Force Sir John Slessor, GCB, DSO, MC

From *Half a Century of Air Power,* a lecture to a course in Military History, Ohio State University, August 1956, page 49, published as Chapter 3 in *The Great Deterrent* by Cassell & Company Ltd, 1957.

KNIGHTS
OF THE SKIES

ARMOUR PROTECTION FOR
BRITISH FIGHTING AEROPLANES

Michael C Fox

Air Research Publications

First published 2006.
Air Research Publications
PO Box 223, Walton–on–Thames,
Surrey, KT12 3YQ
England

Printed in England by
Antony Rowe.

ISBN 1-871187-50-8

Contents

Foreword by Group Captain Billy Drake
DSO, DFC & Bar, DFC (US), RAF

The story of armour protection brings back poignant memories for me – quite literally! After all, one day in the May of 1940, as the German Blitzkrieg swept into France and the air battles against the Luftwaffe became desperate, the armour plate fitted behind the seat in my Hurricane probably saved my life! Earlier, in the November of 1939 and with the Second World War barely a few months old, we pilots of No 1 Squadron knew nothing of how our Commander-in-Chief, Sir Hugh Dowding, and his technical experts had struggled for years with the age-old problem of weight versus performance. Armour plate was heavy and they were reluctant to sacrifice performance – especially the speed and rate of climb we needed to catch enemy aircraft – for the questionable (as it seemed at the time) benefit that the armour, especially rear armour and the complications in fitting it, would provide! All we knew was that air fighting was fast becoming a very dangerous business and that the pilots in our neighbouring squadrons operating the poorly defended Fairey Battle bombers at least had armour plate to protect their backs – we thought that we deserved it too, and proved that our Hurricanes could carry it without difficulty. Whether the initiative of our Squadron Commander was really the direct cause, or just happened to coincide with our turn in a phased installation programme, we soon got our armour – thankfully!

Billy Drake in January 2005 with the armour head plate that at least partially protected him. It was recovered from the wreck site in France by Steve Vizard of Airframe Assemblies Ltd, who arranged for it to be cleaned up, mounted, and who loaned it for the purpose of the photograph.

Armour protection is not something that has previously attracted more than occasional passing interest in military aviation literature – but it is now evident that there is a story to be told. The author, Michael Fox, has therefore done a useful service to the history of the times and to those who took part by piecing together in this book, his first, a chain of events that goes back, surprisingly, to the years just before even the First World War. More surprising to me, though, are the revelations about the thinking in the RAF hierarchy from about 1935 onwards – thinking that delayed the fitting of full armour protection until the bullets were actually flying around the ears of pilots like myself! With the hindsight of nearly 70 years, it is remarkable to think that fighter combats were thought in the 1930s, even by Dowding, to be impossible between the fast "modern" fighters of the day. The air Battles of France and Britain soon proved such an idea to be wrong. The much later events in the skies over Korea, Vietnam and the Falkland Islands have since confirmed that, however high their performance, aircraft will always find ways to fight each other in the struggle for air supremacy. But when we took our Hurricanes to France in September 1939, the German fighters were still based in their own country and did not have the range to escort their bombers in attacks on Britain. Home-based fighters therefore were expected only to have to contend with bombers, while we in France could expect to meet enemy fighters from just across the frontier some 200 km away. Consequently, the rear armour designed for Hurricanes was supposed, when we finally got it, to be removable. We might need it when there were enemy fighters around, who might (supposedly, only if we were careless) attack us from behind, but the Hurricanes (and Spitfires) still based in Britain would not need it – what they needed most was speed to catch the bombers and attack them from astern, so the weight of rear armour was to be sacrificed. As events turned out, we never did get rid of the rear armour – for which many of us, then and later, had reason to be grateful!

Billy Drake
March 2005

Author's Preface, Acknowledgements and Dedication

This is the story of how, for the Royal Air Force in the Second World War, the fitting of armour protection to fighting aircraft in general and fighters in particular came to be one of those "close run things" of which the British seem famed. It is, or at least is intended to be, just a story – a story that encompasses the attitudes, views and decisions of some of the people behind the historic events of British military flying in the years from before the First World War up to the first year or so of WW II. Where parallel events in other nations are touched upon for purposes of comparison with the RAF, or the Royal Flying Corps as earlier it was, these are intended simply to place what the British were doing in the context of what was going on in other air forces. There is no intention, here, to provide a fully researched and exhaustive catalogue, aircraft by aircraft and mark by mark, of the fitting of armour protection – nor is it in any sense a treatise on the metallurgy of armour plate. I am content to leave such details to others – should they so desire. Having been a metallurgist myself once upon a time, I am quite pleased that I have managed to avoid all but a very few minor metallurgical details throughout the text.

In putting together the story of armour protection I have chosen, wherever appropriate – and at my sole discretion – to use words recorded at the time. A consequence is that some of the phraseology and punctuation that I suppose to have been typical of (at least) service life in the times concerned may appear, by modern standards (so far as they may be recognised), somewhat dated. I make no apology for this – nor, I believe – should I. The words recorded at the time give a flavour of the time and must, in my view, better represent the thoughts and judgements of those responsible – even if now they occasionally seem to be a little muddled – than any interpretation that a modern writer can fairly impute other than by way of reasonable and respectful commentary.

The core of the book is primary source material in the National Archives of the Public Record Office, material that hitherto seems to have been largely – if not entirely – unpublished. However, some frustrating gaps in the archived documentation have, perhaps inevitably, been discovered and I trust that the reader will view these with understanding wherever they may appear evident. After all, the story is some 60 to 90 years old. I have particularly appreciated the help of Clive Richards and his colleagues at the MOD Air Historical Branch (RAF) in plugging some of the gaps, but a few have evaded search, particularly in relation to the firing trials on Hurricane and Blenheim aircraft in the 1939–1940 period. If any reader has information that might fill in some of the gaps for any future edition of this book, I would be delighted to hear from him or her.

Notwithstanding historical curiosity, this book is written with a sense of deep respect and admiration of all those who devoted their endeavours and their lives – in many cases quite literally – to the design, development and operation of fighting aircraft. It is not my intention to cast any slight whatsoever upon the memories and reputations of any of the people who are featured in the story. If there happen to be any hostages to fortune in the text that, inadvertently, might in some way give offence, this is entirely unintentional and I unreservedly apologise. The individuals involved were invariably working in difficult wartime and peacetime circumstances. They had to contend with many uncertainties and unknowns that were bound up not just with the domestic and international politics of the day (as if that might not have been enough) but with the tactics, strategies and weaponry of a mode of warfare that had to evolve incredibly rapidly during the space of two World Wars that together lasted some twelve years and spanned, with comparatively minor intervening skirmishes and one major civil war, little more than thirty years. The words of Marshal of the Royal Air Force Sir John Slessor, quoted at the beginning of this book, say it all.

Acknowledgements

No work of this type can be completed without the assistance and co-operation, directly or otherwise, of quite a large number of people and organisations and I am happy to acknowledge their contributions.

It was Paul Richey's book Fighter Pilot, published originally in 1941, that set me on the road to this story, though I cannot now explain exactly how or why. I read his book as a lad, was completely enthralled by it, and the memory of it has stayed with me ever since. I lost my original copy years ago, but discovered Cassell's new (2001) edition around the time that it was published. I can only say that the "Pussy" Palmer incident that Paul Richey recounts sparked something in my mind. I was, at the time, doing some research at the Public Record Office in Kew for a novel featuring military aviation and quite unexpectedly came across the document, reproduced in this book on page 22, that gives independent corroboration at least to the basic story of the incident. The rest, as they say, is (quite literally in this case) history.

One other particular incident deserves special mention. I was well into the book when, almost by accident, I came across the BBC Television programme Billy Drake and the Fighter Boys, that was first broadcast in 2004. I had already been thinking about where I could find a bit of Hurricane armour and there, on the screen, a bit was staring me in the face! Through the good offices of the producer of the programme, John Hayes-Fisher, at the BBC, I got in touch with both Billy Drake who had actually flown the Hurricane that was shot down in France during May 1940 and Steve Vizard who dug up the armour more than sixty years later during the making of the programme. Steve Visard, of Airframe Assemblies Ltd down on Isle of Wight, was wonderfully helpful – bearing in mind that I descended upon him quite out of the blue and as a complete unknown within his circle of crash site excavators, historic aircraft restorers and aviation buffs. He very trustingly loaned me the piece of armour that had been recovered from the site in France and even introduced me to the publisher of this book.

Billy Drake, a fighter pilot throughout the Second World War and beyond, was something else – in every sense. Gracious, charming and ever ready to help, his mind at the age of eighty–seven – when I actually came to meet him in January 2005 – was as sharp as a needle and he was still fit enough to be anticipating another Winter's skiing. As well as suggesting a few helpful changes to the text of my book and authorising the Foreword, Billy helped me in two particular ways that for me were vital. He provided me, through his experiences during the battle of France in 1940, with a context in which to complete the setting my story. More importantly, however, he set my mind at rest. For some time I had been struggling with an area of uncertainty, perhaps even discomfort. The material that I was putting together could in some ways be held to imply quite unintentional criticism of, in particular, someone whom the fighter pilots of the day regarded, by all accounts, with great affection – Air Chief Marshal Sir Hugh (later Lord) Dowding, Commander-in-Chief of Fighter Command from July 1936 until November 1940, just after the Battle of Britain. Billy assured me that in presenting the facts as they were recorded I should not be concerned and I naturally accepted that with some relief. I continue to trust that he was right!

Arthur Sagar, once I had located him in Canada through the kind assistance of Fred Aldworth at the Air Force Association of Canada, responded instantly and very helpfully with several photographs that I might be interested in using in the book – and also with a copy of his own fascinating book of wartime recollections (*Line Shoot*, which is anything but what the title implies!).

I have spent many days absorbed in the National Archives at the Public Record Office in Kew and wish to express my thanks to all the staff there for the marvellous and wonderfully efficient service that they provide. The one occasion when they failed to produce a file for my research was when (I concluded) the Air Historical Branch had called it back to investigate some of the gaps in the records for which I had sought assistance! I am particularly grateful to Paul Johnson, National Archives Image Library Manager, for the reproduction of numerous illustrations from the Archives and for permission to use them.

The reading room at the Royal Air Force Museum at Hendon has looked after me on several occasions and I am particularly grateful to Peter Elliott and all the staff there for their help in providing documents for my research and in answering queries. Likewise the staff at the Imperial War Museum, both in the Department of Printed Books and in the Photographic Archive, have always been ready to help in making available material for my research; I am particularly grateful to Mary P Wilkinson,

Acting Keeper, for the Imperial War Museum's permission to include in my book various extracts from H A Jones' official history of the First World War, The War in the Air, published originally by Clarendon Press and more recently by The Naval & Military Press Ltd and The Battery Press Inc, both in association with the Museum's Department of Printed books. Yvonne Oliver, also at the Imperial War Museum, kindly gave me permission to use numerous photographs from their archive and arranged for copies to be supplied.

Other permissions to use extracts and images from source documents and private collections, as well as the loan or gift of photographs and in some cases a few words of welcome encouragement, are acknowledged with grateful thanks from the following:

Juliet Atkin, Legal & Business Affairs Dept, Chrysalis Books Group Plc (German Aircraft of the First World War, Peter Gray & Owen Thetford; Vickers Aircraft since 1908, C F Andrews; British Aeroplanes 1914–18, J M Bruce; Vickers Aircraft since 1908, C F Andrews & E B Morgan).

Steve Birdsall in far away Australia (The B-17 Flying Fortress).

Heather Brennan, Permissions, American Institute of Aeronautics and Astronautics (Passive Defense – The Protective Armouring of Military Aircraft, Horace J Alter).

Dr Chris Chatfield, Air Britain (Historians) Ltd (Always Prepared, John Hamlin).

Bob Casari, author of Encyclopedia of US Aircraft, Part 1, 1908 to April 6, 1917. Bob, in addition to donating a photograph, was kind enough to read the relevant extracts from my book and suggest some corrections.

Christopher J Coleman, Newpro UK Limited (for Fountain Press) (Russian Civil and Military Aircraft 1884–1969, Heinz Nowarra & G R Duval).

Andrew Costerton, Flight International (various extracts reproduced with the kind permission of Flight International).

John Davies, Managing Director, Grub Street (Billy Drake, Fighter Leader, Billy Drake (with Shores, Christopher); The Sky their Battlefield, Trevor Henshaw).

Ian Drury, Publishing Director, Cassell & Co (Fighter Pilot, Paul Richey; Phoenix Triumphant, The Rise and Rise of the Luftwaffe, E R Hooton; The Great Deterrent, MRAF Sir John Slessor).

Suzanne Galle, Rights and Permissions, University Press of Kansas (The Roots of Blitzkrieg, James S Corum).

Lynn Gamma, Air Force Historical Research Agency, Maxwell Air Force, USA (Louis E Goodier Collection).

Cyndy and Mike Gilley, owners of Do You Graphics in Maryland USA, who supplied me with several images from the NASA archives as well as entertaining me in an exchange of Emails that were both helpful and friendly. Among their staff, Susan Stone actually captured the NARA images, Dottie Siders prepared the digital records and Denise Grogan did the finishing work for the final print-prepared files.

David A Giordino, Modern Military Records (NWCTM), US National Archives and Records Administration, for his help in identifying background material on the post WW1 development of American military aviation.

Nick Grant, Book Editor, Ian Allan Publishing (*Pictorial History of the French Air Force, Vol 1, 1909–1940*, André Van Haute).

Kate Igoe, Permissions Archivist, National Air and Space Museum, Archives Division, Smithsonian Institution (*A History of French Military Aviation*, Charles Christienne & Pierre Lissarague).

Philip Jarrett, who provided various photographs from his extensive collection.

Elaine Maruhn, Contracts and Permissions, University of Nebraska Press (*Arming the Luftwaffe*, Edward L Homze).

Professor John H Morrow Jr, Franklin Professor of History, University of Georgia (*The Great War in the Air. Military Aviation from 1909 to 1921*).

Tamryn North, Contracts Manager, Chrysalis Books Group Plc (for Salamander Books Ltd) (*The Battle of Britain*, Richard Townshend Bickers; *The Illustrated Directory of Fighting Aircraft of World War II*, Bill Gunston).

Michael Oakey, Editor, Aeroplane (various extracts), also for invaluable help and advice regarding the use of various Aeroplane images.

Arthur Owens, lately Subject Librarian, The Lanchester Archive, Coventry University, who provided a much needed photograph of Fred Lanchester.

Geoff Pentland, Manager, Kookaburra Technical Publications Pty Ltd (*Westland Whirlwind*, Bruce Robertson).

Holly Reed, Still Picture Reference, US National Archives and Records Administration.

Clive Richards and his colleagues at the MOD Air Historical Branch (RAF), already mentioned, whom I have pestered more than perhaps I ought but who have nevertheless patiently guided me into areas of the National Archives that I might otherwise never have discovered.

John Schuler, Lanchester Press (*Aircraft in Warfare*, F W Lanchester), who very kindly donated a copy of the latest edition of Fred Lanchester's book, an image from the book and pointed me in the direction of Coventry University in my search for a photograph

NOTE. For anyone who may be interested, the Lanchester Press has a web site at: www.lanchester.com

The new ISBN number for *Aircraft in Warfare* is: 1–57321–017–X.

Peter Waller, Publisher (Books), Ian Allan Publishing (*Bristol Blenheim*, Chaz Bowyer; *Air War over Spain*, Jesus Salar Larrázabal).

Nick Wetton, Permissions Administrator, Hodder Education (*The German Air Force in the Great War*, Georg Paul Neumann).

All reasonable attempts have been made to trace and seek permission from the owners of material quoted, reproduced, or referred to in this book, but in some cases the authors, publishers and/or other sources have not been found. The author and his publisher will be happy to receive information regarding untraced sources not properly acknowledged.

Dedication

This book is dedicated firstly to the honourable memories of all those men in the aircrews of fighting aircraft who played their parts so bravely in and between two World Wars, some of whom – knowingly or not – will have been saved from injury or death by the presence of armour protection in one form or another. Secondly – and by no means least – the book is dedicated to all those men and women who, mainly behind the scenes, contributed to the design and installation of schemes of armour protection that undoubtedly saved lives during the Wars.

I – Introduction
1 Armour, what armour?

Armour protection, mainly in the form of armoured glass windscreens and steel armour plate, was widely employed for the protection of fighting aircraft and their crews during World War II. Many war-time fliers will have had reason to be thankful for such "passive" protection as it is sometimes called. For example, this from an official war-time notice:

"SPITFIRE ARMOUR SAVES CANADIAN PILOT

The armour plated seat and sturdy construction of a Spitfire saved a Canadian pilot – Flight Lieutenant A.H. Sagar of Vancouver – from death when a cannon shell hit his aircraft during a sweep over the Dutch coast. The pilot was unhurt except that he landed with a splitting headache. Sagar was flying low over Holland looking for ground targets with three other Members of the City of Oshawa Squadron [416 Squadron, RCAF] when the cannon shell hit the fuselage and burst behind his seat. "The cockpit filled with smoke" said Flight Lieutenant Sagar, "and I thought the engine was on fire. The explosion blew my radio to bits and burst the panel over my head, but the kite held together and got me home." (1)

Flight Lieutenant (as he then was) Arthur Sagar of Vancouver standing beside his damaged Supermarine Spitfire after he had landed safely at RAF Coltishall on 13th November 1943. (Imperial War Museum, CE.110)

Art Sagar had begun his operational service with 421 Squadron RCAF in the April of 1942. He was appointed to command 443 Squadron RCAF in the September of 1944, after postings to 22 Wing and No 403 Squadron RCAF from January 1944, flying Spitfire Mk IXs and later Mk XVIs. (Courtesy Arthur Sagar)

Flight Lieutenant Sagar had been posted to No 416 Squadron RCAF in August 1943, flying Spitfire VBs and VCs. The Squadron's official Progress Report for the month to 26th November 1943 records that:

"On the 13th eight aircraft of the Squadron proceeded to RAF Coltishall to carry out a Rhubarb [low-level strafing operation] from that station. They were airborn at 09.25 hours and made their way across the North Sea and crossed the Dutch coast just south of Egmond. They encountered light intensive flak from the vicinity of two well camouflaged buildings. Fl/Lt Sagar leading the section was hit by flak rendering his radio u/s and they were forced to abandon the operation and return to RAF Coltishall [at 11.20 hours]." (2)

Art Sagar was taken off operational flying at the end of March 1945 and in the following May returned to Canada, where he later discharged himself. (3)

Certainly, from the outset of the War, fighting aircraft like the Supermarine Spitfire and the Hawker Hurricane were protected against gunfire from the front by bullet-proof windscreens. However, cutaway drawings of military aircraft that were published in prestigious aeronautical magazines like *The Aeroplane* during the late 1930s and early 1940s reveal few if any signs of armour protection other than bullet-proof glass either for the pilots/crews or, incidentally, for vital equipment such as the engines and fuel tanks of the principle fighting aircraft – fighters and bombers – of the day. The Spitfire Mk I illustrated in the 12th April 1940 issue of *The Aeroplane* just before the Battle of France, for example, indicates (rather than actually illustrating!) a bullet-proof windscreen, but nothing more. It is tempting to explain this on the grounds that the artists did not consider such armour important enough to include, especially if its inclusion would have obscured construction features deemed more important, or even that the military authorities of the day preferred not to give away all of their secrets so readily (which may explain the absence of armour in contemporary illustrations of German aircraft), but such an explanation would generally be wrong. Typically, there was no armour

Bullet-proof Hurricane windscreen damaged by enemy aircraft shell–gun fire. Such windscreens protected pilots from what might otherwise have been fatal encounters with the enemy. (Imperial War Museum, C.1656)

to include – at least in the pre-war days when the original of the Spitfire drawing was prepared. But in cutaways published after about mid–1940, armour began to appear as a distinct if perhaps minor feature of fighting aircraft – see, for comparison, the Hurricane Mk I illustrated in the 6th September 1940 issue of *The Aeroplane*. It should not be concluded, however, that armour protection was unknown in the early months of the War. The 11th April 1940 issue of *Flight* included a report on the French Dewoitine D 520 single-seater fighter, "France's fastest fighter", in which it was stated that

> "... The pilot's seat is ... provided with a front panel of armoured glass, ...protection of the fuel tanks by the 'self-sealing' method ... As on the Curtis Hawk 75A, there is probably a sheet of armour plating behind the pilot's seat". (4)

Two weeks later, in the 18th April 1940 issue of *Flight*, there was an article on the Curtis Hawk itself – which actually illustrated the sheet of armour plate behind the pilot's seat. (5) According to Brindley the production version of the Dewoitine D 520, which began production in December 1939 and entered service with the Armée de l'Air in February 1940, did indeed have armour plate fitted behind the pilot's seat. The D 520 clearly had the benefit of the experience in action of the earlier Morane-Saulnier MS 406, as Brindley indicated:

A Fairey Battle bomber undergoing repair or maintenance in 'a workshop in France' shows clearly the back or rear armour fitted in the pilot's cockpit. (Imperial War Museum, C.1126)

"Preliminary combat reports in the Autumn of 1939 showed that the MS 406 suffered from a number of shortcomings. ... Minor modifications were easily effected, such as ... armour behind the pilot ..." (6)

This is the story of how, after decades of discussion in the highest circles of the Royal Air Force command structure and many trials and tests, armour protection finally and very late in the day became an essential "given" in aircraft construction from the early months of the second air war with Germany. Since the Spitfire and the Hurricane, aircraft with fine and well deserved reputations as fighting machines, have already been mentioned, it is appropriate to begin near the end of the story with Paul Richey. Then a Flying Officer with No 1 Squadron stationed at Vassincourt in France with Britain's Advanced Air Striking Force (AASF), Richey recounted in his book *"Fighter Pilot"* (7) how an incident on 24th November 1939 was instrumental in accelerating the fitting of armour plating behind the pilot's seat in Hurricanes, most of which were not at that stage armour protected against attacks from behind. Flying Officer Cyril Dampier Palmer, nicknamed "Pussy", was leading a Section from 'A' Flight. Palmer, attacking a German Dornier 17 bomber that had one engine on fire and from which the rear gunner and the navigator had already escaped, was surprised when the Dornier's pilot suddenly throttled back, slipped onto his tail and put "exactly 34" bullets through the

Hurricane. One of the bullets "penetrated the locker behind [Palmer's] head and smashed the windscreen". (8) Richey continued:

> "Pussy's combat ... had an important sequel that was to save the lives of many RAF pilots. At this time the only armour our fighters carried was a thick cowling over the front petrol tank and a bullet-proof windscreen, while the [Fairey] Battles [bombers] had thick armour behind the pilot – as indeed did the German fighters. After Pussy's lucky escape [he had crashed without injury after the incident] we decided we should have back armour too, and we asked for it. ...the Air Ministry refused our request because the experts maintained that back armour would affect the Hurricane's centre of gravity and lead to flying difficulties.
>
> So the Bull [Squadron Leader Halahan, C/O of No 1 Squadron] ...fitted [back armour from a Battle] into a Hurricane and carried out flying tests. ... The experts were convinced, and back armour was henceforth fitted as standard equipment to RAF fighter aircraft." (9)

The substance of what Richey described is borne out (notwithstanding a disparity in dates!) by a letter, dated 23 October 1939, to Fighter Command Headquarters from the AASF Headquarters in France, presumably on behalf of Air Vice-Marshal P H L Playfair CB CVO MC who then commanded the AASF. (10) It is a matter of record that, some two months after the start of hostilities, No 1 Squadron was one of only two of the Hurricane Squadrons then in France still waiting to have the rear armour fitted. Whether as a result of Squadron Leader Halahan's initiative or coincidentally, a matter to which the story will return later, No 1 Squadron was soon equipped with Hurricanes fitted with rear armour. Soon enough at any rate for Billy Drake who, as another Flying Officer with No 1 Squadron, was saved by his rear armour from possible fatal injury when he was forced to bale out from his damaged Hurricane over France on 13th May 1940 in the early days of the Battle of France. Among other injuries, Drake received wounds in his back and legs from shell splinters and bullets that entered through the hole made for his seat harness straps in his rear armour plate and through other unprotected areas. Drake and the wreckage of his Hurricane were featured in the BBC Television programme *Billy Drake and the Fighter Boys*, broadcast in 2004. The head armour shows a near penetration by a bullet or piece of shrapnel that would to Billy Drake's mind have been the end of him had the armour been less able to resist the impact – or, of course, had it not been there at all! Group Captain Billy Drake retired from the RAF in July 1963; his last posting was to RAF Chivenor as Station Commander. (11)

The frustration over the absence of rear armour protection experienced by the pilots of No 1 Squadron is understandable. The decisions that led to the pilots of fighters and the crews of bombers being provided on a routine basis with the added protection of bullet-proof glass and armour were in fact the results of a debate within the Royal Air Force's Air Fighting Committee (AFC) that had been going on in earnest behind the scenes since 1935. However, the deliberations among the members of the AFC, of which Air Chief Marshal Sir Hugh Dowding (as he then was) was a prominent member from 1936 as Commander-in-Chief of Fighter Command, were successors to a much longer debate. The story of armoured fighting aircraft actually goes back a lot further than the 1930s – to the First World War and, surprisingly, even before that!

1 Imperial War Museum, London: Photograph/caption EC 110.

2 Reports concerning 416 Squadron, November 1941 to March 1946, National Archives of Canada, archive reference RG24, microfilm reel C–12288.

3 Sagar, Arthur, *Line Shoot. Diary of a Fighter Pilot*, Vanwell Publishing Limited, Ontario.

4 "France's Fastest Fighter", *Flight*, April 11, 1940

5 "France's Curtiss Fighter", *Flight*, April 18, 1940

6 Brindley, John F, *French Fighters of World War Two, Volume 1*, Hylton Lancy Publishers Ltd, England, 1971.

7 Richey, Paul, *Fighter Pilot*, (ed Diana Richey), Cassell & Co, London, 2001. (First published by B T Batsford Ltd, 1941.)

8 Richey, ibid, p 38.

9 Richey, ibid, p 39.

10 Public Record Office, AIR 2/5103, piece 29A.

11 Drake, Billy (with Shores, Christopher), *Billy Drake, Fighter Leader*, Grub Street, London, 2002.

Right: Letter from the Advanced Air Striking Force: Additional armour protection for the Hurricane.

(Public Record Office, AIR 2/5103, piece 29A)

(29A)

Copy recd 12th Novr 1939
from Fighter Cmd.

COPY.

Reference:-   Headquarters,

AASF/7100/3/Eng.   Advanced Air Striking Force.

                                               23rd October 1939.

ARMOUR - HURRICANE AIRCRAFT.

Sir,

          I have the honour to refer to the above subject and to state that the question of providing additional armour for Hurricane aircraft, attached to the Advanced Air Striking Force, has been under discussion. It is considered that due to the changed role of the Fighter aircraft attached to this Force, in that they will be engaged with enemy Fighters, it is advisable to provide additional armour behind the pilot's seat.

2.   An experiment has been carried out in which the armour plate fitted behind the pilot's seat of the Battle aircraft has been fitted to Hurricane aircraft. This can easily be done and involves only slight modification.

3.   It is requested therefore that immediate steps be taken to provide the necessary armour plate for the Hurricane aircraft of Nos. 1 and 73 Squadrons.

4.   It is suggested that immediate supplies be made from the stocks of plates already available for Battle aircraft and the necessary modifications for fitting to Hurricane aircraft be carried out before despatch from the United Kingdom. If, however, it is possible to obtain Battle plates which have not been drilled with the necessary holes for the Sutton harness attachment in Battle aircraft they can be drilled to take the Hurricane Sutton harness thereby avoiding unnecessary holes in the armour plate.

5.   The weight of this additional armour is approximately 25 lbs. and has no appreciable effect on the performance of the aircraft.

          I have the honour to be,
               Sir,
          Your obedient Servant,

          (Sgd) ? ? ? W/Cdr. for
          Air Vice Marshal,
          Air Officer Commanding,
          Advanced Air Striking Force.

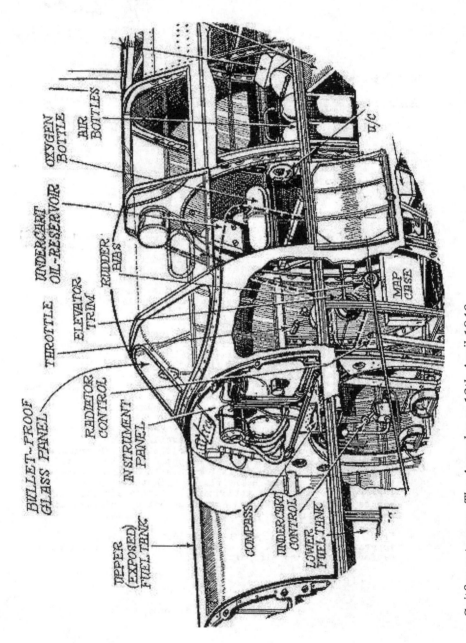

*Spitfire cutaway. The Aeroplane, 12th April 1940.
(Reproduced by permission of Aeroplane Magazine / www.aeroplanemonthly.com.)*

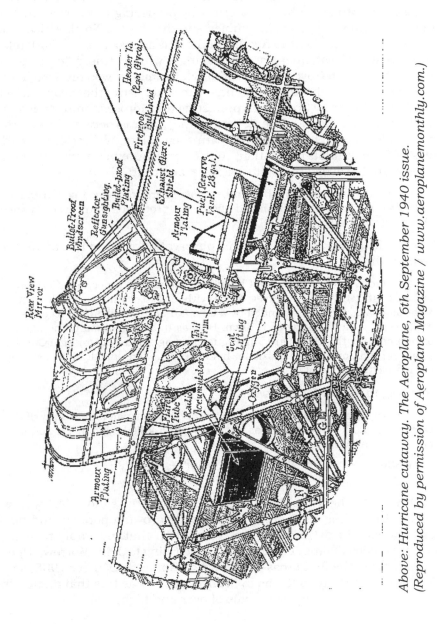

Above: Hurricane cutaway. The Aeroplane, 6th September 1940 issue.
(Reproduced by permission of Aeroplane Magazine / www.aeroplanemonthly.com.)

Rear View Mirror

Bullet-Proof Windscreen

Reflector Gunsighting

Bullet-proof Plating

Firexproof Bulkhead

Header Ta (2gal Glycol)

Exhaust Glare Shield

Armour Plating

Fuel (Reserve Tank, 28 gal.)

Armour Plating

Firing Tube

Radio Accumulators

Tail Trim

Seat lifting

Oxygen

II Trench Fighters of the First World War
2 Shooting at flying machines – A chancy business.

In the June of 1911, French forces occupied the city of Fez in Morocco. Germany caused something of a crisis by proposing to interfere in Morocco, ostensibly to protect her subjects in that part of North Africa. The Germans sent a gunboat to Agadir on the Atlantic coast some 200 miles South-West of Casablanca, later replacing it with a cruiser, to put pressure on the French Government. Although the matter was resolved in the November of 1911, the annual French Army exercise of that year charged the 6th and 7th Army Corps with protecting the Moroccan frontier against attacks from the East. Some 25 aeroplanes, of a variety of types, were amassed for the exercise, together with their pilots. Writing of the early years of French military aviation, André van Haute mentioned that one of the lessons learned from this exercise was that:

> "Reconnaissance aircraft had to be two-seaters, of rugged construction … If possible, the machines should offer some protection to their crews and also to their vital parts. …" (1)

Evidently little heed was paid to this observation, for van Haute went on to record that:

> "… five days after the start of hostilities [between France and Germany, 3rd August 1914] the observer flying with Sadi Lecointe, [a] well-known aviation character, was wounded by a German bullet whilst on a reconnaissance flight at an altitude of 1,200m. He was to be one of many thousands of victims on both sides. [On 15th August] during a bombing mission Garaix, a pioneer aviator, and de Taizieux, his observer, were killed, shot down by German artillery. …" (2)

According to Trevor Henshaw:

> "… Obst R Jahnow was reported to be the first German air casualty of the war on the 12th August. He was shot down and killed, also by ground fire, crashing near Malmedy." (3)

Lucky shots – or signs of things to come?

The Wright Brothers' maiden powered flight over the sands of Kitty Hawk on 17th December 1903 stimulated rapidly growing popular and business interests in the practicalities of aviation that inevitably turned to the military possibilities of aeroplanes. According to John Morrow, (Henri) Farman made the first cross-country flight on 30th October 1908, some 27–30km from Bouy to Reims in France, and it was this that alerted the Germans to the military potentials of overland flights. (4)

In Britain, steeped in a history of wars on the continent of Europe and of the protection afforded by the twenty-two or so miles of the English Channel, nothing could have done more to awaken the minds of the military establishment to the military possibilities of aviation than Louis Blériot's arrival over the cliffs of Dover after little more than a half-hour flight from France on 25th July 1909. Blériot's was the first flight that had crossed national boundaries but was by no means the longest to date, either in time or in distance. But the military establishment appeared, officially at least, more content to observe developments in aviation than to promote or participate in those developments, until the creation of the Air Battalion of the Royal Engineers on 28th February 1911 formalised a place for aviation within the military structure. Unofficially the development of aeroplanes for military use was certainly not being ignored, though the active participants were largely Army and Naval officers who had learned to fly and continued to experiment with flying machines at their own expense.

For the British Army, interest in the possibility of actually shooting at flying devices began to be expressed in the same year that Blériot flew the Channel. At the time, there were doubts about the practicability even of hitting machines flying in the air with ground fire, let alone doing them serious damage. To provide some practical information firing trials, in the first instance against balloons, were initiated in 1910. On 12th April 1910 at Shoeburyness, the Army's artillery firing range on the Essex coast, attempts were made to ascertain the effect of shell detonation waves on balloons. The balloons were of 1,000 cu ft capacity and shells of various sizes were detonated whilst suspended 5ft above the ground and at distances of 25 and 50 yards away from the balloons. Evidently there was no expectation actually of hitting the balloons with shell fire from the ground, but the results indicated that the wave effect from shells exploding nearby had no effect in disturbing the balloons – although their canopies suffered some holing by shell fragments. (5)

A report prepared in 1910 by the General Staff at the War Office indicated that in the USA, too, there was interest in finding out the effect of ground fire on flying devices:

"It was reported in the Press that some experiments were made at Fort Sam Houston, Texas, as to the vulnerability of balloons and aeroplanes. Big box kites to simulate aeroplanes and captive balloons were flown at various altitudes. Both the service rifle and field gun with shrapnel were used. The elevations of the balloons varied between 196 and 400 yards. The firing squads and guns were distant from 500 to 1,700 yards. It was thought that if an aeroplane is to be rendered immune from either small-arm or artillery fire, it will have to be at a greater height than 500 yards [1,500 feet]." (6)

However, these experiments in Britain and the USA were evidently not the only ones being performed at the time, as the (then) weekly journal

The Aero demonstrated in an article on "Aeroplanes in War" by E von Hesser published on 25th January 1911:

> "It was my privilege some six months ago to witness some conclusive tests carried out abroad to determine the most suitable gun to use to repel an aerial attack or reconnaissance.
>
> The test was carried out by towing kites [at 22mph] from the decks of two torpedo boats as targets, and the guns used were howitzers and 15-pound, rapid fire, pedestal-mounted, coast defence guns.
>
> The results obtained were amazing, as out of 100 rounds fired by the howitzer battery one hit was shown, and no hits whatever with the 100 rounds fired from the 15-pounders, and crack companies, too, in charge of the respective batteries.
>
> At present we have nothing to hit with a gun in actual warfare that moves half as fast as a racing aeroplane, ..." (7)

Unfortunately, von Hesser did not reveal the country in which these tests had been conducted and they might well have been in the USA, but he certainly seemed convinced by his observations that there was no gun that could be used effectively to shoot at aeroplanes.

In the May 1911 issue of the same journal, on the subject of "Uses of the War Aeroplane", Harry Harper noted that France, Germany, Russia, America and Japan were all "turning the most serious attention possible to the destruction potentialities of the aeroplane". (8) He listed several possibilities, including:

– attacking supply stores;

– destroying bridges and attacking lines of communication;

– harassing troops in camps at night;

– attacking troops on the march.

With the possible exception of night actions against encamped troops, all of these possibilities were within the decade to be realised with dramatic results. However, like others before him, he was rather dismissive of the vulnerability of the aeroplane to gunfire from below while attacking ground targets:

> "...a few somewhat inconclusive experiments ... have, so far as they have gone, demonstrated the difficulty of hitting an aeroplane ..." (8)

But it was not just the "destruction potentialities" that were receiving attention. In spite of the evidence, the need for and the practicalities of protecting aeroplanes engaged in these activities from ground fire was also beginning to be considered, nowhere more so than in France. A British report on the French Aero Salon in the December of 1911 had observed merely that:

"8. Although a large number of machines are described as "Military type", it is difficult to determine what constitutes this type, but it seems that any machine capable of taking a passenger may bear this title." (9)

However, by the time that the next French Aero Salon opened on 26th October 1912 in Paris, French aeroplane constructors were able to display three types of "military" machines that were not only armed but in which the vital parts were protected by steel armour plate. The November 1912 issue of the journal *The Aero* included a lengthy article on the Salon. Under a heading of "The Military Influence", the article reported:

" … Probably for the first time a serious attempt has been made to armour plate various parts of the machines and fit them with quick firing guns. For the most part the armour is confined to the monoplanes, and consists of chrome nickel steel plates on the sides and under surface of the fuselage, so as to protect the pilot and passenger, the petrol tank and control mechanism. When the fuselage is of the circular section tapering type, such armour plating is of real value, for with such a form there is every possibility of a bullet ricocheting off the surface. On the whole the defensive machines are not numerous, and it is felt that the attempts made to render them impervious to the enemy's bullets are somewhat of an elementary order." (10)

The article went on to describe the three armoured types of French machine, all powered by the 80hp Gnôme engine:

Blériot

"Two-seater armoured side-by-side monoplane … officially known as the type 36, is an entirely new military machine for fast reconnoitring. … A wide girdle of chrome nickel steel two millimetres in thickness encircles the fuselage around the cockpit, and this, together with the circular shape of the body, should prove a satisfactory protection against stray bullets." (11)

Henri Farman

"Military armoured hydro-biplane. … Mounted in the bow is a quick-firing gun, which should be capable of really useful work when chasing an enemy. The sides of the fuselage are formed of two steel plates with bullet resisting material compressed between the two. This armouring extends a sufficient length along the fuselage to give protection to the pilot and passenger and control mechanism." (12)

Morane–Saulnier

"This twin-seater [monoplane] is an army type, with protection given to the occupants and to the control mechanism by a steel plate along each side of the fuselage. Provision is made for mounting a quick–firing gun on the side of the fuselage, …" (13)

The weights and speeds of the three machines were reported as:

Blériot:	826lb (unloaded), 72–74mph
Henri Farman:	1,120lb (with floats and armour), 62mph
Morane–Saulnier:	859lb, 76mph.

According to the article, it was also "believed" that the Blériot had not actually flown.

The British Army did not appear to take much notice of these machines. Already in 1911 Colonel W N Congreve VC, CB, MVO, Commandant of the British Army's School of Musketry at Hythe in Kent, had suggested firing trials at aerial targets with rifles and machine guns – the sorts of guns with which troops on the ground would be equipped and would use to try to defend themselves. The trials began to come to fruition at the end of 1912. In the first of the trials, carried out at Shoeburyness in December 1912, the targets were suspended 100ft below balloons; guy ropes from the bottom corners of the targets were tethered to the ground to steady them. There was apparently no opportunity to fire a Maxim machine gun during these initial trials, but four different marksmen fired rifles at the targets. The intention was to determine the elevations at which the rifles had to be fired, taking into account bullet-drop during flight, in order to hit balloons at various distances and heights. There is no record of the hits on the targets, but tables were drawn up to give guidance on likely firing elevations.(14)

The trials were continued in April 1913 using kites towed by engines running along tracks, in order on this occasion to determine the probability of hitting aeroplanes from the ground with fire from rifles and machine guns. They were carried out initially using 9ft x 8ft sheet steel kites, with the steel nailed onto wooden battens; an insulated gap was left between the upper and lower halves of the kites and microphones were attached to each half to make it possible to tell whether any hits were on the upper or lower halves. Later, 10ft square aluminium kites were used. The towed kites never flew well, barely getting above 60 feet in the air or travelling faster than 20mph, but the results were far from encouraging. Rifle fire by 50 soldiers produced 6 hits from 474 rounds fired; using a machine gun, 2 hits were recorded from a first burst of 250 rounds and a second burst of 183 rounds produced a further 1 hit. Major J Browne, Experimental Officer at the School of Musketry, observed rather skeptically in his report of 2nd May 1913:

> "...it is possible that better results than those obtained on this occasion ... will not be obtained by troops in the field except by chance." (15)

In fact, the British firing trials continued throughout 1913, using rifles, Pom-pom and 13-pounder guns, with mixed results as to the likelihood of hitting and significantly damaging flying devices. (16)

In the meantime, the apparent invulnerability of aircraft was already being tested in action elsewhere in the world. The journal *Flight*, on 4th January 1913, had included a brief report:

"Another casualty in the Balkan War

On the evening of the signing of the armistice, Constantine de Mazurk-iewitch, a volunteer aviator with the Bulgarian Army, was wounded by the Turks while flying over the Tchataldje line. He managed to get his aeroplane back to Bulgarian lines, but died soon afterwards." (17)

The Balkan League (Bulgaria, Montenegro, Greece and Serbia) had declared war on Turkey in 1912 and again in 1913. There was a further report in the journal on 25th January 1913, this time from an aviator serving with the Greek Army in the Balkan theatre:

"... At 1.00pm [on 17th December 1912] [Lt] Moutoussis left to make a flight above Janine [106km from Preveza on the Plain of Nicopolis]. ... During this flight, flying at over 1,600 metres, he threw down bombs, creating a veritable panic amongst the Turkish troops. Many hostile bullets tore the fabric, but the machine continued its flight unaffected. Captain Bares, on the return of Lt Moutoussis, used the same machine, and flew back over Janine, 2,300 metres up. Again several bullets pierced the fabric, but the machine returned to camp unaffected, ...

[Moutoussis] made a second reconnaissance over Janine on a Maurice Farman on 22nd inst, flying over the town at 2,100 metres, and throwing bombs, ... Several hostile bullets reached him, breaking a longeron, but without affecting the machine's flying qualities. He landed at Philippias. ...

... During this campaign of twenty days only three machines suffered damage, and what damage was done was easily repaired." (18)

The message from both of these reports was basically the same – aeroplanes could certainly be hit when fired at, but unless the pilot was actually incapacitated, there was little cause for concern. There was no indication that any of the aeroplanes involved in these events was armoured. Indeed, the probability is that they were not. Notwithstanding the armoured exhibits at the Paris Salon only a few months earlier, exhibits that in at least one case had not actually taken to the air, aeroplane engines were barely powerful enough to lift the machine and its pilot off the ground, let alone any additional pounds of steel plate that might do nothing very useful – and this was a time when the possible military rôles for the aeroplanes themselves were still little more than matters of conjecture.

The British firing trials continued at Shoeburyness on 18th June 1913, against real aeroplanes this time, to ascertain not so much whether they could be hit as the amount of damage likely to be caused by hits from rifle and machine gun fire. In the first trial at 11 o'clock in the morning, a Short tractor biplane, minus engine, was upended on its nose on railway trucks to present its underside towards the firing point. Machine gun fire from a Maxim at 1,500 yards produced the following results:

Short biplane underside used in firing trials on 18th June 1913. Bullet strikes are marked on the lower wings. (19)

Rounds fired at the wings:		500
Hits:	Bottom plane:	83
	Top plane:	45
	(some of these had hit the bottom plane)	
	Engine space:	3
	Pilot space:	3
Rounds fired at the tail:		250
Hits:		5

So far as the "hits" were concerned, according to the report dated 10th July 1913 on these trials:

> "All holes through wing spars, ribs, etc, were clean drilled, and seemed to do little damage." (19)

In the second of these trials, at 3 o'clock in the afternoon of the same day, an inverted Martin Handasyde monoplane, again minus engine, was fired at as if from ahead and below – fifty rounds of rifle fire aimed at the most vulnerable parts of the machine. Presumably to ensure hits, the guns were fired from close range, but the charges in the cartridges were reduced to simulate a retained velocity equivalent to firing from 1,500 yards. The machine was afterwards loaded to 4,200lb as if for flight and apparently "stood the test" – presumably a test to see whether the damaged wings would still bear the load of the aircraft as if flying

Martin Handasyde, used in firing trials on 18th June 1913. Bullet strike marks are evident on the port wing. (19)

– although there were thoughts that the fabric after penetration or tear by bullet strikes might strip off in actual flight. (19) The Superintendent of the Royal Aircraft Factory, the Irish engineer Mr Mervyn J P O'Gorman (later Lieutenant-Colonel M J P O'Gorman CB), was afterwards to note on 24th June 1913 that:

> "As soon as we have armoured the aeroplane ... under the passenger pilot and engine with 1½mm thick alloy steel, it should be practically impossible to stop it or bring it down with rifle, or ... machine gun at 2000ft altitude. That would leave the speed of flight about 70mph and, save for quickfirers say one pounder – the aeroplane could scout with impunity, take photographs etc." (20)

O'Gorman's apparently off-hand mention of armour indicates that despite outward appearances the possibility of fitting armour protection to aeroplanes was in the minds of at last some in the British military establishment.

The absence of engines in the June trials at Shoeburyness was rectified on 19th July 1913 by more firing trials (19) – this time at the Royal Aircraft Factory (Farnborough) against a running 50hp Gnome 7-cylinder single-row air-cooled rotary engine. Rifle fire at 600 yards penetrated a cylinder and the engine stopped at once – the piston shattered and the following spark ignited all the explosive mixture in the crank-case. The immediate conclusion was that any hit on a cylinder would put the engine out of action; any hit on the crank-case might not stop the engine, but would prevent it from being restarted. In further shoots with retained velocities equivalent to ranges of 500, 1,000 and 1,500 yards, cylinder penetration occurred in each case. Additional trials (19) were held on the same date at The Royal Flying Corps' training camp at Netheravon, against an upright-90 degree Vee air-cooled 60hp 8-cylinder Renault engine with a four-bladed propeller, using machine gun fire from a Maxim and a Rexer, as well as four rifles. From 1,100 yards, there were no hits, apparently due to wind. At 600 yards, one hit damaged cylinders and cut high tension wires; another three hit the cooling fan; a further four hit the propeller, necessitating a new one. From 400 yards, the oil pipe was cut away and the crank-case was penetrated twice; other damage included two cylinders penetrated and a badly hit propeller. The engine was not actually stopped, but was judged not to be able to support an aeroplane; oil leakage from the cracked crank-case would eventually have stopped the engine. Other trials at Hythe in July 1913 focussed on the effect of gunfire in damaging bracing wires.

The records do not show what use was made of the results of the British firing trials. The overriding conclusion might very well have been that there was nothing to be done: aeroplanes were going to be difficult to hit from the ground and unless they were fortuitously hit in a vulnerable spot like the engine (or, of course, the pilot) they were unlikely to be badly damaged. However, O'Gorman's earlier and seemingly off-hand reference to British interest in armoured machines turned out to be genuine. Armour protection was certainly a recognised consideration within the Military Wing of the Royal Flying Corps that was created by a Royal Warrant of 13th April 1912 and on 13th May 1912 absorbed the Air Battalion of the Royal Engineers. Major Frederick H Sykes later Major-General Sir Frederick H Sykes CMG, Controller-General of Civil Aviation), Commander of the Military Wing, had given a lecture on "Military Aviation" to the (later "Royal") Aeronautics Society on 26th February 1913. Dealing with aspects of the "Command of the Air", he placed the consideration of armour in context:

> "... the third dimension [climbing] is a severe stumbling block. A fighting machine with its passenger, gun, ammunition, and possibly light armour, is a heavy machine. Every attribute is affected. It cannot, for some time, be as fast or as easy to handle as an unarmed craft. It will climb more slowly, cause more strain on the pilot, and land with less certainty of remaining whole. The difficulties may be circumvented. Many clever designers are working on the problem of an efficient fighting aeroplane." (21)

Successive "clever designers" have continued to work on the problem ever since and will doubtless continue far into the future, though it was to be another twenty years before the problem of weight was effectively resolved.

Moving on to the aerial reconnaissance rôle for aeroplanes, Sykes continued with brutal military frankness:

"... it is often difficult owing to clouds and mist, and there is sometimes a tendency to descend to dangerously low levels in order to ensure correct information or verify that already gained. Bullets will probably quickly correct this tendency in war. ... the Bulgarian flyers think that anything under 4,000 feet unsafe from fire. Bullets, however, must not cause fliers to err on the side of caution when looking for information. The possibility of shrapnel is no excuse for failure. ..." (22)

Sykes even included in his lecture a list of "types of aircraft considered to be required immediately". Among these was:

"... A two-seater fighting machine with speeds of 70 and 40 [presumably mph], to carry a gun, ammunition, light armour, and petrol for 200 miles. ... of good climbing powers." (23)

Sykes, who was to be replaced as Commander of the Military Aviation Wing when war broke out in August 1914, was subsequently to take over from Major-General Trenchard (later Marshal of the Royal Air Force Sir Hugh M Trenchard GCB DSO) in April 1918 as Chief of the Air Staff and head of the newly created Royal Air Force. In 1913 he was clear-sighted enough to recognise that military flights could not be expected to be unopposed in wartime, that military objectives might demand low – and therefore dangerous – flying and that a steely resolve would be necessary in pursuing those objectives. It is interesting to note, however, that in a further lecture to the Society a year later Sykes made no reference to armoured military machines.

Comments on the report of Sykes' first lecture were published in the May 1913 issue of the journal *The Aero*. While there was no real dissent from the views expressed by such an influential figure as Sykes, there was an intriguing response reported from a Captain Wood:

" ... With regard to armoured aircraft, he did not think sufficient was known about them in [the UK]. It had been stated that no such machine had ever yet fired a gun, but the French and Germans had done this, and he believed our own Aircraft Factory had probably more experience of this type of machine than the French or Germans." (24)

The "Royal" Aircraft Factory, as it then was under the umbrella of the Royal Flying Corps, was of course O'Gorman's domain.

The possibilities of work for military aircraft continued to be the subject of wide public speculation and the issue of protecting them began to assume a position almost of accepted fact among the views reported in the aviation press. W Arthur Barr wrote, in an article on "The Flying Gun" that was published in *The Aeroplane* on 11th September 1913:

"It is conceivable that should an aeroplane, [equipped with a gun], settle itself very carefully astride of a perfectly straight trench, the heroic flying

gunner might devote the brief remainder of his mortal span to the clearing
of that trench with some effect, but such a use of aircraft, as an abnormally
mobile sort of gun-carriage, is at least exotic in a military sense, not to say
desperate.

... the only really vulnerable things about an aeroplane are the pilot, engine, propeller, and sundry wires of control and load, of these the first two
are quite capable of being protected, ..." (25)

Notwithstanding that on practical military grounds there would be no
such thing as a "perfectly straight trench", here was yet another early
example of the potential use of the aeroplane as a trench fighter and a
discrete warning of the danger of low flying should that rôle ever be ex-
ercised – but the possibility that vulnerable components of the aeroplane
might also be protected was in effect taken for granted.

W E de B Whittaker, writing on "The Fighting Aeroplane" in the 6th
November 1913 issue of the same journal, took the presumption of protection further:

"All aeroplanes used in war, whether carrying guns or not, will of necessity be armoured. Experiments have been made in France and Russia, with
the result that it has been discovered that sheet steel three millimetres thick
was quite sufficient to turn a rifle bullet at 800 yards. Heavier armour is out
of the question, owing to the already great weights carried in the way of fuel,
gun and ammunition." (26)

As if to press the point home, the journal carried the following item in
the 27th November 1913 issue:

"Spain is still fighting persistently in Tetuan, and it appears that on November 18 two officers flying Maurice Farman biplanes on reconnaissance duties
were seriously wounded by rifle shots from impatient Moroccans. They were
luckily able to return to the Spanish lines without further disaster." (27)

Also in the 4th December issue of *The Aeroplane*, on aeronautics in Spain,
there was a more detailed report dated 25th November 1913 from Mr
Farnall Thurston, who had been superintending the delivery of Bristol
machines to the Spanish Government:

"The Spaniards are taking their military aviation very seriously indeed,
...

As you are probably aware, they have first sent off a number of machines
and some twenty or thirty pilots to Morocco to try to bring their campaign
against the Moors to an end by means of aeroplanes, ..., although two of them
managed to allow themselves to be shot the other day. They were flying a
Farman at about 1,500 feet and appear to have overlooked the fact that the
surrounding hills were about the same height, so that the Moors on them
were able to fire on them practically on the level." (28)

While it is in the nature of all dangerous activities, military aviation
certainly being no exception, that the participants should take care to
eliminate unnecessary risks, the idea that aviators would only get shot

if they allowed it to happen through carelessness was a new line of argument – but one that would be reiterated on future occasions during the First World War and in the years leading up to the Second.

Given articles like those instanced, in respected aviation journals of the day and especially by authoritative and influential figures like Sykes, it is rather surprising to find that while the British military establishment was still exploring the vulnerability of aeroplanes there were farsighted military services elsewhere in the world who were already turning their thoughts not merely to building aeroplanes with some form of armour protection but to employing them. The first service aeroplanes to carry armour – or at least to be specified as armoured – appeared on the scene at about the same time in France, Russia and America, although the success of such machines did not turn out to be as inevitable as the aviation press had hitherto seemed to imply.

W E de B Whittaker wrote on "Some Possible Developments" in *The Aeroplane* on 4th December 1913:

> "In the case of aircraft it seems likely, in France at least, that the Ministry of War will state, for example, that they desire to buy a number of propeller-driven monoplanes ... armoured in the region of vulnerable parts by three millimetre plate, ..." (29)

According to John Morrow, the French army's General Staff had advised the War Ministry a year earlier, at the end of 1912, that:

> "... planes were especially suitable for reconnaissance, rapid liaison, and possibly for attacking dirigibles and troops in dense formations, although effective battlefield operations at altitudes below 800 metres risked serious losses – unless, as Colonel Estienne suggested, airplanes were armoured." (30)

But Morrow also pointed out that:

> "In 1913 and 1914 the French army wasted precious time with ... an abortive policy on armoured airplanes, ..." (30)

Colonel Estienne was an artillery officer and the commander of No 3 Group of the French Aviation Corps created in the August of 1912 and based at Lyon. During 1913 General Bernard was appointed to direct military aeronautics and, acting on instructions from the French War Ministry, he investigated the state of French military aviation, an investigation that led to his appointment as Aviation Inspector in September 1913. Bernard favoured an equipment programme in which all aeroplanes were to be armoured in accordance with Estienne's ideas of 1912. According to Morrow and to Christienne and Lissarague, three prototypes eventually became available in June 1914, including a twin-engined Dorand biplane, but were too heavily loaded for the army's low powered engines and were therefore too slow; few aeroplanes were subsequently manufactured on the basis of these prototypes. (31) (32)

Nevertheless, the Editor of the journal *Flight* seized on the information emerging from France and in his "Editorial Comment" in the issue of 2nd May 1914 reported at great length:

"Armoured Aeroplanes for the French Army

... The latest piece of information ... is that the Air Corps is now in possession of a squadron of armoured aeroplanes, each carrying a quick-firing gun, capable of throwing a shell weighing half-a-pound. These machines are of the monoplane type and are two–seaters, having the vital parts protected by chrome-nickel steel armour, 2½ millimetres thick, which is proof against rifle bullets at a range of 700 metres. They have engines developing 95hp and a standard flying speed of about 62mph.

On paper, these seem to be exceedingly formidable machines and not to be matched in the air service of any other powers. Their armour will enable them to fly with comparative safety at fairly low altitudes, which is good for purposes of observation. According to most authorities the unarmoured machine will have to maintain an altitude of over three thousand feet in order to be reasonably safe from modern rifle fire, while with one reservation, the new French type ought to be able to fly safely over a hostile position at a height of possibly less than two thousand feet. The reservation is ... the danger of the propeller being hit and disabled, ... the weak point from which all machines of the armoured type must inevitably suffer. ... [and] the chances of its being disabled ... would appear to be much greater, since the pilot [of the armoured machine] would certainly be tempted by his armour to fly lower and take more chances.

... there are, even at this early stage of the history of aerial war, several instances on record of pilots and observers being hit by hostile fire without disablement of the machine [in the Balkans and Morocco]. ...On balance, therefore, it would seem that provided the handicap of the lesser speed imposed by the extra weight of armour be not too great, the arguments ... are in favour of the armoured type. ... we shall really not know what are the comparative capabilities of the armoured and unarmoured aeroplanes until they have been taught in the next great war. And that being so, we are not particularly curious to know. ... it will be well that our own military authorities should keep in touch with what is being done in the direction under discussion." (33)

The French interest in armoured aeroplanes evidently waned, as Morrow had pointed out, and it is probably that fact – rather than the rhetoric of Flight's Editor – that had the greater influence on British military thinking. However, Van Haute has recorded that during the ensuing war some French Caudron G4 twin–engined biplanes were protected by armour plating to allow them to fly low-level missions against German targets. (34)

In Russia, the "Delphin" (Dolphin) was, according to Nowarra and Duval, a design by V V Dybovski that appeared in 1913 in which:

The Wright Model F "Tin Cow", U S Army Signal Corps No 39. (Air Force Historical Research Agency, The Lewis E Goodier Jr Collection.)

"... the forward section of [the nose] was sheathed in metal to afford the crew protection from bullets." (35)

Little appears to have come of this machine.

In America, the matter of armour protection appears to have been taken quite seriously for a time. According to Casari:

"In a vain effort in early 1913 to obtain more effective military aircraft, the Army placed orders for three armoured machines, each from a different manufacturer, using foreign engines. ...

From Burgess, a new Burgess-Dunne machine was ordered, the Wright Company was given a contract for their Model F, and Curtiss was to furnish a tractor design. ...

... the Curtiss Armoured Tractor ... is believed to have been a direct derivative of the new Model G tractor designed by the company late in 1912. ... no positive confirmation of this has ever been located.

... The exact configuration of the armoured Curtiss is not known, ... [but] the Curtiss company's attempts to obtain the [French 160hp rotary] Gnome engine ended in a fiasco that ultimately caused cancellation of the contract, the airframe never being delivered. (36)

Of the Wright machine, Casari had nothing more to record other than:

"... The Wright F lumbered through eight months of trials before finally being reluctantly accepted." (36)

Casari described all three machines as having been required to comply with the same specification:

Burgess-Dunne S C No 36 armoured machine. (Courtesy R B Casari.)

"...for a military scout with an enclosed body, chrome steel armour of about .075 inches in thickness for the crew and engine, radio equipment, and having a crew of two with dual controls. Performance requirements included a rate of climb of 2,000 feet in 10 minutes with a 450lb load plus fuel and oil for four hours, a speed range of at least 38–55mph, and the ability to take off and land on plowed ground or in long grass within 300 feet. ...

... To specify an armoured scout for war service under fire was a tremendous step forward ..." (37)

Not so much a tremendous step forward as a remarkable one, for the time! Casari went on to record that the prototype Burgess-Dunne machine was flown at Marblehead harbour, fitted with a central float, on 10th October 1914. The machine, designated SC No 36, was officially accepted on 30th December 1914 and by the spring of 1915 was assigned to experimental work with the Coast Artillery. Because of its flying characteristics, it was never used as a Scout, the purpose for which it had been ordered, and was finally condemned on 18th October 1916.

Little seems to have come of any of these far-sighted initiatives.

Meanwhile, back in Britain, O'Gorman at the Royal Aircraft Factory was already putting his earlier thoughts on an armoured aeroplane into practice. Writing to the Officer Commanding (Sykes), Royal Flying Corps, O'Gorman inquired on 6th October, barely a month after the start of hostilities:

Lieutenant-Colonel M J P O'Gorman CB, Superintendent of the Royal Aircraft Factory. (Public Record Office, AIR 1/728/176/1/1)

F W Lanchester, MICE, Member of the Advisory Committee for Aeronautics. (Courtesy the Lanchester Library, Coventry University)

"Have you seen the new bullet-proof seat, which I am making, ..." (38)

The seat in question was for the BE (Blériot Experimental) 2a, b and c machines and weighed 15lb. Writing then to Major General Sir Stanley Brenton von Donop, Master General of the Ordnance, on 9th September 1914, he stated the position in more detail:

> "... I am getting out an armoured aeroplane and it is of paramount importance to use the minimum possible thickness of armour to withstand German rifle bullets at 1000 feet above the point of fire. The sheet will be heavy so that I propose only to use a sort of tray in the lower part of the aeroplane. (*S of S has approved of the aeroplane*)*. The gunner in the aeroplane would be lying on his face at full length so that the tray could be fairly shallow, the armour used round him would be probably about 7mm thick. The pilot who would be subject to a more oblique fire at a greater range could have thinner armour, about 2½mm (*so save weight of course*)*.
>
> ... I imagine that the upper material protecting the pilot will not be so difficult to hammer up into shape, but the thicker material for the tray will be more difficult unless I can make it say of two trays inside one another of both – say – 1/8 inch thick or more. The rough experiments made here did not seem to show that with the two [kinds of English] bullets the angle of incidence between the wall and the plate makes a very great difference to the

penetration, but there is doubtless some angle at which the bullet glances off. It is of importance that, with a view to trying the working up of the material, I should have a small sample, say about 1 yard square of the material of each thickness necessary for protection

(a) at 1000 feet vertically above the gun,

(b) at 3000 feet horizontally and 1000 feet up.

Could you send this note on to the right quarter for me ..." (38)

(*Author's Note. The wording in italics was added by hand to the typescript letter from O'Gorman.)

O'Gorman appears to have been a thoughtful military engineer who had certainly not let the matter of armour protection rest after the 1913 firing trials. There were exchanges of correspondence as follow-up to O'Gorman's letter up to the end of November 1914 and some trials with various armour plates from steel-makers Thomas Firth & Sons. There is some evidence that the seats intended for reconnaissance aeroplanes like the BE 2c and the BE 8, bullet-proof at altitudes such as 1,800 feet if not 3,000 feet, became a common feature of machines in service, at least during the early war months, as will be seen later. Related papers (38) indicate that although non-magnetic steel armour plate was in the end settled on for use as protection, Duralumin (a lightweight aluminium alloy) was considered as a means for keeping the weight down that would have the additional advantage of being inherently non-magnetic – and so not affect an aeroplane's compass. The papers also include drawings of the proposed armour seat installation in the BE 2a, b and c machines.

Armoured seat for BE 2a, b and c aeroplanes, circa October 1914.
(Public Record Office, AIR 1/ 140/ 15/ 40/ 300)

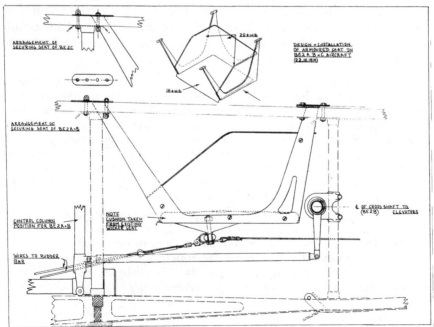

Lanchester used this photograph of a BE 2's skeletal airframe to illustrate the "transparency" of the machine to gunfire. (Courtesy The Lanchester Press.)

F W Lanchester, a member of the Government's Advisory Committee for Aeronautics, wrote a series of articles entitled "Aircraft in Warfare" that were published in the journal Engineering during the period 4th September to 24th December 1914 – in the very first months of the War. Far from the practical approach of O'Gorman, as an early example of tactical thinking about the military implications of aeroplanes the articles were far-sighted in many respects, not least in their assessment of the susceptibility of aeroplanes to gunfire and the rôle that armour protection could play. The articles undoubtedly reflected and encompassed the sorts of ideas and issues that had been the subjects of debate, comment and experiment during the preceding several years and undoubtedly complemented O'Gorman's work. But where O'Gorman was working behind the scenes, effectively in secret within the confines of the Factory, Lanchester presented his ideas in a structured and cogent form to the wider world.

Arguing from first principles, using simple calculations and considering first "attack by gunfire", Lanchester worked out that an aeroplane flying above 5,000–6,000 feet was unlikely to be hit, or at least suffer significant damage, by gunfire from the ground below. He concluded:

> "An aeroplane operating in hostile country is liable to attack by rifle and machine-gun fire, also by shell-fire from anti-aeroplane artillery. It has comparatively little to fear from field artillery owing to the want of handiness of the ordinary field-gun. The "laying" of a field-piece is far too clumsy a business to permit of its effective use on so small and rapidly moving a target as presented by an aeroplane in flight, though it may be effective against a dirigible. With regard to rifle or machine-gun (small bore) fire, calculation shows that aircraft is absolutely safe at an altitude of somewhat over 7000ft; it is in that region that the top of the trajectory lies for vertical shooting [and therefore the bullets would have little or no remaining penetrative energy].

The duties of a strategic scout on long-distance work would, without doubt, permit of flying at such a high altitude, and it may be added that, although absolute immunity is not reached at less than about 7000ft, a solitary aeroplane can only present a very unprofitable target at far lower altitudes. In fact, it may be taken that at, say, 5000ft or 6000ft, the amount of small-arm ammunition required to bring down an aeroplane would be enormous. ... it is evident that for the infantryman or gunner not specially trained, the task of bringing down an aeroplane flying at high altitude is no light one ...

... An aeroplane operating at high altitude will probably need to be hunted and driven off or destroyed by armed machines of its own kind." (39)

Lanchester was therefore beginning to put the prospects of shooting at flying machines onto a more calculated basis than the earlier firing trials had allowed. His reasoning demonstrated that gunfire from the ground could not even be expected to be effective in shooting at "high" flying machines, though there was little here to comfort Sadi Lecointe's unfortunate observer – flying at a little under 5,000ft!

In turning then to "defence from gunfire", Lanchester introduced into the equation the likely work in which military aeroplanes would be engaged and in doing so moved the debate onto an entirely different level:

"It is manifestly not possible for an aeroplane to perform all the duties required of it, in connection with tactical operations at high altitude, and whenever it descends below 5000ft, or thereabouts, it is liable to attack from beneath; in fact, at such moderate altitudes it must be considered as being under fire – mainly from machine-gun and rifle – the whole time it is over or within range of the enemy's lines. Protection from the rifle bullet may be obtained in either of two ways; the most vital portions of the machine, including the motor, the pilot, and the gunner, can only be effectively protected by armour-plate; the remainder of the machine, including the wing members, the tail members, and portions of the fuselage not protected by armour, also the controls, struts, and the propeller, can be so constructed as to be *transparent* [Lanchester's italics] to rifle fire – that is to say, all these parts should be so designed that bullets will pass through without doing more than local injury and without serious effect on the strength or flying power of the machine as a whole; in certain cases components will require to be duplicated in order to realise this intention." (40)

In terms of what Lanchester referred to as the "transparency" of the machine, his reasoning was simply bearing out, knowingly or not, what the earlier firing trials against the Short Tractor and the Martin Handasyde airframes and the conflicts in the Balkans and in Morocco had illustrated – that the airframe could sustain penetration without it necessarily being debilitating, unless by chance a vulnerable component like the pilot or, referring to the follow-up trials, the engine was struck. Indeed, when he republished the articles in book form (41) during 1916, Lanchester included a photograph of a BE 2 machine's skeletal airframe to illustrate the "transparency" to which he referred. (42)

Lanchester was clearly thinking in terms of a shot-gun effect of fire from perhaps multiple sources on the ground below the aeroplane, where the object was to hit the machine somewhere, anywhere, and often enough for the cumulative effect of the strikes and/or the statistical chance of hitting a vital spot to be sufficient to drive the machine away or bring it down. It was evidently not in his remit to consider aerial combats between machines, in which an attacker might be able so to match speed and position with his intended victim as to aim for vital spots and thereby minimise the "transparency" effect. Nor, seemingly thinking of an aeroplane being attacked from behind, did he appreciate the effect that the "harder" components of the aeroplane's structure, like the engine, might have for the machine doing the attacking in actually protecting the softest and most vulnerable component – the pilot – from defensive fire! In this latter point in particular, Lanchester can be forgiven, for it was not until some twenty years later during the run-up to a new war that the potentially protective effect of airframe components (especially the engine) became an official and somewhat distracting tactical consideration. But Lanchester certainly did begin to think of armour protection as a design consideration and in exploring this aspect at some length he foreshadowed a technical debate that was to continue on and off for another twenty-five or more years:

> "It is important to understand clearly that any intermediate course [between stopping bullets with armour and avoiding their effects through transparency] is fatal. Either the bullet must be definitely resisted and stopped, or it must be let through with the least possible resistance; it is for the designer to decide in respect of each component which policy he will adopt. The thickness of armour required will depend very much upon the minimum altitude at which, in the presence of the enemy, it is desired to fly; also upon the particular type of rifle and ammunition brought to bear. There is a great deal of difference in penetrative power, for example, between the round-nosed and pointed bullets used in an otherwise identical cartridge.
>
> If it were not for the consideration of the weight of armour, there is no doubt that an altitude of about 1000ft. would be found very well suited to most of the tactical duties of the aeroplane. At such an altitude, however, the thickness of steel plate necessary becomes too serious an item for the present day machine ... the minimum thickness that will stop a 0.303 Mark VI round-nosed bullet is 3mm (1/8 inch), but if attacked by the modern pointed-nosed Mauser, nothing short of 5mm or 6mm is of avail. ... [at] 2000ft ... the figures become 2mm. ... for the 0.303 round-nosed bullet , and for the pointed Mauser 3mm or slightly over ... it is not expected that it will pay to armour a machine for the duties in question more heavily; thus we may take 2000ft as representing the lower altitude limit of ordinary military flying." (40)

In his article of 25th September 1914, Lanchester turned to the matter of what he could now refer to as "low-altitude flying". He noted first that while the disadvantages were "too obvious to need mention" there were certain military advantages to be derived from low-altitude flying that he felt should be stated. The main advantages lay in the difficulty of spotting from the ground an aeroplane flying low, especially against a dark background like hills, and in the opportunity for the aeroplane to take "an intimate and decisive part in the fray, as, for example, cavalry charging, or infantry with the bayonet". In a remarkably accurate forecast of the wartime developments ahead, he considered that:

> "It might prove of enormous and overwhelming value if at any critical moment, or at any crucial point, it were possible to let loose a few squadrons of aeroplanes each mounting one or more machine-guns, to bring short-range concentrated fire to bear, or alternatively to make an attack by the aid of bombs or hand-grenades. The scene that would ensue, for example, on a congested line of retreat would be indescribable: horses thrown into hopeless confusion or stampeded, mechanical transport lorries holed in a dozen or more vital points, ... gun teams wiped out, infantry decimated; in brief, chaos over endless miles of high road." (43)

Lanchester's graphic descriptions give but the merest glimpse of the actual and horrific carnage of which aeroplanes engaged upon ground attack work were in due course to prove themselves capable and which were to reach their apotheoses in the routing of the polish forces by the Germans in the September of 1939 and the sweeping away of French defences, together with their British allies, in the spring of 1940. But he was not, finally, able to resist exploring the down-side of this powerful contribution to warfare, in terms of "armour for low-altitude and point blank range":

> "The question arises whether it is possible for the aeroplane to fly at a sufficiently low altitude to act effectively in the manner indicated without exposing itself to immediate destruction. The matter is entirely a matter of armour; the unarmoured portions of the machine, which derive their immunity from their *transparency* [Lanchester's italics] to rifle fire, are no worse off at point-blank range than at 2000ft or 3000ft altitude. Taking the altitude as 500ft (a reasonable maximum for the effective execution of the duties contemplated), the thickness of armour necessary is approximately ... 4mm ... for the British service Mark VI ammunition, or slightly over [6mm] in the case of the pointed Mauser bullet, the latter thickness representing a weight of 10lb per sq ft. It is evident that the problem of giving complete protection to the motor, pilot and gunner will become a problem of some difficulty; probably in the present state of the constructor's art the protection would need to be somewhat "scamped" and a certain amount of risk admitted. Whatever economies are effected in armour, the main principle must not be lost sight of – ie, the thickness must not be tampered with; armour too thin for its duty is worse than canvas or brown paper.
>
> ... if and when it is recognised as advantageous and found possible to utilise such low altitudes [as 500ft] in aeroplane tactics – it becomes a question whether it will not be found to pay to "go the whole hog" and fly at the very lowest altitude possible. It may be at once admitted that all the dangers of flying ... will be thereby increased, but danger of the degree in question is a matter of little or no consideration in actual war. ... By following the contour of

the ground, never rising more than 100ft or 200ft, unless to clear an obstacle not otherwise to be avoided, an attack will be made with comparative suddenness, and the machine will be gone out of sight almost before there has been time to bring a gun to bear. Even when under fire it will have a certain tactical advantage in the fact that it will be attacking in a line parallel to which it is flying – it need never miss its target – whereas it itself offers the worst kind of mark for the enemy, combining small size, high speed, disconcertingly short range, in addition to which it is, in effect, a disappearing target.

The further reduction of altitude now under discussion means that rifle-fire must be faced literally at muzzle velocity, and corresponding provision made in the thickness of the armour. For the pointed Mauser bullet, representing the maximum requirement of today, the thickness of plate needed is scarcely less than [9.5mm], and the weight 13lb or 14lb per sq ft. Evidently the question of weight of armour will become a difficulty of a most serious character, and no pretence can be made to give complete protection; the area must be cut down to an absolute minimum." (43)

So Lanchester, though advocating the widest possible use of armour protection, was sensitive to the practical constraint introduced by the weight of the armour plate. But if he appreciated the tactical trade-off between the weight of possible armour and the duty to be performed, he was also careful to recognise – without overstating – the risks inherent in the duties that he was also, echoing Sykes, advocating:

"If one is tempted to be over-influenced by the obvious danger of [very low flying], it is well to recall the exploits carried out as a matter of ordinary experience by cavalry under fire, without the advantage of armoured protection, while presenting a target (man and horse) something like 20 sq ft in area, and with a speed contemptibly small in comparison with that of flight. It is only necessary clearly to admit that in this form of fighting we may have to reckon with serious losses of men and machines, not occasional losses, as at present, but rather such as can be expressed as a percentage of the force engaged." (43)

Looking back with the hindsight of some ninety years, it is difficult to believe – though perhaps it is the way of these things – how such far-sighted and analytical thinking could have been met with so little apparent response from the Royal Flying Corps in the early stages of the War and until those in command were virtually overtaken by events. And yet, if the Germans were not aware of Lanchester's articles, some among them must surely have made the same leaps of logic and imagination, for the record suggests that they were far readier than the British to put what amounted to his ideas into practice!

There was one further and final rôle for aeroplanes that Lanchester thought worthy of consideration: fighting in, rather than from, the air – fighting between the machines themselves. Lanchester did indeed address the problems of "aerial attack and defence" though, as will be seen later, in a way that had more relevance to the preparations of the Royal Air Force for the 1939–45 conflict than to the aerial combats of 1914–18.

He began by establishing the conditions which needed to be fulfilled by the aeroplane constructor as they arose directly from the primary function of the aeroplane: since aeroplanes would find their main use in attacking ground targets, they would need guns that fired downwards especially (though preferably in other directions as well) and armour that enabled them to resist attack from the ground. The first consequence of this starting point was, in any aeronautical engagement, the "importance of the upper berth":

"The machine which is able to attack from above is acting under the conditions for which its armour and armament were initially provided. Beyond this, the taking of the upper position at the start, or perhaps, we may say, before the start, gives the power to outmanoeuvre an enemy, in spite even of inferior speed ... . The initial difference in altitude represents a store of potential energy which may be drawn upon when the opportunity occurs; ... The objective of securing the upper berth, or position, or "gage", ... will probably prove to be, and will remain, the key or pivot on which every scheme of aeronautical tactics will, in some way or another, be found to hang.

The question of employing armour as a protection against attack from above, or against dropping fire, is one which requires consideration on an entirely different basis from that of attack from below. In the latter case, the employment of protection in some degree may be looked upon as essential. The steel employed may be thin and only sufficient to be effective above some prearranged altitude, but, nevertheless, it will be essential. Protection from attack by other aeroplanes, or, more broadly, aircraft, is another question; we may express the utility of armour under these conditions definitely in terms of gun-power.

... let us consider two machines in combat – an aeroplane duel, in fact – and we will take it that at their average distance apart or range the mean number of shots fired by either to score a decisive hit is found to be 600. Now if either aeronaut by the employment of armour or gun-shields, or equivalent device, can reduce the effective target offered by his machine to one-half that previously presented, it will on average take 1,200 shots to knock him out in lieu of 600 without protection. But in order to provide for the weight of his armour he must cut down his armament; he must sacrifice either his gun weight, and with it his speed of fire, or he must carry a lesser total weight of ammunition, and risk finding himself without means of attack, this being virtually synonymous to being without means of defence. If the only alternative were the cutting down of the speed of fire – tersely, if he were to substitute, say, 30lb of armour for 30lb of gun – and if this represent half his total gun capacity, and involve a reduction in his speed of fire by nearly one-half, then the change might be considered as *nearly* [Lanchester's italics] justified, since he would receive two shots for every one he could discharge, but would at the same time be proportionately less vulnerable.

Obviously, *rate of fire* [Lanchester's italics] should be one of the last things to be sacrificed; but the alternative – a reduction of the load of ammunition involves a curtailment of the period of activity, and, as a corollary, an increase in the number of machines required for a given combat duty. Once admit the necessity for such additional machines, and we must estimate the sacrifice, or price paid for the armour, in terms of the loss of fighting strength due to

46

the absence of a section of the air-fleet occupied in replenishing. This is evidently a serious matter under the best conditions – ie, when fighting in the immediate vicinity of the base; if, however, an air-fleet be engaged far afield it becomes still more serious, and the sacrifice of rapidity of fire, rather than reserve of ammunition, might well prove to be the lesser of evils.

The foregoing illustration shows that, tangibly or intangibly, the matter is one of figures, or, at the worst, a balance of advantages not capable of ready numerical expression. It may thus not always be possible to lay it down definitely whether in theory given conditions mean the abandonment of armour or otherwise; but nevertheless the fact is determined by the sum of the conditions, and where theory is dumb the decision will require to be taken on actual experience, as in analogous problems in naval construction." (44)

It is probably fair to observe that Lanchester's thinking in relation to aerial combat was unlikely to have much immediate impact on the fighting men and the designers of their machines. At a time when on the one hand engine power had little to spare beyond getting a machine into the air and gaining modest altitude and on the other there was no real concept of aerial combat and the equipment or performance requirements for machines likely to be engaged in such work, Lanchester offered no solution to the weight problem posed by armour. The trade-off between performance and protection was to prove a vital concern in reality – and to do so for many years to come. But at least he exposed the problem and was prepared to explore the parameters that surrounded it. To the extent that he may have set others thinking, an invaluable service in itself, it is possible to believe that lives will ultimately have been saved as aviation developed into an increasingly crucial and hard-used weapon in the military armoury, not just over the next four years but over the next quarter of a century.

All the theorising and speculation began to be put to the test in the August of 1914. On 3rd August, Germany declared war on France; on 4th August, Britain declared war on Germany. *Flight* reported on Friday 14th August that a Sikorski aeroplane with pilot and two Russian officers was destroyed by rifle fire from Austrian troops on the previous "Tuesday" (11th August) at Cracow. The following day a German aeroplane flying at 1,500ft was brought down in Belgium. (45) Aeroplanes were certainly not invulnerable to fire from the ground, after all!

It is interesting to note that advertisements for armour plate manufactured by Thos Firth & Sons Ltd, a Sheffield firm that had already supplied O'Gorman with some of the armour steel plate for his BE 2 seats, began to appear in issues of *The Aeroplane* from 12th August 1914 onwards. Photographs of bullet-dented plates were supplemented by, *inter alia*, the following text:

"These plates, .104 ins thick, proved themselves bullet-proof when tested at 500 yards range with Service Rifle and Ammunition." (46)

3 The realities of War – Work for the aeroplanes!

The feature of the so-called "Great War" that perhaps distinguished it most clearly from earlier wars was the extent to which manufacturing industry, the product of the industrial revolution, made it possible to introduce a wide range of new weaponry and technical developments to meet the demands of specific battlefields. At sea, there was the widespread use of submarines and the continual struggle for defences against them; the threats and opportunities introduced by aeroplanes led to means for ships to shoot at them, to carry them and even to launch them. Indeed it was the German Naval airships, albeit land based, that began the strategic bombing of Britain as early as 19th January 1915. (47) On the ground, there was a race for more and better artillery, for trench weaponry; tanks, great lumbering machines plated with steel sheets, arrived on the scene, leading to the development of weapons to defeat them. It was in the air, however, where the greatest challenges to inventiveness lay: inventiveness in the ways that war in the new dimension should be waged and in the tools – the men, machines and equipment – required to wage it. Lanchester's theorising was to become reality.

In 1914 and early 1915, aeroplanes had two basic functions: artillery spotting as, in effect, mobile observation balloons; and reconnaissance, including photography, over the battlefield and the enemy positions – in effect, a farther-seeing and more speedy alternative to the traditional light cavalry scouts. The effectiveness of aeroplanes as the "eyes" of the Armies was soon recognised and led inevitably to the search for means to put out those "eyes" – gunfire to combat them from the ground and fighting aeroplanes to engage them in the air. The aerial engagements were at first dictated by the daring and opportunism of individual aircrews in poorly equipped machines, but as the first offensives on the ground soon drew to a halt and the long war of attrition settled in, interspersed by offensive actions by one side or the other that dashed the hopes of short-lived advances on the despairs of stalemates and retreats, additional rôles – prompting new designs for aeroplanes – emerged. What came to be called "contact patrols" attempted to provide better communications on the ground between the forward formations and their headquarters towards the rear; counter-battery work, aimed at spotting the enemy's field-guns; bombing from the air provided the means to strike at the enemy beyond the range of the earth-bound – or ship-borne – artillery; aerial combats, taking literally to new heights the machine-gun that had already wrought so much havoc on the ground, provided an increasingly effective means for depriving enemy machines of the air space in which to work. John Terraine described an early RFC contact patrol:

> "For the [British] attack at Aubers Ridge (9 May [1915], supporting the French at Artois) three radio-equipped aircraft were detailed to report the

progress of the infantry; the latter were to display white linen strips, 7 feet long by 2 feet wide, as they reached successive lines in the German defences. Unfortunately, they did not reach those lines, and the airmen, in the smoke and dust of battle, found the tiny earth-coloured figures of friend and foe beneath them impossible to distinguish." (48)

To see through the "smoke and dust of battle", aeroplanes on contact patrols began to fly lower to distinguish friend from foe and achieve their objectives. But such low flying presented both opportunities and hazards. The opportunities lay in the aeroplanes being able to contribute further to the war effort and support their Army colleagues by shooting up enemy targets on the ground as they presented themselves – troops, gun emplacements and the like. The hazards arose because the aeroplanes found themselves vulnerable to fire from the ground – both rifle and machine gun fire – and, being dedicated to their work, vulnerable also to attacks in the air by enemy machines. It was in the light of these developments, particularly the ground fire, that the practicalities of armour protection began to be considered – all exactly as Lanchester had foreseen.

It is not possible to be certain when contact patrols and especially the ground/trench attacks/fighting work really began; the evidence is a little confused and after all this time the actual timing is not really important to the story of armour protection. But the broad pattern of events can at least be summarised, both from the British and from the German sides. In Volume 2 of the official historical record, The War in The Air series published during the period 1922–1937, H A Jones (49) made his first mention of the use of "trench fighters" by the RFC – "close reconnaissance and trench bombardment" is how he described their work. Among the British aeroplanes available at the start of the allied offensive on the Somme that began on Saturday 1st July 1916, the 4th Army had the following Corps Squadrons at its disposal:

Corps	Squadron	Allotment of Aeroplanes			
		Counter-Battery	Contact Patrol	Trench Fighters (a)	Specific Missions (b)
VIII	No 15 (BE 2cs)	8	3	3	2
X	No 4 (BE 2cs)	9	3	4	2
III	No 3 (Moranes)	4	3	3	2
XV	No 3 (Moranes)	4	Shared with III Corps	-	-
	No 9 (BE 2cs)	-		2	-
XIII	No 9 (BE 2cs)	5	4	4	3

(a) Close-reconnaissance and destructive bombardment.
(b) Destruction of kites, balloons, close photography, etc., and reserve.

It seems, therefore, that the uses of at least a few machines for contact patrol and trench fighting duties were already recognised tactical options by the start of the battle; according to Jones, it was the Battle of the Somme (1st July – 18th November 1916) that first:

> "... [Gave] results which made it clear that this new demand [low flying work] on the air would be a feature of all future ground operations ... A surprising fact that emerged from the fighting in the first phase was the comparative immunity of the low flying aeroplane ... Actually no contact aeroplanes were shot down, although many of them were so knocked about that they had to be dismantled and rebuilt." (50)

On 14 July 1916 at 3.30 pm, during the battle, Captain A M Miller (pilot) and 2nd Lieutenant C W Short (Observer) in a Morane machine of No 3 Squadron were described quite specifically as having harassed German infantry near High Wood to aid advancing British troops by raking the enemy positions with Lewis-gun fire. The aeroplane was badly holed by bullets, but got home. (51) This and other similar attacks by British machines demonstrated that ground attack work of some sort was becoming a more regular occurrence. But Jones noted that according to German sources:

> "... contact patrols had already been introduced by the Germans during the Verdun [21st February – 18th December 1916] offensive ..." (52)

though there was no record on the British side of any actual ground "attack" work by the German machines.

Major Georg Paul Neumann, an officer who served with the German Air Service during the War, writing after the War but a little earlier than Jones and describing the German position from the spring of 1915 onwards, recorded that:

> "On the Western Front in the autumn of [1914] we brought out [an unarmed] biplane L.V.G. which had somewhat better lift [than the 100hp-engined 'reconnaissance machine' that took the field in 1914], but was particularly distinguished in that it could climb and travel faster. ... this machine during the first few months of war did good and useful service, principally reconnaissance and artillery observation ... However, as the war on the ground concentrated more into trenches, and the struggle became stationary with a closed system of opposing lines, this type proved to be unsuitable under changed conditions. The incessant elaboration and development of the tactics and science of trench warfare called so urgently for the rapid production of efficient aeroplanes that one might truthfully say that trench warfare was the father of the modern flying machine. ...
>
> In the spring of 1915 it became clear that the original standard [C type machines designed for general purposes], in spite of all improvements, would have to be replaced by types designed for special purposes, ...
>
> Trench warfare itself brought into existence a specialised type of machine, the 'contact machines', which frequently flew at a height of only 30 or 40 feet. Heavy armour was required to protect the engine, tanks, pilot, and

Halberstadt CL II contour or contact fighter. (Imperial War Museum, Q.66217)

observer from the withering rifle and machine-gun fire to which they were subjected, and this armour could only be carried at the expense of climbing power, flight duration, and quickness of movement. On the other hand, the 2-seater fighting machines which attacked infantry directly with machine-guns, bombs, and hand grenades, had to be as fast as possible and very quick on the controls. For that reason this type was only lightly armoured or else carried no armour at all." (53)

Nothing could be a clearer demonstration of Lanchester's ideas writ large than Neumann's heavily armoured machines flying at "only" 30 or 40 feet! Nor could there be a better description of the two quite contrasting demands for low-flying machines:

– heavily armoured machines for contact work, where the armour was required to protect the crews while passively seeking out and maintaining contact with the troops below and only when this work was completed – or when circumstances demanded it – taking the opportunity actually to attack enemy ground forces; and

– lightly armoured, or even non–armoured, fast and manoeuvrable machines – such as the Halberstadt CL II able to whizz about the battlefield, actively seeking enemy targets to attack.

Neumann continued:

"At the beginning of the long series of C type machines was the first German 'battle plane', which made its appearance at the front in the spring of 1915. In addition to excellent flying qualities, this machine was easy to take off and land. ..." (54)

He did not explain what these "battle planes" were, but they were probably the DFWs and LVGs – unarmoured C types with the 160hp engines
– that Gray & Thetford suggested were, around the end of 1915:

"... modified to include armour sheet underneath the seats and fuel tanks
..." (55)

Indeed, an extract of 20th January 1916 from a French report on the
German Air Service actually mentioned:

"Shields

"Some battle planes have been fitted with shields protecting the observer
and pilot. In certain machines the [nacelle/seats] and petrol tank are protected
by [steel plate/an envelope made of sheet steel] . ..." (56)

Neumann went on to describe the first appearance of the German contact patrols during the Battle of Verdun (21st February – 18th December
1916):

"It was first of all in the summer of 1916 – when our attacks against Verdun,
which had begun so brilliantly, came to a bloody end ... From the moment
when the infantry had left their lines of attack they were almost out of touch
with the higher command and their own supports ... [after] carrier pigeons,
war dogs, etc., failed utterly, ... the flying man was the only messenger that
remained. ...

... The first primitive order referring to this scheme ran as follows: 'Fly
low, reconnoitre the situation with your own eyes, return, and report.' ... the
result was heavy casualties. If the enemy permitted our airmen to fly low,
the machine was soon subjected to concentrated sniping and fire from the
ground, particularly from machine guns, unfortunately only too often with
disastrous results. ...".(57)

It is worth noting that on the British side, O'Gorman had received from
the War Office in the April of 1916 a report (58) by a French Liaison Officer showing that even before the Battle of the Somme the French were
quite well organised so far as armoured machines were concerned. There
were, in principle, five types of machine:

Class A ("Army-corps" all-round work machines), having detachable
7/32 inch thick armour weighing 350lb, intended to give protection
to the crew, radiator, tanks and engine. The only aeroplane actually
mentioned was the twin-engined Caudron G4 machine, capable of
carrying a load of up to one ton.

Class B ("Fighting Scouts"), having a small armoured screen 9/32 inch
thick and weighing 28lb.

Class C ("Battle Planes"), having light armour weighing 70lb.

Class D ("Gun planes") and Class E ("Bombardment"), both types having no armour.

On the actual armour, the report was quite detailed:

"Armouring and Armament

A 3/16 inch armour plate practically protects from the German standard bullet (S type), at a height of 1,500ft. Such plates are now fitted underneath the fuselage, under motor, tanks and crew; and on the sides near the crew, for all "Army-corps" machines.

For aerial fighting, where the Germans now use a new type of bullet (S.M.K.), which, close to the mouth of the gun will go through 9/16 inch of special steel, we now use a small plate of 9/32 inch, in front of pilot. This, or the extra protection given by motor and tanks, ensures absolute protection at close quarters from type S bullet, and practically from S.M.K. at 200 yards."

In Volume 4, Jones described the RFC's ground attacking contribution the following year, at the start of the Battle of Arras (9th April–4th May 1917):

"... aeroplanes had ... gone 'over the top' ahead of the attacking infantry, and, with machine-gun fire and bombs, had helped to demoralise the enemy troops." (59)

John Morrow has described the British attack at Arras as witnessing:

"... the debut of [German] 'infantry fliers', who had evolved from the protection flights for army co-operation planes (Schutzstaffeln or Schustas). These battle fliers (Kampfflieger) or, as they preferred to be called, storm fliers (Sturmflieger), supported the infantry with machine guns and grenades. That summer the Schusta became an effective offensive and defensive weapon, attacking enemy batteries, strong points, and infantry reserves with machine gun fire and light fragmentation bombs. ... During the British attack at Messines on 6th June [1917], ... the German infantry fliers controlled the enemy breakthrough on the evening of the first day.

The infantry fliers took high losses in their dangerous work, as they ranged over the front at 600 metres altitude, buffeted by the drafts of passing shells, and then descended to strafe British troops from 100 metres above the trenches, in the dead zone between the artillery fire from both sides. ...

... On 20th September [1917], when heavy rain and low cloud grounded other units, Schutzstaffel 23 flew alone under the ceiling below 100 metres and returned with their planes so badly riddled that they were out of action for eight days until they received new ones." (60)

So, the RFC's Corps squadrons were building on their work at the Somme and doubtless taking advantage, too, of the observations of the Germans' low-flying work at Verdun, while the Germans too were pressing on with their infantry or battle fliers. British orders were issued for the forthcoming Battles of Ypres (Third, 31st July–10th November 1917) and Cambrai (20th November–6th December 1917) covering bombing and machine-gun attacks. For example, the Battle Orders for Third Ypres included orders issued by Brigadier General P Game from the Advanced General Headquarters of the RFC on 25 July 1917 (GS 21/1) that required on "Z" day (31st July):

"Attacks on aerodromes with machine gun fire

O C 9th Wing will detail five machines, one to attack each of the following [5] aerodromes in the early morning with MG fire from low altitude ...

Machines will start as early as possible in order to arrive at their respective objectives as soon as it is light enough for accurate shooting." (61)

Under Supplementary Orders (a) to GS 21/1, 9th Wing were to detail the following on Z day:

"(a) Two machines to fire on troops, transport, and motor cars from a low altitude ... Machines will be independent of one another. The first two will leave the ground one hour after zero, or as soon after as weather and light permits. The attack will be kept up as continuously as possible throughout the day." (62)

Orders issued on 30th July by Brigadier General C A H Longcroft, commanding V Brigade RFC in the field, included details for single machines to attack each of three aerodromes with machine-gun fire from a low altitude:

"4. Ground Targets

All favourable targets west of ... will be attacked from low altitude. (Not above 2,000 [feet]).

These attacks will be carried out as opportunities occur by machines of Corps squadrons and by scout machines specially detailed for low flying.

Particular care will be taken that no troops are fired at on the ground unless they are unmistakenly identified as hostile.

These machines will also be employed in attacking and driving off enemy contact patrol machines." (63)

Commenting on Third Ypres, Jones noted of these orders and their implementation:

"A new development was the use of single-seater fighters for low bombing, particularly against aerodromes, with the object of keeping the enemy fighters on the ground, at least during the early stages of the offensive." (64)

RFC headquarters' instructions to I Brigade and 9th Wing for the Battle of Cambrai were even more detailed than those for Third Ypres, and allocated specific duties to aircraft like the DH 4 bombing machines and the Sopwith Camel scouts. (65)

It was in response to the British offensive of the Battle of Cambrai (20th November–6th December 1917) that, according to Jones (notwithstanding Morrow), the German counter attack on 30th November involved "battle flights" on a major scale – which apparently came as a rude shock to the British Army.

"The feature of the battle so far as concerns the air services was the development of low-flying attacks on the infantry, and an extension of this activity, in future battles, was foreshadowed. ... The casualties to the low-flying aircraft were high, averaging ... 30 per cent for each day on which aeroplanes were used on this duty.

... The enemy low-flying attacks ... played a part in the success of the German counter-attack ... but [being on the receiving end of such attacks] ... was ... new to the British infantry." (64)

Both Jones and Neumann were in substantial agreement that low flying was effective but dangerous work – and it was work that was beginning to be reflected in statistics, as predicted by Lanchester three years earlier.

The German "contact patrols", intended to maintain contact with the infantry, were vulnerable not only to attacks from the ground but also from British aeroplanes that sought to deny them airspace. To enable their machines to continue with this important work, the German Air Service pursued two different but parallel approaches to the way forward in 1917. One of these approaches was the use squadrons ("Schutzstaffeln" – escort flights) of "escort machines" which, according to Neumann (like Morrow):

"... originally established for the protection of our 'working aeroplanes', were the precursors of the trench-strafing machines. ... These escorting machines remained in the immediate neighbourhood of their companion, and concentrated their attention upon warding off hostile attacks. ... The success which attended their efforts [during September 1917] laid the foundation of that work upon which the escort squadrons were principally employed later – attacks on ground targets. As a result of this new work, they were re-christened with the glorious name of 'storm squadrons' (ie trench-strafing machines). In the course of trench warfare it was found that even when our attacking infantry had succeeded in driving the enemy from his trenches, and at the very moment when their attack was successful, the assault was robbed of its principle moral effect by the failure of our artillery to provide sufficient preliminary protection against the enemy's counter-attacks. This fault was corrected with marked success by the trench-strafing pilots, who flew in front of the assaulting troops at a height of 150 to 200 feet, and attacked the enemy in his trenches with machine-gun fire and hand-grenades. ... However, ... [the enemy's] back areas also had to be dealt with: their artillery, their support trenches, ammunition dumps, the reserves that were being hurried up to the front, their ammunition columns, lorries, trains, etc. This was a rich field for the work of the trench-strafing machines." (66)

The other approach involved armour protection:

"Machines for contact patrol and other work associated with the infantry came more and more into use, and for this purpose the C type also was originally used. In 1917, however, on account of the very heavy losses inflicted by fire from the ground, the machines had to be extensively altered, although the main design was still adhered to. The forward part of the fuselage encased the occupants, engine, and tanks in strong armour-plating of chromium-nickel steel. An entirely new departure in aeroplane construction in 1917 produced a most interesting type, the Junker-Fokker [CL I], which was entirely built of duralumin [an aluminium-base alloy] and had a monoplane wing with internal bracing. ... The all-metal construction was a great protection against fire, and the armour plating, which consisted of one-fifth inch chromium nickel steel, was impenetrable at the closest range. This armour completely encased the engine." (67)

"It was on that front [Flanders, Autumn 1917] that the infantry contact machine was found to be an indispensable weapon of modern warfare. The joint duties of contact patrol and 'ground strafing' earned them the comprehensive designation of 'battle machines'. In the last tremendous offensives in the spring of 1918, ... , whole squadrons ["Schlachtstaffeln" – battle flights] of these 'battle machines' preceded the infantry into battle, wore down the enemy's resistance, destroyed artillery emplacements, and showed our infantry the path to Victory ..." (68)

The course of events may very well have been as Neumann described, though his "path to victory" seems oddly misplaced. Perhaps, having been at the centre of the events he described, Neuman can be excused a little delusion, though his reference to the Junker-Fokker Duralumin-fabricated monoplane machine as having armour plate is not supported by other sources (eg Gray & Thetford). However, Neumann did include a reference to what was clearly an armoured Junker J I/J 4):

"Towards the end of 1917 the advisability of continuing with contact patrol work was seriously doubted owing to the heavy casualties suffered ... through the enemy's very efficient aerial defenses. The men were required to fly a slightly modified C type of machine, which, being quite unprotected, left them completely exposed to hostile machine-gun fire from the ground. ... the aircraft industry came to the rescue with armoured aeroplanes, the so-called 'trench strafing' machine, whose planes, empennage, and fuselage were constructed throughout of metal, while the pilot's and observer's cockpits were so heavily armoured with chrome-nickel steel, that even armour-piercing bullets fired at close range caused nothing more than slight dents. Machines of this type were known to return ... bearing the marks of over thirty bullets, while their occupants escaped untouched ..." (Dyckhoff) (69)

These comments attributed to Dyckhoff, a contributor to Neumann's book, were also over-enthusiastic and time was to prove that the heavily armoured machines were not always as invulnerable as they at first seemed.

As what was to be the last year of the War opened, the ground attack rôle for aeroplanes was well established. James S Corum described the German position:

"By 1918 the German high command was emphasising the role of the 'battle planes' as offensive breakthrough weapons that would substitute for the German lack of tanks in providing mobile fire power and shock effect for the first waves of assault troops." (70)

Indeed, the General Staff of the German Field Army issued specific Instructions, dated 20th February 1918, on the "Employment of Battle Flights". (71)

Also in February 1918, the British GHQ in France issued their own memorandum on fighting in the air which included the following:

4 Choices of Objectives

"(B) Attack of Ground Targets in the Battle Zone with Bombs and Machine–gun Fire

The attack of ground targets ... is an integral part of the aerial offensive designed to weaken the moral of, and cause material damage to, the enemy's troops. It is carried out by fast single-seater machines flying normally at anything from 1,000 to 2,000 feet, either singly or in formation ...

5 Types of Fighting Machines

(D) Machines for Attacking Ground Targets

Machines for this purpose will, as a rule, be single-seaters. Climb is of relatively minor importance, but they require to be fast and very manoeuvrable and must have a very good view downwards. Single-seater fighters can be used for this work, but it is probable that a special type of machine will be evolved in which the pilot and some of the most valuable parts will be armoured. They will probably be adapted for carrying a few light bombs and will have at least one gun, capable of being fired downwards at an angle of 45° to the horizontal, and another firing straight ahead." (72)

This seems to have been the first statement officially issued by the RFC that recognised both the need for special machines for the ground attack rôle and the work behind the scenes to develop armoured aeroplanes. Even so, as Corum recounts, the Germans were one jump ahead of the British, for they already had such machines at their disposal:

"For the three German armies that attacked [at the beginning of their offensive in Picardy] on March 21, 1918, 27 ground-attack squadrons provided support." (70)

But by the time of the Battle of Le Hamel (4 July 1918), the British had learned the lesson and – still with little or no armour for protection:

"The fighter squadrons flew low over enemy lines as soon as the assault had begun, and the pilots made many attacks on infantry, guns, and transport, often from a height of about 200 feet ..." (73)

In the counter-attack during the second Battle of the Marne that followed on 15 July 1918, the RAF (as the RFC had become since 1st April 1918) was also:

"... mainly engaged in attacks against ground targets from low heights. ... German single-seater pilots strenuously contested the allied low-flying activities ..." (74)

Likewise in the British offensive of the Battle of Amiens (8-11 August 1918):

"... As the mists cleared [after 9.00am on 8th August] it was revealed that there was great confusion within the German lines, and exceptional targets were offered to the low-flying single-seater pilots. The battlefield became alive with aeroplanes ...

The main air work throughout the morning of the 8th was ... directed against ground targets ... in the afternoon ... attacks [concentrated] upon the Somme bridges. (75)

Jones recorded that:

"The Royal Air Force casualties on 8th August had been heavy. Forty-five aeroplanes were lost, and fifty-two more were wrecked or damaged and had to be struck off the strength of the squadrons. This was of a total of about 700 serviceable day-flying aeroplanes, and the wastage rate, therefore, was more than [14] per cent for the day. ... of the total of 97 aeroplanes deleted from the strength, 70 belonged to the bomber and fighter squadrons engaged on low-flying attacks against the Somme bridges or ground targets. As the number of aeroplanes so employed was about 300, the rate of wastage for low-flying aircraft was approximately [23] per cent." (76)

In a memorandum issued after the Battle the Fourth Army Commander, General Rawlinson, wrote:

"The important part played by the 5th Brigade [led by Brigadier-General L E O Charlton] , Royal Air Force, in the battle of the 8th August has filled me with admiration. ... The action of low-flying machines, ... though it entailed heavy casualties, had a serious effect in lowering the enemy's morale and inflicting actual losses ... ." (77)

So, by the later stages of the War, Lanchester's rather gruesome foresight had been fully realised and losses from low-flying work had indeed reached statistical proportions – and uncomfortable ones at that. But, then, there is no clear evidence that any of the British machines involved had much – if anything – in the way of armour protection either! Morrow has succinctly contrasted the quite different approaches to low-flying work of the three main air services: British, French and German:

"... The French increasingly risked condemning their revered pursuit pilots to relative ineffectiveness, compared to fighter arms that understood that mass, not individuals, determined the course of the war in the air as it did on the ground.

This cultural bias also helps to explain why French fighters did not engage in ground attack. ... Single-seat fighters were for aerial combat, nothing less. Only after witnessing the effectivenedss of German two-seater fighters did the French decide to develop their own, so that they might have low-level fighter operations while the single-seat elite continued to devote themselves solely to aerial fighting.

By 1917 the British and German commands believed that low-flying attacks were a powerful weapon in battle. British fighter pilots assumed the responsibility for ground attack as well as aerial fighting, as much as they reviled the ... [ground attack] duty. The Germans developed suitable planes for ground attack; the British simply threw in their fighters to supplement their army corps planes; the French did neither, and lagged far behind in effective ground attack operations." (78)

AEG C V experimental semi-armoured ground attack biplane.
(Imperial War Museum, Q.66544)

4 Armour protection in the battlefield

The need for armour to protect aeroplanes and their crews began to appear towards the end of 1915, well before the Battle of the Somme in 1916, and there is evidence of at least an experimental German AEG C V, a modified C IV, machine of this period. As Morrow pointed out:

"One of the reasons for the [German] storm fliers' success was their aircraft." (79)

In the early War years the German Air Service used unarmed "B" types of machine, such as the DFW B I/II of 1914/15, the AEG B I/II of 1914 and the B III of 1915, the LVG B I/II also of 1914/15. Neumann described in detail the broad course of development in the German Air Service's machines for ground attack work:

"Trench-Strafing machines

With the growing practice of harassing the infantry by low-flying aeroplanes, there arose the necessity of developing the C type [the first of the C types having appeared in the spring of 1915 as general purpose machines] especially for this purpose. It was equally important that a machine designed for this object should be fully equipped with offensive weapons such as machine-guns, bombs, etc. and also exceedingly fast and quick on the controls. As a consequence, climbing power and flight duration had to be sacrificed. At first armoured machines with quick-firing guns were experimented with, but they were abandoned later in favour of the new CL [lighter] type ... [which] could attack and escape quickly, and it was also more suitable for aerial fighting.

The Hannoveraner [CL V, or CL 5] and the Halberstadt [CL IV, or CL 4] were among those specially designed to answer this purpose. The former did not survive so long as the Halberstadt because it was not so light on the controls, and because a considerable area of ground was invisible to the observer on account of the excessively wide fuselage. ...

... An all metal machine, the [Junker–Fokker] CL I, was an exceedingly fast monoplane two-seater whose planes were unsupported by any external bracing wires. One advantage of the all-metal construction was the fact that there was no tendency for the wings to tear when punctured by bullets; also, the additional protection [?] afforded to the vital parts and the occupants rendered the machine almost secure from attack." (80)

Neumann seems here again to have been confusing the all–metal but unarmoured Junker-Fokker monoplane machine (CL I) with the armoured Junker J I/J 4 biplane machine, one of a trio of armoured infantry machines that included AEG and Albatros types. Morrow described these machines:

"Powered by the 200hp Benz Bz4 [engine], the AEG and Albatros were modified C types with 860 to 1,078 pounds of additional armour plate for the crew and engine compartments, while the Junkers was all metal and ideally suited to low-altitude operations. Aircrews praised the slow and ungainly Junkers Möbelwagen, or 'furniture van', for the absolute security they offered from machine gun fire from the ground. Though they were vulnerable to enemy fliers above, their operational altitude of 100 metres was too low for flak, which was ineffective below 200 metres." (79)

The Royal Flying Corps seems to have begun to adopt armour protection, at least in the form of bullet-proof seats, almost from the outset of the war. The Chief Ordnance Officer at Farnborough sent a Memorandum to the War Office on 28th September 1914:

"... I have the honour to report that the Officer Commanding, Royal Flying Corps ... has asked me to take up the question of Bullet Proof Seats.

Captain Longcroft, who has just returned from the front, states the present patterns are very unsatisfactory: they are too heavy and do not protect the most important parts. It is extremely rare for an aviator to be attacked by troops vertically beneath him and consequently protection is more important at the sides than beneath.

He recommends that the seats should be bullet proof at 3,000 feet instead of 1,800 and should be scoop shaped to protect the aviator for about 6 [inches] vertically.

Officer Commanding, Royal Flying Corps ... urges that existing contracts should not be disturbed ..." (81)

There was a hand written addition to the Memorandum:

"*Colonel Trenchard has seen a copy of this memo.*"

At this time, "Lieutenant Colonel" Trenchard was still commanding the Military Wing of the RFC at Farnborough and responsible for forming new squadrons for service in France, though in the following November he was to be appointed to command the 1st Wing serving in France. He would, in due course, rise to even greater heights in the RFC and later the RAF.

During 1915, the Royal Flying Corps was also experimenting with the use of armour rather more extensively than the installation of bullet proof seats. The Vickers FB (Fighting Biplane) 5A Gunbus, a two-seater "pusher" with the engine behind the cockpit nacelle to push the machine forward, appeared on the Western Front during 1915 and according to C F Andrews:

" ... at least four [machines] were constructed with armour–plated nacelles". (82)

It is possible that these armoured machines were intended for low–flying work. In aerial fighting, the FB 5 proved to be no match for the Fokker Eindeckers that began to appear in the June of 1915. Like all "pusher" machines, the FB5 was vulnerable to attack from behind and it is unlikely that the armour would have been intended as frontal protection against return fire from enemy machines under attack – the weight of armour on performance well above the ground would have precluded that! The better performing and better equipped, but unarmoured, FE (Farman Experimental) 2b and DH (De Havilland) 2 pusher machines that appeared in 1916 were able to turn the tide back against the Eindeckers.

In the meantime, the British attack that ousted the Germans from the village of Neuve Chappelle in March 1915 had ground to a halt and the German attack that started the second Battle of Ypres had not begun until 22nd April. By this time, armoured seats at least had evidently become more widely used. On 9th April 1915 Lt Col (Temporary) H R H Brooke-Popham in command of 2nd Wing RFC in the Field responded to an enquiry from his replacement as Deputy Assistant Quarter-Master-General (DAQMG) by giving the following as the "general opinion of [presumably British] pilots" on the need for some form of armour protection:

"BE 2's with 70 HP Renault

No armouring beyond the bucket seats such as are now supplied with the BE 2c's. These should be removable. Any additional weight would reduce the climbing powers too much.

BE 2c's with RAF engine

(a) bucket seats for pilot and passenger to be of the same size and shape as the present wicker seats; ie sides and back to come higher than the armoured seats at present supplied. To be made of 3/16 inch steel at bottom and 3/32 inch at the sides and back.

(b) Service petrol tank to be made entirely of armour plate, except the top. Thickness 3/16 inch at bottom and 3/32 inch sides and ends. To be divided into two equal portions, with separate pipes, both to the carburettor and from the lower petrol tank

(c) Carburettor – 3/16 inch armour round bottom and 3/32 inch armour round sides. ...

(d) Sump – to be made of armour plate 3/16 inch bottom and 3/32 inch sides.

This is I consider the maximum that should be put on to an ordinary machine, any further additions will impair the climbing speed to too great an extent.

A few machines might I think be specially armoured for flying low over the enemy's lines.

These might be single seaters of the BE 2c type with RAF engine, and 2½ hours petrol capacity.

The whole fuselage from the back of the pilot's seat up to and including the engine should be enclosed in U shaped armour plate to come round the pilot's back and reach as high as his shoulders and the tops of the cylinders. The propeller boss should also be armoured." (11)

Brooke-Popham later became Air Chief Marshal Sir Robert Brooke-Popham GCVO, KCB, CMG, DSO, DFC; he retired in 1937 as Inspector General of the RAF and was from November 1940 until December 1941 Commander-in-Chief, Far East.

In an interesting though inadvertent vision of a future German machine, the Junkers J I/J 4, Brooke-Popham continued:

"It might be possible to construct the actual fuselage of ¼ inch armour plate and do away with all woodwork and bracing wires. Otherwise I would suggest covering it with the bullet proof compound plate, ...

If practicable the main wing spars and wing struts might be made of steel,..

VOISINS. Sides and back of petrol tank to be armoured with 3/32 inch plate. The bottom is already armoured.

The lower reservoirs of the radiator to be armoured with 3/16 inch plates.

Bucket armour seat to be provided for the pilot." (83)

Lieutenant Colonel C J Burke, commanding 2nd Wing RFC in the Field, also responded on 20th April 1915:

"1. All machines should have bullet proof seats for pilot and passenger. ... The passenger's only should be removable.

2. Speed, ability to turn and climb are, after the above requirements, the best protection.

3. The sump and service tank should be protected by armour on machines for special missions.

4. At present, it seems out of the question to consider further armament, as machines cannot carry all the things that are required for work now. ..." (83)

BE 2c armoured biplane. (Public Record Office, AIR 1/2411/303/4/20)

The extent to which these views either reflected widespread practice (eg armoured seats) or were subsequently taken up is not clear. Certainly there is evidence that several types of Voisin machines were set up for ground attack and/or carried big guns that could hardly have been used for any other purpose – though according to Bruce (84), no British-built Voisins served operationally in France and of the French-built machines in service with the RFC the last left France on 4th November 1915.

There is a note on record, dated 19th June 1915, that the RFC was considering armour plating "the pilot's seat, engines, etc" of the RE 8:

" ... About 90 sq ft" would be required." (83)

Further, on 12th July 1915, Major V Charlton (Commanding Officer of No 8 Squadron, RFC) wrote to the Officer Commanding 2nd Wing RFC:

"1. The value of this armour [plate beneath the fuselage] as fitted to the BE 2c No 2030 cannot be overestimated. It protects carburettor, petrol tanks, throttle and air controls from all shell bursts other than a direct hit, and on these and other grounds gives a feeling of confidence to both pilot and observer.

2. The effect of this armour plating on the flying of the machine is difficult to estimate. It is certainly very slight since the machine with passenger and Lewis gun will climb quite comfortably to 7,000ft in 20 minutes." (83)

It is at least possible that the machine to which Charlton referred was the "specially armoured" BE 2c, though the serial number on the tail fin in the photograph cannot fully be distinguished. Clearly, however, at least some trials on the practicality and value of armour protection were being

AEG J I two-seat ground attack biplane – armoured development of the C IV. (Imperial War Museum, Q.66517)

made in the Field and the fitting of armoured (or, at least, steel) seats during 1915 was not exactly unknown. Indeed, there is a note on record, dated 29th November 1915, that the GOC 1st Brigade RFC

"apparently has some steel seats damaged by rifle or shrapnel fire" (83);

and there is a letter, dated 8th December 1915, from the Equipment Officer 2nd Wing RFC to the Officer in charge of stores at 1st Aircraft Park in France to the effect that:

"A portion of steel seat taken from a machine which is at present on charge of No 6 Squadron is forwarded herewith, and from the reports received from the other squadrons, seems to be the only one at present which has been damaged by bullet. ... The bullets were fired from behind at a range of about 60ft." (83)

According to Bruce (84), it was after one or two British aeroplanes had been brought down by rifle and machine-gun fire from the ground during 1916, that the RFC asked for armoured aeroplanes. Some BE 2c machines, had been provided with armour about and below the cockpits and engines but, contrary to Charlton's view, the weight of the armour (no less than 445lb) and the total absence of streamlining had a detrimental effect upon the machine's performance. It is not clear if Bruce had in mind the machine to which Charlton had specifically referred in 1915. Nevertheless, one of these machines was apparently used by No 15 Squadron and flown on ground-strafing duties by a Captain Jenkins during the Battle of the Somme. Reportedly:

"in three months it was fitted with no fewer than eighty new wings and many other components" (84)

Presumably a testament to the effectiveness of the armour at the expense of unprotected parts – though there could have been little of the original machine left at the end! But, as will be seen later, armour was not necessarily the answer.

A later version of the Vickers Gunbus, the FB 9 "Streamlined Gunbus", appeared in 1916 and

> "Between June 1916 and September 1917 some 95 machines were built and used mostly for training duties at home, ... One FB 9 was especially modified as a trench-strafer with an armour-plated nacelle ..." (85)

This armoured machine and the four earlier FB 5s were the forerunners of more determined attempts to produce an armoured "pusher" for service at the Front.

The use of armoured seats did not entirely disappear from view however. At the beginning of 1917 the Royal Aircraft Factory's new machine, the SE 5, was still undergoing trials and in January some flying trials were held to compare a prototype of the new machine with the 110hp Nieuport Scout and the 150hp SPAD. Perhaps in anticipation of the forthcoming Spring offensive at Arras, the SE 5 was actually fitted with armour, as Lt R M Hill of No 60 Squadron who flew the prototype machine noted in his report:

> "Armour. The back of the seat is armoured; but I am of opinion that a better system might be arranged, which would deflect the armour-piercing bullets so largely used by the Germans since the slightly curved back at present used would not be very efficient for this. If two vertical plates were arranged at an angle with each other forming a V in plan, they could be placed back in the body behind the seat and need not be raised with the lifting seat." (86)

Apparently, the SE 5 was fitted with a device for raising the seat during flight, so that the pilot could get a better view. It is not reported that the armour was anything more than an experiment and was retained in production machines when they entered service with the RFC in the April of 1917. Nor is it clear whether the armour was being thought of as protection against ground fire, perhaps the most likely possibility in view of the increasing use of aircraft for ground attack work (although an armoured floor might then have been more appropriate), or against attacks from behind in air combat. The armour would doubtless have had some value in either case. What is particularly interesting, however, is Lt Hill's suggestion of deflection plates as providing a better scheme of protection, an idea that seems thereafter to have lain dormant until armour protection again became an issue in the latter half of the 1930s.

On the German side, the DFWs and LVGs with armoured seats and tanks were an interim measure pending the arrival of more extensively armoured machines – initially the AEG J I/II and the Albatros J I – during 1917. According to Gray & Thetford, the AEG J I/II armoured infantry contact patrol machines were:

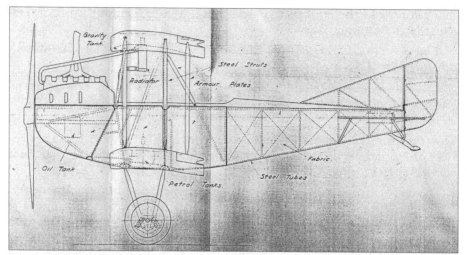

Drawing of the AEG J I/II armoured infantry contact aeroplane.
(Imperial War Museum, Dept of Printed Books, Ref K.89/799)

> "... virtually a C IV re-engined with a Benz and with a modified, armoured fuselage. ... The J Is were not fitted with any forward-firing armament, but two Spandau guns were bolted to tubular brackets on the rear cockpit floor. These fired forward and downwards at an angle of 45° to facilitate strafing of troops and harassing of ground targets, which were the prime duties ...." (87)

In fact, there were two types of armoured AEG machines: the single-engine two-seater ground attack type (J I/II) intended to carry out offensive patrols against infantry and a twin-engine three-seater bomber (GIVk).

An example of the single-engine type was brought down near Hinges, a few miles northwards of Béthune in France, by an RE 8 of No 21 Squadron RFC on 16th May 1918. A report by J G Weir (later Brigadier-General (Temporary) J G Weir CMG, Ministry of Munitions) at the Royal Aircraft Establishment, as it then was, Farnborough described the machine from an examination of the "badly crashed" remains. Weir reported that:

> "The aeroplane is designed for the purpose of carrying out offensive patrols against infantry, and is furnished with armour, which affords protection for its personnel. This armour appears, however, to be more or less experimental." (88)

Weir went on to describe the armour in a technical manner that was remarkably prescient of the debate on armour protection that was to resurface within the RAF nearly twenty years later:

> "Protection for the pilot and gunner is afforded by armour, which is shown in the General Arrangement Drawing in thick lines [in fact the "thick lines" are only just recognisable in drawing reproduced above]. There are three panels at each side, and three panels at the bottom of the fuselage, an ar-

AEG GIVk heavy bomber with a canon in the nose. (Imperial War Museum, Q.67426)

mour bulkhead being placed at the rear of the gunner's cockpit to protect him from behind. The armour is 5.1mm thick, and its total area is 105.8 sq ft. The weight of the armour is thus approximately 860lb.

Careful tests have been made to ascertain the effectiveness of this armour, and the table below gives the ranges at which these plates are safe or unsafe against penetration by bullets of various types. These figures may be taken as correct within the limit of a practical firing test.

The armour is undoubtedly too light to afford protection against British armour-piercing bullets fired from the ground at a lower height than 500 feet, while a machine armoured with it would have to fly at, at least, 1,000 feet to be safe from all but a very low percentage of hits.

Ammunition.	Angle to Normal Degrees	Safe range Yards	Unsafe range Yards
German AP	0	-	600
	15	500	400
	30	400	300
Mark VII P Armour piercing	0 probably	700	600
	15	400	300
	30	300	200
German Spitze	0	150	100
	15	100	50
	30	50	
Mark VII	0	50	
	15	50	
	30	50	

The armour does not appear to have been employed, as it might well have been, in a structural capacity – ie, it is simply an attachment to the framework, to which it adds no material strength. Its appearance seems to point to the fact that it had been added by way of experiment, and that it was of a more or less makeshift character. It had, for instance, evidently been necessary to open out existing holes and cut new holes in the course of erection. The armour is attached by setscrews to clips clamped on the fuselage members ..."

The AEG twin-engine armoured bomber was described in a Technical Commission Report on German aeroplanes and airships:

"The construction is of steel throughout, with the exception of the ribs of the main planes, which are of wood threaded onto steel tube spars. ... The principal feature of the machine is the armour plating, which covers the sides and base of the fuselage, and extends from the nose to the rear of the after gunner's cockpit, behind which a V-shaped panel of plating is fitted. The undersides of the engine eggs are also armour plated. ... The forward gunner is armed with a Parabellum gun, mounted on an imitation Scarff ring. On the floor and arranged to fire horizontally through an arc of about 60 deg is a mounting for a gun – presumed to be about 1½ pounder. This is fixed to a rotatable mounting, which is protected by a semi-circular shield of armour plate, which moves with the gun, as also does the gunner's seat. A second Scarff mounting with Parabellum gun is provided for the after gunner, who manages a 1½ pounder, fixed [it was assumed] to fire downwards through a trap–door in the floor; ... .

The weight of this machine being much greater than the original AEG bomber and the power plant the same, it is presumed that its speed capabilities are lower, but its armament would make it a formidable antagonist and it was evidently principally designed for "ground strafing" purposes." (90)

According to Gray & Thetford, the Albatros J I differed from it's AEG counterpart in that:

"... the whole of the nose was not armoured; only the actual cockpit area being covered with 5mm chrome nickel steel armour on the sides and underneath. To simplify manufacture the armour on the sides was largely in its original slab sheet form, cut to size, and bolted to the structure. To provide maximum protection for the pilot the side armour was not cut away on the front cockpit sides, but to facilitate entry and egress a panel was hinged to fold outwards and down.

... The extreme nose and forward belly panels were of sheet metal, the latter with an additional bulged fairing to encase the engine sump. The panelling adjacent to the Bz IV engine was also fashioned to follow a rounded contour, but these panels were not of armoured sheet. The remaining side nose panels, back to the armour, were of ply. ...

Operating in flights of three to six aircraft from the autumn of 1917 onwards, this class of machine was a continual thorn in the side of the Allied ground troops and artillery batteries as their downward-firing machine guns [two Spandau machine guns fixed to fire downwards at 45° through the floor] viciously probed and stabbed into trenches, gun pits and horse lines." (91)

According to Corum (70), during the Battle of Cambrai and afterwards the German Halberstadt CL II and the Hannover CL II were partially armoured and by the end of 1917 some 10.5% of German machines were for ground-attack – though it is perhaps unlikely that they were all of the armoured types.

The Russians did not entirely forget the possibilities of armour protection, even though Dybovski's "Delphin" made no apparent progress. In the August of 1916, Sikorski's series of "Ilya Muramets" multi-engined bombers came to fruition with the Russo-Baltic produced four-engine Type Ye2, with

> "... the pilot and co-pilot provided with armour plate below and behind their positions. This Type Ye2 was truly a 'Flying Fortress' with defensive armament of eight Lewis guns and a 50mm quick-firing cannon, the gunners positions featuring armour plate protection. Due to the extra weight, the bomb-load was reduced in the Ye2, the armour plate alone weighing some 600lb ..." (92)

The first of the Ilya Muramets had flow in the December of 1913 and during 1914 some 42 had been ordered by the Russian War Ministry, but after the first three were delivered for service trials the aeroplane was declared unfit for military use and the rest of those ordered were cancelled. Development work continued, however, and more than 75 Ilya Muramets were eventually deployed against the Central Powers along the Eastern Front during the Great War. They carried our more than 400 bombing raids between February 1915 and October 1917 – with the loss of only one machine to enemy action! (93)

Some comparisons can be drawn between the Ye2 and Germany's AEG G IV, though the latter carried nowhere near the same extent either of armour or of guns.

5 The Junker "Alert"

At the end of 1917, intelligence reports on Germany's interest in armoured aeroplanes led to a flurry of exchanges in the upper echelons of the British Air Ministry and the Royal Flying Corps. On 10th December 1917 Lord Rothermere (Harold Sydney Harmsworth), whom Prime Minister Lloyd George had appointed as the first Secretary of State for Air earlier in the year, wrote to Brigadier-General D le G Pitcher CMG DSO (Controller, Technical Department, Air Ministry, later Director, Directorate of Equipment and Officer Commanding No 22 Group):

"I understand from confidential information furnished to us that the Germans are concentrating all their energies on the building of armoured aeroplanes. We have direct information from Germany according to which in the newest type of aeroplane the observer sits in a closed compartment of steel provided with peepholes and entirely closed in.

I shall be obliged if you will let me have as speedily as possible a statement on the whole subject of armoured aeroplanes, and exactly what plans we have in hand to counter the Germans in this respect." (93)

Brigadier-General Pitcher soon replied, on 13th December 1917, copying in effect a response prepared by Lieutenant-Colonel/Wing Commander Alec Ogilvie, a Technical Staff Officer with the Ministry of Aircraft Production:

"Information has been received from [the Royal Flying Corps] and agents that an armoured machine for contact patrol work with infantry was on trial.

The machine is called the Junker and is said to be somewhat similar in external appearance to an RE 8. It has a 200 Benz motor and weighs about 4,600lb. The armouring is 1/5 inch thick. The speed is 80–85mph with a ceiling of 10,000 feet or 11,000 feet. Nothing better could be expected for that weight and horsepower.

The German machine has metal wings but it is very doubtful if a metal structure of the flimsy character necessary would stand up to machine gun bullets or to anti-aircraft [fire] any better than a wooden one.

The machine is no doubt a two seater and will be slow to manoeuvre. From a fighting point of view I am of the opinion that a small single seater fighter would be able to shoot down such a machine. The observer would either have to expose himself to repel an attack or try to shoot through a small hole or slit, in which case he would have a very poor chance of success against an active scout.

It is doubted if an armoured machine as described, could be intended for anything but low work. It has never been considered a feasible proposition for ordinary work, owing to the weight of armour. If it were produced and used by the Germans, I consider that a scout would be all over it, as it would be bound to be very unmanoeuvrable.

Junkers J I/J 4 armoured biplane. (Imperial War Museum, Q.90297)

With regard to countermeasures on our part, if the quick firing 1½ lb gun is a success, it is considered that there will be no great difficulty in dealing with the armoured machine. The DH 10, as a short distance gun machine will have a very good performance, somewhere about 120mph at any height below 5,000 feet.

EF [Expeditionary Force in France] have sent us no request for a machine to deal with this, but it is possible that they are thinking of using a short distance twin-engine gun machine [presumably the DH 10, to which reference had already been made] for this purpose.

As regards our own proposals for an armoured machine for contact work, it was originally proposed to make the machine a tractor but in the opinion of the Arial Fighting Committee ... a pusher was decided upon, and on this design the Factory [Royal Aircraft Factory, Farnborough] is engaged. The general characteristics of the proposed machine follow:–

Machine to be a pusher,

The machine to be suitable for flight at a height of 500ft, for shooting at objects on the ground.

The observer to sit in front and the pilot behind.

The engine to be 200 Hispano Suiza ...

Armour to be a single sheet at sides and double sheets at the bottom, suitable for protection of pilot, observer, petrol and engine, against armour piercing ammunition at 500ft ....

3 Lewis Guns in front ... triple mounting if possible.

Single Lewis Gun for firing backwards, for defensive purposes ...

The armouring would weigh 900–1000lb and would be double sheet in the bottom weighing 8.6lb per sq ft, and single sheet on the sides weighing 5.2lb/sq ft ...

Junkers J I/J 4 armoured biplane – the front portion was constructed in armour steel, while the rear portion was fabric-covered on a Duralumin tubular framework. (Public Record Office, AIR 1/2426/305/29/475)

It is not anticipated that this type will be seriously used for trench fighting and this is evidently EF's view who are asking for a high speed single seater fighter specially arranged for this work.

The NE I [night-fighter] machine at [the Royal Aircraft Factory] is being re-designed to carry armour ...

Steps are also being taken to see if the [Sopwith] "Camel" can be armoured; the weight of armour which the "Camel" would carry is at present being investigated." (93)

Major-General Hugh Trenchard, then Commander of the RFC in France, also responded to Lord Rothermere on 13th December 1917, describing two types of aircraft "which should definitely be asked for":

"A. An armoured aeroplane to use near the front line against infantry and troops on the ground. The machine must be a two-seater, with means of firing guns straight downwards and an air endurance of 3½ hours. It would have to be proof against armour piercing bullets, and be armoured on the sides as well as underneath, as there will be direct hits on the sides when the machine is banking. ... Owing to the weight of its armour, this machine would in my opinion not be able to carry any bombs, as to do this it would have to be made too big for use near the front line, and would be an easy target for trench mortars and similar weapons.

B. A machine to be used far behind the lines for dropping bombs as well as for firing on personnel on the ground, at places such as Mannheim, etc. ... this machine would be of no use unless it could be easily flown at night. If this could be done, it would not have to go higher than 8,000 feet. It would not have to be armoured on top; only underneath and on the sides.

Junkers J I/J 4 armoured biplane – the front portion of the fuselage, encasing the engine, the pilot and the observer/gunner was constructed from steel armour plate. (Public Record Office, AIR 1/2426/305/29/475)

... I would allot three of the A type machines to each artillery squadron out here, so as to do the low flying work; ... I would ask that this type might be pressed on with now. ...As to the B type machine; I consider that experiments should be pushed on with as fast as possible in this matter, and six machines made so that they can be tried out ..." (93)

Brigadier-General (as by then he had become) Brooke-Popham DSO entered the fray with a note on Trenchard's views to Pitcher on 18th December 1917:

"I do not think we have got any more information about the German armoured machine than you have, ie, practically nothing. ... As regards aeroplanes for attacking armoured machines, the only thing is to have a gun machine which will, I suppose, have to be a tractor, with the gun firing through the propeller shaft. We rather turned this down a little while ago because it was not then anticipated that the Germans would have armoured machines, but it appears that now we have got to be prepared for it. This machine ... is not the same as the big gun machines asked for [in November 1917], but ought to be the type of our present single-seater fighters with as good a performance as possible. Naturally the performance will not equal the present single-seater fighter, but it will be good enough for the attack of hostile armoured machines which cannot have a very big performance." (93)

The "Junker" machine to which Brigadier-General Pitcher had referred was in all probability the Junker J I/J 4) armoured two-seater biplane which, according to Gray & Thetford (94), entered service with German Infanterie-Flieger units in 1917. Several versions of the remarkable J I/J 4 appear to have existed, differing at least in the designs of their exhaust manifolds. They were intended for infantry contact patrol work and the armour was provided as a defence against ground fire. Two of these machines were examined after the Armistice, one of which was salvaged by British troops apparently near La Vacquerie in France during the German retreat of 1918 and the other had actually been brought down by the French. Armour-piercing bullets from a ground machine-gun had penetrated the armour of the latter machine and caused its descent. In a report on these machines, Brigadier-General Brooke-Popham described the J I/J 4:

> "The Junker is radically different from the usual type of aeroplane, ...
>
> It is evidently a serious attempt to reduce to a minimum the dangers due to enemy action while in flight, and to lengthen the life and endurance of the machine in spite of exposure to bad weather and to rough handling. To this end the machine is armoured, and all vulnerable units, so far as possible, are gathered within the armoured portion. Inflammable materials, and those which suffer rapid deterioration when exposed to rough weather, are almost eliminated. ...
>
> ... The body of the Junker is constructed in two distinct parts – a front armoured portion, and a rear portion built up of duralumin tubes.
>
> The armoured part ... is built of 5mm plate. The Junker is not an ordinary two–seater machine to which armour has been subsequently added, but the armour plate comprises the fuselage ...
>
> The armoured unit houses the engine, pilot, and gunner, and the petrol tank. The vertical cowl surrounding the engine cylinders is of armour plate and is not a mere fairing. The spinner which covers the propeller boss is made of aluminium. The armouring is very thorough, so that the chances of a bullet finding a vulnerable spot are small. (95)

A translated German Instruction Manual, appended to Brooke-Popham's report added:

> "BULLET-PROOF QUALITIES
>
> The wing construction does not include any member which, if damaged might endanger the safety of the whole. The liability of this machine to damage of any kind caused by projectiles is therefore extraordinarily low.
>
> SAFETY AGAINST FIRE
>
> These machines, including rudders and fins, being almost entirely constructed of non-inflammable material, are impervious to incendiary bullets or fires started in the carburettor.
>
> USES AND PROPERTIES OF THE ARMOURED BIPLANE
>
> The armoured biplane is a machine specially constructed for the requirements of infantry contact work.
>
> Special attention has, therefore, been paid to the protection of the engine, crew and wireless. The weight of the armouring is 470kg and, therefore, the climb of this machine is low as compared to a fighter machine, and it requires a longer run at starting and landing. ...

ARMOURING

The armouring consists of a casing (open only at the top) of highly tempered special steel ... made by the well-known "Panzerwerke" of Dillingen. ..." (95)

Weir/Boswell design for a British armoured single-seat biplane. (Public Record Office, AIR 2/731)

6 The British response

Some time around the beginning of November 1917 Sir William Weir, Member of the Air Board and Controller of Aeronautical Supplies, submitted to the Air Ministry details of his "Proposed Armoured Single Seater Biplane":

> "The original purpose of the design is to provide a machine, so constructed as to be practically invulnerable to rifle or machine gun shot. To this end, the vital portions of the machines, viz:– Pilot, engine, tanks, and controls would be enclosed in a tubular bodied fuselage, of non-magnetic, bullet-proof sheet steel. The circular construction would ensure greater protection, by tending to divert the course of shots, which strike the surface, resulting in a "glancing" shot.
>
> Owing to the comparatively heavy nature of the machine, and its consequent limited manoeuvrability its greatest value would be realised in trench raiding, and attacking enemy formations and supplies, behind the lines.
>
> For this purpose two Lewis guns are fixed, one on each side of the pilot pointed down in a line of fire sufficient to clear the propeller. ...
>
> The power unit ... is the 300 HP Napier Triple Four ...The construction of this engine is particularly adapted to the requirements of an armoured machine, owing to the central setting of the propeller shaft, and again because of the comparatively small dimensions for an engine giving such a substantial power. ..." (96)

This ingenious design appears to have been the work of William S Boswell in the Inspection Department of the Department of Aeronautical Supplies. The design was considered by Lieutenant-Colonel Alec Ogilvie, Assistant-Controller, Technical Department (Design). In a letter to Pitcher dated 27th November 1917, Ogilvie concluded:

"... the machine will be of comparatively large size so that the manoeuvring qualities will be poor. The performance is poor as compared with that of a single seated fighting machine. The protection from fire is not complete; as the fuselage and wings are entirely unprotected, and also the pilot's head and propeller are vulnerable; the protection is considerably better than on an armoured machine, but this is counterbalanced to some extent by the lower speed and less performance.

On the whole I do not think that this type of machine would be a satisfactory proposition." (97).

Tellingly, bearing in mind all the communications on armoured seats back in 1915, Ogilvie added:

"... Armoured machines have been tried on the front but the pilots very soon asked for permission to take the armour off as they all preferred safety due to handiness [and] speed rather than that gained by armour ..." (97)

Nothing further seems to have been heard of this proposal, although Ogilvie's criticisms were more than a little harsh – the armoured machines that appeared on both sides during the War had nothing much in the way of performance, except perhaps the later British machines (of which more later), or of protection for the fuselage (aft of the armour), wings, pilot's head, or propeller.

Perhaps, however, Ogilvie was mindful of work already in hand on other types of armoured machine. In France, for example, there was work on the development of a Salmson armoured machine for ground contact work and the RFC received a preliminary description of the machine dated 22nd December 1917. Similar to a type 2 Salmson Army Corps two-seater:

"The whole of the forward portion of the fuselage is armoured, forming a square section "tank" to which the rear [part] is fastened. It is intended to fit a circular plate of 4mm chrome steel between the exhaust crown and the engine itself. A ring of armour is fitted around the engine and hinged armour plate doors are provided opposite each cylinder for valve adjustments etc. Behind the engine are segments of plate to fill in the spaces between the ring and the square sides of the fuselage armour. The armour plate on the sides and top of the fuselage is 4mm thick, and on the bottom 5mm plates are used. The side armour is carried up above the level of the pilot's head, and on top a hinged cover is provided so that he can entirely cover himself in, excepting a slit in front of his eyes like that of an armoured motor car. Sliding panels are also provided in the armour at the side of his head, so that when he likes, he has normal visibility. On either side below these sliding panels there is an armour ledge or flange at [right angles] to the fuselage in which a slit is cut to allow the pilot a view downwards between the aluminium cowling and the side armour without exposing himself. ...

Sopwith TF 1 with a pair of Lewis guns which fired downwards through the floor of the cockpit (the breech blocks are evident in this view of the cockpit area.

(Courtesy Philip Jarrett)

The gunner has armour all round him except on top where a ring mounting will not allow of it. The armour plate over the petrol tank and pilot acts as a wind screen and should protect his head from shots directly ahead. A sliding panel is provided in the bottom armour in front of the gunner, so that he can fire downwards and forwards from a fixed mounting which is provided.

... [The radiator, specially fitted underneath the engine] has armour plate at sides and below, and a louvre of armour plate at the rear. In front of a venetian blind is provided which can be closed when desired.

All the armour at present being fitted, consists of soft iron plate. Messrs Salmson have not yet therefore, experienced the difficulties which are bound to accrue when the time comes to cut and fit actual armour plate.

... the designer of the machine ... anticipates great difficulty in obtaining the necessary armour, and has so far, failed to obtain any." (98)

The armoured Salmson was evidently at the early planning stage. No blue prints were available at the time and details of the machine were apparently changing from day to day. Given the hesitancy with which the British authorities had so far regarded the adoption of armour protection, the rather fancifully extensive and completely untried Salmson scheme – and the weight penalty that it would undoubtedly have entailed – was unlikely to find much support and does not seem to have received further consideration.

However, Lord Rothermere's enquiry of 10th December 1917 had already set wheels in motion. On 5th January 1918, Trenchard wrote to the Director General of Aircraft Production (DGAP) at the Ministry of Munitions:

"It is necessary to get ahead with the question of armoured aeroplanes.

At present we have asked for a small aeroplane for firing at troops on the ground with a slight amount of armour. I would like the Technical Department

Sopwith TF 1 with a pair of Lewis gun barrels visible between the undercarriage struts. Armour plate, outlined here in white, was fitted for the protection of the pilot.

(Courtesy Philip Jarrett)

under you to push ahead with the building of a big armoured aeroplane for experimental purposes." (93)

The DGAP (it happened by then to be Lord Weir!) followed this up on 7th January with a note to the Controller of the Technical Department:

"Three types [of armoured aeroplanes] are wanted:

(1) The partially protected machine based on our standard designs to be pushed forward very rapidly so that we may order sufficient for a small number of squadrons in the early summer.

(2) An armoured aeroplane for artillery work as indicated in General Trenchard's memorandum of requirements for 1919.

(3) A big armoured aeroplane to carry three people. General Trenchard considers this machine must be able to fly and land by night." (93)

It may be that with his "big armoured" machine, Trenchard had something like the Ye2 or the AEG in mind. The "partially protected machine" was undoubtedly the Sopwith Camel TF 1 (Trench Fighter No 1). According to Bruce:

"Sopwith Camels were used so extensively for Ground-attack work, that it was only natural to build a special version for that particular job. The F1 Camel B 9278, originally built by Boulton & Paul, was converted during 1917 into the Sopwith TF 1 by removing the Vickers guns and replacing them by a pair of Lewis guns which fired downwards through the floor of the cockpit. A third Lewis gun was mounted above the centre-section and armour plate was fitted for the protection of the pilot. ... Although the Sopwith TF 1 did not go into production, it paved the way for the later Sopwith Salamander." (99)

Robertson gave rather more details:

> "The initial proposal was to arm a Camel with downward firing guns, pro-
> tected by 700lb of armour and powered by a 110hp Le Rhône which, being
> lighter than a Clerget and taking less fuel, would compensate to a degree for
> the additional weight. ...
>
> ... the project was designated TF 1 ... but already the lines [at Sopwith's
> works] had been cleared of Camels as Snipe production was getting well un-
> der way. Boulton & Paul were ordered to despatch two Camel airframes on
> December 10th 1917, but as these had not arrived some days later, presumed
> temporarily lost on the railway, a machine was allocated from Martlesham
> Heath." (100)

There is no doubt that some Camels were armoured. A Secret Technical
Information Bulletin of May 1918 records in a "chart of additional weights
carried by aircraft" that 12mm armour plating weighing 19½lb/sq ft was
used on the "low-flying Camel". (101)

Meanwhile, the Germans were making more effective progress. Translated
documents from the French Ministry of War, circulated within the RFC
as Intelligence Department Monthly Reports on Enemy Aviation, referred
in the January and February 1918 Reports to several machines bearing
armour that were already in use:

"NEW ARTILLERY RANGING AND RECONNAISSANCE AEROPLANES

[January]

AEG armoured, 160 HP Mercedes engine. In use for infantry work.

Junker armoured two seater also now in use.

ARMOURED AEROPLANES [February]:–

Are used for infantry contact work.

AEG AEROPLANE – Plated with sheet steel 6¼ mm thick underneath and
on the sides of the fuselage (in neighbourhood of pilot) as well as in the rear
of the observer's seat.

Benz 225 HP engine.

Weight of the aeroplane 1,720 Kg.

Horizontal speed comparable to the LVG.

Poor climb and manoeuvrability. ...

ARMOURED ALBATROS – Specially constructed for infantry contact work,
smaller than the usual Albatross.

Benz 225 HP engine.

Armoured in the same way as the AEG.

Speed same as the AEG.

Climb and manoeuvrability better than the AEG. ...

BOMBING AEROPLANES [February]

GOTHA AEROPLANES

Gotha type CV No. 930 brought down on 26/1/18 at Zuydocote.

Span: 24 metres; balanced projecting ailerons.

Two 260 HP Mercedes engines.

Fuselage – Entirely armour plated. Besides the tunnel which allows of fire through a small angle, down to the rear there is a triangular aperture in the rear of the fuselage which allows of a large range of fire to the rear and downwards. ...

FREIDRICHSHAFEN AEROPLANE (FDH)

FDH Type G3 No. 180/17 [4-seater bomber] - landed at Vulveringham

19/1/18, owing to giving of a soldered joint in one of the engine supports. It is identical with the FDH No 177/17 which landed at Soissons, except for the arrangement and number of its petrol tanks. ... Various ingenious arrangements, such as armour plating in the field of the propellers etc. ..." (102)

7 "Pusher" or "Tractor"?

At this stage in the story, it is time to have a look at where the British had got to with their new designs for armoured machines. Whereas the Germans seemed to prefer to get their armoured machines into the field, even if sometimes on an interim or experimental basis, the British approach was much more studied – as was evidenced by Lord Weir's letter of 7th January 1918. (93) The British authorities wanted to be quite clear about what duties the armoured machines would be required to perform, what armament would best suit those duties, what type(s) of machines would be best suited to carry that armament and, if it should be deemed operationally desirable to sacrifice some performance for additional weight, how and to what extent those machines should then be protected from ground fire.

The so-called "pusher" to which references had been made was actually the AE 3 "Farnborough Ram", although a further design subsequently entered into consideration, as will be seen later. A note of 1st February on the subject of the "Ram", sent on behalf of the Officer Commanding the Armament Experimental Establishment at Orfordness to a Lieutenant D R Pye in the Air Ministry's Technical Department, provides some interesting insights into current thinking on the practicalities of engaging targets on the ground:

"... The following are some of the targets [the AE 3] may be expected to engage, arranged in rough order according to their length:–

(1) Trenches.

(2) Trains.

(3) Troops in column.

(4) Road Transport.

(5) Troops in mass.

(6) Gun emplacements.

All targets with the doubtful exception of trains, move so slowly, that as far as manoeuvring the machine and handling the guns are concerned they may be regarded as stationary. Their length therefore has an important effect on the time they can be kept under continuous fire without rapidly traversing or depressing the guns. For example, suppose a machine flying level and with front gun firing at a small target under the following circumstances:–

Height of machine — 300 feet.

Speed — 80mph.

Range at which fire opened — 500 yards.

Range when gun depressed 48° — 135 yards.

[Then] Time of continuous fire — 10½ secs, hardly sufficient to fire off one 100 round drum.

It should also be noted that during the last 3 secs when the range is varying from 230 to 135 yards the good shooting which might be expected from the short range is spoilt by the rapid depressing of the gun – 22½° in 3 secs.

With a gun firing at right angles to the line of flight over the side of the machine, however, continuous fire of almost any duration may be maintained with a very moderate amount of traversing, the pilot flying the machine round the target as centre. The range can remain approximately constant and quite short. Thus, taking the same height and speed as in the previous example, but with a machine circling round the target:–

Range   —— 200 yards.

Rate of turning   —— 1 turn in 28 secs.

Virtual gravity = 1.3g, not sufficient to embarrass the gunner.

It would therefore seem advisable to try to provide a side firing gun, even though it may be rather difficult." (103)

The note states that this argument was taken up with a Wing Commander Robertson and with the Royal Aircraft Factory (RAF) and that it was agreed:

"(1) The RAF to modify the rear mounting so that the gun on it can be used for broadside fire at any rate on one side of the machine and possibly on both sides.

(2) The RAF to make the mounting for the front guns and send to Orfordness for trial in FE 2b. ... ." (103)

The note concluded, perhaps rather late in the day in view of all that had gone before:

"I am having some suitable ground targets constructed, in order to obtain experience of firing at the ground." (103)

Around the same time, in early February 1918, an "outline" specification for an armoured single seater fighter was issued that was obviously to be a tractor machine – there was to be a Vickers gun firing through the propeller as well as two adjustable Lewis guns for downward firing at 45° ± 10°. The specification called for a speed of at least 125mph and if possible 140mph and, especially, for:

"ARMOUR. Front portion of fuselage, including pilot, controls, tanks,

carburettor etc., to be enclosed in armour plate as follows:–

Bottom. Single plate. 11mm.

Sides. Single plate. 6mm.

Back. Double plate. 6 gauge and 10 gauge.

Front. Single plate. 8mm." (104)

There was also to be provision to carry four 20lb bombs and their release gear, so that this might have been some move towards meeting Trenchard's earlier desire for an armoured bombing machine. Sopwiths responded quickly, with a crudely drawn suggestion (104) for the disposition of armour for the machine submitted on 11th February. This

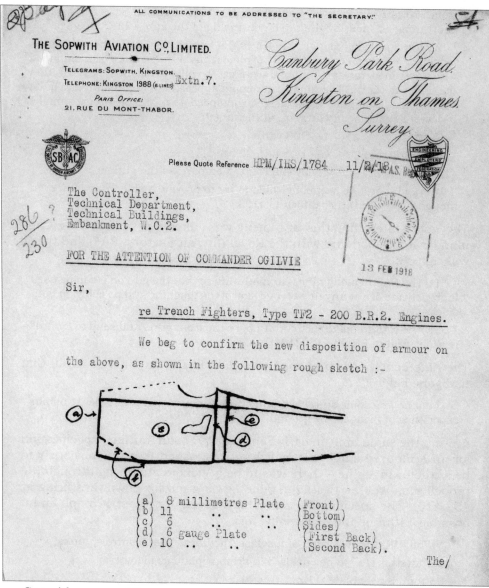

Sopwith proposal for an armoured Trench Fighter – TF 2.
(Public Record Office, AIR 2/1027)

machine, the Trench Fighter No 2 (TF 2) was to become the Sopwith "Salamander".

Meanwhile, the work already in hand exploring the possibilities of armouring aeroplanes received official endorsement at the highest levels. On 6th March 1918 there was a meeting of the Aircraft Development

Committee, attended among others by:

The Secretary of State for Air, Lord Rothermere (in the Chair),

The Chief of the Air Staff (Trenchard),

Sir William Weir (as he was recorded),

Mr Winston S Churchill, Minister of Munitions (at the invitation of the Secretary of State).

Among the decisions reached during the meeting:

"It was agreed that armouring was a most important thing, and that all possible steps should be taken to see that experiments were carried out with a view to producing light armour.

It was thought that the question of producing a large armoured machine should be considered." (105)

On 12th March 1918, following a conversation that day with Lord Weir, Brigadier-General Brooke-Popham (Deputy Quartermaster-General, HQ, RFC) summarised the current position on machines for low flying:

"1. There are three types ... now being designed:–

(a) The Sopwith Camel.

(b) The Sopwith TF 2 with BR 2 engine [Salamander].

(c) The RAF 2-seater Pusher [AE 3].

2. With regard to the Sopwith Camel, it has been decided that the downward pointing gun is impractical and that [the Expeditionary Force (EF)] will take the ordinary Sopwith Camel with two Vickers Guns firing forward. It is considered that armour, as originally fitted to the Camels, is still wanted, even though the guns are now firing straight ahead. The period during which these machines will be actually using their guns on trenches, will be in the neighbourhood of one or possibly two minutes, whereas the time during which they will be exposed to fire from the ground, will amount to 20 minutes or more. Therefore, if the armour is wanted in the case of downward pointing guns, it is wanted in the case of machines with guns pointing straight ahead.

3. With reference to the Sopwith TF 2 this is a single seater heavily armoured machine, having 600 pounds of armour. The question arose as to whether the guns ... should be pointing downwards or firing straight ahead. In view of our experience on the Sopwith Camel, there seems no doubt that they must be placed firing straight ahead. In this case, a gun on the top plane will not be required, as the other guns can be used for fighting other machines. It seems doubtful whether this machine will be as good for shooting into trenches as the Sopwith Camel, as it will be heavy and less manoeuvrable. Being a single seater it will be of little use for trench reconnaissance.

4. With reference to the Factory 2-seater [AE 3], this is a pusher with the Engine Pilot and Gunner protected by armour. The Gunner has two Lewis Guns which can be fired downwards at an angle of 45°, also the single gun firing backwards for protection against hostile machines.

5. It is considered that for immediate use, the Sopwith Camel with two Vickers Guns pointing straight ahead and with a small amount of armour,

ie, 170 pounds, should be turned out for low flying. For the future the RAF 2-seater should be pushed on with as rapidly as possible and it is considered that this machine will be more likely to meet the EF requirements, than the Sopwith TF 2." (104)

Actually, according to Robertson (106), the first armoured Camel had already been flown to Sopwith's testing aerodrome at Brooklands on 15th February, with 5 gauge armour plate and ballast to make up the weight of the 11 mm plate that had been ordered for the next two. After brief trials, it was flown to the Expeditionary Force in France on 7th March and returned to Brooklands in mid-March with the endorsement that a machine firing forward at a small angle of depression covers a far greater killing area than a machine in level flight with acutely depressed guns.

The view of the Expeditionary Force clearly held sway, for on 13th March (104) there was a discussion between Trenchard (CAS), Brooke-Popham and the Controller, Technical Department (CTD) during which it was decided primarily:

– That provision should be made for two squadrons of Camels like those examined by the Expeditionary Force, but with forward-firing guns.

– To stop work on any Salamanders that were not too advanced in construction, owing to the view that the loss of manoeuvrability would not be compensated by the increased protection from the armour. The first machines were to be completed for trials with the Expeditionary Force, but with forward-firing guns.

Nevertheless, they could not quite abandon the original idea of a "narrow-fuselage" machine with downward-pointing guns and there would be a "serious effort" to get out such a design. The two-seater pusher was also to be brought forward "as rapidly as possible". However, Ogilvie was evidently not happy with the decision to abandon the Salamander in favour of the armoured Camel and was influential enough to express his views. He responded on 22nd March (104), pointing out that:

– The Camel with armour as examined by the Expeditionary Force would be too weak and dangerously tail heavy.

– The standard Camel, with forward-firing guns, would only be able to carry armour as a plate under the pilot's seat.

– The TF 2 would not be seriously unmanoeuvrable and the first machine would be flying in 2–3 weeks, with correct weight of armour.

– The narrow-fuselage/downward-firing machine was impracticable "in a tractor for any engine which would be available".

– The two-seater pusher might, subject to engine availability, instead be a single–seater.

On 25th March the Controller of the Technical Department advised (107) that, with the armour protection required, the Salamander should be able to achieve a speed of about 130mph – though rather less than the

140mph hoped for. He also advised that, as a result of experience with the Camel, the downwards-firing Lewis guns originally specified for the TF 2 had been altered to two Vickers guns firing through the propeller. (In respect of the original requirement for downward-firing guns, it is notable that the Germans had already abandoned the idea for the Junkers J I/J 4, "due to the impracticability of aiming at ground targets from a low height, owing to the aircraft's speed. (94) With this armament, it was thought also that the proposed upwards firing Lewis gun would be unnecessary, though a Lewis gun mounting could be fitted if required. He considered that the armament as previously proposed would give protection for the pilot, tanks, etc, against vertical fire from the ground with armour piercing bullets and against oblique fire from the sides, front and rear.

On 5th April, details emerged from the Technical Department of the AE 3 armoured pusher. (104) With the pilot sitting behind the gunner, as close together as possible in the nacelle to reduce the weight of armour, and designed to fly at 500ft for attacking infantry, the machine would have:

- a Sunbeam Arab engine; estimated aeroplane weight of 4,250lb;
- ground level speed of 95mph and climb rate of 320ft/min;
- double plate armour (outer 10 Gauge, inner 5 Gauge) on the bottom, single plate armour (5 Gauge) on the sides, front and back of the nacelle;
- two Lewis guns firing from straight ahead to vertically downwards and a horizontal traverse of about 20° each way, with a single Lewis gun on a pivot mounting firing backwards over the top plane; and
- fuel capacity for 3 hours flying.

There was also a general outline of the Salamander:

"The machine is to be similar in general arrangement to the [Sopwith] Snipe, but the front portion of the fuselage is to be made of armour plate [as previously specified]. No internal struts or bracing are required in the front portion of the fuselage.

... 2 Vickers guns firing straight ahead ... " (104)

A note (108) from Orfordness (Capt F W Musson, Officer i/c No 1 Section, Orfordness) to the A-CTD* on 9th April reported that trials on an FE 2b pusher fitted with the proposed AE 3 front gun mounting found the general arrangement:

"... very suitable for engaging ground targets of all descriptions ...",

though

"... better results could doubtless be obtained on isolated posts with the guns firing over the side ..."

*Assistant-Controller, Technical Department.

However, he raised a doubt about the defensive capability of the AE 3 that was to have repercussions later:

"A low flying machine such as the AE 3 must normally be attacked from above by [enemy aircraft] and the two forward guns are therefore useless for defence. If only one other gun can be carried with the protection it would best be mounted upon some type of rocking pillar such as is used in FE's; this should be fitted in the rear of the gunner's nacelle and would be used by pilot or observer according to circumstances. ..."

On 13th April W Sydney Smith (Superintendent, Royal Aircraft Establishment – as it had by then become – Farnborough) sent a note (109) to the Assistant-Controller Experimental & Research Department, Air Ministry (attention Lieutenant Spring), reporting discussions with Captain Musson and pointing out *inter alia* that:

– It was not possible to put much more armour in the front of the AE 3, as the centre of gravity was already as far forward as was desirable.

– Concerning the considerable amount of weight used in providing a double–bottom to the whole of the nacelle, Musson had doubted the effectiveness of the double armour as the main attack on a low flying aeroplane came from the sides. It was possibly preferable, therefore, to improve the side armour at the expense of the bottom.

– The arrangement of the guns had already been approved by the Technical Department at the mock-up stage, but the concern about defence was considered "very important" and they were:

"... drawing out another scheme for an entirely different arrangement for the front part of the body incorporating an armoured turret with the double gun Scarfe ring."

8 Guns forwards or downwards?

The results of extensive experiments on ground shooting at Orfordness were reported on 17th April 1918. (110) It was assumed that ground targets were of two types, isolated points like defended shell holes and long continuous targets like roads and trenches. Shooting trials were carried out at a large flag lying on the ground to represent an isolated point and at a sand trench 4ft wide and 200 yards long with traverses, communication trenches and the like. The machines used were:

- a Sopwith Pup and a Camel, each with fixed guns firing ahead;
- a Sopwith Camel with fixed guns shooting downwards at a depression of 45°;
- a Bristol Fighter with standard armament; and
- an FE 2b with twin guns arranged as in the proposed AE 3.

So far as the scouts (the Pup and the Camel) were concerned, the Expeditionary Force views were confirmed – the downwards-firing guns were inferior to those firing straight ahead. The experiments indicated that:

"... under good conditions a scout with fixed guns [firing directly] ahead can get at least 50% of the shots into a 30ft diameter group by getting well above the target and diving at 45° or more. Without practice at this particular form of attack there seems a tendency to approach at a flat angle and fire is almost certain to be opened at an excessive range and the bullets fall short.

For attacking a trench the scout also appears able to get effective shooting on a length of about 50 yards long in each dive; the sand trench used ... was very well traversed ... and in this it was possible to get rather less than a quarter of the shots under reasonably good conditions." (110)

The two-seater Bristol Fighter was flown at about 400ft and the observer/gunner fired downwards over the side with a single gun and using a wind vane sight: about one quarter of the shots could be got into the trench – 6 or 7 per 100 yards. For attacking an isolated position (the flag target), the method employed was for the pilot to fly round the target at as constant a speed as possible, thus giving the observer an easy shot over the side on a constant bearing to the machine. With the sight corresponding to the machine's speed, "very deadly" shooting was found to be possible and could be maintained continuously for as long as the ammunition lasted – practically all the shots were within a 30ft diameter circle. The experiments showed that to get the best results on isolated positions:

"... the pilot should have a little training in flying round objects so as to keep them on a constant bearing. If he does this the Observer has the easiest shot possible as he hardly has to traverse his gun at all to hold the sights on the target. For this work the most convenient speed for a Bristol Fighter is 80 mph. .... In addition ... this method of shooting offers the enemy who is being attacked a most difficult target as he has to traverse very rapidly and make a large allowance to keep pace with the machine circling overhead." (109)

Sopwith TF 2 Salamander armoured single-seat "tractor" Trench Fighter. (Imperial War Museum, Q. 67368)

No proper shooting trials were possible with the two-seater pusher fitted with the AE 3 mounting, because of unsatisfactory sight compensation. However, tests with an Aldis Sight indicated that in attacks on long continuous targets the proposed scheme would be superior to shooting over the side of a tractor, owing both to the greater ease of using the guns and also the better protection provided by the armouring. Even so, unless the mounting could be modified to allow shooting over the sides of the nacelle as well, the circling method employed so effectively by the Bristol Fighter in attacks on point targets would not be possible. Such a modification would provide "the ideal arrangement for attacking ground targets of all types".

With no armoured machines actually available to Orfordness at the time, notwithstanding the objectives of the experimental programme, there were no comments on how the weight of armour might affect the tactics to be adopted or even whether the armour would afford complete protection against fire from the ground – though there is no record of how the latter would have been judged.

The overall conclusion was that the two-seater tractor was to be preferred over the pusher as the basis of an armoured machine. The former would be likely to have better performance and had the additional benefits of being able to continue to harass the objective as it left the target, thereby greatly reducing the chances of being hit in the back, and of being less likely to be surprised and shot down from behind by hostile aircraft.

9 The Sopwith Salamander

In the meantime, work on the TF 2 had progressed and the name "Salamander" was confirmed to Sopwiths by the Air Ministry with effect from 9th April 1918. The first (E5429) of six prototypes, E5429–5434, was delivered to Brooklands on 26th April, for the maker's flying trials due to commence the following day; the trials were reported to have been "very satisfactory" (104). The first machine was flown to France by a Captain Allen on 9th May for service trials at No 1 Air Supply Depot on 11th May; it crashed on 19th May and was struck off charge. There is a note (107) of 1st May on file, to the GOC RAF in the Field (by then Major General, later Marshal of the Royal Air Force Sir, John Maitland Salmond KCB CMG CVO DSO), that appears to provide some advance details of the prototype sent to France, especially:

- the armour plates, though of the correct thickness and weight, had not undergone final hardening in order to save time and so were not at that stage bullet-proof;
- the plates were designed to give protection against vertical (upwards) and oblique fire at a height of 100ft;
- the handiness of the machine was something that ought to be tested, though the machine was judged safe to be "put through any possible manoeuvre while a maximum speed of 130mph is not exceeded, and is safe for any but the most violent manoeuvre up to a speed of 150mph";
- no bomb racks or release gear had yet been fitted.

There was, in addition, an interesting aside:

> "It is realised that the downward and forward view is not so good as could be obtained in a pusher machine, and it is requested that the advantages of the machine being a tractor may be balanced against this disadvantage. The question of armouring a single-seater pusher is under consideration ..." (107)

Clearly, therefore, the two-seater AE 3 was not the only armoured pusher in prospect.

The field trials with the Salamander were obviously a success because Ogilvie, whilst still awaiting an official report from France, felt able to advise the Controller of the Technical Department on 25th May 1918 that:

> "... it is understood from General Brooke-Popham that the [first] machine is considered very satisfactory and is likely to be called for in production ... subject to some improvements in directional and lateral controls, a larger rudder and gearing of ailerons." (110)

By then, however, the Air Ministry's Aeroplane Supply Committee had already agreed (on 23rd April) that a contract should be placed with

Sopwiths for 500 Salamanders – though only two production machines were ever to reach France by the time of the Armistice. (84),(100) Some 77 Salamanders were supposed to have been delivered to the RAF by 19th September (110); the disposition of aircraft and engines on charge of the RAF at 31st October 1918 shows that in fact, out of a total of 20,890 machines of all types, there were 2 Salamanders actually in service with the Expeditionary Force in France and 37 "at Home", of which 35 were at aircraft constructor parks and contractors. (111)

It is of passing interest to note that a "temporary specification" (107) for the Salamander's armour was issued on 27th May and included a fairly detailed inspection procedure which included firing tests on the hardened plate. The procedure stipulated that the tests were to be made with a German service rifle, "the barrel of which is in good condition, and not unduly worn, ...". The firing test conditions were:

Thickness of plate	Ammunition (German)	Range, yards	Angle to normal Degrees
11 mm	AP	75	15
8 mm	AP	250	15
6 mm	Spitze	100	0
6 & 10 gauge	AP	200	15

The 6 and 10 gauge compound plates were to be clamped together with distance pieces, to leave an air space of 3¾ inches between them, presumably representing the double-plated bottom that had apparently been retained in the Salamander design. The 10 gauge plate was to be nearest to the rifle and was expected to be pierced by each bullet, but the rear plate was to resist the bullets. During the tests, six rounds were to be fired at each plate and all were to be stopped – unless hitting a stressed area caused by a previous shot.

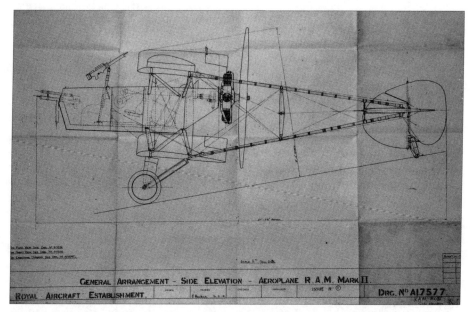

GENERAL ARRANGEMENT – SIDE ELEVATION – AEROPLANE R.A.M. MARK II.
ROYAL AIRCRAFT ESTABLISHMENT.
DRG. Nᴼ AI7577

Royal Aircraft Factory AE 3 "Farnborough Ram" armoured Two-seat "pusher" Trench Fighter. (Imperial War Museum, Q. 68061)

10 The Farnborough Ram

Three prototypes of the AE 3 "Farnborough Ram", based on a Royal Aircraft Factory 1917 design for the NE 1 night fighter, appear to have been completed between March and May 1918 (84). The NE 1 itself was a comparatively heavy and slow machine, having a performance that was judged not good enough for service as a night fighter.

The first two prototypes were fitted with Arab engines and the third with a BR 2 engine. One of the Arab-engined prototypes was sent to Orfordness for testing during May and a report was issued on 21st June. (112) It carried two Lewis guns firing downwards and ahead for the observer and, following the earlier suggestion, a third Lewis gun mounted on the bulkhead between the pilot and the observer to be used by either according to circumstances. The performance of the machine was evidently unacceptable:

"The machine has twice been taken up with the full military load, and on each occasion was only got off the ground with difficulty. In the air it is scarcely manageable and practically useless for either attacking ground targets or for defending itself if attacked by other aeroplanes." (112)

As part of the programme of tests, comparative trials were carried out with the AE 3 flown light and an unarmoured Bristol Fighter:

"Each machine was sent out on a definite reconnaissance at about 500 feet and while thus engaged, scouts, varying in number from one to three, were sent off to try and make a surprise attack. In every case the scouts were observed coming in the distance and only once did a scout effect a surprise. This occurred to the AE 3, the reason being that the observer, though aware that scouts were overhead, could not entirely give up the reconnaissance to watch them and one scout happened to attack when the observer had decided to carry on with his job for a moment: actually the pilot saw it first, but not till it had spent some time under his tail." (112)

Perhaps on this evidence the crew of the AE 3, rather than the machine itself, were at fault, but the report damagingly concluded from "the opinion of the pilots, and especially the observers concerned" that:

"While there is any likelihood of attacks being made by HA [hostile aircraft] we consider that a tractor will make the most suitable type of armoured two-seater for attacking ground targets. If the risk of attack by HA were negligible the pusher would undoubtedly be the better machine. The AE 3 with the Arab engine is too heavily loaded for service use." (112)

This appears to have been the end for the so-called "Ram" and none saw any service.

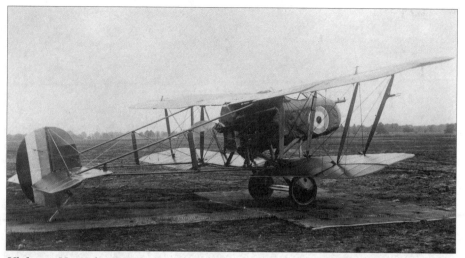

Vickers Vampire Mark II armoured single-seat "pusher" Trench Fighter. (Imperial War Museum, Q. 67006)

11 The Vickers Vampire and the Sopwith Buffalo

Two other British aircraft feature in the armour story, the Vickers Vampire and the Sopwith Buffalo, both of which appeared towards the end of the War.

The Vampire was, ironically, something of a precursor of its jet-propelled namesake that entered RAF service in 1946, in that it was a twin-boom pusher. The Vampire that began its flying trials in the Mk I version at Joyce Green near Dartford in Kent on 27th September 1918 (113) was an armoured single-seater trench fighter originally fitted with a 200hp Hispano-Suiza engine. A 230hp Bentley BR 2 rotary engine version, became the FB 26A Vampire Mk II. According to Bruce (114), the nose of the Mk II nacelle was a little blunter and shorter and the engine was mounted well forward in order to keep the centre of gravity in the right place. The armour plate was fitted inside the nacelle structure, the pusher arrangement enabling both pilot and engine to be protected by the armour. The basic scheme (115) was as follows:

Pilot's back	Double plate 5 and 10 gauge
Pilot's sides	Single plate 7mm
Bottom of cockpit	Single plate 11mm
Front of cockpit	Single plate 7mm
Carburetta casing	Single plate 11mm
Disc on engine nose plate	Single plate 7mm
Total weight of armour	460lb

Sopwith Buffalo armoured two-seat "tractor" Trench Fighter, presumably the second prototype (H5893) with the armour extended aft of the gunner's position. (Royal Air Force Museum, B581)

According to Andrews & Morgan (116), six machines were originally ordered under contract in 1917 but only three (B1484–1486) were built at Vickers' Bexleyheath works, one having been used by No 141 Squadron. It was B1485 that was modified as the FB 26A. The Vampire was abandoned once the decision had been made to adopt the Salamander as the standard trench fighter.

According to Bruce (117), (118), the Buffalo was a two-seat tractor machine with the BR 2 engine, structurally derived the Salamander, that was regarded as a Trench Fighter though officially designated as a Contact Patrol machine. Two examples are recorded, the first prototype (H5892) having been sent to France for evaluation also on 27th September 1918 and returned to England on 26th October 1918. The entire forward portion was constructed of armour plate which, on the first prototype, terminated at the back of the observer's cockpit. The second machine, H5893, had the armour plate extended by one bay further aft. After the war, both prototypes were assigned to the Expeditionary Force in Europe in April 1919, H5893 eventually crashing. The Buffalo was probably the nearest British equivalent to the Junkers J I/J 4, but the arrival of the Armistice prevented its entry into service with the RAF.

12 Progress during the First World War – A retrospective

The story of armoured fighting aircraft during the War appears to have been confined essentially to machines involved in and latterly designed for work near the ground, where shooting from troops and gun emplacements on the ground posed the main threat, although the possibility, even the likelihood, of attack by other aircraft could not be ignored. Nothing can illustrate better the ingenuity of the German Air Service, or its ultimate though honourable futility, than the sequence of armoured machines that culminated in the Junkers J I/J 4 – which, incidentally, was so extensively armoured that it would have protected the crew and engine from attack by other aeroplanes as well as fire from the ground. According to Gray & Thetford (94), there were various further prototype German machines and later developments that reflected the continued ingenuity of their designers in the later stages of the War – but which made little or no contribution to the actual fighting.

On the British side, the development of armoured machines followed an approach that was initially somewhat *ad hoc* but later became more methodical, thorough and – in its contribution to the War effort – effectively fruitless. Compared with the Junkers J I/J 4, over 200 of which were built and which began to appear towards the end of 1917, the limit of British technical ingenuity could reasonably be said to have been the proposal that was put forward by Sir William Weir at around the same time – and which was quickly dismissed by the military aviation establishment. The British authorities were more firmly committed than were their German counterparts to the principle that their Corps machines should above all be fighting aeroplanes, capable of defending themselves from air attack. It was this principle that saw the end of the Farnborough Ram. Ironically, the Weir/Boswell design, with its apparently enclosed tubular crew/engine compartment would, like the Junkers J I/J 4, at least have been protected by armour against attack from behind, even if it could only actually defend itself from air attack by turning on the enemy attacker – just as the Salamander would have had to do and the Ram could just as easily have done! However, there are clues to the fact that attack specifically from the air was not entirely excluded from British thinking on armour protection. A survey of Royal Aircraft Establishment aeroplanes developed during the war, compiled by Observer Officer A J Insall after the war, recorded that for the SE 5 scout machine:

> "Armour plating was fitted behind the pilot's head." (119)

It is not clear whether or not the armour mentioned was a standard installation, was different from the armoured seats reported by Lt Hill at the beginning of 1917. Nor is it definite that the armour was intended to protect against fire from enemy aeroplanes – it could equally have been intended to protect the pilot's head against return fire from ground targets once they had been flown past. The SE 5 was a well reputed fighting Scout, but there is no doubt that after the events of 1916 fighting machines of all types were thrown into ground attack work whenever the occasion demanded, irrespective of whether or not (most often the latter) they had any armour protection. Another clue was buried in the detail of Fighting Instruction No 9, drafted by Major C F Dixon MC and issued by the Central Flying School probably in 1917 (the Instruction itself is undated). Fighting Instruction No 9 was concerned primarily with formation flying in relation to air combat, but it contained an interesting paragraph that is relevant:

> "One important factor which is bound to have great effect on Formation Flying in the future is the improvement in Aerial Gunnery. At present owing to the impossibility of fighting at a distance, machines must come within very close range in order to bring about decisive combat. When two formations thus meet in Aerial Combat they become hopelessly intermingled and keeping station is impossible. Therefore it will readily be seen that for the present one cannot lay down definite regulations for manoeuvre during a fight. With larger calibre guns, improvements in sights, and protective armour, the "away boarders" tactics of the days of Drake and Raleigh will give way to the present day "Jutland Battle" manoeuvres." (120)

The though of fleets of heavily gunned and armoured fighting aeroplanes firing at each other as they lumber past in lines, rather like the inconclusive sea battle of Jutland in 1916, seems a ludicrous analogy today and should have done even then. It was of course in 1805 when Nelson unconventionally broke through the line of the combined French-Spanish fleet off Cap Trafalgar, turning the engagement into a series of individual close-quarter battles like those of Drake and Raleigh against the scattered Spanish Armada in 1588, that was a key factor in achieving so momentous a victory! It is possible to see some remnants of Dixon's "Jutland" scenario in the lengths that the RAF went to during the 1930s to develop formation attacks against enemy bomber fleets; time was to prove Nelson, Drake *et al* to be the better teachers.

The seemingly intractable conflict between weight and performance, the installation of armour having a detrimental effect on both, was undoubtedly the overriding issue for the British authorities. The comparison below suggests the extent of the penalty imposed on at least the speed element of the performance of German armoured machines by the extra weight carried, as compared with the British armoured machines. The German machines listed (except the AEG GIV) were two-seaters, compared with the single-seater Salamander and Vampire, but even allowing for the additional weight of the extra man and his equipment/accommodation, the Buffalo two-seater still had a speed advantage over the German machines. While superior engine performance in the British machines may have been a factor, all the machines listed were fitted with engines of around 200hp, so it could only be weight that was the determining factor. Put simply, the Germans were evidently prepared to accept some sacrifice in performance for the protection afforded by armour; the British were not – an attitude that was to have repercussions for the defences of British aircraft right up to the start of the next war with Germany!

COMPARISON OF KEY AIRCRAFT IN THE WW I ARMOUR PROTECTION STORY

Aircraft Type	Engine (hp)	Unloaded Weight (lb)	Loaded Weight (lb)	Maximum Speed (mph)
RFC/RAF (cf Bruce)				
Sopwith Buffalo	230	2,178	3,071	114
Sopwith Salamander	230	1,844	2,512	125
Vickers Vampire (F.B.26/26A)	200/230	1,470/1,870	2,030/2,438	121
German Air Service (cf Gray & Thetford)				
Hannover CL III[a]	180	1,577/1,732[b]	2,378/2,572[b]	96
Halberstadt CL II[a]	180	1,701	2,493	103
Albatros J I	200	3,075	3,978	87.5
Albatros J II	220	2,259	4,239	87.5
AEG J I/II	200	3,201/3,256	3,828/3,883	94
Junker JI(J4)	200	3,724/3,885	4,787	97
AEG G IV	2 x 260	5,280	7,986	103

[a] Unarmoured.

[b] Captured machine.

1   Van Haute, André, *Pictorial History of the French Air Force, Volume 1, 1909–1940*, Ian Allen Ltd, London, 1974, p 15.
2   Ibid, p 26.
3   Henshaw, Trevor, *The Sky their Battlefield*, Grub Street, 1995, p 19.
4   Morrow, John H Jr, *The Great War in the Air – Military Aviation from 1909 to 1921*, Airlife Publishing Ltd, England, 1993, p 7.
5   Public Record Office, AIR 2/4, File 87/31.
6   Public Record Office, AIR 1/729/204/5/62, Aeronautical Reports (Foreign Countries) A 1533.
7   Von Hesser, E, *Aero (The)*, Vol II, No 88, 25th January 1911, p 71.
8   Harper, Harry, *Aero (The)*, Vol V, No 98, May 1911, p 37.
9   Public Record Office, AIR 1/729/176/5/69.
10 *The Aero*, Vol VI, No 116, November 1912, p 321.
11 Ibid, P 322.
12 Ibid, P 327.
13 Ibid, P 328.
14 Public Record Office, AIR 2/4, File 87/504, Piece 45A
15 Ibid, Piece 4A.
16 Public Record Office, AIR 1/763/204/4/180.
17 *Flight*, Vol V, No 1, 4th January 1913, p 21.
18 *Flight*, Vol V, No 4, 25th January 1913, p 89.
19 Public Record Office, AIR 2/4, Pieces 3a-c and 12A.
20 Ibid, File 87/1212, Minute Sheet No 7, Minute 31.
21 Sykes, Maj F H S, *Flight*, Vol V, No 10, 8th March 1913, p 278.
22 Sykes, Maj F H S, ibid, p 279.
23 Sykes, Maj F H S, *The Aero*, Vol VII, No 121, April 1913, p 103.
24 *The Aero*, Vol VII, No 122, May 1913, p 146.
25 Barr, W Arthur, *The Aeroplane*, Vol V, No 11, 11th September 1913, p 297.
26 Whittaker, W E de B, *The Aeroplane*, Vol V, No 19, 6th November 1913, p 500.
27 *The Aeroplane*, Vol V, No 22, 27th November 1913, pp 576–577.

28 *The Aeroplane*, Vol V, No 23, 4th December 1913, p 603.
29 Whittaker, W E de B, *The Aeroplane*, Vol V, No 23, 4th December 1913, p 598.
30 Morrow, op cit, p 30.
31 Ibid, p 31.
32 Christienne, Charles & Lissarague, Pierre, *A History of French Military Aviation*, Smithsonian Institutional Press, Washington DC, 1986, p p 46–48.
33 *Flight*, (Vol VI, No 18), No 279, 2nd May 1914, p 456.
34 Van Haute, op cit, p 35.
35 Nowarra, Heinz J & Duval, G R, *Russian civil and military aircraft 1884–1969*, Fountain Press London, 1971, p 23.
36 Casari, R B, *Encyclopedia of US Aircraft, Part 1, 1908 to April 6, 1917*, Robert B Casari (Publisher), 1970, Volume 2, p 83.
37 Ibid, Vol 1, p 48.
38 Public Record Office, AIR 1/140/15/40/300.
39 Lanchester, F W, Aircraft in Warfare, Part III, *Engineering*, September 18th 1914, p 367–368.
40 Ibid, p 368.
41 Lanchester, F W, *Aircraft in Warfare–The Dawn of the Fourth Arm*, Constable, London, 1916.
42 Ibid, Plate IV.
43 Lanchester, F W, Aircraft in Warfare, Part IV, *Engineering*, September 25th 1914, p 392.
44 Lanchester, F W, Aircraft in Warfare, Part VIII, *Engineering*, October 23rd 1914, p 514.
45 Flight, (Vol VI, No 33), No 294, 14th August 1914, p 837.
46 *The Aeroplane*, Vol VII, No 9, 26th August 1914, p 193.
47 Terraine, John, *White Heat – the new warfare 1914–1918*, Guild Publishing, 1982, p 190.
48 Ibid, p 194.
49 Jones, H A, *The War in the Air – Being the Story of the Part Played in the Great War by the Royal Air Force*, Volume 2, Clarendon Press, 1928, p 198
50 Ibid, pp 232–233.
51 Ibid, p 229.
52 Ibid, Appendix VII, pp 464–470.
53 Neumann, Maj George Paul, *The German Air Force in the Great War*, (translated by J E Gurdon), Hodder and Stoughton Ltd, London, 1920, pp 36–41.
54 Neumann, Ibid, p 41.
55 Gray, Peter & Thetford, Owen, *German aircraft of the First World War*, Putnam, 1962, p xiii.
56 Public Record Office, AIR 1/731/176/6/9.
57 Neumann, op cit, pp 193–196.
58 Public Record Office, AIR 1/731/176/6/12.
59 Jones, op cit, Volume 4, 1934, p 129.
60 Morrow, op cit, pp 216–217.
61 Jones, op cit, Volume 4, 1934, Appendix VI, p 419.
62 Ibid, Volume 4, 1934, Appendix VI, p 420.
63 Ibid, Volume 4, 1934, Appendix VII, pp 421–422.
64 Jones, op cit, Volume 2, Appendix VII, p163.
65 Jones, op cit, Volume 4, 1934, Appendix IX, pp 424–426 and Appendix XI, pp 431–433.
66 Neumann, op cit, pp 204–206.
67 Neumann, op cit, pp 43–44.
68 Neumann, op cit, pp 197–198.
69 Neumann, op cit, pp 199–200.
70 Corum, James S, *The roots of Blitzkrieg, Hans von Seeckt and the German military reform*, University Press of Kansas, 1992, pp 15–16
71 Jones, op cit, Volume 4, 1934, Appendix XII (Employment of Battle Flights), pp 433–438.
72 Jones, op cit, Volume 6, Appendices, Appendix XX, Fighting in the Air, Clarendon Press, 1937, pp 94–95.
73 Ibid, Volume 6, p 417.

74 Ibid, Volume 6, p 414.
75 Ibid, Volume 6, pp 437–441.
76 Ibid, Volume 6, pp 445–446.
77 Ibid, Volume 6, pp 463.
78 Morrow, op cit, p 276.
79 Morrow, op cit, p 219.
80 Neumann, op cit, 44–45.
81 Public Record Office, AIR 1/765/204/4/241.
82 Andrews, C F, Vickers Aircraft since 1908, Putnam, London, 1969, p 51.
83 Public Record Office – AIR 1/2151/209/3/256.
84 Bruce, J M, *British Aeroplanes 1914–18*, Putnam, 1957.
85 Andrews, op cit, p 56.
86 Public Record Office, AIR 1/731/176/6/5.
87 Gray & Thetford, op cit, pp 9–12.
88 Weir, J G, Report on A.E.G. Armoured Aeroplane,
    Royal Aircraft Establishment, 1918. (IWM reference K89/799).
89 Public Record Office – AIR 1/470, Technical Commission Report on
    German Aeroplanes and Airships, 1919.
90 Gray & Thetford, op cit, pp 39–41.
81 Nowarra & Duval, op cit, p 41.
92 Nowarra & Duval, op cit, pp32–34, p 52.
93 Public Record Office – AIR 2/57.
94 Gray & Thetford, op cit, pp 154–157.
95 Public Record Office – AIR 1/2426/305/29/475, Report on the Junker
    Armoured Two–seater Biplane, Type J.I., 1919.
96 Weir, Sir William, Proposed Armoured Single Seater Fighter Biplane,
    Public Record Office – AIR 2/731.
97 Public Record Office, AIR 2/731, Piece 3A.
98 Public Record Office, AIR 1/2391/228/11/140.
99 Bruce, op cit, p 582.
100 Robertson, Bruce, *Sopwith – The man and his aircraft*, Air Review Ltd, 1970, pp
     112–114.
101 Public Record Office, AIR 1/2130/207/100/2,
     Secret Technical Information Bulletins No 21.
102 Public Record Office, AIR 2/2670.
103 Public Record Office, AIR 2/1530, Piece 9A.
104 Public Record Office, AIR 2/1027.
105 Public Record Office, AIR 1/2418/305/3.
106 Robertson, op cit, p112.
107 Public Record Office, AIR 2/1029.
108 Public Record Office, AIR 2/1530, Piece 41A.
109 Ibid, Piece 43A.
110 Public Record Office, AIR 2/1530.
111 Jones, op cit, Volume 6, Appendix XLI.
112 Public Record Office, AIR 2/1530, Report No A/99, Piece 64a.
113 Public Record Office, AIR 1/2418/305/5.
114 Bruce, op cit, pp 694–697.
115 Public Record Office, AIR 1/2418/305/5.
116 Andrews, C F and Morgan, E B, *Vickers Aircraft since 1908*, Putnam, 1988, p 509.
117 Bruce, op cit, pp 629–630.
118 Bruce, J M, *The Sopwith Fighters*, Arms & Armour Press, 1986, p 64.
119 Public Record Office, AIR 1/727/152/7, folder 152/3.
120 Public Record Office, AIR 1/727/152/7, folder 144/2.

III The inter-War years: 1919 to August 1939
13 The 1920s – A comparatively peaceful interlude

In the aftermath of the Great War, the future of the Royal Air Force hung in the balance. The Royal Navy and the Army wanted what they chose to regard as their shares of the flying machines and of the monies allocated in the Treasury's budgets to peace-time military flying, together with its associated research and development; neither saw any need for a separate air force during times of acute financial stringency for the military arms. Faced with these threats to the RAF's continued existence and with the additional problem created by the absence of any foreseeable prospect of a major new military conflict, it is perhaps understandable that much of what had been learned during the Great War no longer seemed to be important. Trenchard's clever response was to find a new rôle for his still fledgling independent Service – a rôle that for modest expenditure actually saved money elsewhere. The new rôle was colonial policing from the air: substituting, for the Army in particular, RAF squadrons that were capable of quickly delivering effective attacks from the air against fractious tribesmen at distances and over terrain that could neither easily nor as quickly be traversed by ground troops. The nature of the work in which the RAF became engaged provided little opportunity to practice and improve upon the air fighting tactics of the earlier conflict – there was no aerial opposition, there were no battles in which they could intervene. The opportunities for aerial operations were at best sporadic. The operations in which the RAF was involved were therefore confined to the attacks on ground targets. In spite of the fact that the tribesmen and other hostiles that they confronted were held often to be, individually, good shots, the provision of armour protection – something that had proved to be more of a distraction for the British aircrews than a positive benefit during the War – was certainly not a factor that in these circumstances was likely to be uppermost in the minds of the peace-time authorities. The immediate military value of the policing work might have been limited, but the longer term strategic benefits to the RAF were much more significant. There was a period of stability, of ticking-over operationally, in which a sound – but, importantly, fully independent – infrastructure for the young Service could be built up. Training centres for air and ground-crews were expanded and were not confined simply to producing immediate cannon-fodder for the Front; the suppliers of future aircraft and the equipment to be carried by those aircraft could be nurtured and the development of a variety of different designs for military aircraft could be explored on a more leisurely basis.

Elsewhere, the situation was different. The American Army Air Force for example, having had nothing in the way of aircraft to contribute to the

European conflict, actually pursued the development of ground-attack and infantry-liaison aircraft after the cessation of hostilities. According to James C Fahey (1), in the years immediately following the War several types were produced in small numbers with this work in mind:

Aircraft Duty	Aircraft Type	Gross Weight (lb)	Top Speed (mph)	Year Ordered	Number Produced
Type IV-Pursuit-Ground attack (PG)	Aeromarine PG-1	3,918	124	1920-21	3
Type VI-Ground Attack (GA)	Eng DIV GAX	9,813	115	1919-20	2
	Boeing GA-1	9,740	105	1920-21	10
	Boeing GA-2	9,150	98	1921-22	2
Type VII-Infantry Liaison (IL)	Orenco IL-1	5,686	107	1919-22	2

Peter M Bowers described the Aeromarine PG-1 as a "true sesquiplane" (a biplane with a lower wing area much less than, in this case less than half of, the upper wing area) and with a 37mm canon firing through the propeller shaft, although he made no mention of armour. (2) According to Bowers, there was also a Fokker PW-5, a one-piece high-wing mono-plane otherwise similar to the German war-time Fokker D VII fighter aeroplane, production of which extended to two prototypes and a test order for a further ten machines. The PW-5 was depicted as having had removable armour plating. The designation "PW" referred to "Pursuit, Water-cooled". (3)

Louis Bruchiss described the Boeing GA-2 and its background thus:

"That the U.S. Army Air Forces even in the early '20's was aware of the necessity of designing and building flying arsenals is evidenced by the Boeing GA-2 of 1922. This is believed to have been the first "Flying Fortress", and it was proposed mainly for trench strafing. It followed one of the two schools of thought regarding the most effective uses of aircraft in the type of warfare developed during the first world conflict. One group advocated the use of manoeuvrable pursuit aircraft to dive and strafe the trenches with their machine guns, while the other group believed that a low-flying, heavily armored airplane could do much more damage and be less vulnerable to rifle or machine gun fire from the troops in the trenches.

The armament of the GA-2 airplane consisted of the following: 37mm. canon, .50-caliber machine guns, a brace of .30-caliber guns, an armored turret, and 1,600lb of armor plate. The canon was mounted just above the landing gear spreader struts, and had a field of fire 60° from vertical. Two .50-caliber machine guns above the canon had a downward sweep to 60° from vertical and 15° from horizontal. The other .50-caliber gun was carried in a rear tunnel in fixed position, and operated by remote control, or by the lower gunner. Scarff-mounted Lewis guns completed the armament." (4)

In the GA-2 it is possible to glimpse a vision of things that were to come, not so much in the ground attack rôle but in the shape of the multi-gunned Boeing B-17 and B-29 heavy bombers of the next major conflict.

Aeromarine pursuit/ground attack PG-1 aeroplane. (US NARA Image 342–FH–3B–32364–8289AC)

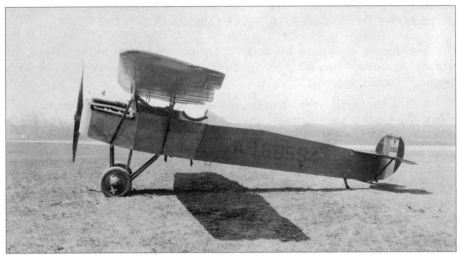

Fokker armoured pursuit/water-cooled PW-5 aeroplane. (US NARA Image 342–FH–3B–32437–168437AC)

Bruchiss did not seem to have been aware of the much earlier Russian machine, the Sikorski Type Ye2 "Flying Fortress" (cf Chapter 4).

Nothing came of the specialised American ground-attack aircraft of that time. G R Duval explained the demise of the PG-1 thus:

"...officially classed as a Pursuit-ground attack aircraft, the Aeromarine PG-1 first flew in 1921 ... The heavy armour-plating with which it was fitted caused excessive vibration, making it unpleasant to fly, and the three machines constructed were mainly used for experiments in weapons installation." (5)

An explanation of the demise of the GA-2 came from Group Captain M G Christie CMG DSO, an Air Attaché with the British Embassy in Washington, who sent a note on 22nd April 1924 to the Directorate of

Boeing GA-2 Trench Strafer. (US NARA Image 18–WP–18747)

Air Intelligence at the Air Ministry in London in which he described the state of the American Air Service. He included a reference to what were termed "attack" aircraft:

"... the armoured types, ie the single-seater P.G.I with 300hp Wright H-3 [engine], the two-seater triplane GA I with twin-Liberty engines and the two-seater biplane GA II with 700hp W-1 motor have failed to give satisfaction and are now being discarded. Meanwhile, the DH 4B with Liberty motors carry out the bulk of the Attack Squadrons' work but the De Havillands are not well suited to Attack Tactics. It is hoped that one of the two-seater types called for in the new specifications for Corps Observation machines will provide a plane well adapted to Attack Aviation, but it is realised that one built around an aircooled motor would be more desirable." (6)

The situation is confirmed in an Air Intelligence Report on aviation in the USA in 1925, under a section entitled "Ground Attack Aviation":

"This branch of military aviation was separated from 'pursuit' aviation back in 1921, when a special organisation known as the 3rd Attack Group was formed at Kelly Field, Texas, for its development. This group originally consisted of four 'attack' squadrons, but two of these have been temporarily disbanded since the summer of 1924 owing to shortage of officers.

The multi-gunned armour-plated machines, type 'G-A', introduced in 1921 for 'ground attack' as an experiment, have been abandoned. The armour plating which extended on both sides and beneath the floor of the fuselage merely made the machine unwieldly and slow, ie, an easy prey to armour piercing bullets from the ground and to fighting planes from above; the marksmanship of the downward fire of flexibly-mounted machine guns was found to be difficult and inaccurate. It is generally felt that a speedy but very manoeuvrable unarmoured two-seater with an air-cooled engine carrying light bombs, two or preferably four fixed guns for the pilot and two flexibly mounted for the observer, is the ideal ground attack plane." (7)

Evidently the Americans were not losing sight of the desirability of a specialised ground attack aircraft but, in preferring a nimble unarmoured two-seater, they were pretty much in the position that the RAF found itself in during 1917–1918. There should be no surprise, however, that the RAF had been keeping an eye on progress in the USA. Indeed, some two years earlier than the Air Intelligence Report, on 30th May 1924, Air Vice-Marshal Sir W Geoffrey H Salmond KCMG CB DSO, the Air Member for Supply and Research (AMSR), minuted Air Commodore J M Steel CB CMG CBE, the Deputy Chief of Air Staff (DCAS):

"... I minuted you on this matter in connection with the USA ground strafing organisation. I repeat this minute herewith.

The form of aircraft attack detailed in [Christie's note] is undoubtedly a very important one and I am fairly convinced that the development of air operations will eventually result in our incorporating some form of ground strafing organisation in the RAF.

The Salamander was an indication during the war of the necessity for this form of development. If we take into account the great potential use of gas, ground-strafing and smoke screens, it is extremely likely that the Americans are well advised to take the initiative in the formation of a special unit for exploring this line of development.

At present we have no types of machines which can be considered similar to the GA type, nor are we developing any armoured machines. The development of the .5 [inch] gun, which can penetrate 1 inch of armour plate (40lb per sq ft) with normal impact and ½ inch with 45 degree impact makes the problem of armouring machines almost prohibitive. In any case, a .5 bullet would be extremely damaging to any part of the structure if hit.

The air cooled engine would be more efficient for these types of operations than the water cooled, owing to the fact that it is less liable to damage under these circumstances. Probably, therefore, armouring of aircraft for this purpose will have to be disregarded and reliance placed more and more on speed and manoeuvrability.

Whether the machine adopted should be a two-seater, such as the "dormouse", or a single-seater is a matter for consideration. A two-seater for such work could leave behind a lot of military load it has to carry at present owing to its other duties but which would not be required for ground-strafing, such as oxygen, R/T, electrical equipment and heaters. The advantage of the two-seater would be that it could afford a certain amount of protection. On the other hand, the single seater should be faster and, therefore, might rely on its own manoeuvrability for protection.'

It has been suggested that it would be worth while investigating whether detachable armour could not be easily fixed to an aircraft when such aircraft were required solely for trench strafing or similar low flying duties." (8)

It is not apparent that the RAF ever did form a special unit to consider the development of aircraft for ground work but the issues raised in this minute, especially the idea of detachable armour, were to be raised again in a new debate on armour protection in the latter half of the 1930s and the run-up to the Second World War.

The Royal Air Force in the 1920s

For the RAF, its aircraft contractors and its equipment suppliers, low fly-ing work as a valuable battlefield tactic – and with it the rôle for armour protection – appears to have slipped (like the Trench Fighters themselves) from official view after the Armistice in 1918, presumably because no actual "battlefields" in the Great War sense presented themselves. All was not entirely lost, for there were serving Officers with experience of the Great War who were not quite prepared to let the idea of armour for aircraft engaged in such work die. Squadron Leader Bernard E Smythies DFC, a student during 1922–1923 at the Royal Air Force Staff College in Andover, wrote an essay in which he recounted some of his experiences while serving during the War:

"11. **Low Flying**:–As Cambrai [November 1917] was the first battle in which the Squadron [No 64, flying DH 5s] had taken part, and also the first in which low-flying aeroplanes were used in quantity for the attack of ground troops, the following impressions recorded at the time may be of interest:–

(c) Armour to protect the pilot from underneath would have been desir-able. Performance under 1,000 feet would probably not be interfered with to any great extent.

The machine must be light on controls, as protection is only obtainable at present by zig-zag tactics.

19. **Aircraft Attack against Ground Targets**:– Subsequent to the battle of Cambrai, a great development occurred in the use of low-flying aeroplanes, such duties becoming during the battle periods almost the normal rôle of single-seater scouts. ...

(a) Low flying in strongly protected areas is unpopular with scout pilots. This is only to a small extent due to the risk of machine-gun fire from the ground; it is partially attributable to the inability to defend oneself against attack from enemy aircraft above, though this can be remedied by providing an escort for protective fighting duties. ..." (9)

In a similar Essay to the Staff College in the same year, given by Squad-ron Leader Keith R Park MC DFC who was subsequently to command No 11 Group of Fighter Command in the thick of the Battle of Britain, the subject of ground strafing was also, though briefly, mentioned:

"Ground Strafing is carried out best by small, fast, and handy scouts hav-ing two or more fixed guns firing forward. If two-seaters are to be employed they should be armoured and have additional guns." (10)

Park did not explain why he thought that two-seaters should be protected by armour but not single-seaters doing the same work, although the im-plication was that the nimbleness of the single-seaters was alone consid-ered sufficient for their protection against ground fire while also enabling them to defend themselves against possible attack from enemy aircraft. Towards the end of the War in which Smythies and Park had so recently been engaged, the adjudged inability of the two-seater Farnborough Ram "pusher" to defend itself against attack by enemy scouts whilst engaged in ground work had been given as the main reason for its cancellation in favour of the single-seater Sopwith Salamander "tractor". In terms of being capable of defensive fire against air attack while engaged in ground work, the two-seater Sopwith Buffalo "tractor" would seem to have been a better prospect that either the Ram or the Salamander. The fact that all three machines had armour behind the pilot/gunner seemed to have little relevance when considering attack from the air; it reflected merely the possibility that there could be fire from the ground once the aircraft had passed its target or from other troops passed over. There does not seem to have been any appreciation of armour as a means of protection in aerial combat; guns (except for the Ram) and manoeuvrability were the things that really counted and they could not be sacrificed for the weight of armour – a view that was to persist almost until the opening shots of the next war!

Smythies, Park and their colleagues were keeping alive memories of the actualities of the War, albeit within the confines of the Staff College – though, perhaps importantly for the future, at least in the minds of their co-students. The Air Ministry itself, however, was not yet able to give up completely on armour protection – though it was soon to try. On 10th May 1924 Sir Bertram Cubitt wrote on behalf of the Army Council at the War Office to the Secretary of State at the Air Ministry, referring to a lecture on anti-aircraft defence delivered at the Centre d'Etudes de l'Aeronautique at Versaille in France:

"... [the] lecturer presses for small calibre automatic artillery for dealing with low–flying aeroplanes, ...

In order that this question can be considered further, the Army Council would be glad to be informed regarding the latest developments in armour for aircraft and what the ideas of the Air Council are for the future in this respect." (11)

The response from the Air Council came on 27th June in a letter from J A Webster, a Principle Assistant Secretary at the Air Ministry, in which Cubitt was informed in no uncertain terms that:

"... it is not the present policy of the Air Staff to use armour to protect aeroplanes." (12)

The letter set out "the various considerations which have weighed with the Air Council in adopting this policy". These considerations were stated in detail and formed the text of a policy document that was subsequently issued as Staff Memorandum No 24 of 27th June 1924. The Memorandum, the full text of which is reproduced below, tells its own story of how the RAF's thinking had settled on the subject of armour protection:

"POLICY REGARDING ARMOUR IN AIRCRAFT.

1. The question with regard to the use of armour for protection of aero-

planes has been considered by the Air Council and the various considerations which have weighed with them in adopting their present policy are
summarised below:–

(a) If an aeroplane is armoured underneath only, it sacrifices some of its
manoeuvrability and performance without obtaining any compensating immunity from attack by hostile aircraft. It would be shot down from the air with
greater ease than if it were unarmoured. Alternatively a force of fighters would
have to be provided to protect it, and this is considered to be uneconomical
and contrary to the accepted principles of air warfare.

(b) If armoured above, below and at the sides the aeroplane would be quite
unable to perform satisfactorily any duty necessitating high flying, such as
photography or fighting. It is also a matter of doubt whether an aeroplane
could be armoured sufficiently against attack from the air.

(c) Armoured aircraft would be quite unable to take the offensive against
enemy aeroplanes owing to their poor performance.

(d) Low flying is only one of the duties which aircraft may be called upon
to carry out in army co-operation. Every aeroplane in a squadron working
with the Army must be able to perform any of the several different types of
work which may be required by the Military Commander.

(e) An armoured aeroplane [the Salamander] was produced at the end of
the war and was tried out in Egypt, Iraq and India, but as the consensus of
opinion was that it was unsatisfactory, it was not adopted.

(f) Manoeuvrability and high performance are considered to give the best
defence against all forms of attack. If they are sacrificed to secure immunity
from one form of attack the aircraft is made more vulnerable to all other forms
of attack. For instance, if a machine gun is produced which will pierce our
armour we shall have sacrificed much to gain nothing.

2. The Air Council do not at present intend to use armoured aircraft.
Their policy would, however, be closely reviewed should a much lighter form
of armour be devised, or other improvement made which would enable the
extra weight to be carried without so great a loss of performance. (13)

It was noted in Webster's letter, though not carried over into the Memorandum, that a further consideration had been:

"... in some measure because the French, so far as is known, are not experimenting in this direction." (12)

The blunt terms of the Memorandum were evidently intended to close
the argument between weight and performance, an argument that had
waged since about 1915, once and for all; it was again not quite able to
succeed. In a later essay for the Staff College, during the 1926–27 year,
Squadron Leader G B A Baker MC contributed the following:

"The [German] ground fire became amazingly accurate during the last
months of the war ... The writer notes that of the last seven flights of the
war, he was hit in five. Possible developments of ground fire may seriously
impede low flying aircraft in the future and call for particular armouring of
the under surfaces." (14)

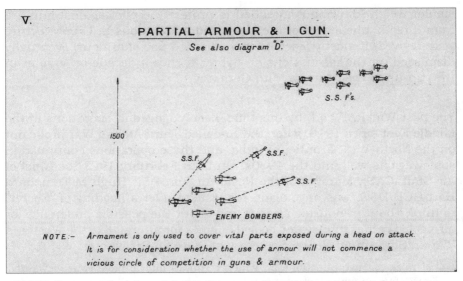

Gibbs' diagramme of tactics for the use of partially armoured aeroplanes. Air Publication 1308. (15)

Pilots attacking ground targets in the next war, targets protected by German Flak batteries, would have been sympathetic to Baker's comments and thankful that the lesson had, by then, been learned!

On the same course, Flight-Lieutenant G E Gibbs MC addressed the subject of "Fighter Squadrons in Air Defence" and considered that armour had a role to play in this work too. (15) Considering the defence of Great Britain and the tactics to be used by day fighters, he took the view that there were two aspects to repelling attacks from bombers in well-packed formations:

– Firstly, the formations had to be broken; and

– Secondly, the scattered bombers could then be dealt with by single-seater fighters (SSFs) given the "fullest liberty" to use individual initiative and mobility.

Somewhat dismissive of the standardised attacks then being taught for squadron formations against bomber formations, he suggested that the key to a successful defence was the first aspect – disrupting the bomber formation. He proposed a number of methods whereby this might be achieved, amongst which were the use of:

– strong armoured "ramming" aeroplanes, and

– partially armoured aeroplanes carrying one gun.

Gibbs' diagrammes of such tactics illustrated clearly what he had in mind. The Gloucester Grebe was a twin-gunned biplane single-seater fighter that served in the RAF from 1923 until 1929. Taking this machine as an example, Gibbs showed how one of the guns might be replaced by a similar weight of armour intended to protect the pilot against gun fire from directly ahead. All of the ideas and suggestions in Gibbs' lecture were revived, if mostly (except for the limited use of armour) eventually dismissed, in the discussions on fighter tactics a decade or so later in the run-up to the next war with Germany.

The post-War RAF had, by this time, been engaged in operations in the Middle East since 1919, when the so-called Third Afghan War broke out on the North-West Frontier of India, and these operations continued in some regions well into the 1930s. On 25th February 1928 the Chief of Air Staff (CAS), Marshal of the Royal Air Force Sir Hugh M Trenchard Bart GCB DSO, was once again requested under a heading of "Secret" to think about armouring aircraft and about the possible preference for air-cooled rather than water-cooled engines for aircraft like the Westland Wapiti. Sir Samual Hoare, Secretary of State for Air, wrote:

"I raise ... two questions on which I should like to have your views at leisure, but on which I do not ask for an early reply until pressure on your time is less acute than at present.

Have we considered, and if we have not, might it not be worth considering, the development of a general purpose machine for use in suitable theatres, and particularly in Iraq and the Sudan, where the bulk of air operations are not (I assume) carried out at very high altitude, with some form of light armour plating underneath. I do not know whether this would mean the inclusion of this item in the next specification we put out for such a machine or whether it might not be feasible to incorporate some such plating in the modern machines of improved performance which we are now introducing in place of the DH 9A? This plating might take various forms, since I assume lightness is a fundamental consideration, eg, if anything approaching bullet proof thickness would be too heavy, would some light metal fitment designed to make a bullet glance off be practicable? As to the expanse of the plating, it would, I imagine, be confined to the bottom of the fuselage, and according to weight, might aim at (1) protecting the pilot only so that machines would not be likely to be shot down out of control, or (2) both pilot and engine, or (3) pilot, observer and engine.

In this same connection is it not the case that an aircooled engine is much less vulnerable than a watercooled engine in the sense, not that it presents a smaller target, (although from the ground I suppose that it does so), but that a bullet might perfectly well put one cylinder out of action without completely stopping the engine, whereas, particularly in a hot climate, a watercooled engine is likely to seize up almost immediately if the watercooling system is badly penetrated.

This may point to the development of aircooled rather than watercooled engines for use in the theatres I have in mind. I note that the "WAPITI" as opposed to the "FAIREY IIIF" has such an engine.

I dare say there have been full discussions on these points for months past, and that you are contemplating something on these lines, or have rejected any such proposal as impracticable for the time being, but I have not heard of

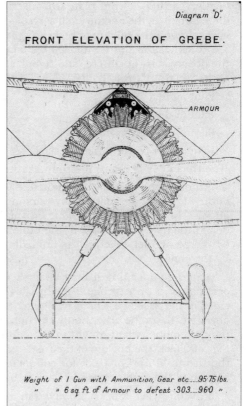

Diagram "D".

FRONT ELEVATION OF GREBE.

ARMOUR

Gibbs' drawing showing how one of the guns might be replaced by a similar weight of armour intended to protect the pilot against gun fire. Air Publication 1308. (15).

Weight of 1 Gun with Ammunition, Gear etc....95·75 lbs.
" " 6 sq. ft. of Armour to defeat ·303....960 " .

any such discussions nor seen any papers on the subject, ... If the proposal for light armour is impracticable at present, should we not consider it as an ultimate desideratum in future machines?" (16)

Advice on 6th March 1928 to the CAS from the Air Member (of the Air Council) for Supply and Research (AMSR), Air Vice-Marshal Sir John F A Higgins KCB CB DSO AFC, pointed out that:

> "... Memorandum No. 24 puts the reasons which have led us to disregard armouring aeroplanes. It is not quite applicable to the present question as it brings in the point that armouring a machine would be a definite disadvantage in fighting enemy aircraft.
>
> At the same time the main principle holds good. To provide armour is definitely to detract from the performance of the machine, and to do so to a very considerable extent.
>
> The total weight of armour used in the "Salamander" was 627lb. Part of this was to protect the pilot's back (I presume against enemy aircraft*) and can

---

* An unexpected, though not unreasonable, "presumption", though there had been no previous mention of protection against air attack from behind. The fitting of armour behind the pilot's back in, for example, the Salamander had appeared previously to be concerned with protecting the pilot against return ground fire from astern once he had passed the vicinity of his objective.

be disregarded. A front plate was also included, which I think could also be disregarded as the engine itself serves for frontal protection. All the remainder is essential if the pilot is to have any protection which is worthwhile, though the thickness of the bottom plates could be reduced and the protection of the observer is, of course, additional. ... the following is a detailed estimate of the weight of armour necessary for the "Wapiti":

Pilot alone	391lb
Pilot and observer	667lb
Pilot and main petrol tank	543lb
Pilot, main petrol tank and observer	819lb

The thickness is 6mm, the thinnest armour which would be of any value.

I think, if the question is studied, it will be clear that in the ordinary form of direct attack against enemy personnel on the ground, which is a diving attack, the provision of armour on the bottom of the fuselage alone would be of little use. Practically all the bullets directed at the attacking aeroplane by the personnel which is the immediate object of the attack will be caught by the engine.

Generally speaking it may be expected that bullets which would hit the occupants of an aeroplane in this form of attack would come through the sides of the fuselage – fired by enemy personnel who are not the immediate objective. If, on the other hand, the nature of the attack is the precision dropping of bombs, which might in the countries alluded to take place at 2,000 to 4,000 feet, the bottom of the fuselage becomes a more vulnerable point so that it would appear that, for complete protection, both the sides and the bottom of the fuselage would have to be armoured.

If the observer is to be protected in the prone bombing position the weight of armour required would be even more than in my estimate of that required for the "Wapiti".

It is instructive to consider ... facts ... as to casualties caused in Iraq, India and Palestine during the past seven years by hostile action ... . It will be seen that, although pilots and observers have been wounded on a certain number of occasions, the great majority of crashes or forced landings were not caused by the pilot being wounded or killed, but by parts of the engine or aeroplane being hit. The logical inference would seem to be that it is more important to protect the engine, petrol tanks, oil tanks, etc, than to protect the pilot, but the armour required for this would be altogether prohibitive.

If then we ignore the question of protecting the engine, we may consider the case under four headings:

(a) Are we to protect the pilot only?

(b) Are we to protect both the pilot and the observer?

(c) Can we sacrifice the weight necessary for either (a) or [...] (b)?

(d) Is light protection against, eg, a glancing bullet worth while?

I should say that the answer to (c) is that we cannot. The weight we sacrifice, even to protect the pilot only, is equivalent in petrol to something like two hours range at cruising speed.

One of the most important points for the machines used in the countries specified ... is range and extra tanks had to be fitted to DH 9As in order to make them a serviceable machine for desert conditions.

I consider the answer to (d) should be "No". The probability would be that we should still sacrifice a good deal of weight and that the protection afforded would be of little value.

... I consider the real way to consider [the question] is on broad lines. A certain amount of useful load can be carried. Are we going to use this load to the best advantage by taking some of it for purely defensive purposes? Is it not in accordance with first principles to use it all for directly offensive purposes such as longer range, more bombs, more guns or more ammunition? Having regard to the small number of casualties which armour would have prevented, should we not, by providing it, rather be handicapping the work of the RAF in these countries as a whole than be helping it?

In my opinion there is no doubt that we should.

As regards the question of the air-cooled engine in comparison with the water-cooled one, it cannot be gainsaid that the air-cooled one is the less vulnerable and the main question is what loss of performance can we accept? On all other grounds the air-cooled engine is preferable to my mind. It is easier to maintain and overhaul and limited experience we have had with it in hot countries shows that a modern air-cooled engine will run as well as a water-cooled one. We have not, however, really had enough experience to be certain of this and I think before making up our minds finally we should await the experience of the "Wapiti" with the Jupiter engine in Iraq." (17)

The CAS evidently concurred with these views and advised the Secretary of State accordingly, with an almost verbatim Minute, on 13th March 1928. The casualties to which Higgins referred were appended to the CAS's Minute and are reproduced here in Table 13.1 overleaf. (16)

The AMSR's advice on armour protection is quoted at length not only because it is a further illustration of the level of detail upon which the official resistance to such protection was based, but also because it demonstrates the extent to which Trenchard's doctrinal philosophy of unremitting aggression had embedded itself in the minds of his officers and successors – nothing should be allowed to stand in the way of taking the attack in its fullest measure to the enemy. Nevertheless, it would be churlish to deny that by having recourse to relevant casualty statistics the AMSR and the CAS had taken a reasonable military view that the risks of harm to the aircrews concerned in actions in Iraq and elsewhere resulting from the use of unarmoured aircraft were not high. Out of the 30 incidents listed in Table 13.1 as occurring over a period of nine years, there was only one possible case in which the loss of the aircraft was specifically (though questionably) attributed to pilot injuries (the DH 9A that crashed in Iraq on 6th October 1922). Of course there were other injuries to crew members over the period and it remains a speculative possibility that those might have been prevented or reduced

Table 13.1. Casualty statistics from the Middle East, 1920-1928

Date	Command	Type of aircraft	Remark
			CASUALTIES WHILST FLYING
7.1.1920	India	Bristol Fighter	Passenger wounded.
1.2.1920	India	Bristol Fighter	Pilot wounded.
?.4.1920	Palestine	Bristol Fighter	Pilot shot through both legs after bullet had passed through port wing and port exhaust pipe …
24.10.1922	Iraq	Sopwith Snipe	Crashed on roof of hostile town during raid: pilot killed.*
3.2.1923	India	Bristol Fighter	Observer wounded.
14.8.1924	Palestine	Bristol Fighter	Pilot wounded.
14.8.1924	Palestine	Bristol Fighter	Passenger wounded by bullet which had previously gone through petrol tank.
14.9.1924	Iraq	Bristol Fighter	Pilot wounded.
24.9.1924	Iraq	Bristol Fighter	Pilot and passenger wounded.
18.4.1925	Iraq	Bristol Fighter	Crashed in flames on bomb raid: petrol tank believed to have been shot through: pilot and passenger killed.*
9.12.27	Iraq	DH 9A	Passenger wounded.
20.2.1928	Iraq	DH 9A	Brought down by enemy fire: pilot killed.*
			*No definite details as to whether occupants were hit.
			CASUALTIES IN OR AFTER CRASHES ATTRIBUTED TO ENEMY ACTION, EXCLUDING * ABOVE
14.6.1920	India	Bristol Fighter	Bullet in engine: forced landed: pilot and passenger wounded by rifle fire whilst escaping.
19.6.1920	Iraq	DH 9A	Petrol tank hit: passenger injured in subsequent crash.
6.10.1922	Iraq	DH 9A	Crashed: due to pilot becoming unconscious or shot: not determined.*
21.3.1925	Iraq	DH 9A	Pilot and passenger killed in crash after an engine failure attributed to enemy fire.
			OTHER FORCED LANDINGS OWING TO ENEMY ACTION (NO CASUALTIES)
21.2.1920	India	Bristol Fighter	Bullet in oil tank and cam shaft.
13.4.1920	Iraq	Bristol Fighter	Petrol lead to carburettor shot through.
28.11.1922	Iraq	DH 9A	Bullet in radiator.
5.2.1923	Iraq	DH 9A	Bullet through petrol tank.
3.?.1923	India	DH 9A	Bullet through petrol pipe.
14.3.1924	Iraq	DH 9A	Shot down: no details.
4.9.1924	Iraq	DH 9A	Bullet through petrol tank.
25.6.1925	Iraq	Sopwith Snipe	Ailerons shot away.
27.6.1925	Iraq	DH 9A	Bullet through radiator.
29.7.1925	Iraq	DH 9A	Bullet through sump and radiator.
7.10.1926	Iraq	DH 9A	Bullet in engine.
?.10.1927	Iraq	DH 9A	Bullet through main spar (possibly did not forced land).
30.1.1928	Iraq	DH 9A	Bullet in radiator.
22.2.1928	Aden	Bristol Fighter	Camera hit by bullet (possibly did not forced land).

by the presence of armour protection. The fact remains, however, that there was little in those comparatively insignificant (except to the crew members concerned!) events to set against the downsides of armour.

The AMSR's advice also illustrates an element in his thinking that was to influence Dowding's attitude to armour protection in the years ahead – the protection afforded to the fighter pilot by the engine in front of him, when fired at from the front either by ground forces under attack or from an enemy aircraft under attack. The issue under discussion was clearly low flying ground attack work but Dowding, who in his turn became the next AMSR and subsequently Commander-in-Chief of Fighter Command, was in due course to espouse the protection afforded by the engines of his Hurricanes and Spitfires as a necessary means of defence when engaging enemy bombers and facing return fire from their gunners.

But the issue still did not go away. By the October of 1928 the provision of bucket seats for the Wapiti, made from bullet-proof plate as an interchangeable alternative to the standard seats in order to give some reasonable protection from ground fire, was actively being considered. Discussions were held with the Wapiti suppliers at Westland Aircraft Works and with the steel suppliers Hadfields Ltd, Vickers-Armstrongs Ltd and the English Steel Corporation. The result of these discussions was a programme of trial installations and firing trials set for the end of 1930, using two seats of 5mm nominal thickness armour plate. However, when one of the seats was subjected to firing trials on 6th January 1931 at Woolwich Small Arms Range, it was concluded that neither the seat nor its back were acceptable; the second seat was not shot at. (18) Air Vice-Marshal Hugh C T Dowding, in his new capacity as the AMSR, became involved at this time – an involvement that was to last until the matter of armour protection was finally settled in the months leading up to 1940. Dowding, working in collaboration with Sir Noel Birch at Vickers-Armstrongs Ltd, was particularly interested in encouraging firing trials to determine whether parachute packs might provide sufficient additional bullet stopping power to permit the use of armour plate even thinner than 5mm. Vickers' own test results reported to Sir Noel on 26th June 1931 demonstrated that with plates of 3mm, 3½mm and 4mm, bullets were indeed stopped by a parachute: out of a total parachute thickness of six inches, the bullets penetrated only two inches. On 13th June 1931 Dowding had already taken the step of querying Air Staff policy regarding the provision of bullet-proof seats for pilots. Referring to the 1924 memorandum and summarising the current position regarding experimental work, he sent a note to the Deputy Chief of Air Staff (DCAS), Air Commodore C S Burnett:

"I am not quite clear as to the Air Staff policy regarding the provision of bullet proof seats for pilots.

2. ... The position [regarding Memorandum No 24 and Air Staff policy] was reviewed in 1928 as the result of a pilot being shot by rifle fire from the ground in Iraq, ... As a result of discussions between Sir John Higgins* and Lord Trenchard, it was decided to investigate the possibilities of an armoured bullet-proof bucket seat for aircraft and instructions were given accordingly by Sir John Higgins ... . Some seats were obtained and tested and the results [were not encouraging].

3. ... it is now proposed to order further modified seats and a requisition has accordingly been raised ... . I have ordered these requisitions to be held in abeyance pending discussion with you.

4. I take it that however light and efficient armoured bucket seats might be, they would never be universally adopted (eg for interceptor aircraft).

5. On the other hand you may be able to say that you would like a certain number of bucket seats for certain types of aircraft used in India and Iraq, provided that they could be produced at a certain weight and be made bullet-proof against service ammunition at a certain range.

*Air Marshal Sir John Higgins had retired as AMSR on 1st September 1930.

6. Suppose, for the sake of argument, that a bucket seat could be provided for the Wapiti weighing 40lb and bullet proof at 100 yards, how many of these, if any, would you wish me to order?

7. At present we are carrying out some experiments of our own with Hadfields' plate at Westlands and Vickers are carrying out some experiments on their own initiative with our knowledge and implied consent. If there is no reasonable prospect of an order being forthcoming, I scarcely think it fair to encourage Vickers to pursue their experiments." (19)

Burnett's reply was as blunt as the earlier letter from Webster and Memorandum No 24:

"... Armour seats are not required." (20)

Consequently and ironically on 26th June 1931, Dowding felt constrained to write to Sir Noel:

"... now in a position to let you know the ideas of the Air Ministry about the armouring of aircraft.

Each type of aircraft can carry only a definite amount of useful load and it is in accordance with basic principles to employ all this useful load offensively, ie by carrying more petrol, more bombs, more guns or more ammunition. The very small proportion of casualties which could be obviated by the use of armoured seats is not considered to be commensurate with the loss of offensive power entailed by their adoption.

It has therefore been decided that armoured seats are not an Air Force requirement.

Of course, this is not to say that for certain specific operations (such as desert control in Iraq) armoured seats might not be employed at some future time ..." (21)

This effectively killed off further official experimental work although, with Dowding's knowledge, Vickers-Armstrongs Ltd continued to experiment with armour for seats until mid-1935.

Armour protection in theory

It can only be concluded that the works of the Giulio Douhet were not widely read or regarded within the Royal Air Force during the late 1920s or even, as it turned out, the 1930s. Just as Lanchester had been something of a champion for armour protection by arguing its importance from basic principles at the start of the First World War, so during the 1920s and early 1930s a new champion emerged – the Italian General Giulio Douhet. General Douhet (1869–1930) was an early supporter of strategic bombing and the military superiority of air forces as, indeed, though perhaps quite independently, was the RAF's Lord Trenchard. Douhet served in World War I, organising Italy's bombing campaign, but was court–martialled for criticising the Italian high command by publicly declaiming Italy's aerial weakness. He was released when his theories were proven true by the defeat of Italian arms by the Austrian Air Force at Caporetto. He was later recalled and was promoted (1921) to general. In 1922 he was appointed head of Italy's' aviation programme by Benito Mussolini. (22) According to Eddy Cassin (23), Douhet's involvement with the Italian Air Force began around 1909. By 1911, the Turkish Empire was in it's death throes while Italy was keen to rebuild her empire of the past and seized the opportunity presented to them. In a conflict with Turkey that lasted from 1911 to 1912, Italy invaded Turkish possessions in Libya, the Italian Army sending a complement of aircraft commanded by Douhet that recorded a number of "firsts";

- the first bombing mission (November 1911),
- the first aerial reconnaissance (October 1911); and
- the first aircraft shot down (by Turkish rifle fire).

Frustrated by the inability of his superiors to see the merits of a strong Air Force, Douhet subsequently retired from active military service after the Great War and turned to writing as a means for developing and publicising his views on military aviation. General Douhet published "The Command of the Air" in 1921 and followed this with "The probable aspects of the war of the Future" (1928), "Recapitulation" (1929) and "The war of 19—" (1937), all of which were subsequently issued as a single volume. (24) Douhet's theorising was largely concerned with strategic bombing and is therefore outside the scope of this book, but he was incidentally a firm proponent of armour, as the following extracts illustrate.

"Combat planes [by which he meant escorts to clear the way for bomber formations], like bombers, ought to be capable of carrying a substantial load in addition to an adequate supply of fuel. This increase in the carrying capacity of the combat unit should be made use of for increasing firepower and, if possible, armour protection. ... A certain amount of protection may be afforded by armour-plating the vital parts of the plane with light metal alloys. Certainly it would be absurd to expect complete armour protection against all possible hits; but it is not too much to expect that a very light armour–plating would deflect a great many bullets." (25)

"An aerial battle is fought by fire action between warplanes, The fitness of a plane for aerial battle is determined by its power of attack and defence. In aerial battle a warplane may be attacked by enemy fire from any direction. ... To withstand enemy fire, the greatest measure of self-protection is needed. Therefore, other things being equal, the advantage lies with the plane which is more heavily armoured. ... Therefore, a warplane should possess to the maximum degree compatible with technical exigencies, the following four characteristics: *armament, armour protection, speed,* and *radius of action*. [Douhet's italics]" (26)

"The purpose of armour protection is to conserve the power of the [combat aeroplane] by reducing its vulnerability. Obviously, as between two planes with equal armament, the one with the best armour protection has twice the offensive capability of the other, because it can keep up its offensive power twice as long in the same action, or double its power for the same period of action. The characteristic of protection has not only a material but a moral

General Giulio Douhet.
(Source: Archivio Storico Aero-
nautica dell' Ufficio Storico
AM)

value, and it is erroneous to think that the weight used for armour protection is always a waste of power and material, even though it may exist at the expense of armament itself." (27)

"If armour protection is considered necessary for a combat plane, there is no reason why it should not be equally necessary for bombers." (28)

"... it is best that the bulk of an Independent Air Force be made up entirely of battleplanes designated for [both] aerial combat and for bombing offensives against the surface. ... it would be better if the characteristics, or at least some of them, were *elastic* [Douhet's italics]. For instance, since radius of action, armour protection, and armament can be translated into carrying capacity, and since the sum total of the weight of these in a given plane is constant, the weight of any of them may be increased at the expense of any or all of the others. ... Consequently, it would be very useful to have these details in the construction of battleplanes to allow of easy alteration of these characteristics." (29)

It is a measure of the realism of Douhet's thinking that his comments about the weight of armour, the possible use of plates for deflecting rather than stopping bullets and the morale issue were all points that were subsequently to find voice in a key RAF committee of the 1930s. However, as in the Great War, the trade off between the weight of armour and the performance/armament of a fighting aeroplane was an equation with which the higher echelons of the RAF continued to struggle for many years to come.

It has to be appreciated that Douhet's idea of a "combat plane", a plane "capable of carrying out destructive actions against enemy aircraft in the air ... entrusted with clearing the air of enemy obstacles", (30) was not what by the end of the 1930s would have been described as a "Fighter" or "Pursuit" aircraft. Douhet was thinking more in terms of a composite aircraft, which he chose also to call a "Battleplane", that he envisaged as a bomber type that could fly a little faster, a little higher and a little further than the bombers being escorted and with a flexible load of both bombs and defensive armament, so that it could fight off any enemy aircraft that attempted to attack the bombers but otherwise carry on like a bomber. Indeed, he felt that the flexibility should be designed into the Battleplane to allow for easy alteration in the light of service demands. Germany's Messerschmitt Bf 110 Zerstörer ("Destroyer") that first flew in 1936 was something of an early attempt to fill the escort aspect of the Battleplane rôle and the British De Havilland Mosquito was certainly flexible enough to fulfil several of the other aspects – and as a night fighter did, indeed, fulfil something of the escort rôle in protecting the British bomber streams during night raids over Germany. However, it was long range American fighters like the North American P-51 Mustang and the Republic P-47 Thunderbolt that really perfected the daylight escort rôle.

Focussed on the imperative of taking the battle to the enemy, Douhet was not a great fan of pure fighters in the defensive rôle, deeming them an ineffective means of locating and attacking enemy bombers that could appear from anywhere at any time. In this respect at least, therefore, he failed to envisage the sort of defensive tactics that Dowding's Fighter Command would later employ so effectively for Britain in the summer of 1940 – against the hoards of hitherto unstoppable German bomber formations – and the central contribution of radar to those tactics. His failure was understandable, given the political circumstances and the technology of the day, but he was by no means alone – the emerging German Luftwaffe made the same mistakes with what turned out, for them, to be disastrous consequences!

14 The 1930s – A decade of modernisation

To the extent that the 1920s can be said to have been a decade of exhausted military slumber, at least among the major air forces of the world, the decade that followed – encompassing as it did the invasion of Abyssinia by Italy, the civil conflict in Spain and latterly both the Sino-Japanese and Russo-Japanese engagements – saw a progressive awakening to the dangers posed by the growing military might and belligerence of Germany, Italy and Japan. The development of aircraft for the RAF was inevitably dictated by the prevailing theories and perceptions of what the rôle of the air arm might be in the event of a new war. The deliberations that surrounded the question of armour protection for the crews of bombers and the pilots of fighters were no exception. But by the mid-1930s, British thoughts began once again to turn to the real possibility of a new war with Germany – or even France – and the strategy, tactics and equipment necessary to prosecute a war involving the fast modern aircraft then coming off the drawing boards were subject to more insistent scrutiny. The Air Ministry specifications of the 1930s that stimulated the development of aircraft like the Hurricanes and Spitfires, destined to make such vital contributions to Britain's survival during 1940, made no provisions for protective armour – or even for bullet-proof windscreens. Nor was it the practice to make any provision for fitting such protection to their precursors, aircraft such as those of the Hawker stable (e.g. the Hart day bomber that entered service with the RAF in 1930, the Demon and the Fury day fighters that followed the Hart into service in 1931) – or even, save eventually for a bullet-proof windscreen, the out-dated Gloster Gladiator biplane that was even so to serve the RAF with distinction during the Nowegian campaign (April–June 1940), the Battle of France in May/June 1940 and in the heroic defence of Malta later in 1940.

The situation was again different in other countries. During the 1930s, for example, the Russians made considerable progress in armouring aircraft. In 1933 Polikarpov, in charge of a design collective at Factory No 36, produced a single-seater biplane fighter, the TsKB-3, in which:

"... The pilot was provided with an armoured seat." (31)

Production began in October 1933 as the I-15 and by November 1936:

"... the I-15, known as the 'Chaiko' ('Gull') to the Russians and 'Chato' ('Snubnosed') to the Spaniards, ... went into action over Madrid ... and aquitted itself well in combat." (31)

But the I-15 was not Polikarpov's only success at this time:

"Polikarpov's second fighter design of 1933, produced almost simultaneously with the I-15 (TsBK-3) and destined for equal fame ... designated as the TsKB-12 ... [became] ... the I-16." (31)

Polikarpov I-16. (Imperial War Museum, RUS 345)

Whether or not the original I-16 carried any armour, the later Type 5 version embodied

> "... new 9mm armour protection for the pilot ..." (31)

The I-16 began to arrive in the Red Air Force late in 1934 and by November 1936, nicknamed 'Mosca' ('Fly') by the Russians and 'Rata' ('Rat') by the Spanish Nationalists, I-16s were carrying out their first combat flights in Spain and they later fought against the Japanese in August 1939. (31) There is independent corroboration of the latter in a British Intelligence Objectives Sub-Committee report dated 31st October 1945 of an interview with Major (EC) Taneo Koinumaru, a research metallurgist in special steels at Japan's Army Air Technical Research Laboratory at Tachikawa:

> "The first investigations of the practicability of using armor in aircraft were begun during the Sino-Japanese war, but serious efforts were not applied until 1939 when the Russo-Japanese conflict was underway. At this time some of the Russian aeroplanes were found to be using armor sheet. The requirements for armor installations in Japanese aircraft did not become urgent, however, until the outbreak of the war with the United States." (32)

A ground-attack version of the I-16, the Type 18, was:

> "... armed with four PV-1 machine guns mounted in the fuselage and arranged to fire obliquely downwards. Two more PV-1s were mounted in the wings, and the underside of the engine bay and the cockpit were armoured ..." (33)

There was also an Arkhangelski designed SB (fast bomber)-2 of around 1933/34 in which the pilot had armour protection. The SB-2 flew on the Republican side during the Spanish Civil War. (34) And:

"Perhaps as a sequel to the failure of the VIT-2 [Airborne Tank Fighter, developed from the TsKB-44] was the production of a small number of armoured ground-attack aircraft, known as the SPB(D), in 1938-39 ... officially designated as a fast dive-bomber." (35)

The RAF in the 1930s

Eventually Marshal of the Royal Air Force, Sir John Slessor became a Deputy Director of Operations and Intelligence at the Air Ministry in 1937. After the War, quite revealingly, he was rather disparaging of Douhet's theories of strategic bombing:

"All we early RAF officers were alleged to sit up late every night learning the words of General Douhet by heart. We may have had his book in the Staff College library, but, if so, I never saw it." (36)

Sir John Slessor was also honest enough to admit that "before 1939 we really knew nothing about air warfare". (37) But while Slessor pleaded ignorance of Douhet, there were others in Britain's armed forces who did not.

Lt-General N N Golovine, in his 1936 book "Air Strategy" (38) devoted a whole chapter to a critique of what he called "Douhet's Doctrine". His main criticism, for he too did not appear to be much of a fan of Douhet, was that the Italian general had completely failed to take into account the air defences that an attacking bomber force would face, especially anti-aircraft fire from the ground. However, Golovine was not convinced either about the practicalities of the so-called 'Battleplanes'. He questioned the practicability of armouring them without losing too much in the way of performance and quite bluntly noted that it was not only the body of the aircraft – that at least in principle could to some extent be armoured – that was at issue. The wings, for example, would remain unprotected and therefore vulnerable. Although he suggested that designers were actually working on the development of suitable means for armour protection for their aircraft, it is not at all evident that this was necessarily the case. However, it is certainly true that there was uncertainty about the stopping power of armour plate of a thickness that could realistically be carried by aircraft without unacceptable loss of performance.

Golovine was evidently something of a theorist of air warfare himself and in 1938 he published in book form (39) a series of earlier papers originally published in *The RAF Quarterly*. In a paper originating in October 1937, he addressed the "fighter-versus-bomber" issue in terms of aircraft design and went so far as to propose that an Independent Air Force capable of defensive and strategic operations should comprise four types of aircraft:

– A high performance three-seater "Bomber", with a maximum speed at 16,000 feet of around 325mph, a range of 1,200 miles and a bomb load of 2,240lb. Though it was armed with three large-bore machine guns, one in the nose firing forwards and two firing astern (one dorsal and the other ventral), Golovine himself was not exactly enthusiastic about the defensive capabilities of his bomber without supporting escort aircraft.

- A heavily armed three-seater "Destroyer" with three shell-firing guns, armoured shields and bulkheads, a maximum level speed at 16,000 feet of about 350mph and a range of 1,200 miles, intended to escort the bombers in composite squadrons or flights.

- A small, short-range, single-seater "Interceptor" or fighter with four large-bore machine guns, intended to attack enemy bombers. The maximum speed of the interceptor at 16,000 feet was judged to be about 390mph and the range 650–800 miles. There would be two armoured bulkheads, a conical one in the nose to protect the fuel tank and a second one behind the pilot's seat.

- A lightly armed two-seater "Scout" or "Fighter Leader", a strategic air reconnaissance aeroplane rather than a fighter or bomber but capable, in "modified" form of being used as leading a large fighter formation. The maximum level speed of the scout at 16,000 feet was envisaged as being 414mph, with a range of 1,200 miles, but with the modifications necessary to make it suitable for use as a Fighter Leader – such as more powerful armament and armour protection as on the destroyer or interceptor – the maximum speed would be reduced to 400–405mph.

For those aircraft types to be armoured, propellers made from armour steel were also envisaged, as protection for the engines.

Reflecting on the evolution of the single-seater fighter during the First World War, Golovine was in no doubt that success in future aerial combats would once again depend primarily upon the speed advantage of the attacking aircraft. Furthermore, arguing from what he termed "speculative and hypothetical reasoning", much as Lanchester had done more than two decades earlier, he concluded that in respect both of performance and armament scout and fighter aircraft should be twin-engined designs.

Golovine's proposals were in some respects quite similar to the ideas of Douhet that he was so ready to disparage. Where, for example, Douhet had suggested more heavily armed bombers to escort the main bomber force, Golovine was suggesting his destroyer with (in effect) its shell-firing guns in place of bombs. To an extent, these suggestions were in due course to be realised. Here again, the Messerschmitt Bf 110 was something of a cross between Golovine's destroyer and his scout; while on the Allied side, the twin-engined De Havilland Mosquito could easily have fitted (and actually did fit!) any of the rôles from scout to bomber, twin-engined aircraft like the post–1945 De Havilland Hornet, the ill-fated Westland Whirlwind and never operational Welkin were indeed "interceptors".

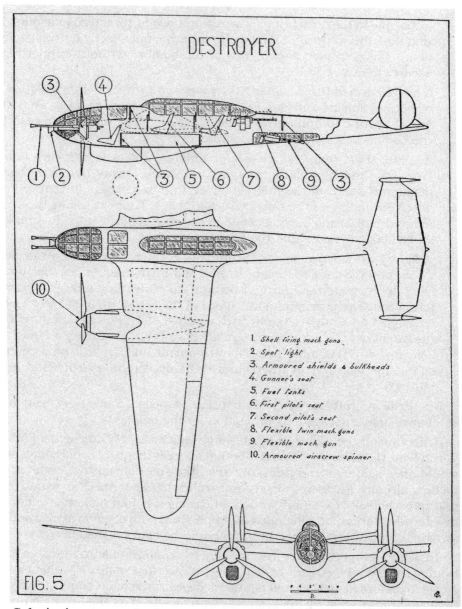

DESTROYER

1. Shell firing mach. guns
2. Spot-light
3. Armoured shields & bulkheads
4. Gunner's seat
5. Fuel tanks
6. First pilot's seat
7. Second pilot's seat
8. Flexible twin mach. guns
9. Flexible mach. gun
10. Armoured airscrew spinner

FIG. 5

Golovine's armoured "Destroyer". (Courtesy Mirrorpix)

However, the story is in danger of running ahead of itself and it is necessary to step back a year or two in time. In the middle of the decade a fortunate coincidence came about in the juxtaposition of two, as it turned out, crucial events. The first was the creation, in November 1934, of a new and high level RAF think-tank – the Air Fighting Committee (AFC). The second was the appointment some twenty months later, in July 1936, of the far-sighted and determined Air Chief Marshal Sir Hugh Dowding as Commander-in-Chief of the RAF's newly created Fighter Command.

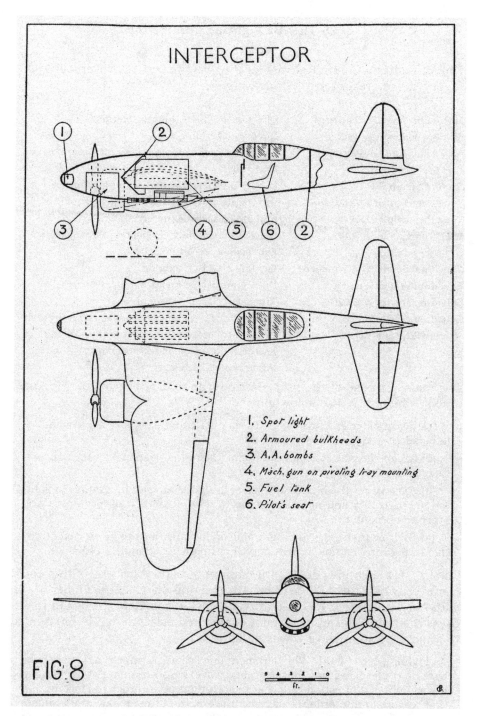

Golovine's armoured "Interceptor". (Courtesy Mirrorpix)

15 The Air Fighting Committee

The Air Fighting Committee met for the first time on 1st November 1934. Among those present at the time were:

Air Commodore C L Courtney	Directorate of Staff Duties, Chairman
Air Commodore A W Tedder	Director of Training
Air Commodore L A Pattinson	Air Officer Commanding Armament Group, Eastchurch
Group Captain R H Peck	Deputy Director, Operations and Intelligence
Wing Commander R D Oxland	Directorate of Operations and Intelligence
Wing Commander R H M S Saundby	RAF Staff College, Andover
Wing Commander A H Peck	Officer Commanding Air Fighting Development Establishment, Northolt
Wing Commander H A Whistler	Fighting Area HQ, Uxbridge
Squadron Leader R Sorley	Directorate of Operations and Intelligence
Squadron Leader W E G Bryant	Armament Group, Eastchurch
Squadron Leader W E G Mann	Air Fighting Development Establishment, Northolt
Captain (RNAS) F W Hill	Department of the Air Member for Supply and Research, Research and Development (Armaments), Secretary

The main purpose of the first meeting was to agree terms of reference, among which were the following:

"(1) To consider and investigate the offensive and defensive fighting tactics to be adopted by all types of aircraft.

(2) To consider the specific equipment (including weapons) for the successful conduct of fighting tactics, ...

(3) To consider the broad outlines of design of aircraft in relation to fighting requirements and also in relation to the installation of armament and other equipment, ...

(4) To draw up a general programme of investigations to be carried out by the Air Fighting Establishment and the Armament Group...." (40)

The first few meetings dealt with matters outside the scope of this book. However, when the AFC held its 4th meeting on 12th December 1935, with Air Commodore A S Barratt CMG MC in the Chair, it began to address the issue of armour when it considered a recommendation related to attacks by successive waves of fighters:

"Fighting Area (W Cdr Whistler) mentioned that aircraft often have to hang back on the level, waiting for the second wave, longer than might be thought. It was always a question of trying to get up speed in order to close in. For that reason, and in order to increase the length of time pilots could remain in position, a request had been made by Fighting Area for a little armour to be placed in front of the pilot, and for a thick Triplex windscreen, in order to increase the amount of protection already provided by the engine." (41)

It was noted that the extra weight (about 6lb per square foot) would mean a reduction either of the performance of the aircraft or of the number of guns carried – though the general feeling in the Committee seemed to be that "... the average pilot would probably prefer 8 guns with the protection of armour than 10 guns without it". (42) With reference to the request for a bullet-proof windscreen, it was reported that trials with a Bristol Bulldog aircraft had shown that a Triplex windscreen three inches thick and weighing about 13lb would be needed to stop a Mark VII ordinary bullet. Reportedly, "About double the weight would be required to stop an armour piercing bullet." (43)

Naturally the AFC, like Douhet earlier, recognised that the effect of the weight of armour protection (steel plate or glass) on the performance of aircraft was a factor for consideration. What the discussion at the meeting began to illustrate was that there was a further and perhaps more significant factor – the view that dog-fighting amongst opposing fighter formations, like the aerial battles of the First World War, was a thing of the past. According to the thinking of the day, it would simply not be possible for the so-called "high speed" fighters in prospect like the Hurricane and Spitfire, to engage in aerial dog-fighting. However, in a definite divergence from Douhet, an attacking bomber force was not regarded as necessarily invulnerable and it was the primary job of fighter aircraft to concentrate on intercepting the bombers – the aircraft that would actually inflict the damage on the ground – rather than engage in fighter-v-fighter combats. According to the "modern" theory, worked out through air exercises early in the 1930s, fighters were expected to attack bomber formations preferably from astern, so that defensive fire from the bombers would be directed at the fighters from directly ahead – from which direction the mass of the engine would surely provide a good measure of protection for the pilot. This is evident from the recommendation of the meeting – that a memorandum should be prepared for the Committee on the possibility of providing

"... a small amount of armour protection in addition to that provided by the engine, to withstand fire from an angle of 20° on either side." (44)

Such an angle of fire would, of course, be met from whichever direction the bomber was attacked, provided that the bomber had guns capable of being directed to oppose the attacking fighter, though the deflection shooting necessitated by attacks other than from directly ahead or astern was definitely discouraged as too difficult for the RAF's fighter pilots!

AFC Reports, Nos 21 and 19

On the bomber front, AFC Report No 21 of 23rd June 1936 summarised the position:

"SECRET

NOTES BY [THE DIRECTORATE OF OPERATIONAL REQUIREMENTS] ON ARMOUR PROTECTION FOR THE PILOT OF BOMBER AIRCRAFT

I. DIRECTIONS FROM WHICH ATTACKS MAY BE EXPECTED.

It is anticipated that the largest number of attacks will come from a narrow cone astern. Attacks may also be made from ahead and below, and from the beam.

II. DEGREE OF PROTECTION

The ideal protection should therefore be all round, which is obviously impracticable, so we must be content with protection of the pilot's body and head from the primary zone of attack, ie astern.

III. WEIGHT OF PROTECTION

The weight of a seat with an armour plate back and extension piece to protect the head would be about 135lb (6 sq ft at 22.5lb per sq ft). In addition adequate padding would have to be introduced between the armour and the pilot's back. The seat should be readily detachable, so that it can be changed if hit. A seat of this nature would give protection against .303 inch ammunition (including [Armour Piercing (AP)]) only.

IV. THE GUN ARMAMENT OF FOREIGN FIGHTERS

The provision of a seat as outlined in paragraph [III] might be considered for the partial protection of the pilot, if rifle calibre weapons only were to be encountered. Foreign Fighters are, however, already armed with .5 inch and .8 inch (20mm) guns which would require armour of about 1 inch and 1½ inch respectively to afford protection in comparison with 5/8 inch armour which suffices against .303 inch ammunition. The weight of the protection to keep out these larger calibres would be most serious.

V. CONCLUSIONS

It is concluded therefore that:

Partial protection could be afforded against rifle calibre ammunition for a weight of about 135lb.

Such protection would be of limited value in view of the present gun equipment of enemy fighters.

Protection against .5 inch or .8 inch calibre guns is impracticable.

In Heavy Bombers there are two pilots as well as the Automatic Pilot; it is considered therefore that if armour protection is to be given to anyone, it should be to the lone tail gunner. This unfortunately is impracticable on the score of weight so far aft of the [centre of gravity]." (45)

Little comfort there for the crews of bombers!

On the fighter front, the memorandum recommended at the 4th meeting of the AFC was issued as AFC Report No 19 of July 1936. More comprehensive than Report No 21 for bombers, No 19 considered both bullet-proof glass and armour plate. On bullet-proof glass, the Report was not encouraging:

"(i) 8-ply glass 2½ inch thick will resist a hit from a .303 inch AP bullet at normal angle at 100yds range. If another hit occurs within 2 inch of the first, penetration is probable.

(ii) There is a serious loss of light transmission through glass of this nature, only 48% of light being transmitted.

(iii) The weight of this glass is 32.5lb per square foot, and an additional layer of celluloid is necessary at the back to prevent splinters flying backwards.

(iv) There is no distortion with safety glass but refraction is present.

(v) Safety glass cannot be curved.

(vi) When struck by a bullet, the safety glass is "starred" over a radius of 4 inch from the point of impact.

It seems obvious from a study of the above characteristics of safety glass, that the use of such material for protective windscreens is impracticable, particularly so when it is borne in mind that the windscreen frame must be very robust, and therefore the members of it of wide section, in order to resist the shock of impact. This feature will still further reduce the vision of the pilot." (46)

On the subject of armour plate as protection from frontal fire, Report No 19 noted that:

"A 14mm* plate gives protection against .303 inch AP ammunition at normal impact at 100 yards. The weight of this protection works out at 22.54lbs per square foot. If protection at a striking angle of 20° to the normal is acceptable, a plate of 9mm, weighing 14.5lbs per square foot would be sufficient. In fitting armour plate to existing aircraft considerable difficulties are likely to be encountered in the matter of installation layout, strengthening of members to withstand impact blows, and rendering the armour readily detachable for replacement after being hit. It is considered that to obtain a really practical layout of the armour, the use of such protection must be borne in mind in the design of the aircraft from its conception." (46)

Clearly there was much in this thinking that was akin to Douhet's theories.

In considering the problem of giving protection to the pilot, the Report (No 19) made a number of assumptions:

"(a) Protection is required from shots dead ahead and up to 20° on the bow.

(b) That the pilot is already protected by the engine from the waist downwards.

(c) That not less than 4 square feet of armour will be necessary to cover the pilot's body and not less than 2 square feet to cover his head and neck.

(d) That protection must be 100% against .303 inch AP ammunition at a range of 100 yards." (46)

The Report went on to postulate that there were 3 "degrees" of protection to be considered:

* Author's Note. The random switching between imperial and metric units is in the original document.

(a) Protecting the pilot's body only, leaving the head unprotected.

(b) Protection of the pilot's body and as much of his head as possible when using a small armour sighting box for protection of his head.

(c) 100% protection of pilot." (46)

Interestingly, the third option (c) involved using both option (a) and the safety glass windscreen already suggested to be impracticable. Given that the aims of the protection, as stated in the Report, were "to enable and encourage the attacking pilot to press home his attack with minimum risk of personal damage" and "to minimise casualties among fighter pilots", the Report entered into a series of intricate arguments based on the "eight-gun fighter". These concluded that while armour protection (possibly including a retractable "sighting box" plate through which the pilot could peer) would enable the pilot to press home his attack, albeit with restricted vision and provided that his engine was not put out of action, the protection should be designed – as for the bombers in the earlier Report and as suggested by Douhet – into the aircraft at its conception. Given, as appears to have been previously agreed, that an eight-gun fighter would be able to produce a lethal density of fire in 2 seconds at a range of 300 yards whereas for a bomber being attacked lethal density from a four-gun turret would be achieved in the same time at 200 yards range, the Report argued that:

"...it appears that it would be of advantage to the Fighter pilot to be provided with armour protection, so that he has not only a range advantage over the Bomber, but can, if required, close the range with impunity and outclass the Bomber in density of fire." (46)

Even then:

"... if the equivalent weight of armour protection be utilised in mounting more guns, the Fighter can outclass the Bomber in density of fire, without approaching the zone of lethal density which the 4 guns of a Bomber's tail turret are capable of commanding." (50)

So, the technical experts were broadly accepting the case for armour and even introducing the new concept of the "sighting box". Just why the experts were concerned about four-gun turrets on enemy bombers, however, is not clear. Foreign designs for bombers of the time did not (nor were they later to) feature four-gun turrets or tail gun positions, but British designs for a new range of heavy bombers certainly did. Consequently, it is evident as early in the Committee's work as 1936 that it was labouring under a particular difficulty. Included in the make up of the Committee were representatives of both fighter and bomber interests, both groups of whom were trying to solve the same problems of protection from their opposite perspectives. This difficulty is something that is dealt with more fully in a later chapter.

Somewhat helpfully, from the perspective of the bomber interests, the Report observed – as long forgotten firing trials had clearly demonstrated

back in 1913 and experience in the Middle East had more recently illustrated – that the engine, as well as being a source of protection for
the fighter pilot, was also a source of vulnerability. This observation was
actually put to the test in response to a recommendation from the earlier 5th meeting of the AFC held on 9th March 1936. Trials were carried
out at Shoeburyness on 21st April 1936 that involved firing four .303
Browning machine guns from 600 yards for two seconds (37 rounds per
gun) head on (ie, in the "no deflection" position) at each of two running
aircraft engines, in an attempt to prove whether "the .303 bullet is useless against an aircraft engine at any range". (47) The engines were a 14
cylinder air-cooled Jaguar radial with a wooden airscrew in an Armstrong
Whitworth Siskin airframe (the Siskin was a single-seater fighter that
entered service with the RAF in 1924) and a 12 cylinder water-cooled
Lion with a metal alloy airscrew in a Fairey IIIF airframe (the Fairey was
a two-seater, single engine, biplane that entered service with the RAF in
1927). Although the accuracy of fire was not good, owing to unsuitable
gun mountings, the results were deemed to be worth reporting. The basic
conclusions were:

"(i) [That] 2 seconds firing from 4 Browning guns, firing AP ammunition at a
range of 600 Yards is capable of stopping a radial engine within 3 minutes.

(ii) That irregular running will be evident before this time and may prevent
the fighter pilot pressing home his attack to short range, or maintaining his
aim.

(iii) The water cooled Lion engine was not stopped by gunfire, but would
have seized from lack of water and/or oil. The shooting against this engine
was poor and, in fact, only 1 bullet hit the engine, the rest of the hits being
on auxiliaries. With this particular type of engine, where the carburettors and
magnetos are at the back, the only chance of causing immediate stoppage
appears to be break–up of one or more of the front cylinders which present
a very small target.

(iv) From an inspection of the type of damage caused on these engines,
there seems no reason to believe that an equally effective result would not
have been obtained with ordinary ball .303 inch ammunition. The striking
energy at this range is 712 foot lbs and it has been held in the past that 100
foot lbs should cause vital engine damage.

(v) There can be no doubt that the .303 ... bullet has the power to cause
rapid stoppage of an aircraft engine at a range of 600 yards IF IT HITS THE
RIGHT PLACE*. There are only a limited number of vital spots, and our aim
should be to produce the highest possible density of fire and so increase our
chances of hitting these vital spots. It appears that there would be no object
in using the .5 inch calibre which, by virtue of greater weight and slower rate
of fire, reduces the density, and only gives the same result as the .303 inch
when a vital spot is hit." (48).

These trials were conducted from the point of view of a bomber wishing
to defend itself against a single-engined fighter. The 1913 firing trials
against engines clearly envisaged trying to bring down aircraft with

* Author's Note. The upper case text, doubtless to emphasise the point, is in the original
Report.

ground fire, aerial combats between aircraft having not then been envisaged; in the Middle East, all the aircraft brought down by enemy action were from ground fire, there being no opposing aircraft with which the RAF could engage. Nevertheless, the basic conclusion was inevitably the same – whether by ground fire or fire from enemy aircraft, engines and the aircraft that they powered could be defeated.

The Air Fighting Committee – the 6th Meeting

Air Marshal Sir Hugh Dowding, as AOC-in-C Fighter Command, made his first appearance on the Committee at its 6th meeting held on 28th July 1936. Having Reports 19–21 to hand, the main purpose of the meeting was to discuss whether armour (or some other) protection should be provided for the pilots/crews of fighters and bombers. R D Oxland was by then a Group Captain and a Deputy Director, Operations and Intelligence, at the Air Ministry. In the discussion on bullet-proof glass Oxland, whilst admitting that no tests had yet been done on an actual aircraft, was of the opinion that the disadvantages of the bullet-proof glass for fighters – weight and vision impairment – outweighed the advantages. Group Captain L L MacLean (Officer Commanding, Air Fighting Development Establishment, AFDE, Northolt) supported concerns over the pilot's vision and Air Commodore L A Pattinson (AOC Armament Group, Eastchurch) concluded that any bullet-proof screen would have to be retractable and only put into position when the pilot had selected and lined up on his target. Pattinson pointed out, however, that the whole issue depended upon what weapons a potential enemy would be using – larger calibre guns would be likely to render any form of protection useless. Dowding is recorded as having expressed the view that:

> "... the fighter was already in possession of certain points of superiority which gave him such an advantage over the bomber [greater volume of fire, smaller cone of dispersion with each gun, protection from the engine] that it was open to question whether his prospects need be further improved by making him more safe, particularly if, by doing so, his efficiency would be impaired". (49)

Dowding envisaged that combats between high speed aircraft of the future would almost invariably resolve into stern chases. Since the eight-gun single-seater fighter already possessed three great advantages over the bomber, the pilot's head was really the only vulnerable point that needed to be considered. A square foot or so of glass, the weight of which would hardly be material, was all that would be needed – provided illumination and vision were not seriously impaired – and this should be verified in the air, by day and by night, not just on the ground as had apparently been the case thus far. The Committee therefore concluded that further trials were necessary to test the effects on visibility (by day and by night) through different thicknesses of glass and to ascertain the effects of both ordinary and .303 inch AP ammunition on the different thicknesses of glass at various ranges and angles of impact.

Turning to armour protection for fighters, Dowding continued to doubt that any more protection than that provided by the engine was necessary in a single-seater fighter and that protection of the engine itself would not be practicable – other, perhaps, than by means of a small area of thin deflecting armour plate in the nose region, especially for twin-engined fighters such as the Westland Whirlwind then being developed. He also thought that an armoured spinner for deflecting bullets might be a possibility. Dowding's comments initiated some fairly deep thinking that reveals just how complicated the consideration of armour was becoming:

– In war, the supply of airframes tended to outstrip engines, so anything, like armour protection, that could be done to lessen the wastage of engines (particularly water–cooled engines) was worth considering, even a light armoured spinner.

– The angle from which firing at the fighter was most probable from a bomber under attack, the assumption being dead ahead and within 20° of that, affected the necessary area of plating required.

– The thickness of the plating and whether the plating should be flat or curved would depend upon whether the intent was to stop or to deflect bullets.

– If cross fire from a formation of bombers was to be expected, where should the armour on fighters best be positioned? In the case of flank fire, the further that the pilot was from the armour plate the less protected he would be and the protection either from the engine or from armour plate would be less as the range decreased – so ought the pilot to be encouraged not to press home his attack to very close range (300 yards being about the correct limit) in order to simplify the protection problem?

– The hardness of the metal used for the armour might be an issue; very hard metal might shatter, so perhaps a hard surface on a soft inner core was worth investigating – or perhaps, instead of steel, aluminium or even compressed cotton wool!

Some tests had apparently already been done by the AFDE on compressed cotton wool only a few days earlier and justified further trials, though the results of much earlier trials on cotton wool mixed with resin had reportedly been found to be unsatisfactory. Such materials, as a possible substitute for or adjunct to armour plating would be further investigated.

The Committee then addressed the question of armour protection for the personnel of bombers, especially the tail gunner, since according to Oxland:

"… it was almost impossible to do more for the pilot than provide armour plate behind his back and under his seat and even this presented considerable difficulty. Frontal protection in addition was out of the question". (50)

It was thought that an armoured bulkhead amidships would protect the majority of the crew (and perhaps a petrol tank in the fuselage) from a stern attack, but what then of the tail gunner who would be particularly vulnerable in such an attack – should he be left to take his chances, with the knowledge that his fellow crew members were better protected possibly affecting his morale, or should he be withdrawn forward behind the bulkhead and work his guns by remote control. In any case, irrespective of armour, in the hail of bullets to be expected from the fighters practically everything in the bomber was likely to be hit – and some foreign fighters were known to be armed with 20mm guns! Perhaps, therefore, the axiom should be that speed was the bomber's best form of defence. It is to be noted that Dowding was, from a home defence point of view, apparently "glad" to hear that armouring bombers presented such difficulties, as it was the one thing that would counter the devastating effect of his eight-gun fighters attacking from astern. (51) Of course, as the eventual new war progressed and losses due to enemy action increased, German aircraft were increasingly armoured. The He 111H-3, for example, made use of armoured bulkheads to protect the rear gunner, though the gunner was already positioned conveniently forward of the bulkhead and not – as in the British and American heavy bombers – right at the tail end!

Finally, at the meeting, the Committee looked at the results (AFC Report No 20) of the trials of armour-piercing ammunition against running engines. The conclusion was that while the trials were to be considered conclusive, in that ".303 inch ammunition is sufficiently effective to cause rapid stoppage of an aircraft at 600 yards," (52) more work was needed with normal and explosive bullets. All in all, therefore, there was much more work to be done.

Protection of Fighter Aircraft

On 9th October 1936 Air Commodore O T Boyd OBE MC AFC (Air Officer Commanding No 1 (Bomber) Group), for the Officer Commanding Fighting Area, sent a comprehensive note to the Headquarters Air Defence of Great Britain entitled "Protection of Fighter Aircraft":

" In view of the now generally accepted principle that Fighter Aircraft should attack normally from the 'no deflection' position astern of raiding aircraft, I am of the opinion that it is possible to afford fighter pilots a certain amount of protection from enemy fire in the line of attack without serious loss of efficiency in aircraft performance.

2. During the last war it was found that the morale and confidence of pilots of SE 5 aircraft and others fitted with water-cooled engines affording protection to the pilot from ahead, was very much greater than in the case of pilots of pusher aircraft, who were more exposed to enemy fire during the attack. If, in addition to the protection already afforded by the engine in fighter aircraft, the upper part of the front of the aircraft was rendered bullet proof, pilots would be protected completely from fire along the line of flight. By this

means not only would the lives of pilots be preserved, but the confidence produced by the knowledge of the protection would induce coolness in the attack out of all proportion to the possible small loss in aircraft performance due to the slight additional weight involved.

3. In order to render the upper fore part of the aircraft bullet proof from the line of flight, a bullet proof windscreen would be essential. The remainder of the fore part could be rendered bullet proof either by providing an armour plated dashboard capable of resisting bullets striking at normal, or by introducing thin armour plating into the structure of the aircraft, capable of resisting bullets striking the aircraft at the angle from which they would be fired from a formation on the defensive.

4. According to the data at my disposal, ..., a 2lb dashboard of a [Bristol] Bulldog can be armour plated to resist .303 inch ball ammunition striking at normal, by the addition of only 7.7lb in weight, and the same dashboard can be 'proofed' against armour piercing ammunition by the addition of 24.4lb. A certain amount of protection against cross fire from other aircraft in the formation being attacked, could be provided by the provision of side plates measuring approximately 2 sq feet and weighing from 12.5lb to 35.2lb each, according to whether protection is required against ball or armour piercing ammunition. Having regard to the speeds at which it is hoped fighters will be able to 'close', however, and the fact that 'cross' fire will have to allow for deflection, I am of the opinion that the provision of such protection should be regarded as a refinement of the principle of protection and resorted to only if performance and the design of the pilot's cockpit permit.

5. With regard to the bullet proof windscreen, trials carried out by my staff in conjunction with the Triplex Company, revealed the fact that a 1½ inch plate weighing 20.5lb will resist .303 inch ball ammunition striking at normal at ranges within 100 yards, while a 1¾ inch plate, weighing 24.25lb resists the same ammunition striking at normal at a range of 30 yards. ...

8. With a view to keeping down the weight factor to a minimum and to avoid interference with the fundamental design of the aircraft, I consider that the side plates mentioned in paragraph 4 could be dispensed with. I therefore, strongly recommend that in future types of fighter aircraft armour piercing proof windscreens should be provided and that either the dashboard be rendered AP bullet proof or the upper structure of the fore end of the fuselage be rendered proof against armour piercing bullets striking the aircraft at the angle from which they would be fired from a formation on the defensive. ...I am ... satisfied that some additional weight to provide protection for the pilot is amply justified." (53)

The Air Fighting Committee – 7th Meeting

At the 7th meeting of the AFC on 19th October 1936, the deliberations continued. (54) On the subject of bullet-proof glass, it was noted that further trials with 2½ inch glass had not added significantly to the earlier results, though Dowding referred to correspondence of his own with the Air Ministry concerning 1½ inch thick glass being proof at 200 yards range. It was agreed that there should be two more trials, one at Orfordness (presumably a firing trial) and the other, in flight by day and by night, on a Gauntlet by the Air Fighting Development Establishment at Northolt.

The debate on armour plate got no further than recognising that there were two types: homogeneous and cemented (ie surface hardened). Conclusion – more trials!

In the December of 1936, the AFC received an "Extract from a report by an experienced pilot (possibly French) in the service of the Spanish Republican Army". Originating apparently on 8th October 1936, only three months into the war in Spain, it contained the remarkably apposite observations that:

"We have now reached the point where air warfare takes the form which characterised it in 1918 – mass attacks of four to six heavy bombers (3-engined Junkers, Caproni), escorted by flights of fighters in groups of three or four aircraft in echelon, protecting the bombers at three different altitudes.

The pilots of the single seaters which we encountered seem to be extremely well trained in formation flying and air gunnery. They are generally good at manoeuvring, but avoid individual encounters. Nevertheless, we several times gained a clear advantage over them in single encounter, mainly because of the good climbing quality of our machines, which enabled us to take advantage of our height in making a sharp turn and then diving down upon them." (55)

Describing the Potez 54 multi-seater bomber then in service with the Republican forces, the Extract continued:

"... it is very difficult for a multi-seater bomber to avoid the attacks of a single-seater fighter and the only means of effective protection rests with the single-seater escort. ... Multiseaters are highly vulnerable particularly if powered with air-cooled engines. ... Since the majority of attacks are from the rear, it might perhaps be possible to envisage the provision of armour protection at any rate for the cockpit of the first and second pilot upon whose lives those of the rest of the crew and the return of the aeroplane from enemy territory depend; this armouring could be limited to a covering for the back of the seats shaped to fit the form of the pilot when seated at the controls. It does not seem likely that the weight of this armour would be such as to have any detrimental effect on the performance of a heavy bomber and the increase in moral and material security which it would afford the crew, on the other hand would, in our opinion be most valuable.

The damage caused by steel-core bullets is considerable. These bullets have several times been known to traverse the whole length of the fuselage of a Potez machine tearing off metal splinters which in turn become projectiles capable of inflicting minor injuries on the occupants of the aeroplane. The holes made by these projectiles in sheet metal covering have sometimes been as much as 20cm in diameter." (55)

The "mass" attacks by "four to six bombers" were hardly the onslaughts that Douhet had earlier envisaged or that the Air Ministry was currently speculating about. Nevertheless, the Report supplied clear and recent evidence that the days of dog-fighting were not yet over, while exposing the vulnerability of unarmoured day bombers.

It is not clear to what extent, if any, this report had any direct impact on thinking in the RAF but – coincidence or otherwise – on 1st December 1936 Air Vice-Marshal C Courtney CB CBE DSO (Director of Operations and Intelligence and Deputy Chief of Air Staff) summarised the position in a note for Sir Edward Ellington GCB CMG CBE (Chief of Air Staff) in response to a query from Dowding on 2nd November:

> "It is true that the adoption by foreign countries of armoured protection for their bombers may render our 8 gun fighters ineffective. This is one of the reasons why we are developing single seaters armed with four cannons (Specification F37/35 [Westland Whirlwind]). ... it must be remembered that all parts of the enemy aeroplane will, we hope, be vulnerable to the shells fired from a cannon whereas the parts vulnerable to machine gun fire are limited to the crew, the tanks and possibly the engines. ...
>
> A good deal of work is being done on [the armouring of bombers]. It at once became obvious that we knew very little about the possibilities and characteristics of the latest designs of armour plating, and investigations are now proceeding to ascertain the most satisfactory material as well as the best angle at which it should be set so as to economise in weight. We are also carrying out research with materials such as compressed cotton wool which seem likely (if used in conjunction with armour) to enable us to reduce the weight of plating. It seems necessary to make further progress with this work before we undertake the installation of armour in our bombers. Moreover, in the opinion of the Technical Department it would be impracticable to incorporate armour plating in existing designs of bomber aircraft without causing serious difficulties due to shifting the centre of gravity. It is unlikely that adequate protection behind the crew could be provided at a weight less than 250lbs which would have to be placed a long way behind the centre of gravity. Although we are pressing on with the experimental work as fast as possible, it should be added that the general consensus of opinion at the sixth meeting of the Air Fighting Committee was opposed to the armouring of bombers in view of the probability of serious detraction from other qualities." (56)

Courtney's recollection of the 6th AFC meeting was not entirely accurate, for the Committee had been not so much opposed to armouring bombers as "against armouring on a large scale" pending further investigations. (57) Furthermore, when Ellington sent his reply to Dowding on 2nd December, enclosing Courtney's note, he commented:

> "... As the note mentions, certain trials of plates are being undertaken, and in the meantime the only armour required in any of our specifications is the requirement that armour protection should be provided for the pilot in the latest heavy bomber specification, ie the four-engine one issued recently. ..." (58)

Dowding, in his new capacity, responded to a copy of the DCAS's note on 11th December 1936. He made some rather inconclusive comments on cannon guns, but on the armouring of bombers he was much more incisive:

"I think this is a typical instance where the desire of experts to discuss nothing but 100% protection against every possible form of attack is hampering progress towards a practical degree of protection against probable forms of attack.

2. I regard the figure of 250lb "a long way behind the centre of gravity" as perfectly fantastic.

3. I have a statement from Vickers that their 3/16 inch plate will keep out an ordinary .303 bullet at 350 yards. This plate weighs (according to Vickers' figures) under 8lb per square foot, and 4 square feet of plate would protect the pilot's back and head.

4. This minimum degree of protection, at a cost of 30lb disposed near the centre of gravity, would surely add enormously to the efficiency of a bomber, because even if the gunner were killed the pilot could still drop his bombs and bring the machine back to safety on many occasions.

5. I should like to suggest that without delay a machine of the [Hawker] Hart type [single-engined day bomber] which is due for disposal should be fitted with protection for the pilot as indicated above, and should contain dummies representing the pilot and air gunner. This machine should be erected in flying position and fired at with a machine gun from a range of 400 yards. A screen should be erected immediately beyond the aircraft and fire should be continued by short bursts until "lethal density" has been obtained, (say an average of one bullet in 3 square feet. The effect on the pilot and air gunner should then be examined.

6. The fire could then be continued until a sufficient density of pattern has been obtained to give us statistical data as to the probability of vital parts of the machine being put out of action by a given number of rounds.

7. At this, or at a later stage, means for the protection of the air gunner could also be tested. A bulkhead plate in 3/16 inch steel would weigh about 70lb, and would be at a distance of about 8 feet from the centre of gravity." (59)

And so, long after the initial firing trials during 1911–1913, first at balloons and kites, then at engine-less machines and finally at running engines, Dowding could see that there was a need for a new set of trials to be fitted into the AFC's programme of experiments: firing trials at armoured aeroplanes! The Great War had undoubtedly presented the most realistic and the ultimate testing environment; armoured aircraft, mostly German (a minimal number, at best, of partially armoured British machines appear to have seen service during that War!) and including even the massively armoured Junker J I/J 4, had been brought down – but that had been nearly 20 years before and the results of such extreme "trials", few as they probably were, had become lost in the mists of time. What was now needed was, or at least turned out to be, a series of firing trials against more modern aircraft that might somehow reflect attacks by the new eight-gun fighters that were soon to become available. Ironically, the chosen target in these trials had both advantages and disadvantages. The Hawker Hart day bomber was, indeed, a modern (for

1936!) aircraft in terms both of construction and of performance, though the latter would have no bearing on the static trials envisaged by Dowding, and Harts had actually seen service over the North-West frontier from 1932, in Aden in 1935 (they would see service again in Palestine in 1938 and were still, technically at least, in service in the Middle East in 1940). But, apart from the use of metal components rather than wood in much of its construction, the Hart was still a largely fabric-covered biplane not greatly removed in terms of design from the machines that fought in the Great War. Nevertheless, the Hart it was to be in the first instance – though Dowding was later to reflect upon the wisdom of his choice and a heavily understated question mark was actually registered at the time (16th December 1936) within the Operational Requirements Directorate (OR III), to the effect that:

> "... later on a trial of this nature against an all metal aircraft might be of value." (60)

May 1937 saw the emergence of some results of the trials and experiments agreed within the Air Fighting Committee, in the form of a progress report, AFC 35.(61) The 1½ inch glass was not coming out too well, impacts from both AP and ball ammunition causing splinters and pulverised glass to be detached from the rear face. The glass was therefore suggested to be scarcely "protection" – though Dowding would later query this point. Visibility through the glass was, however, good and both 1½ and 2½ inch glass plates were to be tested on a Gauntlet, or a Gauntlet fuselage. It was also noted that an armoured bulkhead was being included in a new single-seater fighter currently under design – presumably the twin-engined Whirlwind – in which the pilot would be otherwise unprotected (by the engines). Neither cotton wool nor silk were found to be as effective as an equivalent weight of armour plate.

The Air Fighting Committee – 9th Meeting

AFC Report No 35 was briefly considered by the AFC at its 9th meeting on 9th June 1937.(62) Dowding, referring to the Report is recorded as having expressed the following views:

> " ... this report embodied the implied conclusion that the glass was no use because splinters became detached from the rear face of the windscreen if struck by a bullet. ... this was the wrong way in which to regard it. The proportion of hits on the windscreen to rounds fired would be extremely small, and in any case it was better to be struck by a splinter of glass than a bullet. It might be necessary for a pilot to drop out of the fight because he could not see to aim, but it did not follow that he would necessarily be a casualty, and he would probably be able to fight again the same day."

> ... [He] therefore thought that the report, as far as it went, was satisfactory, and said he would like to see bullet-proof glass fitted in six aircraft without delay ... and flown in all weathers, in order to ascertain if there were any hitherto unexpected difficulties." (63)

He was also keen to see the trials on the armoured Hart fuselage expedited, it being unnecessary for the Hart to be in flying condition; a simple "lashed-up" arrangement was, in his view, all that was required to test the effects of bullets.

The Air Fighting Committee – 10th Meeting

The 10th meeting of the AFC on 16th July 1937 touched only very briefly on the subject of protection. Dowding nevertheless considered that, if the trials with the Gauntlets proved to be satisfactory, bullet-proof glass windscreens would "certainly be required in Gladiators", notwithstanding difficulties with installation. He reportedly :

> ".... considered that this matter ought to be tackled immediately, as it was essential for the glass to be very well bedded if it were to achieve the object of stopping the bullet. ... emphasised the necessity for ascertaining without delay whether the optical qualities of the glass were satisfactory, and to confirm that the reflector sight could be used with it, as, if successful, the glass might be required on a very large scale." (64)

The suggestion from Bomber Command that bullet-proof glass might be fitted to gun turrets was deferred, pending the completion of the windscreen trials, noting again that the glass could not be curved.

The Air Fighting Committee – 11th Meeting

The 11th meeting of the AFC was held on 4th November 1937. Progress on obtaining the armour plate for the Hart trials and the bullet-proof screens for trials on six Gauntlets was reported; all items were due to be delivered during November. The size of the screens under consideration for the Gauntlets was 12½ inch x 12½ inch and the thickness 1½ inch –2½ inch. It was also reported that a design for the installation of a 1½ inch panel in the windscreen of the Gladiator had been passed from the aerodynamical point of view and that contract action could therefore proceed. Dowding appeared by this stage to have become a little concerned over the extremely slow progress on the glass windscreens. He:

> "... hoped that every effort would be made to hasten it. ... noted that the size of the panel appeared to be on the large side, and said he had only visualised protecting the pilot from getting a bullet plumb through the face. ... would not, of course, object to an extension of the protection if found possible, but not if it meant enlarging the windscreen to an inconvenient size or spoiling the performance of the aeroplane." (65)

On the understanding that the proposed size of the windscreen presented no difficulty, the Committee gave instructions that six of the bullet-proof panels should be ordered for the Gladiators, as well as for the Gauntlets.

An instruction from the Air Ministry to Vickers (Aviation) Ltd, to fit out a Hawker Hart fuselage with armour plates (4mm plate of homogeneous steel) and service equipment (including a dummy pilot and observer/gunner), was issued on (or about) 10th November 1937 (66). The proposed positions of the three armoured bulkheads were behind the pilot and behind the observer/gunner. This meant that the pilot was protected from a stern attack by bulkheads B and C, yet from a frontal attack only by the engine, whilst the observer/gunner was protected from both frontal and stern attacks by bulkheads B, C and D. The corresponding programme for the firing trials actually stated, as Dowding had earlier proposed, that the armoured bulkheads were deliberately arranged to protect the crew from a stern attack only. So, from Dowding's point of view, the trials were designed to demonstrate the extent to which the armour might reduce the vulnerability of the bomber to attack from astern. For Dowding, the implication was that, if the armour worked, he would have to revise either his fighter tactics centred on attacking bombers from astern or fit guns big enough to defeat the armour.

Information from abroad

There had not at this stage been any suggestion of fitting back armour to fighters, although the stopping capability of the armour plate would in principle be just as valid for fighters as for bombers for a given type of ammunition. But of course, the evidence from Spain notwithstanding, "modern" fighters were still not expected to engage in dog-fights with each other; the only threat would come from the bombers in front of them that it was their business to engage! Further information from abroad seems unlikely, too, to have had little impact. A confidential note of 16th November 1937 from an engine manufacturer's agent in Paris gave:

"... a brief report on armouring of military aircraft ... with particular reference to the Spanish Civil War.

General remarks: The majority of reports from Spain agree on one point – mainly that the defensive fire of bombers is only efficient when the line of fire coincides roughly with the axis of flight of the aircraft [presumably directted ahead or astern]. Even French experts ... are adopting this view, though it is a condemnation of the heavily–armed bombers so popular with the French Air Force.

Thus the only defence of the medium or heavy bomber is speed." (67)

The report went on to point out that several possibilities for front armour protection for fighters had been suggested before: an armoured spinner or propeller boss, proposed by the Frenchman C Rougeron, and a rather more extensive armouring scheme apparently already patented by M Rabatel of Hispano-Suiza. The agent was reportedly not greatly impressed with either of these suggestions. He therefore felt it appropriate to suggest an alternative scheme:

"... The armour, of tapering thickness would protect a much larger portion of the engine [than the Hispano-Suiza scheme] – in any case from shell splinters and rifle-bore bullets striking at an acute angle. If the total weight allows a further small increase, a thin armour shell can be provided to protect the pilot.

A difficulty remains, namely the protection of the radiator. Movable steel shutters complicate controls, fixed ones may upset the airflow. Moreover the direct impact of a 0.5 inch bullet would certainly shatter the whole assembly, especially one with movable shutters.

Another point to be borne in mind is the resistance of aircraft [presumably propeller] blades to bullet impacts. According to German sources, experiments with magnesium blades gave rather unfortunate results." (67)

The report concluded:

"The "V" liquid cooled engine can be protected fairly easily, which is not the case of the air-cooled radial. From the Military point of view armour plating now appears to be an essential feature of an efficient [single-seater] fighter.

The same scheme is applicable to a twin–engine, long-range fighter.

The fast bomber will probably need the same protection in the event of an engagement with twin-engined fighters armed with rear guns. ..." (67)

For 1937 these were somewhat far-sighted and controversial views. The establishment was already inclining to air-cooled engines as being less vulnerable than liquid-cooled ones, but then there was no thought yet about protecting the engines and essential components such as the radiators. Neither, too, was there any consensus yet about the use of armour to deflect rather than defeat bullets and only defeat splinters. But the suggestions did not go down well with the authorities and Hill minuted DArmD on 23rd December 1937:

"One scheme [Hispano-Suiza] of armouring which is in essence a return to the Sopwith Salamander in which 11mm armour was used. [A] bulkhead is necessary if cross fire from the wings of a squadron is considered.

If the armour is arranged on the Spitfire in this manner the weight is estimated to be 900lb and would give protection against ... 303 AP at reasonable ranges. If fire from directly abeam is ruled out the side panels can be thinner and the weight reduced to 470lb. ...

The second [agent's] scheme is more difficult to apply and protects the engine at the expense of the pilot if cross fire even at fine angles is considered. The scheme is estimated to cost 475lb in weight.

Neither scheme uses the armour really economically and it is considered that a useful amount of protection against 303 AP could be obtained for 210lb on an aircraft of the Spitfire dimensions." (68)

A further minute, from "CR2", of 30th December 1937 added:

2. We are always interested in questions of armour, as applied to both fighters and bombers.

... I do wish we could get reliable information as to whether armour is being applied to the latest types of aircraft engaged in the Spanish War, ...

3. As you know. Our present policy is to ask for a measure of protection

RADIATOR
SHIELD

▨ ARMOUR STEEL 0·4"   10 m/–   16 in

▨ ARMOUR STEEL TAPERING
FROM 0·4" to 0·1"   10 m/– – 2.5 a/f · 16 – 4

Armouring scheme suggested by an engine manufacturer's agent in Paris.
(Public Record Office, AIR 2/3233, piece 1B)

for pilots of single-seater fighters, that is protection from a cone of 20°. We accept the engine as being armour in itself.

4. For home defence purposes I think it is reasonable since if single-seater fighters are hit in the engine they should have a fair chance of getting away with a forced landing ... The question of armour is becoming so important that we should make every effort to find out what is being done by foreign powers ..." (69)

Wing Commander H V Rowley, on the Air Staff in the Directorate of Operations and Intelligence, added his own minute "5" to these comments, confirming that indeed the schemes put forward by the agent did not appear to be "economical". These comments, reflecting evident frustrations at the poor quality of the information coming out of Spain, effectively brought an end to the agent's contribution to the armouring debate.

An undated position paper, presumably of about this time and apparently provided by Wing Commander H E P Wigglesworth DSC (Deputy Director, Directorate of Intelligence (2)), gave further information on the situation in Spain and elsewhere – though of the usual tentative nature:

USA   Is so far not interested in [the problem of armour].

USSR   It is believed that the standard Russian reconnaissance bomber – R.5 – is fitted with special grooves to take steel armour plates to protect the vital parts of the cockpit and engine when the aircraft is employed on low flying duties. The replacement for the present R.5 will probably be similarly constructed, but confirmation of this point is lacking.

There is one report from Spain which states that the Russian I.16 ... is armoured to protect the pilot. We have fairly full information on this type – including that obtained ... by Wing Commander Wigglesworth (AI.2) last year – but no other evidence that it has been modified in this connection even for low flying work. The Spanish report cannot, of course, be entirely ignored, but it is considered extremely unlikely particularly from constructional considerations that the pilot is specially protected.

The other Russian fighter (biplane) in Spain – I.15 – is also reported to be armoured behind the pilot's position. This is an obsolescent type, and according to our information it is in no way armoured, but it is possible that some local modification has been effected in Spain to provide protection as suggested and with this type may well be a practical proposition.

Japan   According to the information available to us, no aircraft in the Japanese Air Services is armoured, and there is no indication that projected types will be protected." (70)

In the meantime Wing Commander R V Goddard, an Officer on the staff of the Assistant Director (Major A R Boyle OBE MC) in the Directorate of Operations and Intelligence (Air Intelligence Branch AI 3), in a note to the Deputy Director of Intelligence on 2nd December that could well have taken into account the position paper, reported:

2. As far as we know no first line aircraft in {other] countries ... are armoured with the exception of a few examples in Spain, from which country we have had several reports about armour being fitted and the desirability of it.

3. It is reliably reported that the Italian fighter [Fiat] C.R.32 [all-metal biplane] has been fitted with an armour plate silhouette behind the pilot which weighs 130lb. It has also been reported that the I.16 fighters are armoured about the pilot's position. I think we can accept this as being true ...

The American Air Attaché in Valencia has stated that the Russian R.5 ground attack aircraft has protective armour under the cockpit and around the vital parts of the motor.

4. There is evidence to show that armouring has been effective in protecting pilots in combat." (71)

The Russian "R.5" was the Polikarpov R-5, the Rasante (Leveller), a two-seater light attack biplane that saw service on the Republican side during the Spanish conflict. However, the RAF was already exploring the possibilities and limitations of armour protection in laborious detail and there was little in any of the reports to cause the Air Fighting Committee to jump to any sort of meaningful conclusions.

16 January to May 1938 – Firing trials and experiments

1938 was a year during which Germany began at last to flex its growing military muscle to serve its expansionist plans: Austria was annexed in March and, following the Munich Crisis in September, Germany reoccupied the Sudetenland, precipitating the partition and later dismemberment of Czechoslovakia. It was a year, too, in which No 111 Squadron stationed at Northolt completed its conversion to Hurricanes in February and No 19 Squadron received the first production Spitfires at Duxford in August.

Firing trials against the Hart day-bomber

Unaware of the military tensions and political upheavals that were soon to follow, the RAF's first firing trials against the armoured Hart fuselage were carried out on 6th (Part I), 14th (Part II), and 25th (Part III) January 1938 by the A&AEE at Martlesham Heath in Suffolk; a Report was issued on 17th February. (72) The trials were designed to:

- find the effect of incorporating thin armour plate in the fuselage of an aircraft with the object of protecting (i) the crew, and (ii) the pilot only against a stern attack;
- determine the adverse effect if any on the aircraft structure when a large plate (D, see page 149) or a small plate (B, see page 149) stops a .303 inch bullet;
- demonstrate that the resultant bullet grouping fired from an eight–gun fighter which produces a density of 1 per 4 sq ft in the neighbourhood of the pilot's cockpit would cause other damage to the remainder of the aircraft and the protection afforded to the crew by the usual items of equipment installed in a light bomber;
- ascertain the approximate range at which the armour plate is penetrated and the type of damage which results from machine gun fire at various ranges;
- determine the typical bullet distribution on an aircraft of modern type (Blenheim) when the fuselage is subjected to a bullet density of 1 per 4 sq ft.

Three sets of 4mm thick hard homogeneous armour plate were made available for the trials, specified as being capable of resisting .303 inch Mk VII ball ammunition at a striking velocity of 1,730ft/sec with a fair margin of safety. Totalling 110lb in weight, each set comprised three plates:

Plate No	Approx. weight	Design position
B	20lb	Behind the pilot's head and shoulders.
C	37lb	Behind the pilot's body and joining up with plate B.
D	53lb	Behind the observer's cockpit and affording him protection when sitting down.

One set of the plates was actually fitted to the Hart fuselage, the others being used directly for firing trials against the plates themselves.

In Part I of the trials, on 6th January, one of the spare bulkheads 'D' was erected as a target in the same position as in a Hart fuselage – with the main portion sloping away at 20°. Single shots were fired from a service rifle with Mk VII and Armour Piercing (AP) ammunition, presumably as if from behind a Hart. The results are summarised in Table 16.1. (73)

Table 16.1. Firing trials, 6th January 1938, against armour plate

Range	Ammunition	Effect on plate
200 yards	2 shots Mk VII	Two bulges, no cracks or penetration.
	1 shot AP	Clean through.
350 yards	2 shots Mk VII	Slight bulges, otherwise no damage.
	1 shot AP	Plate perforated by core. Core probably broken up.
400 yards	2 shots Mk VII	Slight mark on plate.
	1 shot AP	Clean through.

To check the results at 200 yards, one shot of Mk VII ammunition was fired from 100 yards; the result was a bulge similar to that obtained at 200 yards.

In Part II of the series of trials, on 14th January, a further 10 shots of Mk VII ammunition were fired at the bulkhead D plate from 200 yards. In all cases the plate was bulged at the back. There was one small crack on the front side where two shots were close together and in two cases the surfaces at the back of the bulges were starting to crack. This was apparently "normal and does not indicate failure". One further shot was fired from 100 yards, the result being similar to those from 200 yards – as in the 6th January firings. (74) The official report of the trials actually failed to mention that the same armoured bulkhead fired on previously was the target for rounds from a German Mauser 7.92mm rifle fired at a range of 200 yards. The ammunition used was of two types: SA Ball (German Service) and Kynoch. Two shots of the German ammunition resulted in broken bulges with holes smaller than the bullet but which had probably let most of the bullet through, according to the hole and splash markings on a card behind the plate. Two shots of the Kynoch ammunition gave similar results, but the holes in the plate were slightly smaller. (75)

Part III of the series of trials was carried out on 25th January in two distinct parts. In the first part a stripped "armoured" Hart fuselage, fitted with all the usual light bomber equipment and two dummies for the pilot and observer, was anchored down in a flying position in a corner of Orfordness aerodrome and fired at with Mk VII ammunition from various ranges using a tripod-mounted Browning machine gun. There were ten shoots at the target, each burst being fired so that at least three hits might be expected on the fuselage. The first four shoots were made with plates B and D in position; for the final six shoots, plate D was removed

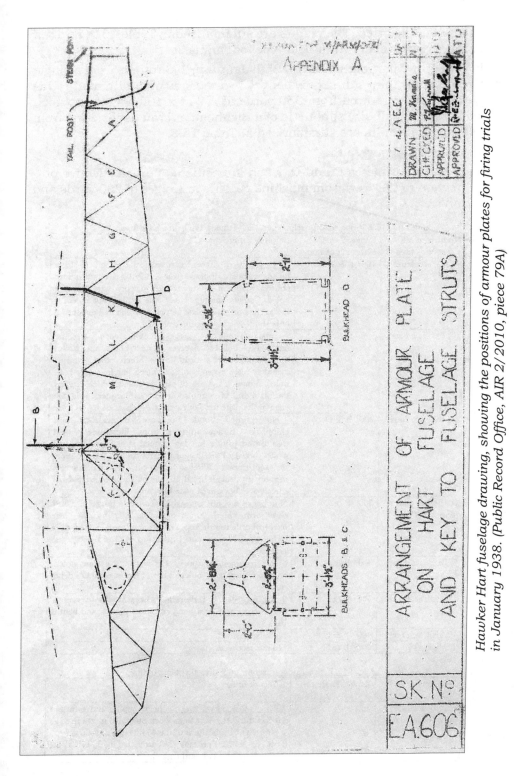

Hawker Hart fuselage drawing, showing the positions of armour plates for firing trials in January 1938. (Public Record Office, AIR 2/2010, piece 79A)

and plate C inserted. The results are summarised in Table 16.2; injuries to the "crew" are shown in bold type for emphasis.

In the second part of the trial on 25th January, 293 rounds from a single Browning machine gun, equivalent to two seconds of fire from an eight-gun fighter, were fired from 350 yards at a 20ft x 10ft target on which was drawn a half-size silhouette of a Blenheim aircraft as if viewed from astern. The results are summarised in Table 16.3.

The conclusions were that:

– the armour plates B and D, when in position, afforded effective protection to the crew from machine gun fire at ranges of 200 yards and above;

Table 16.2. Firing trials (machine gun), 25th January 1938, on a Hart fuselage

Number of Mk VII rounds fired	Range, Yards/ Plates in position	Effect of firing
4, Ball, as a burst	100/ B & D	4 hits recorded. Aft and forward rear bay vertical struts holed. Starboard diagonal strut A holed. Starboard rudder control wires cut. Port/starboard diagonal struts e,f/f,g holed. Camera aperture cover entered, but not holed. 3 hits at the bottom of plate D, one of which had punched a hole about ¾ inch in diameter.
10, Ball, as a burst	100/ B & C	Number of hits not assessable. Observer's parachute holed by 4 bullets; **observer's chest holed and bullet entered observer's right knee.** Much other damage, including rear oxygen bottle and Lewis gun magazine both holed. 3 hits on the top of plate B, two of which cracked the plate and in conjunction with earlier crack split the edge of the plate for a distance of 2 inches.
12, Ball, as a burst	200/ B & D	7 hits recorded. Wooden portion of tail incidence wheel chipped - **bullet splinter from incidence wheel penetrated pilot's left leg.** Lateral strut supporting tail wheel holed. Port diagonal strut holed. Dry battery stowage ripped. Wireless cage cut. Wooded traverse support for cockpit holed. Engine bulkhead holed. 5 shots spread over bottom of plate D - dents only visible.
10, Ball, as a burst (Shoot "IX")	200/ B & C	Number of hits not assessable. **Gunner's parachute and right arm holed.** Much other damage, including rear oxygen bottle nozzle knocked off and bottle dented, port rudder control wires cut. 1 hit at top of plate B (plate just cracked).
5, Ball, as a burst (shoot "II")	300/ B & D	4 hits recorded. Starboard Lewis gun magazine holed. Starboard Jury strut holed. 2 hits at top of plate D - dents only.
12, Ball, as a burst	300/ B & C	2 hits recorded. **1 bullet in right arm of observer.** 1 bullet struck top right hand corner of plate C and bent it back.
12, Ball, as a burst	400/ B & C	No hits recorded.
12, Ball, as a burst	400/ B & C	No hits recorded.

TABLE 16.3. Firing trials (machine gun) on a Blenheim outline.

Number of Mk VII rounds fired	Range, Yards	Effect of firing
293, Ball, in a series of bursts	350	43 hits recorded on the Blenheim outline and a further 187 on the 20ft x 10ft framework on which it was fixed as a target. The distribution of the 43 hits was as follows: Port engine, 12. Port tank, 7. Turret, 1. Fin, 3. Tail plane, 3. Fuselage, 14. Starboard tank, 3.

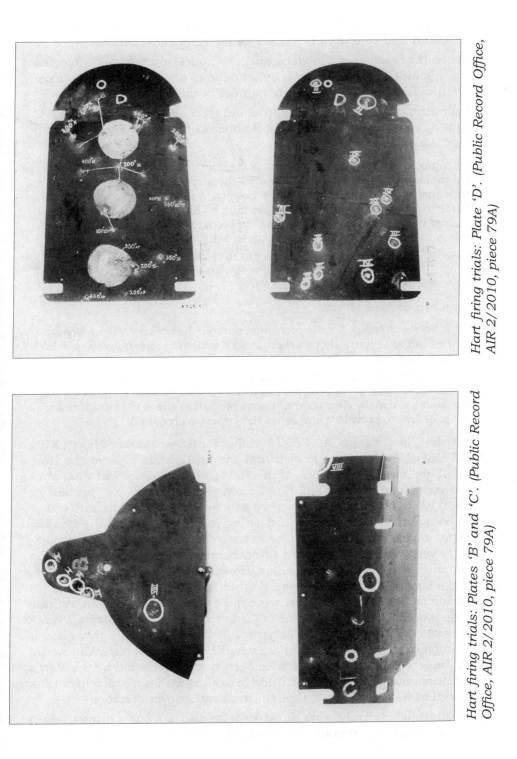

Hart firing trials: Plate 'D'. (Public Record Office, AIR 2/2010, piece 79A)

Hart firing trials: Plates 'B' and 'C'. (Public Record Office, AIR 2/2010, piece 79A)

– the protection afforded to the crew when plate D was removed and plates B and C were in position was not so effective; and

– when the fuselage of a *modern* [author's italics] aircraft was subjected to machine gun fire giving a bullet density of 1 per 4 sq ft, damage would also be caused to the remainder of the aircraft.

Following the firing trials on 25th January 1938, Air Commodore A C Wright AFC at the headquarters of Bomber Command wrote to Captain Hill on 24th February:

> "... [the C-in-C] asked me to take up the question of the protection of the fuel tanks in the wings of aeroplanes. In the aircraft we are likely to get in the future large quantities of fuel will be carried in tanks in the wings, and it is therefore probable that, in this position, on an attack immediately from the rear in the line of flight, aircraft will be brought down through lack of fuel unless the tanks are to some extent protected.
>
> Are you considering fixing deflectors in the plane aft of the fuel tank in the wings? If suitably placed they would weigh very little, and might go a long way towards protecting these tanks." (76)

Hill replied on 2nd March:

> "... No requirement for the protection of tanks has been brought forward by the Staff at present, though there is little doubt that the question will be raised before long.
>
> ... If we can get points like [the projectiles to be armoured against and the direction of attack] settled the provision of a suitable plate is fairly easy since the tanks are usually clear of adventitious protection due to the structure and the plate has to provide the whole of the protection required." (77)

The C-in-C in question, Air Chief Marshal Sir Edgar Ludlow-Hewitt KCB CMG DSO MC, will have known that the firing trials against the Hart did not include the protection of the fuel tank. Ludlow-Hewitt was, after all, a member of the Air Fighting Committee and when not present in person he was certainly represented at meetings of the Committee that had both authorised the trials and agreed the objectives and the detailed programmes involved. It must be assumed, therefore, that the protection of wing tanks had cropped up in Bomber Command as something of an afterthought and that Ludlow-Hewitt was quite sensibly registering the issue for future consideration. In fact, the January 1938 series of firing trials against the Hart were quite literally the opening rounds in the evolution of a programme of firing trials on various aircraft types that extended well into the war years. At this early stage, therefore, it was merely sufficient to determine whether or not armour plate would stop bullets that had not otherwise been held or deflected by the Hart's structure and fittings. Hill's attitude to dealing with the problem of tank protection was to turn out, though, to be rather over-confident.

Quite independently, 13th January 1938 also saw some firing trials at Orfordness against aircraft structures comparing the damage from 20mm

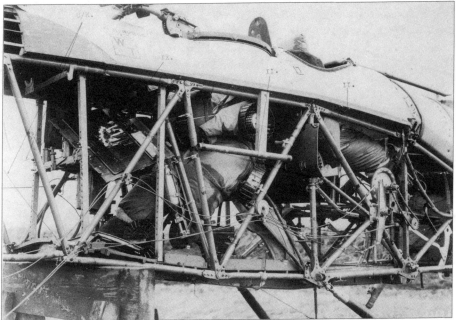

Hart firing trials: bullet strikes on the fuselage components. (Public Record Office, AIR 2/2010, piece 79A)

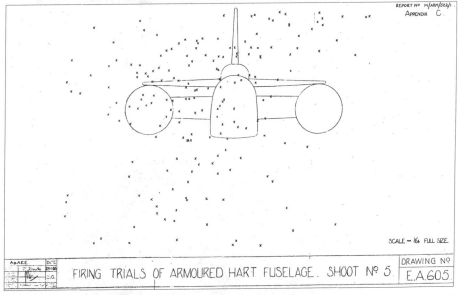

Bristol Blenheim half-size outline used for firing trials. (Public Record Office, AIR 2/2010, piece 79A)

Viastra aircraft wing, lower and upper surfaces, showing the effects of 37mm cannon shells. (Public Record Office, AVIA 18/524)

Type 224 "Spitfire", showing the effect of a 20mm cannon shell and subsequent fire. (Public Record Office, AVIA 18/524)

cannon, 37mm cannon and .303 inch machine gun explosive projectiles. The object was to determine the effects of explosive ammunition on both running engines and the aircraft structures. Two aircraft, with their engines, were used: a Handley Page G4/31 general purpose biplane and a Supermarine Type 224 F.7/30 "Spitfire" (the gull-winged early version!). There were also firings at an all-metal wing of a Vickers Viastra, small twin-engined, transport aircraft. The cannon were fired at 200 yards range and the Lewis machine gun at 50 yards. In "the absence of the A&AEE Assessors", those charged with carrying out the trials declined to report any conclusions, but the report did at least give details of the bare results of the gun fire. For example:

– Trial "L" and "L1" comprised the firing of first one round, then a further two rounds, from the 37mm cannon at the underside of the all-metal wing of a Vickers Viastra twin-engined transport aircraft, placed so that the wing was normal to the line of fire as if the aircraft were a bomber fired at directly from below.

– Trial "M" comprised the firing of one round from the 20mm cannon at the Type 224 "Spitfire" with its engine running at maximum revolutions. The point of aim was the front cylinder on the starboard side of the engine, a Rolls-Royce Goshawk. The engine was hit, caught fire and the aircraft was badly damaged in the subsequent conflagration. (78)

Further firing trials on the Hart fuselage with 4mm thick armour plates as before were carried out on 8th March 1938, using a Browning machine gun with .303 inch AP ammunition and also using a German 7.92mm Mauser rifle with ball ammunition and a muzzle velocity of 2,880 ft/sec. The official conclusions (79) were, once again:

– that the fuselage and equipment deflected a considerable number of bullets and decreased their impact velocity;

– against the .303 inch AP ammunition, the 4mm plates in the B and C positions and the protection provided by the fuselage and equipment combined to give approximately 80% immunity to the pilot at ranges greater than 200 yards and the fuselage/equipment also provided "some small protection to the observer" – although the observer/gunner was hit once in the leg; at 300 yards, in the absence of plate D, the observer/gunner was hit once in the chest, while a bullet also passed through plate B and the pilot's collar;

– against the .303 inch AP ammunition, the 4mm plates in the B, C and D positions gave approximately 80% protection to the whole crew at ranges greater than 200 yards;

– the .303 inch AP ammunition, though slightly more destructive than the earlier .303 inch ball ammunition, was not considered heavy enough to provide lethal effect against the protection afforded by the armour, fuselage and equipment – although it was noted that the type of fuselage used was "not typical of the modern fuselage now in use"; and

– ten deliberate shots from the Mauser rifle at 300 yards did not appear to be any more destructive than the .303 inch rounds, though the tests were done with only plates B and C on position. Not surprisingly, the poor old "observer/gunner" suffered – one round ended up in the Lewis gun magazine in his lap, a second went through his left arm and a third went into his left leg, as well as holing his parachute!

Rowley, writing to the Deputy Director of Operational Requirements (DDOR) (by then Group Captain Saundby) the day after the trials that he had witnessed, had some interesting observations to make about the effect of the aircraft's structure on the different types of bullets:

"3. The first object of the trials was to find out the behaviour of the fuselage and equipment as a whole when struck with AP ammunition. This type of ammunition when striking the struts of the Hart or fittings usually disintegrates, the core travelling on by itself but not always in a straight line, and at a considerately reduced velocity. The result is that occasionally AP does cause slightly greater damage to struts, owing to the fact that the core may be moving sideways; but if the AP strikes any part of the aeroplane structure before hitting the armour plate it will not usually penetrate the armour bulkhead.

4. At the conclusion of shoot No 1 there were five holes through the armoured bulkhead out of a considerable number of hits. In spite of this the

gunner appeared to be untouched; at any rate he was no more than scratched by fragments. Apparently the core of the AP bullet is moving so slowly after penetrating the bulkhead that it is virtually harmless. I would point out that there is a considerable amount of structure and equipment between the bulkhead and the gunner.

5. In the shoot using Mauser ammunition (not AP) the bullets travelled in a much straighter line, after hitting struts and equipment, than the AP. In this trial the gunner's armoured bulkhead was removed and several shots went through the gunner, which is only to be expected, but the pilot's armour was hardly dented." (80)

He was satisfied, too that:

"6. ... The trial showed clearly that in the case of the Hart the fuselage and equipment did reduce the impact velocity or deflected the cores of the AP bullets sufficiently to make the armour plates worth while."

On the merits of using such an "obsolete structure" as the Hart, he was inclined to think the trials

"... rather a waste of time although on the other hand there are many foreign aircraft, particularly the Italian ones, which use a comparable fuselage structure and from this point of view I suppose the information will be worth while."

Nevertheless, he felt that another series of trials against a more modern aeroplane structure was now necessary, such as a Blenheim or a Whitley bomber – the latter because not only was the structure more similar to the size of foreign bombers, but also because it would be easier to get inside the fuselage to follow and mark the tracks of bullets.

Saundby drew the whole series of firing trials against the Hart to a conclusion in a Minute offering his views ostensibly on the Report (72) of the January trials. Saundby's views are reproduced in full below:

The effect on Aircraft Structure

"We may dismiss this by saying that the target (which suffered considerably) was not representative of modern practice[;] modern airframes will withstand a tremendous number of hits from solid .303 inch bullets.

Armour Plate

The trials proved that 4mm homogeneous plate will resist .303 Mark VII ball ammunition at ranges down to 100 yards. This ammunition gives [a muzzle velocity (MV)] of 2,440ft/sec to a 174 grain bullet.

The report does NOT* state that at the end of the trial, shots were fired at the plate at 200 yards range using two types of Mauser ammunition (MV 2,880ft/sec with a 145 grain bullet, and MV 2,490ft/sec with a 198 grain bullet) and both types penetrated the plate.† In this connection it should be noted that the standard Italian ammunition gives an MV of 2,494ft/sec to a 207 grain bullet, which indicates that this ammunition would also penetrate this type of plate.

---

* Saundby's emphasis.

† This is the additional trial (79) to which earlier reference has been made.

157

The trial proved that .303AP ammunition penetrates this plate at 400 yards. Further trials are being held using AP ammunition at different ranges against the plate fitted in the Hart fuselage, to establish the obstruction effect of the aircraft structure and equipment.

Effect of Equipment

Even in a small aircraft such as the Hart, the equipment gives some useful protection; in larger aircraft with more equipment and more structure, a still higher percentage of bullets will be deflected or stopped before reaching a vital spot. This point must be borne in mind when considering Part III of these trials against the silhouette of the Blenheim. A considerable number of bullets appear to have hit the starboard engine and crew, but bearing in mind that the shoot represented conditions of a stern chase, I doubt if more than a very small percentage would have actually penetrated to a useful target, owing to odd obstructions in equipment and structure. We have asked for a trial against a complete modern aircraft to clear up this point.

Lessons from the Trials

(a) Fighter Aircraft

This trial has, I think, established one fact, and that is that 4mm homogeneous plate is not good enough for the bulkhead in a twin-engined fixed gun fighter. Such aircraft may expect to be hit by AP ammunition at 200 yards range, which, assuming the hit is at 20° to normal, requires a 7.3mm plate weighing 11.7lb/sq ft to resist it, which in the case of an aircraft like the Westland [Whirlwind] means a total weight of 94lb.

(b) Bomber Aircraft

Until we can establish the obstruction effect of the equipment and structure of a modern aircraft, it is difficult to know what we could do in the way of armour protection. I think the best compromise would be to fit a conical deflector bulkhead of 4mm plate amidships, which would give some degree of protection against attacks by fixed gun fighters, except for the unfortunate tail gunner, but protection from a turret fighter is impracticable.

Conclusions

These trials have not materially affected our opinions. These are as follows:

(i) In a twin-engined fixed gun fighter, the best possible protection must be provided, for its moral[e] effect if no other.

(ii) In other aircraft we can provide the crew only with some degree of armour protection against .303AP and none against the .5 inch calibre which the Italians use extensively. Against 20mm guns no protection can be given against AP projectiles but a 4mm deflector should give a high degree of protection, from astern, against [high explosive] projectiles and fragments.

(iii) Protection as in sub-para (ii) can only be given if attacks are limited to stern chases, but as soon as turret fighters are introduced, armour protection of the crew becomes impracticable.

(iv) Probably the most vulnerable part of a modern bomber to both small and large calibre fire is the petrol tanks, the area of which amounts to a considerable percentage of the whole structure. There is no possibility of being able to provide armour protection for these if they are carried, in accordance with our normal practice, in the wings except perhaps to a limited extent against attacks from astern.

(v) It is the old story of gun versus armour and, owing to the great weight of armour that would be required, the gun is in my opinion so far ahead at the moment that, except in the case of the fixed gun twin-engined fighter, armour is not worth considering." (81)

Saundby's views were conclusive and doubtless persuasive for the time, but they were also questionable and representative of the limited thinking that typified the higher echelons of the RAF. While the Hart fuselage was certainly not typical of the construction of the modern aircraft then beginning to come into service, there was no evidence to suggest that modern airframes would in fact "withstand a tremendous number of hits from solid .303 inch bullets". That was a leap of faith that could only, in the end, be tested in battle – as indeed it was, with somewhat mixed results – but it was not a justifiable argument at the time.

Saundby's views clearly reflected high hopes for the Whirlwind, but just why it alone should be targeted for "the best possible protection" was another leap of faith too far. Surely every fighting aircraft type, fighter and bomber, should have merited the best protection scheme that was operationally desirable in each case and at the same time was practicable, having regard to the effects of the weight penalties of the various protection options on the fighting qualities of the aircraft. Thus, protection in front of the pilot of a Hurricane or Spitfire might be operationally desirable against return fire from an enemy bomber under attack, but be obviated as an additional measure by the existing, inherently protective, presence of the engine. The Whirlwind, with no engine in front of the pilot, would by contrast merit additional protection for the same operational desirability. Saundby undoubtedly knew this, so the "... best possible ..." expression can probably best be put down simply to an unfortunate choice of words.

Much was also being expected of the attack capabilities against enemy bombers of the turret or turreted fighter, the Boulton Paul Defiant in the RAF's case. Its ability to attack from any quarter realistically avoided anything that could practicably be done by an enemy to protect their bombers with armour and their defence would have to rest mainly upon the efforts of their own gunners. By the same token, there was equally little in the way of practicable armour protection that could be done for the Defiant since it could receive fire from any direction!

The fuel tanks of bombers, filling large amounts of internal wing space, were an obvious source of vulnerability. However, the ultimate solution of self-sealing technology already existed – though it, too, incurred a weight penalty. It is notable, therefore, that Saundby did not feel it an appropriate option for comment.

Saundby's conclusion (v), on the gun versus armour, is perhaps the most instructive of all in terms of the attitudes of the day. Notwithstanding the smokescreen of the weight of armour, he and his colleagues had been brought up on the Trenchard doctrine of unremitting offence. The gun was an offensive weapon and armour was defensive, or at least "passive".

Air Vice-Marshal D C S Evill, Senior Air Staff Officer at the Headquarters of Bomber Command, wrote to Saundby on 31st March 1938 about armour protection for bombers. He wanted to know what protection might be practicable in terms of weight. Saundby replied on 8th April 1938:

> "We are not neglecting the problem of armour plating and have asked for a further series of trials to be carried out against modern aeroplanes fitted with various forms of armour plate. ... As you know so far we have only been able to do shooting trials against the Hart. I hope the next trials will be done against the Blenheim which, of course, is much more representative of modern aeroplane construction. ..." (82)

Dowding's initial comments on the firing trials were submitted to the Air Ministry in a letter dated 22nd April 1938. (83) In his view, the "outstanding lesson" from the trials was that "practically complete protection" of the pilot and gunner of a two-seater aircraft could be obtained for an additional weight of about 80lb of armour plate – the desirability of affording this degree of protection to "bomber and other aircraft likely to be attacked by fighters" should therefore be considered by the Commanders-in-Chief of Bomber and Coastal Commands! However, by then he had some quite reasonable reservations:

- The Hart fuselage was an obsolescent type and modern enemy aircraft would probably not provide the same forest of struts, cross-members, etc.
- No light had been thrown on the problem of protecting the petrol tanks, or of engines if mounted otherwise than in the fuselage, though in the Hart they were anyway both protected against attack from astern by the armour plates. If bombers were to operate over distant objectives and return safely, it was obviously necessary to protect the tanks and engines as well as the crew.
- The rudder and elevator controls and surfaces were not present during the trials.

It might seem surprising that he had not acknowledged these limitations when pressing for the Hart to be used back in the December of 1936, but the Hart had then still been fairly "modern" by the Service standards of the day and by 1938 the concept of "modern" aircraft construction had changed quite significantly. He did, though, find it "abundantly clear" that, from the fighter's point of view, it was necessary to reconsider what would constitute "lethal density" of the fighter's bullet pattern. There were other useful lessons: it was desirable to increase the muzzle velocity of machine guns and to provide them with as much ammunition as was practical. It was evident, essentially, that he was not as confident as Saundby about the inherently protective capabilities of the equipment and structure of "modern" enemy bombers and more inclined to expect those capabilities to be supplemented by some measure of armour protection. Dowding was therefore reasonably confident about the outcome of the trials so far, if also a little cautious:

> "I think that when we consider the difficulty of protecting the personnel, the tanks, the engines and the controls of an aeroplane against the effect of a high density of machine gun fire, we shall find that the modern high-performance multi–gun fighter is a type which will be useful for many years to come.
>
> We must, nevertheless, look ahead to the possibility of the production by Continental nations of types completely immune to small calibre machine gun fire.
>
> In this case we must be prepared to attack by means of an explosive shell."(83)

Events by then barely two years away were to prove him substantially correct. However, Dowding was aware of other experiments, perhaps those carried out in January 1938, apparently indicating that 20mm and 37mm shells would only occasionally and accidentally produce decisive damage to aircraft wings – although such a description hardly accords with the damage actually reported from those trials. While, therefore, he was not prepared to neglect the possibilities of rockets and two- or three-pounder shell guns, he recognised that there were practical complications with each and looked forward to the results of further experiments.

But events were already moving on. A note from the Director of Armament Development, Group Captain G B A Baker, dated 16th May 1938 (84) drew attention to proposed firing trials, scheduled for June 1938, on a modern aircraft – a fully equipped Blenheim bomber (presumably without bombs!) – as well as on self-sealing, as a more practicable alternative to armour-protected, tanks. Baker also proposed using a larger calibre solid bullet, rather than increasing the muzzle velocity (apparently difficult) or employing explosive shells that might explode before penetrating far enough into the fuselage to damage something critical.

17 AFC Report No 51

A very comprehensive discussion paper (AFC 51) (85) on the armour protection of military aircraft was issued to the members of the Committee
with effect from 20th May 1938. The paper began by outlining a number
of principle assumptions:

    – Foreign powers were known to be using bullets similar to those used by
British aircraft: principally the .303 inch/7.7–7.9mm bullet, as ball, AP or
incendiary. All were used in the Spanish Civil War, the incendiary bullet being extremely successful. All countries were looking at larger calibre weapons
of 20mm and upwards, designed to fire explosive or solid ammunition and
fairly rapid developments were expected. The weight of armour plate thick
and strong enough to resist perpendicular attack by 20mm AP projectiles at
short range was considered to be prohibitive, so that it was impracticable to
provide protection against such ammunition. Nevertheless, limited protection against fragments from explosive shells might prove valuable, if only as
a bursting screen that localised the effect of shells and prevented damage to
vital parts, and in any case the .303 calibre weapons would not be completely
replaced by larger calibre guns for some time.

    – On-going trials of anti-aircraft (AA) shells fired at Blenheims indicated that
the structure of modern aeroplanes stood up very well against the fragments
of AA shells and that such fire had "little chance of bringing aeroplanes down,
except by a direct hit or by a fragment striking vulnerable parts, such as the
crew, engines and tanks". However, based on a reported 9.5mm thickness
of plate required to stop the average fragment from a 4.7 inch shell bursting
120ft away, it was calculated that 5,624lb of armour plate would be necessary to give complete, all-round, protection to an Avro Manchester (the twin-
engined and disappointing forerunner of the very successful four-engined
Avro Lancaster) – a weight that would comprise too great a proportion of the
disposable bomb load. In view of the prohibitive weight of armour required to
protect against large calibre and AA shells, coupled with the fact that Germany
("the most powerful of our potential enemies", according to the paper) did not
at that time use .5 inch ammunition, the Notes were thereafter confined to
protection against .303 inch ball and AP ammunition.

    – Alternatives to armour plate, such as tightly packed cotton wadding,
were dismissed as not so economical in weight as the plate.

    – Considering types of attack of fighters ("ours" or "theirs") against bomb-
ers, experimental work at the Air Fighting Development Establishment had
apparently shown clearly that attack from single-seater fighters was "only
likely to be successful when delivered approximately from astern". Since the
complete protection of bombers against turreted fighters (i.e. the Boulton
Paul Defiant) would require a prohibitive weight of armour, as demonstrated
in the case of the Manchester, and since also no foreign powers were likely
to employ such fighters for some years, further consideration of protection
was restricted to that of bombers attacked from astern and fighters meeting
defensive fire from ahead while engaged in stern attacks.

    – Armour plate could of course be mounted normally to the flight path of
a bullet or set at an angle. Charts demonstrated that the most economical

method of applying armour plate protection against .303 inch AP "will be obtained if the plate is mounted at 40° [where practicable], and weighs 9.2lbs. per square foot." So, once again, it seems that Douhet's theorising was not too far wide of the mark!

– The range from which attacks would be delivered and at which armour should be protective was taken as 200 yards.

– In single-engined fighters, the engine would afford reasonably adequate protection for the pilot's body.

The key arguments were:

– Firstly and generally, that the metal construction of most modern aeroplanes, together with the equipment inside the structure, provided a measure of protection and the metal skin on the fuselage presented such a very fine angle when viewed from astern that it might deflect bullets (especially AP) quite easily. The protective effects of the aircraft structure had already been demonstrated in the Hart trials.

– Secondly and also generally, even limited armour protection would give great moral support to the crews of fighters and bombers – the fighter pilot would undoubtedly press home his attacks at closer range to make sure of the kill, while the bomber crews would be more likely to reach their objectives in the face of enemy opposition.

– Thirdly, so far as bombers were concerned:

– Protecting the tail gunner was difficult owing to effect of the weight of armour so far aft on the centre of gravity of the aircraft, but the gunner was nevertheless very exposed and even limited protection would give great moral support. Such protection was envisaged as comprising limited use of bullet-proof glass and strips of armour plate.

– For the crew forward of the tail gunner, a sloped armour plate was envisaged, large enough to cover the cross-sectional area of the fuselage immediately aft of the wireless telegraphy (W/T, or radio) operator.

– Second only to the protection of the crew, reports from the Spanish War indicated that modern aeroplanes were very vulnerable to attack from incendiary bullets and large numbers were destroyed by fire. The choice between economically armoured and self-sealing tanks was still the subject of experiments, there being little to choose between them in terms of weight.

– For engines, firing trials had already amply demonstrated that air-cooled engines were remarkably resistant and the application of armour was considered hardly worth while, although several possibilities were presented. Water-cooled and sleeve-valve engines were far more vulnerable and more work was needed.

– Fourthly, so far as fighters were concerned, three configurations were considered:

– Turreted fighters (ie the Boulton Paul Defiant, first flown in prototype on 11 August 1937) were devised to deliver attacks from any direction and were correspondingly likely to be shot at from any direction, so either the armour would have to give all round protection – already dismissed as prohibitive for bombers – or, equally unacceptably, attacks would have to be limited to stern attacks only. The conclusion was that consideration of protection by armour plate would serve no useful purpose, except to the limited degree envisaged for the turrets of bombers.

– Fixed-gun single-engine fighters (eg the Hurricane, the first deliveries of which reached No 111 Squadron at Northolt on 15th December 1937, and the Spitfire, the first delivery of which reached No 19 Squadron at Duxford on 4th August 1938), where most of the pilot's body would already be protected by the engine in the astern attack, so that the addition of a small bullet-proof glass windscreen of comparatively negligible weight afforded adequate additional protection. In view of design difficulties and the effects on centre of gravity, it was doubted that it would be economical to provide armour plate for the protection of the engine – especially bearing in mind that the fighters, as defenders, would normally be operating over their own country! In the Hurricane, where the main tanks were situated behind the main spar in the wings, armour plate of proportionately small weight for their protection appeared to be very worthwhile. However, the Spitfire's tanks were behind the engine and presumable would need no extra protection, though for both types of aircraft self-sealing tanks appeared to provide the best solution.

– Fixed-gun twin-engined fighters (there was only one being built – the Westland 37/35 Whirlwind, not flown in prototype until 11 October 1938), were to be fitted – from the prototype stage – with armour plate in the fuselage in front of the pilot and a bullet-proof windscreen as essentials, as well as armour in front of the main spars in the wings to protect the tanks.

Whether it was the lessons of the war in Spain that were beginning to leak through to the thinking of the experts, or the hardening of opinion as to both the desirability and practicability of armour protection, such protection was clearly becoming an acceptable option. Inevitably, it seems, the paper concluded that further experimental work was required to settle outstanding issues: how best to protect the tail gunners of bombers; the best methods of providing armour plate for protecting bomber crews and the tanks and engines of both bombers and fighters. However, summaries of the weights of armour estimated to be required for various levels of protection for the aircraft and engines in Bomber Command's stable had already been drawn up for inclusion in AFC 51 as "Appendix F", from which Tables 17.1 and 17.2 are extracts.

The significance of these data really lay in the additional information relating weights of armour to the bomb loads of the various aircraft for a nominal range of 2,000 miles (1,000 miles in the cases of the Battle, Blenheim and Whitley). For example, in the case of the Battle, compared with a bomb load of 1,000lb the 122lb of vertical armour (350lb against AP ammunition) required to protect the crew space and its single engine represented 12% (35%) of the bomb load. In the case of the Wellington, to take another example, against a nominal bomb load of 4,500lb some 269lb (773lb) of vertical armour would be required to protect the crew space – 6% (17%). However, if the Wellington's two engines were to be protected as well, then some 2,171lb of vertical armour comprising 48% of the bomb load would be needed to give total protection against just ball

Table 17.1. The Application of Armour to Bomber Aircraft
Minimum range 200 yards   Fire parallel to flight path
No allowance for fastenings
No allowance for protection given by structure

Aeroplane	Weight (lbs) of Armour to protect main crew space		
	Against ball ammunition	Against AP using a vertical plate	Against AP using a sloped plate
Battle	122	350	228
Blenheim	134	386	252
Wellesley	102	294	192
Lysander	128	368	240
Wellington	269	773	504
Vickers B1/35 (Warwick)	269	773	504
Harrow	333	957	624
Whitley	205	589	384
Avro P13/36 (Manchester)	230	662	432
Handley Page P13/36 (Halifax)	282	810	528
Short B12/36 (Stirling)	333	957	624
Supermarine B12/36	256	736	480

ammunition. Taken to extremes, the 1,269lb of vertical armour required to give total protection to the Blenheim against ball ammunition would completely eliminate the 1,000lb of bombs that it was designed to carry – even sloping plates (828lb) would leave precious little room for bombs unless the engines were left to chance and only the crew (134lb of vertical armour) were to be protected!

The Report was nothing if not comprehensive. Weights of armour required to give protection to various types of engines were included, on the assumption that the armour plates would have the same cross-sectional areas as the engines themselves. Thus, for example the Bristol Pegasus engine (Wellesley, Wellington) would require 192lb of plate, the Rolls-Royce Peregrine (Whirlwind) would require 94lb and the Rolls-Royce Merlin (Manchester/Lancaster) would require 100lb. Presumably, the weights referred to single engines, so that for multiple-engined aircraft the weights would have to be similarly multiplied. There was, however, an interesting note:

Table 17.2. The Application of Armour to Bomber Aircraft
Minimum range 200 yards   Fire parallel to flight path
No allowance for fastenings
No allowance for protection given by structure

Aeroplane	Total Weight (lbs) of Armour for complete protection (crew and engines) against ball ammunition		
	Using vertical plates	Using sloped plates	Using deflector plating for tanks and engines
Battle	350	228	Protection given by crew bulkhead
Blenheim	1,269	828	454
Wellesley	791	516	Protection given by crew bulkhead
Lysander	128	368	Protection given by crew bulkhead
Wellington	2,171	1,416	960
Vickers B1/35	2,503	1,632	1,217
Harrow	2,189	1,428	999
Whitley	-	-	-
Avro P13/36 (Manchester)	2,712	1,776	1030
Handley Page P13/36 (Halifax)	2,834	1,848	1029
Short B12/36 (Stirling)	3,422	2,232	1550
Supermarine B12/36	4,194	2,736	1416

"Armour plate for engine protection may be applied by using deflector plating applied all round the engine nacelle. Figures have been worked out for one aeroplane, the Wellington, and if armour of 12swg [2.64mm] thickness be used, the weight works out at 184lb, which makes an interesting comparison with the weights given [in the tables]." (85)

It is again not clear whether the weight for the deflector plating was per engine or for the whole aircraft (ie the two engines of the Wellington), but it is assumed to apply per engine. Neither is it clear whether the plating involved was armour steel or a lightweight alloy such as Duralumin (basically aluminium alloyed with a few percent of copper). The reference to the thickness of the deflector plating in terms of Standard Wire Gauge (ie "12swg") at least suggests that Duralumin may have been envisaged – see Chapter 18 below. Nevertheless, the Report undoubtedly gave the members of the AFC considerable food for thought, particularly at the next meeting.

Given the comprehensive nature of the report, especially the detailed assessment of armour requirements for bombers, it is rather odd that work was going on elsewhere in Bomber Command that seemed unaware of the data presented in AFC 51. Bomber Command's Operations Requirements Committee had been working for some time on a basic design for "the ideal bomber" and throughout 1938 a series of drafts for a specification were circulated. A draft of March 1938, Air Staff paper BC18, gave proposals for the content for the specification and included the following:

Armour

35. Up to the present time very little work has been done in the way of providing armour for bombing aircraft. With the advent of larger bombing aeroplanes, having a large disposable load, armour plate becomes practical politics.

36. To be of any use against even .303 Armour Piercing bullets, the weight of armour must be very considerable, for an armour plate box proof against the .303 AP at 200 yards, capable only of accommodating the pilot, would weigh approximately 1,200lbs. This effectively puts it out of court for smaller aircraft. It would, for instance, more than absorb the entire bomb-carrying capacity of type 'A'. On the other hand, if the full bomb load were 12,000lbs (type 'C') it might well be worth sacrificing 20% – say 2,000lbs of bomb load for that weight of armour, if by doing so you could increase the chances of the aircraft reaching the target and getting back again by more than that percentage. Moreover the moral effect of a certain amount of armour would be very valuable.

37. It appears, therefore, that it is practicable to provide bombers of type 'B' and larger with armour against the .303 bullet. If enemy fighters use larger calibre weapons, however, it will be quite impossible to provide adequate armour in any aeroplane within the upper limit of size, especially if a proportion of AP ammunition is used by the enemy fighters." (86)

Although three types of bombers are mentioned in this extract, five broad types were actually being envisaged, all with a nominal range of 2,000 miles and classified according to performance.

Table 17.3. The Ideal Bomber.
Table of Performances

	Take off 700 yards over a 50 ft screen		Take off 1,000 yards over a 50 ft screen		Gross weight, with bombs (lbs)
Type	Bomb load (lbs)	Cruising speed (mph)	Bomb load (lbs)	Cruising speed (mph)	
A	1,000	265			18,000
B	2,500	270	8,000	266	35,000
C	4,000	275	12,000	270	55,000
D	8,000	280	20,000	275	80,000
E	18,000	275	44,000	270	160,000

Heavy bombers like the Halifax and the Stirling would fall somewhere between types 'C' and 'D', while the Avro Lancaster still some years ahead would come in at around type 'D'.

Strictly speaking, of course, the paper was quite correct in paragraph 35: little had indeed been done in actually providing armour protection for the bombers listed in AFC 51. Appendix F of the AFC Report merely set out what was calculated to be needed in the way of armour to give limited protection to the aircraft considered – and, of course, what the cost would be in terms of weight. But, even so, a considerable amount of work had in fact been done in putting together the basic data against which protection schemes could be devised and their comparative merits and penalties considered.

Paper BC18 was discussed by the Operations Requirements Committee on 11th August 1938, with AV-M Douglas (ACAS) in the chair; Air Marshal Sir Wilfrid Freeman (Air Council Member for Development and Production) and ACM Ludlow-Hewitt were present. The proposed specification was broadly accepted, with a few modifications which *inter alia* emphasised that the armour was only to protect against .303 ammunition (ball and AP) and described the protection scheme as comprising:

> "... a small armoured control cabin and an armoured bulkhead aft to give some protection to the crew (from the point of view of morale it would be undesirable to give armour to the pilot and none to the crew. ..." (86)

It was not thought possible to armour all the fuel tanks, but it was suggested that the tanks could be sub-divided into jettisonable subsidiary tanks.

18 June to December 1938 – Deliberations of the Air Fighting Committee – Practical Progress

The 13th meeting

So, fifteen months before the German invasion of Poland signalled the outbreak of the new World War, where had the RAF got to after all this experimental work? Well, at the 13th meeting of the AFC on 2nd June 1938 Dowding and his colleagues met to consider AFC Report No 51. A key point, to be settled at the outset, was the question:

"Q1. Whether the data provided in AFC 51 justified the limitation of discussion ... to the provision of protection against .303 inch and .5 inch ball and AP ammunition only ..." (87)

The decision, as cautionary as many of the AFC's discussions and conclusions, was in effect a 'yes' for the day

"... but that ultimately the question of protection against a larger projectile might have to be considered." (88)

Ludlow-Hewitt attended for the first time in his capacity as AOC-in-C Bomber Command. He was reluctant to accept the weights of armour for bombers given in AFC 51, reasoning that these weights were determined on the basis of the armour stopping the penetration of bullets striking normally (ie at an angle of 90°) to the plane of the plate. He believed that for bullets striking plates set at an angle to the line of fire, intended to deflect rather than resist the bullets, thinner and therefore lighter plates would suffice. Captain Hill supported Ludlow-Hewitt by reporting on

Air Chief Marshal Sir Edgar Rainey Ludlow-Hewitt KCB DSO, MC, PSA. (Imperial War Museum, C.1013)

preliminary trials on 1st and 17th June which showed that even Dura-lumin plates, when set at an angle to the line of fire, were proof against AP ammunition at 200 yards: 10swg (Standard Wire Gauge) at an angle of 77° and 12swg at 80°, compared with 4mm of steel plate at 65°. (89)

Addressing the question of the probable armament that foreign aircraft might use, Dowding was inclined to disregard conclusions (apparently from France, though the AFC Minutes do not include a source reference) that for a diving fighter attacking with 20mm guns, the enhancement of the effect of the bullets by the speed of the aircraft would "ensure that the bomber would be brought down". (90) He continued to believe that Britain's experiments with 20mm and 37mm shells justified the deduc-tion that they would not necessarily bring aircraft down. It is difficult to understand now how Dowding could so readily have been prepared to disregard the results on the shell firing trials against aircraft structures back in the January of 1938. After all, 20mm and 37mm shells had been shown seriously to damage flying surfaces, while a single 20mm shell hit on the engine and the ensuing fire had been enough to wreck a prototype type 224 "Spitfire". But, of course, there was no clear evidence yet that potential enemy aircraft would mount such cannons and, in any case, the practicalities of defending against such guns seemed to be just too difficult to contemplate. So, while the Committee continued to explore the possibilities for bombers of deflecting and/or multi-layer (eg herring-bone) armour as protection against .303 and .5 inch bullets, Dowding was more interested in what practical means an enemy could take to stop .303 bullets (since, he considered rightly, the Committee had already decided against the use of .5 inch by British aircraft). However, it was noted that there was a "paucity of information regarding the armaments, ammuni-tion, protective measures and tactics of aircraft of foreign powers", (91) the importance of the acquisition of such information being stressed. Once again, there was reference to trials on Blenheim fuselages, but no direct reports seem to have survived.

The Committee then turned to the assumption that the protection of bombers should be designed to resist attacks by fighters from astern at 200 yards range. Dowding seemed to be fixed on the idea that fighting at high speeds necessitated stern attacks, believing that while fighters might open fire at about 400 yards range it would be rare for the new types of aircraft to close to less than 200 yards. So, for further experiments on protection, 200 yards was accepted as the minimum range – though Ludlow-Hewitt was thinking not so much of complete protection for his crews, but more of sustaining their morale. He was prepared to rule out attacks from turreted fighters – though it is not clear whether this was because all-round protection for bombers was so unthinkable or because there were no foreign turreted fighters in prospect. It is perhaps worth noting that while "turreted" fighters of something like the Defiant type were not envisaged in Germany, the Messerschmitt Bf 110 certainly had a manually aimed machine gun in the rear cockpit for stern defence that could be swung from side to side through a limited arc and could therefore provide for some attempt to fire at bombers in passing. In the event, no final decisions were made concerning the protection of bombers, though Dowding is recorded to have made a particularly interesting comment on hearing from Gp Capt Orlebar (OC Air Fighting Development Establishment (AFDE), Northolt) about experiments with Hurricanes in stern attacks against admittedly slow targets:

> "these results were very promising ... Against a slow bomber armoured from astern, the attack from below would be a practical method. It was considered doubtful, however, whether similarly good results would be obtained against a Blenheim ..." (92)

In the event, of course, Blenheims in both fighter and bomber rôles were very severely treated by German fighters, as well as by ground fire, during the Battle of France in May/June 1940. The quote, in effect, reveals just how elementary the "abstract" thinking among the members of the AFC turned out to be – and perhaps just how far the actual fighting lessons of the earlier World War and the war in Spain were being disregarded (or simply forgotten!) under the weight of expectations for the so-called "modern" aircraft, bombers as well as fighters. It also indicates an element of double standards in Dowding's thinking: he felt that the Blenheim would better resist attacks than the out-dated Hart type but did not apparently go on to wonder about the comparative resistance of modern enemy bombers like Germany's Heinkel 111 to attacks by his own fighters. And time was slipping by!

The protection of bombers was discussed at some length. The tail gunner's position was regarded as "very exposed", though problematic. After considering the limitations of the types of turrets then being developed – basically the Boulton and Paul, Frazer Nash and 'Wellington' types – it was agreed that investigations in liaison with designers should start immediately on the lines suggested in AFC 51:

– A bullet-proof glass window for the Boulton and Paul type; and

– A bullet-proof glass panel, supplemented by a sheet of armour to protect the lower part of the gunner's body, for the Frazer Nash type.

For the bomber crew in forward positions, there seemed to be a general reluctance to accept the indications of the Hart trials in the absence of direct trials with a modern aircraft like the Blenheim; further discussion was deferred pending such trials.

For the protection of fuel tanks, discussion was again deferred pending the Blenheim trials in which the possible protection afforded by stressed skin wings could be investigated. It is interesting to note that concern over the fuel tanks seemed to be focussed on the maximisation and conservation of fuel rather than with the likelihood of fire!

Finally, for the bomber, the protection of the engines was discussed. In the light of the tests done on running engines, concern focussed on the effect of bullets coming in not from the front but from the rear and into the ancillary apparatus like pumps, magnetos and distributors. The possibility of stiffening the fairings behind the engines with thick Duralumin or thin armour plate added a further dimension to the Blenheim trials.

For the single-engined fixed-gun fighter, whilst again expressing dissatisfaction over the delay in connection with the supply of bullet-proof glass screens for trials on Gauntlets and Gladiators, Dowding reaffirmed that he did not wish to press for any more protection for the pilot than that provided by the engine and a bullet-proof windscreen. He also concluded that, apart from the possible provision of an armoured spinner, it was not worthwhile attempting to armour the engine. In view of trials showing that AP ammunition offered little advantage over ball ammunition against engines – according to Captain Hill representing the Air Ministry "...neither type did very much damage, and several hits were necessary before the engine was stopped" (93) – it is possible to sense some consternation in Ludlow-Hewitt's subsequent question:

> "... the most likely form of attack which the bombers would have to meet would be from astern, which implied that the principal target presented to them would be the engines of fighters. [since] .303 ammunition, the present standard ammunition of the bomber, was of little use against this target, what, then, was to be used?" (94)

The response was that while a 20mm gun, perhaps with a delay-fused shell, might be effective, an idea that Ludlow-Hewitt found far from satisfactory, the "main function of the bomber's armament was to force the enemy fighters to keep a respectable distance away. Saundby, observed that less than 10% of the fights in the First World War had produced lethal effect and thought that "the bomber could still hope to keep the fighter at a sufficient distance to make fighting inconclusive. [The bomber] also had a chance of firing the fighter's tanks or of killing the pilot". (95) Ludlow-Hewitt was clearly not satisfied with these remarks and recorded:

> "a formal request that research be carried out with the definite purpose of investigating the question of how the bomber could best be protected against the single-seater fighter, every type of gun and ammunition available being tried." (96)

For the twin-engined fixed-gun and the turreted fighters, the recommendations in AFC 51 were accepted, except that in the latter type Dowding preferred additional ammunition rather than an equivalent weight of armour.

Dowding's remarks during the meeting had clearly unsettled Ludlow-Hewitt for, on 25th June, he wrote to the Director of Staff Duties (DSD, Air Commodore R P Willock) at the Air Ministry:

"... The C-in-C Fighter Command contended that against frontal attack [by a fighter] the engine afforded almost complete cover to the pilot, petrol tanks in the fuselage, and main aircraft controls. He stated that trials had shown that a considerable time elapsed before a running engine could be put out of action by machine gun fire from ahead. ... Such a state of affairs, if correct, is of vital concern to this Committee since the main target presented by the modern monoplane fighter attacking directly from astern would be the engine. ... It is obvious that the Bomber Command cannot accept a state of complete helplessness against the single-seater fighter. ..." (97)

The following day, 27th June, Dowding himself wrote to the Secretary at the Air Ministry:

" ... at a recent meeting of the Air Fighting Committee I gave as my opinion that Fighter Pilots in single-engined aircraft needed no protection beyond that of the engines and a screen of bullet proof glass.

2. Further consideration has led me to revise this opinion as regards the Hurricane, and similar conditions are likely to arise in the case of the Spitfire.

3. The low-wing monoplane, with its comparatively low set in-line engine, will leave the throat and chest of the pilot exposed except in so far as incidental protection is provided by the header tanks and other obstacles.

4. The alternatives appear to be to fit a shallow bulkhead in the upper part of the fuselage or to provide a deflecting plate upon the upper line of the cowling as far back as the cockpit. " (98)

Whether Dowding had got wind of Ludlow-Hewitt's letter or had been prompted to change his mind as a result of some other influence is not known, but the evident fact is that Dowding had come to appreciate that there were limitations to the protection afforded by the engine and the windscreen (albeit fortified) upon which he had been inclined so confidently to rely.

Saundby, responding officially to Ludlow-Hewitt via the DSD on 20th July, argued as follows:

"... When we consider that a modern fixed gun fighter such as the Hurricane can fire all its ammunition in 20 seconds, and can hope to build up lethal density against a bomber in a very few seconds, it would appear that the chances of the bomber escaping by stopping the fighter's engine is remote ...

We have never thought that the proper target of the bomber's guns was the fighter's engine; on the contrary, we have been inclined to regard the engine as a shield between the bomber's fire and the real vitals – the tanks and the pilot. What has really altered the balance against the bomber is that the weight and performance of fighters is now such that the carrying of the small amount of armour necessary to protect the pilot and the tanks *can be arranged without difficulty* [Author's italics]. The remedy is to arm the bomber with a gun which can penetrate the engine and the armour alike, and this we are proposing to do by modifying existing turrets to carry the 20mm Hispano gun ...

It would, however, be misleading to leave this subject without pointing out that the bomber, by reason of his greater disposable load, can by means of armouring make itself even more immune from fire than can the fighter. There is no reason why the crews, the tanks and the engines should not be protected from .303 fire from fixed gun fighters, and, in fact, it is our intention to do so as far as possible." (99)

There could have been little in these exchanges to ease the mind of the C-in-C Bomber Command and Saundby's view on the potential for the relative immunity of the bomber can (at least now) be seen as unreasonably optimistic!

Blenheim firing trials

Flying trials were carried out between 1st March and 28th July 1938 to determine the most promising tactics for Hurricane type aircraft in Home Defence attacks on monoplane bombers and for Harrow, Battle and Blenheim types in defence against German aircraft of the "Hurricane class". While the subsequent Report, AFDE Report No 9 (100), mainly dealt with the tactics to be used by attackers and defenders, it expressed on the one hand the view that:

"53. The need for armour was very apparent particularly for gunners in the rear turrets [of bombers] who had an extreme sense of exposure to fire."

Also for bombers, the trials:

"... clearly showed the need [inter alia] for:

109 (iv) armour against the stern attack – particularly for rear turrets ..."

Meanwhile, the first firing trials on a Blenheim aircraft (K.7150) took place during the period 5th–7th July 1938 at Orfordness. They were regarded as a continuation of the Hart trials. As in the Hart trials, the Blenheim was completely equipped for service use, with standard condemned equipment and dummies for the pilot, the navigator and the air gunner in full flying clothing with parachutes. It was fitted with armour plate directly behind the pilot's seat and behind the starboard wing petrol tank; the armour was 4mm thick and specified to resist .303 Mark VII ammunition at about 300 yards with a fair margin of safety. The objects of the trial were:

(a) to find out the behaviour of the aircraft and equipment when struck with .303" Mark VII and AP ammunition:

(b) to find out if the aircraft and equipment deflected the bullets or reduced the impact velocity sufficiently to make the use of the 4mm plate worthwhile.

The Blenheim was anchored down in flying position with the wheels retracted and its tail pointing directly towards the firing points, as if attacked from astern. Using tripod-mounted Browning and Vickers guns, the programme of firing was in three parts:

(i) a series of shots with .303 inch Mark VII ammunition, at ranges of 200, 300 and 400 yards;

(ii) a series of shots with .303 inch AP ammunition, at ranges of 200, 300, 400 and 500 yards; and

(iii) a second series with .303 inch Mark VII ammunition, fired at a range of 500 yards in long bursts to a total of 2,000 rounds to simulate the full load of an eight-gun fighter.

The numbers of rounds in (i) and (ii) were such as to obtain standard density (one hit per 4 sq ft). The trials were witnessed by, among others:

Air Chief Marshal Sir Hugh C T Dowding	Fighter Command
Air Commodore K R Park	HQ No 11(Fighter) Group, Tangmere
Wing Commander C E Williamson–Jones	Bomber Command (Engineering)
Wing Commander F J W Mellersh	No 25 (Armament) Group (Training Command), Eastchurch
Squadron Leader R V M Odbert	No 25 (Armament) Group (Training Command), Eastchurch
Group Captain R V M Saundby	Deputy Director of Operational Requirements (DDOR)
Wing Commander H V Rowley	Directorate of Operational Requirements
Group Captain G B A Baker	Director of Armament Development (DArmD)
Mr R S Capon	Deputy Director of Research and Development (Armament) (DDArmD)
Captain F W Hill	Directorate of Research and Development (RDArmD)

From the results, it was noted that:

	"Deflection	Penetration
(a) [Bullet strikes] on the side of the fuselage	33	61
(b) [Bullet strikes] on the top deck of the fuselage	14	25
(c) [Bullet strikes] on the upper wing surface	24	169
(d) [Bullet strikes] on the upper part of the cowling	7	80

From which data it was deduced that:

(a) the sides of the fuselage deflected 35% of all strikes on the sides of the fuselage,

(b) the top of the fuselage deflected 36% of all strikes on the top of the fuselage,

(c) the upper wing surface deflected 12% of all strikes on the upper wing surface,

(d) the upper part of the engine cowling deflected 8% of all strikes on the upper part of the engine cowling.

The small percentage of strikes deflected by the upper wing surfaces and the upper part of the engine cowling in comparison with those deflected by the sides and top surfaces of the fuselage may be accounted for [by] the fact that the bullets strike the surfaces of the former at a greater angle. The tail structure had shielded the lower portion of the fuselage to a considerable extent, similarly the rear wing surface flap mechanism and heavier spar fittings had shielded the lower portions of the engine and under-carriages.

> The damage to the gunner was noticeably concentrated on his head and shoulders above the level of the main ring of the cupola, and on his feet which were near the fuselage skin, and not shielded by the tail structure. One of the two port rudder control wires had been severed but the controls were still workable. It was noted that AP ammunition is more readily deflected and more likely to strip and break up, whereas ball ammunition has a tendency to mushroom and make large holes." (82)

The "damage" to the gunner was something of an understatement. A draft set of notes on the trials was more explicit:

> "The rear gunner's cupola was blown to pieces and the gunner hit 10 times in the legs, 10 times in the body and five times in the head. ..." (82)

The following conclusions were reached:

> (a) A small increase in the weight of the skin plating behind the tanks and in the upper surfaces of the fuselage would give a useful amount of protection against .303 inch Ball and AP ammunition.

> (b) Armour plate of 4mm thickness behind the pilot's head and upper portion of his body would also give adequate protection against the .303 inch ammunition of both types.

> (c) If the gunner in the turret was to be adequately protected, some form of armour scuttle or bullet-proof glass for the cupola and armour protection for the gunner's feet were essential.

> (d) The maximum fire from an eight-gun fighter was not sufficient to render the controls of the aircraft ineffective.

> (e) The AP ammunition appeared to be no more effective that the Ball ammunition.

Saundby, summarising the results for the Director of Armament Development (DArmD) in a note on 28th July, in advance of the official Report, advised:

> "2. ...we can certainly say that the trial has proved clearly that the aircraft structure provides a definite measure of protection for the pilot and also that the rear gunner is extremely vulnerable.

> 3. We are most anxious to take advantage of the results of this trial as soon as possible and to provide some form of protection for both pilots and gunners. ..." (82)

He later, on 28th July, went so far as to raise the possibility with the DArmD of a specially constructed armour chair for the pilot, but no doubt mindful of the time that it would take to get this organised, he suggested:

Blenheim firing trials – view from astern. (Public Record Office, AIR 20/12)

Blenheim firing trials – view from ahead. (Public Record Office, AIR 20/12)

"As an immediate step, a piece of armour plate behind the pilot's seat, such as was used in the trials, would be satisfactory." (82)

He also recognised that protection for the rear gunner was a much more difficult problem and thought that, pending trials with two Fraser Nash turrets that were apparently being planned, some sort of visor protection would be worth exploring.

Air Vice-Marshal Douglas (Assistant Chief of Air Staff) wrote to the Chief of Air Staff (Air Chief Marshal Sir Cyril Newall) and to the Deputy Chief of Air Staff (Air Vice-Marshal R E C Peirce) on 16th September 1938, reporting on Blenheim trials:

"2. The main features of the Report would seem to be:

(a) The large number of hits with .303 ammunition that can be obtained on a modern aircraft structure without causing material damage;

(b) The fact that a comparatively small amount of armour plate placed in suitable positions will produce quite a high degree of protection against attack from astern.

(c) The next trial that we are carrying out is with 20mm Hispano guns against a Blenheim fuselage. ..." (82)

Dowding himself wrote to the Under-Secretary of State at the Air Ministry, on 19th September 1938, giving his own observations on the Blenheim trials. He noted that the undercarriage had been damaged – one wheel had dropped down and both tyres had been punctured repeatedly. He thought that the damage should be kept in mind in relation to British bombers. He also observed that much of the perspex in the gunner's cupola had broken away and disappeared and reckoned that in the air the slipstream would have swept it all away. (82)

Newall responded on 7th October 1938 to Douglas' 16th September note, wondering whether sufficient was now known about the protection afforded by armour to incorporate it as a requirement in one new specification, or even in specifications such as 12/36 (Short Stirling) and 13/36 (Handley Page Halifax and Avro Manchester). (101) Douglas advised Newall on 18th October 1938 that armour plate was being specified in the requirements for various new types of aircraft, such as the Hawker F.18/37 (Hawker Typhoon), the Westland F.37/35 (Whirlwind) and the Gloster F.9/37 (twin-engined canon fighter, which never went into production). He also advised that action had been, or was being taken, to incorporate "on the highest priority" a measure of armour plate protection in the following aircraft: Hurricane, Spitfire, Battle, Blenheim, Hampden, Halifax, Harrow, Manchester, Stirling, Wellington, Vickers B.1/35 (Warwick) and the Gladiator. Apparently, protection for the Lysander and the Wellesley were still under consideration. (82)

Notwithstanding Newall's concern about the protracted nature of the tests and trials, new firing trials were conducted against Blenheim K.7168 on 28th October 1938 at Orfordness. The object this time was to assess the effect of .303 inch, both AP and ball, and 20mm solid shot on the Blenheim with engines running and armour fitted. There was a secondary object, to assess the effect of the solid 20mm shot on a self-sealing fuel tank taken from an Airspeed Oxford aircraft.

The Blenheim, fitted with two Bristol Jupiter VII engines was set up in flying attitude and fired at from directly astern and slightly below at ranges of 300 yards for the Browning .303 inch machine gun and 200 yards for the 20mm cannon, but the cannon shells were reduced in charge to represent firing from 700 yards. It was armoured with 4mm plate behind the "pilot", head high; a 10 gauge (0.128 inch) Duralumin deflector shield aft of the upper gunner's turret, 10 inch high and 18 inch wide; the wireless (W/T) operator was protected with two 4 inch wide horizontal strips of 10 gauge Duralumin, intended to catch shots skating along inside the fuselage, and two deflector shields some 10 inch wide. Thus there was a large space in the centre, behind the W/T set that was unprotected. On the starboard main plane there was 10 gauge Duralumin plating from the wing root to the outer edge of the engine nacelle, the top of which was also protected; the engine and the fuel tank on that side were therefore protected on top from .303 inch ammunition striking at an angle of less than 20° and 15° respectively. The Oxford self-sealing tank was installed in the port wing and was otherwise unprotected. There were several points of aim:

– the port wing (unprotected): three burst, each of 15 rounds, of .303 inch ball ammunition and one 15 round burst of 303 inch AP ammunition;

– the starboard wing (protected on the top surface): two 15 round bursts of .303 inch ball ammunition;

– the fuselage: three 15 round bursts of .303 inch ball ammunition and one 15 round burst of 303 inch AP ammunition; and

– a series of single shots with 20mm solid ammunition at various points of aim on the aircraft.

A preliminary report from Sq/Ldr I E Brodie to his Commander-in-Chief in Bomber Command concluded:

"16. On a previous trial it was found that when .303 bullets enter an Oxford aircraft type of self-sealing tank, the holes made are sealed over and no petrol is lost. It is likely that on the trial on the 28th October ... some bullets did strike the self-sealing tank, but confirmation is required; in any event no leaks occurred. It is unfortunate that no hit on the self-sealing tank was obtained with the 20mm solid shot but it is likely that a hole would not be sealed over.

17. It now seems likely that protection for petrol will be provided by self-sealing tanks rather than extra plating because such a tank weighs only about 50lb more than 10 gauge Dural (as provided at this trial). The advantage of

the tank being self-sealing is that no matter from where an attack is delivered protection for the petrol is given, whereas with extra plating, protection is only given from an attack from a small area astern. However this tank would shorten the range by about 60 miles, its external size cannot be enlarged in Blenheims and its cubic capacity would be less. ...

18. It is again evident that 10 gauge Dural is enough to deflect .303 ball and AP ammunition when the angle of attack is less than 15°.

19. On the other hand except where a graze (in its literal sense) is obtained by 20mm shot, neither the aircraft skin, nor 4mm armour, nor 10 gauge Dural will be any protection even at 700 yards.

20. Provided the oil and petrol tanks are protected this trial again showed that when attacked from directly astern, a large number of .303 hits are required to cause lethal damage except to the gunner. The number of hits and grazes obtained was 55 and 11 respectively out of 150 rounds fired. Of these, only 4 really affected the aircraft and crew, ie two in the oil tanks and two in the gunner's head. Steps are now being taken to provide armour plate shields for attachment to a gun or mounting to protect the gunner from the eyes downwards, and I now understand that action will now be initiated to provide a gunner with some form of "tin hat" or upper protective plate – he will then virtually have only an eye slit open to bullets from an enemy at whom he is firing. ...

21. I was again impressed by the damage inflicting power of the 20mm projectile in comparison to .303. As a member of a bomber aircraft I'm now quite certain that I would far prefer to be up against a fighter armed with say 8 Browning [machine] guns than against one with say three 20mm [cannon] guns. This takes into consideration the smaller number of projectiles that would be fired by the cannons. I believe the Air Ministry has reached a similar conclusion and is now going for the 20mm cannon. ..." (102)

The case for self-sealing tanks, if not yet conclusively made, was at least firming up as a result of these trials. They left little room for further doubt, either, about the destructive capabilities of the 20mm cannon – nothing could be more telling than Brodie's stated personal preference for going up against Browning machine guns rather than cannons. But the confidence inspired by the trials in the ability of the aircraft structure and equipment to withstand machine gun fire would turn out to be somewhat illusory. Fighting aeroplanes would, in due course, prove themselves capable on occasions of returning to base after sustaining incredible amounts of damage. Yet, in the early stages of the war, aircraft like the early Blenheims would also prove themselves very vulnerable to attacks by German fighters like the Messerschmitt Bf 109 equipped with machine guns and the Bf 110 equipped with a mix of machine guns and 20mm cannons.

Brodie, in a covering Minute (31st October 1938) to his report, had two further comments of interest to make:

"I hear that a scheme for putting protective or armour plate in Manchester aircraft is now being put in hand but only 200lb extra weight is at present contemplated.

... the RAE Assessor present at the Shoeburyness trial recently carried out [apparently on 6/7th October 1938] with explosive 20mm projectiles (instantaneous fuses), assessed the damage inflicting capabilities of that shell as:

25% hits would immediately be lethal and an additional 25% hits would prevent the aircraft from reaching home again."

The hearsay about the Avro Manchester (the forerunner of the Lancaster) suggested that protection was beginning to be taken seriously as a service requirement. The information from the RAE Assessor was, by itself, more confusing than helpful – if 25% of hits were lethal (to some of the crew, to the aircraft?), why were another 25% needed to bring the aircraft down? The comment was evidently intended, though, as a further confirmation of the destructive capabilities of 20mm shells.

Supplementary trials were carried out at Orfordness on 3rd November 1938, in which French 20mm high explosive (HE) shells were fired at Blenheim K.7168. The intention was to compare the results with those obtained with solid (ie "inert") shot on 28th October. The Blenheim was once again set up in the flying level position and fired at from the near astern direction. According to a preliminary report (103) from RD Arm, the results were as follows:

- Two rounds were fired against the port engine, which exploded near the point of impact on the rear wing surface. A 90° butterfly fragment pattern resulted but the only important damage was the holing of the oil tank and serious damage to one magneto.

- Two rounds were fired at the starboard engine, which exploded on the reinforced plating. One wrecked the flap gear and another holed the oil tank. A fragment pierced the fireproof bulkhead but did not damage the engine.

- One round was fired at the starboard tank, which exploded on the reinforced plating and several fragments pierced the rear spar wall and the rear wall of the tank. The tank was blown approximately spherical and lifted the two 10swg plates off their fastenings. ... This spectacular damage was thought to have been caused by ignition of petrol vapour above the water in the tank.

- Five shots were fired at the fuselage. Those that struck the tail plane did no serious damage and those that struck the side produced dense local patterns but no serious damage.

- A single round was fired at the self-sealing tank in the port wing, a number of fragments penetrating the top surface. As the water had drained away, there was little evidence of bursting.

Although a detailed examination was not possible by the RD Arm representative, it appeared that the crew were unhurt even though one shell had exploded 2ft ahead of the gunner. The general impression was that the trial was much less favourable to the ammunition than previous trials. The damage appeared to be more localised, with fewer large sized fragments. Brodie later concluded (104) that for a tail on shot a solid projectile was much more effective "and indeed 50% lethal", whereas from other angles of attack the explosive shell was 50% lethal and more effective than solid shot "could be expected to be". Although he was once again rather unhelpful in his use of "lethal", Brodie made some interesting further observations:

"... For a bomber it therefore appears that HE shell of this calibre is sufficiently lethal against fighters. But

... it may be that fighters will have to be armed with a gun larger than 20mm, or carry HE in some 20mm guns and solid shots in others, the use of either depending upon their angle of attack.

One thing stands out and is encouraging to bombers; fighters firing .303 (any type of bullet) or HE 20mm can have little hope of bringing down a bomber from astern and within 15° of the bomber's fore and aft axis."

The first two of these observation were little more than fanciful. It was not unreasonable to take the view that bombers, particularly in formation, would have the opportunity to fire at attacking fighters at angles other than head on and would therefore benefit from 20mm HE ammunition – but there was no reasonable prospect at the time of British bombers being armed with such guns although the possibility was under discussion. Likewise, the there was no realistic prospect of fighters being equipped with a selection between HE and solid shot, although during the war it was not uncommon for guns to fire some combination of alternate rounds of ball, incendiary and armour piercing ammunition; later, fighters were to be equipped with combinations of machine guns and cannons or cannons and rockets.

It is all too easy, with the benefit of hindsight, to be critical of Brodie's conviction that bombers would be relatively safe from fighters firing .303 and 20mm HE ammunition in regulation stern attacks. Yet there was already a war raging in the skies over Spain in which bombers were proving vulnerable to attacks by fighters using a variety of ammunition. The problem was that too little information of any value was coming out of that conflict to guide officers like Brodie and the members of the Air Fighting Committee.

Hawker Hurricane

AFDE Report No 9 on the flying trials also had something to recommend for in the way of armour protection for fighters like the Hurricane:

> "111. Armour above the engine to protect the pilot is required." (100)

Discussions at Hawkers in Kingston took place on 21st July 1938 to consider a proposal to introduce armour plate for the protection of the Hurricane pilots. Among others attending the meeting were: Dowding, Saundby, Hill and especially Mr Sydney Camm of Hawker Aircraft Co Ltd. It was Sydney Camm, of course, who designed the Hurricane. Dowding opened the meeting and explained that:

> "... the modern view on air fighting tactics was to have the fighting aeroplanes protected in front of the pilot as a defence against fire from ahead. The superior speed of the fighter aeroplane would render it less vulnerable from attack from the rear. Armour plate other than in front of the pilot would be too heavy to contemplate to give effective protection ...." (105)

Although the report of the meeting recorded no requirement or suggestion specifically for firing trials to test the proposed scheme of armour protection, these can be inferred because Minute 9 noted that RD Arm 1(c) (ie Captain Hill) would submit a scheme for:

> "... a proposed programme of tests to determine the thickness of armour plate required and the effect of the 10 gauge Duralumin protection." (105)

Some six weeks later, on 9th September 1938, Hill advised the Officer Commanding A&AEE at Martlesham Heath that Hurricane airframe L.1550 was being forwarded to Orfordness for use in connection with firing trials. (106) The aircraft had been struck off charge from No 111 Squadron after a crash landing at Northolt, on 14th July 1938, with undercarriage retracted (ie "wheels up") owing to engine failure.

On 23rd September Douglas himself was evidently getting a little concerned about the seemingly interminable extent of the trials and tests that were not thus far leading to direct action. He wrote to the Air Vice-Marshal A W Tedder CB, Director General of Research and Development (DGRD):

> "In the last eighteen months we have carried out a considerable number of experiments in connection with the use of armour protection in aircraft, with the general result that the fitting of quite thin gauge armour or deflecting plate will prove effective against astern attack from rifle calibre machine-guns.
>
> 2. Although there is, no doubt, much experimental work to be done, I feel that we should without delay apply the information now at our disposal to the protection of aircraft in the Service.
>
> 3. I think you will agree that in the present disturbed state of Europe we should all feel very much happier if our Hurricanes and Spitfires had an armour plate apron in front of the pilot, and our Battles and Blenheims an armour plate bulkhead behind the gunner and possibly some protection for the tanks.

4. I am most strongly of the opinion that we should take immediate action to provide some simple form of protection, which, though not 100 per cent effective, would, if we became involved in hostilities, provide some very great value. I suggest, therefore, that we should aim at all the above named aircraft in service to be so equipped, no matter how rudimentary a manner, by the 1st January 1939." (82)

The ACAS was informed by Saundby on 2nd November 1938 that firing trials on the Hurricane were being progressed:

<u>"Hurricane</u>

2. An unserviceable Hurricane has been completely equipped with the proposed armour layout, including bullet proof windscreen, and will be subject to firing tests on Thursday, 3rd November 1938.

3. Hawkers are proceeding with the preparation of the modification scheme but have not yet completed the design for the windscreen frame, ...

4. The new windscreen may have some effect on the flying characteristics of the aeroplane but this cannot be proved until the modification has been flown.

5. The armour equipment will also increase the gross weight of the aircraft, the effect of which will be to lengthen the take-off run, which is already too long. The VP [variable pitch] airscrew is expected to provide a satisfactory solution to this problem.

6. The increase in weight is not, however, very large and I doubt if the effects will be noticeable." (82)

He also reported progress on other aircraft:

<u>"Spitfire</u>

7. A conference was held recently at which a scheme of armour protection was agreed and the works are now getting this out in detail. The form of protection consists of a new fuel tank, which has one bulkhead of steel armour and top surface of thick section intended to deflect the .303 bullets. There is also to be a bullet proof windscreen. ...

<u>Blenheim</u>

8. ... The [firing trials] showed that armouring would provide a reasonable means of protection against .303 ammunition. Two weak points in the scheme were disclosed at the oil tank and the cupola of the rear turret (exposing the gunner's head). The scheme is being modified to provide better protection at these points.

<u>Battle</u>

9. A scheme of armour protection has been discussed with the constructor and is now being prepared.

<u>General</u>

With the exception of the Westland [Whirlwind] and the Blackburn Botha, schemes of armour protection are being prepared for all other bomber and fighter types subsequent to (and including) the Wellesley. Armour protection schemes for the [Whirlwind] and the Botha will be considered ... during the coming week." (82)

It should be appreciated that for the Spitfire, as for the Hurricane, the protection schemes being envisaged were intended as a defence against fire from ahead – as from a bomber under attack. Consequently, the firing trials against Hurricane L.1550 were designed specifically with this scenario in mind.

The first Hurricane trials were carried out on 3rd November 1938 and witnessed by among others, Saundby, Rowley and Hill. Brodie circulated a report (104) on 8th November that enclosed a "Preliminary Note" (107) from RDArm (Captain Hill). The Hurricane was anchored down in flying position in a corner of Orfordness aerodrome, with the wheels retracted, with the engine towards the firing point and with a dummy pilot in the cockpit. It was fired at nose on, at various ranges, to test three schemes for protecting the pilot and petrol tank:

"Scheme A

– A 4mm bulkhead forward of the reserve petrol tank in front of the pilot;

– A reinforced cowling between the fireproof bulkhead, between the engine and the reserve tank, and the base of the windscreen; and

– A windscreen panel of 1½ inch bullet proof glass.

Scheme B

– A reinforced cowling from the base of the airscrew to the base of the windscreen; and

– A windscreen panel of 1½ inch bullet proof glass.

Scheme C

– As for scheme A, except that the reinforcing consisted of a band 16 inch wide in the centre from the fireproof bulkhead to the base of the windscreen."

Scheme A was tested with bursts of fire from a Browning machine gun, firing ball ammunition, at 400, 300 and 200 yards range. No rounds struck the reinforced cowling, but two reached the armour bulkhead without damaging the coolant header tank. The plate was dented slightly. The pilot was struck in the foot by rounds passing under the bulkhead – these would have been stopped by the propeller boss, had it been fitted. The screen was struck at the shorter ranges, but was not penetrated. Some rounds entered the cockpit through the temporary wooden frame at the base of the screen.

Scheme B was tested with burst of Browning fire from 200 yards. One round penetrated the joint in the front section of the cowling and the petrol tank was holed, but not the header tank. Some rounds entered under the front edge of the cowling and the screen was hit again. The protection was judged to be inferior to Scheme A. As a supplementary test, the nose of the aircraft was dropped by about 3° and the cowling was fired at with a rifle. Hits were obtained, but the bullets were easily deflected in all cases without damage.

Scheme C was also tested with bursts of Browning fire from 200 yards. The headed tank was badly holed and further rounds reached the armour plate, but there were no penetrations. The screen was again hit without penetration. As a supplementary test, AP ammunition was fired from 200 yards with a rifle. Rounds passed through the now empty header tank and some reached the armour plate. Part of one bullet core penetrated the plate but only slightly dented the petrol tank.

Overall, some 220 rounds were fired with either the Browning or the rifle. There were 22 hits on the front of the engine, 32 hits through the nose and bottom cowling, 10 hits in the radiator and 8 hits in the header tank – most of these were judged to be ultimately lethal to the engine, but not necessarily immediately so. The "pilot" was hit 6 times, but had the windscreen been properly fixed only twice would the pilot have been hit by bullets striking the side windscreens. The windscreen was hit 5 times, stopping the bullet on each occasion.

Hill's preliminary note had concluded that Scheme C gave the most efficient protection, in terms of weight and ease of installation. However, the official conclusion was that Scheme A gave the best protection, with 4mm armour being adequate, provided that the screen panel was properly fixed and that there was more effective protection for the petrol tank. The engine, felt to be impracticable to protect, was reported to be very vulnerable. The report recognised that all three schemes depended to a great extent on the effectiveness of the bullet-proof windscreen, although the screen had certain disadvantages as well:

– the additional weight might affect the performance of the Hurricane and entail some redesign to compensate; and

– should the screen be hit during actual combat, the pilot's forward visibility would be considerably reduced, making night landings particularly dangerous and effectively ruling out any further participation in combats.

Consequently, on 11th November Hill reported to Hawkers that as a result of the trial:

"... the scheme of protection selected comprises:

(i) The rear piece of 10swg cowling ie between windscreen base and the header tank.

(ii) The 4mm armour plate bulkhead.

(iii) The windscreen [1½ inch Triplex].

In the case of the last item ... the windscreen frame will have to be carefully designed to prevent rounds getting into the joint between the frame and the cowling and thus damaging the pilot." (108)

The Mechanical Test Department actually proposed on 23rd November an Addendum to Brodie's preliminary note on the Hurricane firing trial, in which it was suggested that there should also be:

"... an armour plate immediately behind the airscrew when the usual two blade wooden airscrew is fitted.

If a [metal variable pitch] airscrew is fitted some protection will be required in addition for the boss of the airscrew, and the plate behind the airscrew can then have a corresponding lightening hole behind this protection." (109)

The official Report (110) of the firing trials was actually issued on 30th November 1938. The results, after hand-written adjustments to compensate for the inadequate fitting of the windscreen in a temporary softwood frame and the absence of the airscrew boss, are summarised in table 18.1.

Table 18.1. Programme of firing trials and summary of damage sustained by Hurricane

Type of armour	Range in yards	Burst No	Ammunition and number of rounds	No of strikes	Result
A	400	1	15 Ball	0	
A	400	2	15 Ball	3	Negligible damage.
A	400	3	15 Ball	2	Negligible damage.
A	400	4	15 Ball	11	Negligible damage.
A	300	1	15 Ball	9	Negligible damage.
A	300	2	30 Ball	15	Pilot knocked out (once). Engine stopped due to loss of coolant (once).
A	200	1	45 Ball	22	Engine stopped due to loss of coolant (19 times).
B	200	2	45 Ball	20	Pilot killed (once). Engine stopped due to loss of coolant (once). Reserve petrol tank holed.
B	200	3	5 Ball	3	Pilot killed (once).
B	200	4	5 Ball	5	Pilot knocked out (once).
C	200	1	10 Ball	10	Pilot killed (twice). Engine stopped due to loss of coolant (once).
C	200	2	10 AP	10	Engine stopped due to loss of coolant (five times).

Note:

A = 10G duralumin rear top engine cowling, rectangle of bullet-proof windscreen + 4mm steel bulkhead.

B = 10G duralumin front and rear top engine cowling + rectangle of bullet-proof windscreen.

C = 10G duralumin sheet 16"x26" over header tank and reserve petrol tanks + 4mm steel bulkhead between.

Hurricane used in firing trials – damage, port side. (Public Record Office, AIR 2/3353, piece 36A)

The damage sustained by the Hurricane (as illustrated in the photographs) is presumably the totality, after all the bursts had been fired. Evidently, from the table, at ranges of 300 yards and less both the pilot and the engine appeared to be extremely vulnerable. However, the bullet-proof windscreen had been poorly set up; the glass was mounted in a soft wood frame that did not match the contour of the engine cowling and allowed bullets to penetrate where they would have been resisted by a proper frame. This accounts for several hand-written adjustments to the figures in the original table from which Table 18.1 above is reproduced. Indeed, the official Report concluded:

> "4. The number of hits obtained on the pilot during [the] trials cannot be accepted as a guide to the effectiveness or otherwise of the scheme of protection provided, since on examination it is apparent that a number of these hits are from bullets which penetrated the mock-up frame-work provided for the laminated glass 1½ inch windscreen." (110)

However, the bullet proof glass itself evidently proved comfortingly resistant to bullet penetrations and the view (undated) of Group Captain G B A Baker (DArmD), seeking to correct an impression left by the report, was that:

> "It is at least probable that when the screen is properly fitted at the correct distance from the pilot the protection will be adequate." (111)

The photographs of the damaged Hurricane do not appear to show the bullet proof windscreen, suggesting that the one(s) used in the trials had either been simply rested in front of the existing windscreen or attached so that it or they could be easily removed after the firing. The key prob-

Hurricane used in firing trials – damage, starboard side. (Public Record Office, AIR 2/3353, piece 36A)

lem exposed by the trials, that of bullets entering to cockpit area under and around the "lashed-up"bullet-proof windscreen, was the subject of detailed exchanges.

During a further meeting at Hawkers works on 2nd December 1938, the firm undertook to introduce the agreed scheme on production aircraft after, in effect, the first 400 produced. For the 200 or so likely to be in service by 31st December 1938 and the further 200 that would be in service by the time that the scheme (scheme 'A') was in production, a cruder scheme (scheme 'B') was agreed that service units could incorporate: items (i) and (ii) as for scheme 'A', but for (iii) a modified Triplex windscreen and simple attachment. An interesting piece of information that emerged from the record of the meeting was the actual weight effect of replacing the two-bladed fixed-pitch wooden propeller with either a De Havilland Variable (two-Pitch or a Rotol Constant Speed wooden bladed propeller. The additional weight of the De Havilland (247lb) or the Rotol (180lb) propeller was considered more than enough to allow the 50lb of forward ballast, needed to correct the centre of gravity in aircraft fitted with the fixed–pitch propeller and some 140lb of armour (80lb) and other equipment (40–60lb) aft of the cockpit, to be discarded. (112)

However, it became evident by 10th December that Camm was reluctant to implement scheme 'B', on the grounds that there would only be a small difference in installation time before the armoured aircraft came off the production line. But the Air Ministry was insistent that scheme 'B', even if further simplified, should be implemented as:

"... some crude measure of protection was most urgently wanted on Hurricanes already in service."

While the debate in favour of fitting bullet-proof glass windscreens had evidently been hardening in the AFC and could be said to have been recommended, it is by no means clear that there was yet any definite agreement that these to be fitted as standard; as for deflecting armour, the debate seemed still to be unsettled.

Boulton Paul Defiant

The "turreted fighter", the F.9/35 Bolton Paul Defiant, did not escape attention. Captain Hill visited the works of Boulton Paul Aircraft Ltd on 19th September 1938, to investigate the question of fitting armour protection to the Defiant. He sent a note on 4th October 1938 to the ACAS, pointing out that armour protection had not been called for in the original specification (nor, though, had it been called for at the design stage for any of the aircraft then coming to fruition) but had been raised later! He took the view that:

"... On looking into the matter the provision of armour protection in this aircraft does not appear worth while for the following reasons:

(i) Owing to an increase of 700lb in the estimated weight of the engines, the aircraft is close to its weight limit.

(ii) The pilot is the member of the crew who is most exposed, but adequate side and overhead protection would be difficult to install and would ruin his view.

(iii) The gunner is already afforded a considerable degree of protection by the guns and turret structure.

(iv) Finally, with a battery of four 20mm guns, this fighter should be able to engage the enemy at a range at which the enemy's machine gun defences should be comparatively ineffective.

4. It seems to me therefore that it is not worth while putting in armour which can do no more than protect the crew from attack from very limited angles of attack. The answer is, I suggest, that the pilot can choose his direction of attack so that he is in one of the enemy's "blind spots", and he can also outrange machine gun defensive fire.

5. I suggest therefore that we should give up the idea of armouring this aircraft ..." (82)

However, the contractor was visited again on 26th October 1938 and on the reckoning that "protection against counter fire ... is not very expensive in weight", the following possible scheme of protection was discussed:

"[A] Thus, for the pilot:

(i) A windscreen panel 12 inch x 12 inch – 23½lb.

(ii) Decking over the oil tank increased to 10swg and extended to the windscreen base – 8lb.

(iii) A plate in the panel behind his head – 17lb.

Total – 48½lb.

B. For the Gunner

The turret itself is well arranged for protection but a face plate 9 inch x 6½ inch would give confidence – 6lb.

C. For the oil tank

The [coolant] radiator is reasonably protected against fire from above as is also the oil radiator but the oil tank is rather exposed. A plate on the upper part of the fireproof bulkhead in conjunction with A (ii) above would protect this item for a weight of about 13lb." (114)

Consequently, Hill's suggestion of abandoning the idea of armour for the Defiant seems to have been disregarded and, during a further meeting at the contractor's works on 19th December 1938, the following protection scheme was actually agreed:

"(a) <u>Windscreen</u>. Bearing in mind the methods of attack which are likely to be used by this aircraft, it is considered that the pilot will not be subject to fire directed at his windscreen from ahead ... no front armouring in the form of bullet-proof glass or tough Dural over the oil tank to be mounted in front ... already endorsed by C-in-C Fighter Command.

(b) <u>Armour at back of Pilot</u>. ...4mm magnetic armour protection approximately 3½ sq ft should be fitted behind the pilot, covering the whole bulkhead down to the decking. [On] the question of incorporating this armour ... the firm are already redesigning the strong front framework behind the pilot. This new design will not appear on production aircraft until after the 30th at the earliest.

(c) <u>Turret</u>. ...a small piece of armour protection 6½ inch x 10 inch (9mm magnetic) should be fixed below the gun sight arm. Possibly also a piece of bullet-proof glass in front of the sight bar and sight." (115)

Hill is not recorded as having been present at the two later meetings. The proposed installations for the Defiant were not, however, to be officially approved until 24th February 1939. (116) The agreed scheme was thereafter fitted to all Defiants, according to a note of 25th January 1940 (J Hanson), (117) notwithstanding that A H Jones (for the Director of Technical Development) had advised Boulton Paul Aircraft Ltd on 15th January 1940 that "... armour protection for the Defiant is not required". (118) It does not appear that this "decision" was ever put into practice, any more than was the suggestion from Hill. Indeed, in June 1940 thoughts were turning to incorporating "additional" rear armour protection. (119) The "four 20mm guns" to which Hill had referred were never to be installed; the armament was to remain as four Browning machine guns throughout the Defiant's service life.

Gloster Gladiator

The biplane Gladiator was already obsolescent as a front-line fighter in 1938 and the AFC could therefore be excused for largely neglecting the aircraft in their deliberations, preferring to focus their attention on the

Hurricane, Spitfire and the radical Defiant. However the Gladiator, which was in service with the RAF at home and in the Middle East as well as with the Belgian Air Force, had been thought useful as a vehicle for trials of bullet-proof windscreens and flight trials for this purpose were carried out at by the AFDE at Northolt on 9th November 1938. These found that the visibility and general view for landing was not as good as with the standard screen but, even so, no great difficulty was experienced in landings by day or by night, neither was there any diffusion effect by night. It is notable that it was not thought necessary to carry out any firing trials on the Gladiator.

Fairey Battle

The Fairey Battle bomber seemed, towards the end of 1938, to embody the highest aspirations of the Command in the short term. It had begun life as the prototype monoplane two-seater Fairey Day bomber to Specification P.27/32, but went into production as a three-seater day bomber to revised Specification P.23/35. (120) Discussions on possible schemes for armour protection were held at Fairey's Stockport works on 13th October and 22nd November 1938. The first of these visits served to rough out provisions for protecting the Battle. For the rear gunner, there would be a 6mm plate mounted in the cockpit to give some chest protection "from fire at quite considerable angles"; (121) there was nothing yet for his lower body and legs. For the pilot, it was considered that:

> "This position can be protected adequately by means of a 4mm plate in the seat back. This can be accommodated by a slight modification to the upholstery." (121)

It was not until the second visit that account was taken of the redesign of the Battle as a three-seater, with an extra 45 gallon petrol tank in the fuselage. Whatever the reason, the November meeting occasioned a revised protection scheme. A new armour template for the Battle pilot's seat back was devised, one that would be fixed to the seat and go up and down with it. It was now shaped to protect the pilot's head as well and it was thought that the template should be increased in size "to protect a large pilot"(122), subject to avoiding fouling the Sutton Harness that strapped the pilot in his seat. For the navigator/bomber, it was:

> "... assumed that his position in action is lying down in the well, as it is impossible for him to sit in his seat when the gunner has the cockpit cover open for firing. It is suggested that he could be protected by two panels of 10 gauge Duralumin on the flat bottom of the fuselage below his legs and stomach, and that curved outer fillets of the same material could be fitted on either side of the centre section fairing in place of the standard panels." (122)

For the rear gunner/wireless operator:

"A template had been prepared which fitted the contour of the fuselage and gave protection roughly from the third rib down to the waist. The plate ... is absolutely as big as it can be, and already interferes to a certain extent with the deflector bag when the gun is in certain positions. From the waist to the knees aft there is a W/T set. The only possibility of further protection is two shin guards fitted onto No. 10 bulkhead, but this would restrict access to the generator and accumulator. ... For protection of the gunner's face an armour plate measuring about 6 inch x 3½ inch would have to be mounted on the gun, but it is doubtful if the gun could then be worked, or whether sighting would be possible. ... There does not seem to be any method of protecting the gunner's head, except by some sort of steel helmet (for use in action only) ..." (122)

Finally, for the petrol tanks (two main tanks in the centre section and a further 33 gallon tank in the port wing):

"... No provision has been made ... for the protection of the tanks as the aircraft is already considerably overloaded. A possible method of protecting them would be to fit a 10 gauge Duralumin cowling as a cover instead of the normal skin of aircraft, which is at present about 20 gauge." (122)

There was a further meeting at Fairey's works in Stockport on 20th December 1938, at which the protection scheme discussed on 22nd November was discussed and modified as follows:

"1. Armouring scheme

(a) Pilot is to be protected by means of a flat seat back of 4mm non-magnetic [armour plate] 3ft high and 1½ft wide (weight approximately 28lb) bolted on to the front face of the existing seat back, its lower edge to be 1ft above the parachute seat. Suitable slots will be arranged to allow the Sutton harness straps to be brought through.

(b) Rear gunner and W/T operator. Some protection for the gunner's face is desirable, but it is not possible unless the plate is mounted on the gun. The problem should be examined by [the Royal Aircraft Establishment, RAE].

To protect his chest a flat plate (6mm magnetic weight 15lb) is to be fixed immediately forward of the forward gun cone support. ... (Size of plate 23in wide at base and 11¾in high at centre). ...

For the gunner's legs two shields, fitted on No 10 bulkhead, in 4mm magnetic [armour plate] are proposed. Approximate size 18in x 14in, 12lb each. Between these shields are the camera and the W/T set. The height of these shields is limited by the slide for the W/T tray. They should be fixed in as simple a manner as possible so that they can be removed to allow of changing the W/T set.

(c) Navigator and bombaimer. To give some measure of protection against fire from below it was agreed to fix a flat plate of 10 gauge dural over the existing floor on which he lies when at his action station. The plate is to extend from 1ft behind the rear edge of the bombaimer's aperture to the rear spar. Approximate area 3ft 6in x 2ft, weight 12lb.

3. Recommendations

(a) Authority to the firm to proceed (as agreed) immediately with a trial installation (in mild steel plate) ... They will bear in mind that the armour must be so designed as to make its fitting by service units a simple matter.

The firm undertook to complete this trial installation and production drawings by the end of January [1939]. Sets will then be ordered to cover all Battles in service units and production aircraft.

(b) RAE to be asked to examine question of face protection for gunner." (123)

The effect of the armour and other equipment on the centre of gravity and landing/take-off runs was also considered. With a total weight of armour and fixings of 85lb, no centre of gravity difficulty was thought to arise. With an all-up weight of 11,967lb, the take-off ground run was reckoned to be 350 yards – acceptable as an overload case. However, at this weight the reserve factors for some parts of the undercarriage were reduced; flying factors for non-acrobatic flight were considered adequate, but the landing factors were considered more serious – no landing at that weight was to be contemplated and even take-off could be critical. The concern over landing may have been exaggerated because no allowance seemed to be made for the reduction in weight resulting from fuel usage during flight. The concern over take-off at the overload weight appears to have been justified.

Firing trials against a running engine

Meanwhile, some new trials had been carried out at Martlesham Heath on 30th October 1938 against a running engine – in this case a sleeve-valve Perseus No 252 radial engine. The object was to determine whether a sleeve-valve engine was more readily damaged by machine gun fire than an engine of the poppet-valve type. The engine, mounted in a Bristol Type 120 aircraft fuselage, was fired at from a rifle at 150 yards range using .303 inch AP ammunition. From the results, it appeared that the cylinders of a sleeve-valve radial engine were indeed less vulnerable to .303 inch AP gun fire than those of a radial engine with poppet valves and the damage to the pistons was no greater. It was recognised, also, that the sleeve-valve cylinders had the advantage of not having overhead valve gear and tappet rods that, on a poppet-valve engine were known to be a source of vulnerability. Moreover, the induction pipes on the sleeve-valve engine were well shielded by the cylinder barrels – thought to be a definite advantage as a high percentage of poppet-valve engines was attributable to air leaks through holed induction pipes.

The 14th and 15th meetings

While the debate in favour of fitting bullet-proof glass windscreens had evidently been hardening in the AFC and could be said to have been recommended, it is by no means clear that there was yet any definite agreement that these were to be fitted as standard; as for deflecting armour, the debate seemed still to be unsettled. The 14th (29th November 1938) and 15th (7th December 1938) meetings of the AFC were mostly concerned with matters other than armour protection. There were however, at the 14th meeting, further discussions on lethal density, cones of fire and attack formations/methods which interact with the subject of armour protection and are therefore of interest. Dowding believed that the Germans were going for protection by speed rather than armour or guns – the modern German bombers had only a single gun and no turrets – and he did not believe that the gunners would be able to put their heads out of the cockpits at modern speeds like the 342mph of the "latest Junker", presumably the Junker Ju 88. (125) He felt, however, that:

> "… it was necessary, at present, to ignore the enemy's return fire when coming to a decisive range from astern, and he was anxious to have a bullet-proof windscreen and deflecting armour (as previously recommended) so that a chance shot should not put the fighter out of action." (126)

The Minutes of the meeting also record that Dowding:

> "…said he felt that the simplest form of tactics was the best until the enemy had done something to defeat it. As long as we had unarmoured bombers to compete with, he considered that the principle should be to ignore the return fire until the relative optimum range was reached, and then to let loose a shot-gun effect in order to bring the enemy down.
>
> … He would like the "flat astern" attack, which was very simple, to be regarded at present as the normal standard method for the eight-gun fighter, and he pointed out that it could not be expected, particularly under war conditions, that all units could be trained up to the highest pitch of efficiency. It was quite conceivable, however, that armouring on the part of the enemy might necessitate different methods, and it was therefore necessary to know how best to use an eight-gun fighter against an armoured bomber. …" (127)

Bearing in mind the general preference for the astern "111" attack (the "111" being derived from the work of No 111 Squadron at the Air Fighting Development Establishment), Dowding:

> "… thought it quite probable that the enemy would use very large numbers of aircraft for [attacks on Britain], but that they would probably despatch formations from separate aerodromes and attempt to rendezvous over here. It was not an easy matter, as we had found, to organise large formations.
>
> There was, of course, another possibility, …, that the enemy might come over in a very long column, squadron behind squadron, (say 200 yards apart) with armoured fighters in the back row with turrets and unlimited ammunition. This would make the whole formation a very difficult one to attack from behind, and in these circumstances the "111" attack would obviously be most valuable. Incidentally, the adoption of a "column" formation would present an excellent target to the [anti-aircraft] guns.

The logic of what Dowding said, or was trying to explain, is not clear from these minutes. It is by no means obvious that the "111" attack – from astern and climbing up from 2,000–3,000ft below in the no-deflection position, the preferred method for the more highly trained pilots – would be particularly "valuable" in either scenario, but especially the latter with armoured enemy escort fighters breathing down the necks of Dowding's Hurricanes and Spitfires. Indeed, the members of the Committee went on to explore methods of attack at length. The important point, however, is that he was at least anticipating escort fighters – and armoured ones at that – with which his own fighters would have to tangle!

Earlier in the meeting, with the "beam deflection" attack being ruled out on grounds of inadequate equipment and sighting arrangements, the "flat astern" attack was regarded as the "ordinary simple or standard" attack for less experienced pilots. When approaching from astern, the "vic" formation of three fighters was preferred to any form of echelon. Dowding's position was that as training in these methods of attack improved:

> "... he hoped to be able to adopt the ideal principle of <u>always doubling fighter for bomber</u>* in the firing line. As the fighters were smaller than the bombers, an equal formation of fighters could easily be got into the same space. Supposing that at first they found difficulty in matching one for one, they could always match one against two, and providing they took the precaution of armouring their aircraft against the weak and erratic fire which they might expect from the present German bomber, he did not think they would suffer any great disadvantage from that comparative loss of fire power." (129)

Although Dowding must have been thinking of front armour as protection in the "flat astern" attack, the role of armour as a means for protecting his fighters whilst engaging enemy bombers in any scenario seems to have become firmly embedded in his thinking by this time.

The armouring of bombers was at least touched upon during the 14th meeting:, it was briefly noted that "all bombers were being examined with a view to putting in armour wherever practicable". (130) This was evidently true for the Fairey Battle but, for the Bristol Blenheim bomber, no signs of armour protection had yet emerged. The discussion on bombers went a little further:

> "73. The C-in-C, Bomber Command said he would like to restate the strong arguments in favour of <u>protecting the tail gunner</u>*, both on moral and physical grounds, and pointed out that if this man were to be shot, he could not be replaced. DDOR (Group Captain Saundby) said that all possible steps were being taken to meet this requirement, both on present and new types, but he mentioned that armouring of the tail turrets, which was admittedly highly desirable, unfortunately presented the worst difficulty on account of the extra weight in relation to the centre of gravity. A committee was at present touring the works to try and reach decisions on the spot.
>
> ...

*Report's underlining.

75. The C-in-C, Coastal Command (Air Marshal Sir F Bowhill) asked for further enlightenment on the general policy regarding armour*. He gathered that the Germans were adopting larger calibre guns. In this case would not the armour which it was proposed to put on our new aircraft be useless?

76. In reply ..., it was stated that the intention was to armour against ammunition up to .5 inch calibre. It was not practicable, on account of the weight involved, to provide armour which would be proof against anything larger, eg the 20mm gun, but even so, it was considered that the existence of armour as contemplated would afford a certain amount of protection against anti–aircraft shell fragments." (131)

The overall conclusion that can be drawn from the AFC meetings up to this point and the overall debate on the subject of armour protection is that, as in the earlier war, nobody in the RAF seemed prepared to make the final decisions without conclusive evidence of what might be justified – nor did there seem to be any undue haste, despite the urgings of the Chief of Air Staff back in October! A part of the problem was the seeming fixation within Fighter Command that the Hurricanes, Spitfires and Defiants would confine themselves to attacks on bombers – that there would be no place for fighter-v-fighter combats. However, a Russian article on air combat during the wars in Spain and China, dated 22nd July 1938 and circulated to the AFC as Report No 54, was quite definite in its accounts of mass air battles and fighter-v-fighter engagements. (132) Notwithstanding that the Russian article made no mention of armour protection, there can be little doubt that it was being fitted at least to some aircraft. Jesus Salar Larrázabal, for example, who was eleven years old when the Spanish Civil War broke out and whose brother flew on the Republican Government's side during the conflict, reported the experience of another pilot, Francisco "Tarazona" Toran. While flying a Mosca ("Fly") over Pinell on 30th October 1938, Tarazona was attacked by a Fiat after blacking out during his attack on another Fiat:

"The slamming impact of bullets on the armour plate behind me was the first thing to register as I recovered. I quickly glanced behind to discover a Fiat firing from scarcely fifty metres ..." (133)

Larrázabal's book, which included the incident originally recorded in Tarazona's own book Sangre en el Cielo ("Blood in the Sky"), was not published until after the Second World War. What the incident seems to reaffirm, however, is that the RAF was receiving little intelligence about – or taking little notice of – the experiences of participants in the air battles over Spain. Such reports as there were showed that dog-fighting and ground attack work were by no means things of the past; seasoned air fighters were realising, perhaps for the first time, that armour provided at least a measure of protection against gunfire in circumstances when

*Note. The underlining is in the original document.

air attack could not be avoided – but more especially when the gunfire came not from ahead but from behind!

To be fair, however, the Committee had their minds set on a war scenario that was quite different from the comparatively local, small scale, operations that typified the aerial contributions to the internal Spanish conflict. The Fighter Command interests led by Dowding were responsible for the tactical defence of the realm against Douhet-like hoards of supposedly invincible incoming bombers and already had the basic tools to do the job – the Spitfire and the Hurricane. The Bomber Command interests led by Ludlow-Hewitt were responsible for putting, or at least trying to put, into the air just such hoards of strategic bombers to strike at distant targets in Germany or elsewhere, but it could hardly be said that the tools to do the job were anything like available – deliveries to the Command of the first of the four-engined heavy bombers, the Short Stirling, did not begin until the August of 1940. The Committee therefore had to struggle with real and serious conflicts of interests among its members. On the one hand, there was the possible effectiveness of armour – in boosting the morale of the aircrews and the ability of their aircraft, fighters or bombers, to achieve their objectives, return safely and go off again – to be set against the consequential and inevitable loss of strike capability (armament, duration, range and overall performance) of the aircraft resulting from the weight of the armour. On the other hand, there was a fundamental and inevitable conundrum that bedevilled the AFC: if the fighter could be protected effectively against defensive fire from the bomber, how then was the bomber to defend itself against the attacking fighter; if the bomber could be so well armed and protected as to be able to beat off the fighter or withstand its fire-power, how then was the fighter to stop it?

These conflicts of interests were to be resolved in the fullness of time: huge increases in engine power enabled aircraft to carry greater loads; with improved navigation and bombing aids, British bombers sought the protective cloak of night and the accompaniment of friendly night fighter intruders; with the advent of the long range escort fighters, American bombers – themselves bristling with guns and bolstered by extensive armour – gained protection during the daylight hours. But these developments were some years away and it has to be remembered that Britain was not yet even at war with anybody, nor was there any conclusive view that there was going to be a new war with Germany. But political developments in Europe were inexorably moving towards a new conflict. The Germans had already annexed Austria in the March of 1938 and the Munich Crisis of September 1938 initiated the partitioning of Czecho-slovakia – the Sudetenland was occupied by Germany in October and in November much of what had been Ruthenia was ceded to Hungary. The "peace for our time" with which British Prime Minister Chamberlain had returned from Munich, an agreement with Germany that was to be followed in December by a similar agreement between France and Germany, was destined to be short-lived.

19 The ground attack rôle

One thing that the AFC failed to do at this time, if with the benefit of hindsight it is fair to call it failure, was to foresee the role of aircraft – and particularly nominally "fighter" aircraft – in a ground attack supporting rôle – what nowadays would be called "close air support". Ground attack work developed into a powerful weapon for offence and defence during the later phases of the Great War and, was destined to do so again in the war soon to come.

The reason for this lack of foresight is quite evident from the AFC's deliberations: it was simply not a concept in the RAF's tactical and strategic thinking. The crucial components of the fighting arms of the RAF were seen as the fighters and bombers. The Fighters comprised the "Home Defence Force" and their job was to shoot down intruding enemy bombers. The bombers were the real strategic arm; their job was to penetrate enemy territory and bomb appropriate targets, in the course of which operations they were expected to defend themselves against attacking enemy fighters. The job of destroying enemy fighters and bombers on the ground in their own territory would be the function of the British bomber, not of the fighter. Dowding was to say so himself, at the 17th meeting of the AFC on 31st May 1939. (134)

The reluctance to envisage fighters like the Hurricane and Spitfire in ground operations was fully encapsulated in AFC Report No 59, "The Rôle of the Field Force Fighter", of 25th April 1939. While making no mention of armour protection, the Report is of interest because it explains in detail the reasons why the Field Force Fighter – the primary duty of which was to shoot down bombers – was judged to be "ill suited" to secondary duty in the close support rôle. Extracts from the text of Report No 59 are

Henschel Hs 129B single-seat ground attack aircraft. (Imperial War Museum, HU2724).

reproduced as Appendix B. It is true that the RAF developed two light bombers, the single-engined Fairey Battle and the twin-engined Bristol Blenheim, that were thrown hurriedly into the rôle of tactical Army support in 1940, but such a possibility had not featured in the AFC's more strategic deliberations so far as bombers were concerned.

Armour protection, being a defensive measure, was seen by some in authority as working to counter aggression – much as parachutes had been viewed during the Great War – and, as well, incurred operational penalties. But, after the Battle of Britain, fighter operations over occupied territories took on increasingly (and increasingly effectively) the ground attack rôle and thereby completely confounded the precepts of AFC Report No 59. The aircraft – initially Hurricanes and Spitfires and later aircraft like the Hawker Typhoon and Tempest V, the North American P-51 Mustang and the Republic P-47 Thunderbolt – carried the barest minimum of armour, relying instead more upon speed and manoeuvrability to evade fire from the ground than upon armour to withstand it – as in the Great War, at least on the British side!

On the German side, the lessons of the previous war were neither neglected nor forgotten. Throughout the 1920s and early 1930s the German military worked secretly to perfect a style of warfare that matched fast-moving ground assault, spearheaded by tanks and specialised troops with close air support – ultimately revealed to the world in the Polish campaign of 1939 as "Blitzkrieg" (Lightning War). Under a programme of development that arose from the 1933–34 winter exercises, the ground-attack or close air support rôle was to be split between light and heavy types of dive-bombers. The former, the Schlachtflugzeug (battle planes), were updated CL types – relatively small single-seater machines with machine-guns and small bombs that were, in effect, what would later be termed "fighter-bombers". The Henschel Hs 123 biplane, that first flew in 1935 and saw service in Spain, Poland, the Balkans and Russia, was the main result. The heavy dive-bomber, initially termed the Stürzbomber and later the Stürzkampfflugzeug or Stuka, was to be a two-seater machine with heavier bomb load and the result was the Junker-designed Ju 87. (135)(136) There is no indication that, at that stage of development, either of the two types were envisaged as being armoured. The official specification for the armoured Schlacht aircraft was issued in December 1937 in response to the Condor Legion's limitations in tactical operations against ground targets during the Spanish Civil War. Two designs resulted (137): the Henschel Hs 129 and the Focke-Wulf Fw 189 Uhu ('Owl'). The Hs 129 design, a single-seater twin-engined machine, first flew early in 1939 and entered service in 1941. Especially in the Hs 129B variant, the aircraft, with its very small and heavily armoured cockpit for protection against ground fire, saw service mostly in Russia where it proved to be an excellent tank-buster. A report from Squadron Leader C C Wheeler on the "Developments in armament and protection found in

The pilot's cockpit of the Henschel Hs 129B was extensively armoured, with 12mm plate front and rear, 6mm plate sides and bottom, and a 3 inch windscreen. A 6mm horizontal plate ran from the top of the nose to the base of the windscreen. The lower halves of the engines were protected with 5mm plate, as were the oil coolers under the wings. (Imperial War Museum, CH 15613)

German aircraft subsequent to 1st October 1942 and up to 31st March 1943", described the protection scheme in detail:

"The pilot's cockpit, ..., consists entirely of armour plate, the thickness being 12mm front and rear, with 6mm sides and bottom. A top horizontal plate runs from nose to windscreen, also 6mm.

A bullet-proof windscreen about 3 inches thick is provided.

The lower half of the engines are protected from astern by 5mm plate and auxiliaries have additional armour plate.

The oil coolers situated under the wings are protected by 5mm plates at the sides, bottom and in the shutters." (138)

The Fw 189 design, a larger twin-engined three-seater machine with twin booms intended for reconnaissance as well as close-support, first flew in July 1938 and began pre-production delivery in September 1940. It, also, performed well in Russia after the invasion in June 1941. (138)

It is perhaps ironic that the need for specialised aircraft in the ground-attack rôle that led the Germans, fighting with the Nationalist forces in Spain, to develop the HS 129B and the FW 189 was also recognised by the Russians fighting against them with the Republican forces and led

Focke-Wulf Fw 189A reconnaissance and close support aircraft.
(Courtesy Phillip Jarrett)

to the development of the Illyushin IL-2. The Russian situation has been succinctly described by Nowarra and Duval:

"The Munich Crisis of 1938, and intelligence reports of the mass production of tanks and armoured vehicles in Germany lent additional urgency to the Soviet requirement for an Army close-support aircraft in the anti-tank rôle. The original specification of 1935 [for an aircraft of high performance, suitably armed and equipped for attacking armoured vehicles and heavily

Ilyushin Il-2.M.3 "Shturmovic" armoured ground attack aircraft.
(Imperial War Museum, RR 2221)

defended strong-points] was reissued as a top priority ... Illyushin's prototype, designated TsKB-55 or BSh-2 (BSh – Armoured Assaulter) was a 2-seater monoplane ... the entire forward fuselage was virtually an armoured box accommodating the engine, fuel tank, and crew, ..." (140)

In fact, as Nowarra and Duval explained, State acceptance trials for the BSh-2 did not commence until the Summer of 1940 and concerns were expressed about its stability and that it was under–powered. Illyushin's crash programme led to a new prototype, the TsKB-57, produced in under four months, as a single seater with thicker armour plate fitted behind the pilot. The TsKB-57 first flew on 12th October 1940 was ordered into production in March 1941 as the IL-2 "Shturmovic". The Il-2 became available as a two-seater in 1942, with a rear gunner to protect against attacks from astern, and in its twin 37mm anti-tank cannon version went on to devastate the German tank units during the 1943 Battle of Kursk.

20 1939 – The last months of peace

January 1939

And so, at last, the fateful year 1939 arrived – towards the end of which a new war in Europe would begin and, within some two years, would spread to the wider world.

On 2nd January 1939, Wing Commander J C M Lowe of Air Intelligence 1(g) sent a Note to Air Intelligence 3(b) regarding the position in Germany:

"1. There have been varying contradictory reports regarding Armour Plate Protection in German aircraft:

(a) A report secured about the beginning of this year stated that it appears possible that nickel steel plates with .3% of Zirconium about 1 & 2mm thick may be supplied as armour plates for Junker aeroplanes. This metal is imported from the U.S.A.

(b) A report dated 9/11/38 is to the effect that as far as is known no decision has yet been made as to the extent to which armour plates will be used in aircraft. The question is still under consideration. ...

(c) A report dated 9/12/38 states that as a general rule armouring of German aircraft is non-existent. Experiments have been carried out but the increased weight makes it prohibitive. In some of the bombers armour plating of absolutely vital parts round the cockpit is being tried, but in no case is this plating more than 4mm to 5mm thick. The types of machines being experimented with are unknown.

(d) A report of May 1938 is to the effect that as a result of experiences in Spain a shield protecting the pilot's back and instruments is built into all German fighters. It is a concave shaped shield having an area of 1 square metre, 3.55mm thick. It is a composite plate having 5 layers ... The shield is stated to afford protection against medium MG bullets.

(e) A report dated 17/12/38 has just been received to the effect that certain Heinkel and Italian Alfa-Romeo fighting aircraft employed in Nationalist Spain on ground strafing and "chain" attacks on enemy infantry positions are armour plated as protection against rifle and machine gun fire from the ground. The armour is of light weight laminated composition of a total thickness of 4mm, extending from a position underneath the fore part of the engine for a distance of about two thirds the length of the fuselage towards the tail. Rudder and control wires are similarly protected against rifle and machine gun bullets by being encased in tubes of composite metal armour plate.

In addition pilot's and observer's cockpits are protected from behind by a 4mm laminated metal plate which joins the armour running lengthwise along the bottom of the fuselage and extends to the top of the fuselage in the form of a bulkhead. The pilot's cockpit is also protected by similar metal plates on each side, which afford a certain amount of protection for the controls and instrument panel.

N.B. It appears that the plate described here may be the same as in (d), which is lighter than the same thickness of ordinary plate.

2. Although the conditions of air warfare in Spain are very different from those which would prevail in a European war, in that the additional weight of armour is not an important factor [presumably in Spain], it seems fair to assume in spite of X* that the Germans are at least considering some form of protection, particularly if the composite plate is efficient, since it is comparatively light." (141)

* Note. The hand-written reference to "X" was explained by a corresponding and obviously much later addition to the end of the document:

"It was reported in March, 1939 that as a general rule modern German aircraft are not fitted with armour plating."

An Intelligence report, undated but possibly the Report of 9th November 1938 to which Lowe referred, purported also to give some information on the situation in the German Air Force at the time:

"1. Source was asked if he could give any information on the use of armour plates in aircraft.

2. He reports that, as far as he knows, no decisions have yet been made as to the extent to which such plates will be used. The question is still under experiment and consideration.

3. Some of Junkers Bombers have been fitted with these plates. The process of fitting takes about two hours.

4. The plates will protect the engine, petrol tanks and pilot's cabin. The area they cover varies, in some cases they only give protection from the front; in others, from sides and rear.

5. The plates are usually 2mm, sometimes 3mm thick and will keep out machine-gun bullets." (82)

The level of hard information in both Lowe's note and the Intelligence report was very poor and it is unlikely to have generated much excitement in the minds of experienced and knowledgeable Officers like Dowding and Saundby. There was nothing upon which to base any judgements that would be likely to alter either the proposed schemes for, or the rate of progress on, the armouring of British aircraft.

The early weeks of January also saw a consolidation of what had been achieved during 1938. The ACAS (Douglas), in a draft Minute dated in January to the Director General of Research and Development (DGRD), Air Vice-Marshal A W Tedder, considered:

"1. ... that the schemes put forward by the Armour Plate Sub-Committee are, in general, satisfactory and it is confirmed that the corresponding loss of fuel and/or bomb load is acceptable. In the Stirling, Halifax and Manchester [bombers] the protection of the tanks accounts for a large proportion of the total weight devoted to armour plate and I understand that the tank protection will be so designed as to be removable by Service Units should it be found that this extra weight is not worth carrying.

Air Marshal Sir R H M S Saundby CB MC DFC AFC. (Imperial War Museum, CH.14544)

2. The following order of priority will meet our requirements:

Fighters	Bombers and G.R.	
Hurricane	Blenheim*	Botha
Spitfire	Battle*	Beaufort
Westland F.37/35	Hampden	Armstrong Whitworth 18/38
Defiant	Hereford	Stirling
	Wellington	Halifax
	Whitley IV and V	Manchester

*Minimum protection for crew is first consideration

3. I have confirmed [elsewhere] that it has been decided to abandon the scheme for armour plate protection for the Blenheim fighter." (82)

On 18th January Saundby, appointed as Director of Operational Requirements (DOR) with effect from that date, sent a note to Douglas (ACAS):

"   I think that the arrangements made by the [Armouring] Sub-Committee which dealt with armour plate protection are, in general, satisfactory. All the firms have been most helpful and are now engaged on the design of the necessary templates, etc. I think it would be best in the interests of quick production to accept all the schemes as submitted by the Sub-Committee.

2. It is true that we may have to accept reductions in bomb loads or range on the Stirling, Halifax and Manchester. What this reduction will be depends entirely on the behaviour of the aeroplane in flight. Frequently we find that aeroplanes can be over-weighted considerably without unduly affecting the length of take-off.

3. Although the total weights required for armour plate protection on the Halifax, Stirling and Manchester appear at first sight somewhat alarm-

ing, they represent a very small proportion of the maximum all-up weight of these aircraft in the overload case. The total weight of the armour plate for the Manchester amounts to .6% of the total all-up weight. In the Halifax it amounts to 1% and in the Stirling to 1.2%. By contrast the 80lb of armour plate protection required for the Hurricane appears quite modest, yet in this case the weight of the armour plate amounts to 1.35% of the total all-up weight.

4. I would explain also that the Sub-Committee took great care to ensure that the design of the armour plate protection was such that it can be applied easily and with the minimum of structural modifications. I am informed by Mr Serby (Chairman of the Sub-Committee) that as regards the Stirling, Halifax and Manchester, it will be possible for Service Units to remove the tank armour plate should we find that the weight imposes undue limitation on bomb load or range. In these aircraft the protection of the tanks accounts for a very large proportion of the extra weight.

5. Regarding the DGRD's request for an order of priority, I would suggest that the order laid down in [the ACAS's draft Minute of January] should meet our requirements with certain additions... ."

A Minute of 20th January 1939 from Douglas to Tedder (DGRD), included his confirmation that the Blenheim fighter would not be armoured.

The Air Fighting Committee – the 16th Meeting

The AFC began the year with their 16th meeting on 20th January 1939 and dealt mainly with interceptions by night.

February 1939

Another round of firing trials against Blenheim aircraft was held on 2nd February, in which the damage sustained from .303 inch ammunition was compared with that from 20mm high explosive (HE) ammunition. In the trial with .303 inch Mk VII Ammunition, the eight Brownings of a Hurricane fired 150 rounds each at a Blenheim from astern, at a range or 500 yards:

(a) The Blenheim was not put out of control but would have had to land immediately as both petrol and both oil tanks were holed. The tanks had been filled with water, but it was judged that there would have been a likelihood of fire if the petrol/oil tanks been filled with their usual contents and had incendiary ammunition been used.

(b) All tyres were punctured.

(c) The air gunner was killed (twice); the pilot was definitely not hit, but the navigator may have been hit once in the arm.

(d) The armour plate was not penetrated.

(e) The fuselage was so gashed that extensive repairs would have been necessary before the aircraft would have been fit to fly again. (142)

In the trial with 20mm HE shell, a single Hispano cannon was used, firing at a range of 500 yards at a second Blenheim from astern. Firing single shots 14 hits out of 18 shots were obtained. Had the aircraft been flying it was estimated that the 14 hits would have been obtained out of 60 shots fired:

(a) The tail plane and elevators were so badly damaged that it was believed that the aircraft would have been uncontrollable after the fourth hit.

(b) The air gunner was killed but the pilot and navigator were unhurt.

(c) Both petrol tanks quickly drained and one oil tank was badly damaged, but no obvious damage was done to either engine.

(d) The armour plate was not penetrated." (142)

These trials on the Blenheim were to be followed by numerous others throughout 1939, examining the effects of variations in the protection schemes and the ammunition used, most of the results being no longer on file.

The Modifications Committee (Airframes, Airscrews and Miscellaneous Equipment) had been involved in the process of approving the schemes for installing armour protection and in the Minutes of their 385th meeting on 8th February 1939 it was recorded that:

"The Committee considered modifications relating to the armour protection of aircraft following detailed investigation by the Armouring Committee and DGRD's and ACAS's approval of [that] Committee's recommendations. The Modifications Committee agree that action should be taken... . They were informed that any consequent increases in the weight of the aircraft beyond the maximum permissible would be met by adjustments in load to be referred to in the Weight Sheet Summaries, together with references to changes in centre of gravity. The modifications covered [*inter alia*]:

Battle	4mm plate pilot's seat back
	6mm chest plate for rear gunner
	10g Dural flooring for bomb aimer
	4mm plate bulkhead behind
	[wireless telegraphy (W/T)] set at bottom of fuselage.
Blenheim (Bomber only)	4mm plate pilot's seat back
	4mm plate on top front spar for navigator
	4mm plate bulkhead aft of W/T set for W/T operator, and present gun ramp replaced by 4mm plate.
Defiant	4mm plate attached to existing bulkhead behind pilot." (82)

There were details, too, for all of the other aircraft listed earlier by the ACAS.

March 1939

On 15th March 1939, Wing Commander Rowley wrote to the Chairman of the Modifications Committee chaired by Mr J E Serby, a Senior Scientific Officer at the Royal Aircraft Establishment:

"1. ... it is agreed that no armour should be included on the [prototype Defiant] except those items for which design alterations must be made now in order to avoid a redesign after prototype completion.

2. Regarding your proposals ..., it is considered that the total weight of 613lb for armour plate protection is not acceptable. In a turret fighter of this type we must either sacrifice armour plate altogether or else we must provide a limited amount of armour designed to protect the crew when attacking from the most favourable position. We consider that the most favourable tactics likely to be employed by this fighter will be the attack from the no-allowance or the near no-allowance position, that is, from behind or below the enemy bomber. We think it is worth while making a detailed investigation into the provision of protection against bombers' fire directed from 15° on each side.

3. This requirement could be met approximately by providing a large bullet-proof glass windscreen for the pilot, plus some bullet-proof cowling and the weight involved would probably be ... about 86lb. For the gunner ...[the armour] would amount to 66lb, the total weight of armour coming to about 152lb. This is relatively a small proportion of the all-up weight of this aeroplane and, although protection would be limited, we consider the moral support given to the crew justifies its provision. We shall not require protection for the tanks. ..." (82)

Around this time, possibly in March, the Air Ministry issued a "Secret Advisory Note on how armouring may affect design". The text of this Note, which accepted as "present policy" the provision of armour protection for bombers and fighters, is reproduced in full as Appendix A.

April 1939

A new report (143) became available on the experiences of French and Spanish pilots while fighting on the Republican side against the Germans and Italians in the Spanish Civil War. Prepared by Squadron Leader A P Berkely at the Air Ministry following interviews in France during 13th–15th April, the report had some interesting things to say about armour protection. From conversations with a Senior Carreras Ledeux, a Spanish Republican bomber (Potez 54s) pilot of some 5,000 hours experience, it appeared that owing to the nature of the civil war there had been little fighter-v-bomber action and most of the actual fighting has been fighter-v-fighter. In the early days of the war a large number of Republican fighters had been shot down in air combat. In these circumstances pilots experimented with various types of armour plating to protect them when attacked from behind and below. Cannon guns had been used in the German Bf 109 and in the front cockpit of the Heinkel He 59. After the arrival of the German Bf 109, with its cannon-gun, the damage caused by its explosive bullets caused a severe drop in the morale of the pilots and the thickness of the armour was increased to 7mm. The pilots were unanimous that this protection had saved many lives. It was not clear whether they believed that 7mm armour plating offered complete protection against a 20mm cannon projectile.

The aircraft that first came from Russia had no armour and this was fitted in Spain. Later batches of fighters that arrived from Russia, were, however, fitted with armour plating. The Russians had decided upon this as a result of experience gained in Spain. Berkely indicated that it had been confirmed by inspection of the aircraft which landed in France that both the I-16 and I-15 in Spain were fitted with armour plating 7mm thick to protect the back and head of the pilot. The only Republican aircraft that was armed with a cannon gun was apparently the Gordou (a dive–bomber) and explosive bullets were used. All the Republican fighters in Spain had used guns of 7.7mm calibre. The Russian guns had a rate of fire of 1800 rounds per minute. The maximum calibre used in Italian fighters was 12.7mm.

The key message from the report was the need for rear armour to protect the pilots of fighters in fighter-v-fighter actions rather than in fighter-v-bomber actions. Dowding had been arguing all along that the job of the fighters was to shoot down bombers and that for "modern" fighters dog-fighting was a thing of the past. Here, however, was direct evidence that in actual battle the situation was quite different and, although fighters like the I-15 and I-16 on the Republican side might hardly have been what Dowding would have regarded as "modern", the Bf 109s in the B, C and later E-1 variants that supported the Nationalists certainly were!

May 1939

Tests were carried out at Martlesham Heath on 3rd and 5th May 1939, to examine the possibility of fitting some form of armoured face plates to protect rear gunners. The tests were carried out using a Lysander; plates were fitted to the Vickers .303 machine gun Mk II installed on a rocking pillar mounting.

On 4th May there was a firing trial at Orfordness against a Blenheim. The effects of .5 inch ball and AP ammunition from a Vickers machine gun at 400 yards range were compared with the results obtained earlier using conventional .303 inch ammunition. A particular feature of this round of trials was that two different types of self-sealing tanks were tested, Henderson and SEMAPE.

The Air Fighting Committee – the 17th Meeting

The 17th meeting was held on 31st May 1939. (144) The prospect was clearly in mind that some contingents of the RAF's forces might soon be stationed in France as part of a new British Expeditionary Force, supporting French and Belgian forces in repelling a German attack. The main intention was to clarify views on the role and characteristics of what was termed the "Field Force Fighter" (FFF), as distinct from the "Home Defence Fighter" (HDF). The FFF would be required over the battlefield and in conditions where there would be armies on the ground below and reconnaissance going on – and so would be liable to meet other fighters. The HDF would be stationed in Britain, to defend the homeland against attacks by enemy bombers – presumably unescorted bombers! Dowding argued that the FFF was primarily required not only to shoot down enemy aircraft (which was generally agreed) but, like the HDF, would have to catch and destroy those likely to do the most harm, ie bombers. Consequently, as long as the FFF could catch and shoot down enemy bombers, some sacrifice of manoeuvrability in individual combat could and must be accepted. Hence, the FFF might not be a very suitable weapon against enemy Army co-operation aircraft that were reckoned to be of the lightly loaded manoeuvrable types; he thought that such types as the Lysander would be able to look after themselves against modern fighters. However, Dowding concluded that as in the course of other work the FFF would frequently be coming up against enemy fighters and might often be caught unawares, the time had come to provide *all fighters with back armour against surprise!* (145) This seems to have been quite out of the blue. He even mentioned the Spanish War, in which fighters often did not catch the enemy bombers but were left to dog-fight with their escorting fighters, so perhaps the April 1939 report from combatants in Spain had finally convinced him that fighter-v-fighter combats were not only possible but likely – at least in the battle zone.

Inevitably, this realisation then led Ludlow-Hewitt to raise the matter of escorts for British bombers and whether this should be a further role for the FFF, much against the wishes of Dowding. It might perhaps seem a matter for some relief in the light of the approaching conflict with Germany that the Committee finally decided that:

> "the primary purpose of the FFF is to destroy enemy aircraft in the air ...[and] should be capable of intercepting the enemy aircraft of highest performance likely to be encountered in its sphere of operation." (146)

Note. The underling is in the original document.

But the Committee, in emphasising "performance", were really thinking primarily of high speed and only secondarily of manoeuvrability. Perhaps having in mind the weight of back armour in relation to speed and manoeuvrability, though this is by no means clear, the Committee then turned to the likelihood of the FFF being attacked from the rear. It was argued that as the FFF would not be required to carry out offensive patrols far over the enemy lines back armour, though desirable, was not essential – but this was countered by the view that if the fighters were to shoot down enemy aircraft, they would have to go to the place where they were most numerous, even far over the lines, in which case back armour was essential. Dowding pointed out that if the enemy aircraft were far behind their own lines they would not be doing actual harm – and the job would be one of destroying them on the ground, which would be the work of the bomber. But then it was also noted that in Spain most of the destruction of enemy aircraft on the ground had been effected by fighters equipped with forward-firing guns (like the Salamander that had been developed for ground work in the Great War) and using explosive ammunition. So armour was a factor to be considered for the FFF.

The question of armour continued to see-saw between the supposed differences in the requirements for the FFF and the HDF. The Chairman of the Committee (Douglas) even suggested that back armour, if it was to be fitted to meet FFF requirements, should be removable, so that it could be taken out for HDF operations: "... It was not considered desirable to complicate Home Defence Fighters with permanent rear armour, but it was desirable to be able to fit it rapidly in case a proportion of the Home Defence Fighters were sent overseas", (147) a view with which Dowding seemed actually to agree! However, Dowding also:

> "... expressed the view that the time was not too far distant when, in the event of war, <u>fighters would be met over [Britain]</u>*. He thought that either a long range fighter would be developed by the enemy, or that the Low Countries might be occupied and used as forward landing grounds. He considered that the unescorted bomber was going to prove such a hopeless proposition over this country, from the enemy's point of view, that he would have to do something about it." (148)

Note. The underlining is in the original document.

The final decision, however, was that detachable rear armour should be included as a requirement for the FFF and that the possibility of such armouring for the Hurricane and Spitfire should now be investigated – and this was May 1939, remember!

June 1939

Quite suddenly, therefore, the debate had taken a new turn and Rowley soon got the ball rolling when, on 2nd June 1939, he minuted D Arm D 1(c):

> " I spoke to you yesterday about the discussion of the [17th] AFC meeting on the subject of the Field Force Fighter, and I explained that there may be a requirement in the future for detachable armour plate to protect the backs of pilots in Hurricanes and Spitfires. There may also be a requirement for armour plate to protect the rear of the tanks in the Hurricane, but I am not

in favour of this if we can get self-sealing tanks for the same or only slightly greater weight.

I do not want you to look at this as an official Air Staff requirement at present, and I will take no action until I receive the formal Minutes of the meeting, but as I said you may wish to do a little preliminary investigation on your own. It is probable that the armour plate if required will have to be detachable, because it will not be needed for home defence purposes." (149)

The AFC had, of course, "decided" that rear armour would definitely be looked at for the FFF, but not for the HDF.

15th June saw more Blenheim firing trials at Orfordness, this time using French 20mm Hispano HE ammunition at 200 yards range. There were more trials on 26th June at Shoeburyness, using 20mm Hispano solid (inert) practice ammunition fired at 200 yards range. On this occasion, the petrol tank in one wing was to be 2/3 full of petrol and the oil tank full of oil, both tanks being protected with ½ inch thick SEMAPE self–sealing material. The petrol tank in the other wing was to be 2/3 full of water and protected by a 4mm armour back plate.

July 1939

Rowley, wrote to Wing Commander V B Ranford in the Directorate of Equipment on 4th July 1939, noting that sets of armour protection for the Blenheim bomber were becoming available for retrospective fitting along the same lines as for Hurricanes:

"We look on it as a matter of highest importance that there should be no delay in getting the bomber armour plate installations fitted to Service aircraft. Every set fitted may save lives. ..." (150)

On 13th July 1939 Ranford, replying to Rowley, gave the position regarding the supply of sets of parts of armour plating for four types of aircraft:

Blenheim

Instructions have been issued to Messrs Bristols to put in hand a sufficient number of sets of parts to cover production aeroplanes and for retrospective application to those already delivered. ... the firm have not yet reached the stage where armour plating is being installed in production Blenheims. ...

Battle

The question of fitting armour plate ... has been put to Bomber Command as to priority of application, ie, in production or in service.

Wellington

The stage has just been reached whereby contract instructions can be issued to cover the necessary number of sets both for production and retrospective action ...

Spitfire

An advance order for 200 sets of [presumably front] armour plate ... was placed with Messrs Supermarines in January last [1939] ... ." (150)

Saundby was to minute on 28th August 1939, in response to a query from Douglas, that instructions to proceed with the design of detachable rear armour for the Hurricane were given on 17th July 1939. (151)

On 22nd July 1939 L T G Mansell, Deputy Director of Aircraft Production (DDAP), was advised that:

"... news is already available regarding the Hurricane and Spitfire. [for the Hurricane] 125 sets of [front] armour have been or are now being fitted to aircraft at Squadrons by firm's working party. Probably this number has increased during the last few days.

In the case of the Spitfire, however, the situation is not so promising. No aircraft in production have yet been delivered with [front] armour fitted and the firm do not anticipate to start doing so until about the middle of August. There are, however, at their works about 200 sets of the bulk-head armour plate already available. ... only a part of the modification but there is no technical objection to its being fitted without awaiting the residue of the modification." (150)

The DDAP reported on 26th July:

"To date 189 Hurricanes are fully [front] armoured at Units [squadrons].

The output of armour protection sets at Hawkers is now in the region of 10 sets a week and this will be increased as material becomes available.

Regarding Spitfires, the 308th and all subsequent aircraft will be fully [front] armoured. This means they will commence to come out of Supermarines in the early part of August.

There are already not less than 100 sets of armour plate available for fitting at Units but bullet-proof windscreens and dural [Duralumin] sheets for petrol tanks cannot be supplied [until] mid August.

I suggest it would be better to wait until whole sets are available before commencing the work at Units." (150)

Also on that date, Wing Commander Ranford was given an update on the earlier four aircraft types:

"BLENHEIM

Modification 566 – Armour plate (pilot and Navigator)

The present position is:

56 sets are now available for fitment.

15 sets will be available on 26th instant.

15 sets will be available on 29th instant.

20 sets per week will be available during August (excepting the one week works closed period).

... Of the above mentioned quantities, 20 sets will be delivered for spares immediately, and thereafter at the rate of 20 sets per week.

Modification 589 – Armour Plate (Rear Gunner)

This is a much later introduction, and information will be forwarded when enquiries are pursued further.

BATTLE

Faireys , Stockport

Armour plate is now being received from Messrs Hadfields. The 10 gauge plate on the Bomb Aimer's Floor has proved satisfactory. Further supplies of armour plate are now awaited from Hadfields before incorporation into aircraft, so that continuity will be assured.   Present proposal is to incorporate in the 765th aircraft.

Austins

The present proposal is to incorporate armour plating in the 379th aircraft.

The firm ... are using 8 gauge [Duralumin] as an alternative [for the bomb aimer's floor], there being no technical objection to this.

VICKERS-ARMSTRONG – WELLINGTON. Position at 20/7/39.

Aircraft from machine L.4292 and onwards are being equipped with fixed fittings to take armour protection at the first pilot's, W/T operator's and rear gunner's stations. Fittings for wing tank armouring are not yet available.

[Subject to delivery] it is proposed to introduce complete armour protection on the first Mark I.A. aircraft, viz, the 181st machine in the production line.

VICKERS-ARMSTRONG – SPITFIRE. Position at 11/7/39.

The requirements are substantially in three parts, viz:

     (i) Armour plate fireproof bulkhead.

     (ii) 10 gauge Duralumin sheet over fuel tank.

     (iii) Bullet–proof windscreen.

Approximately 150 armour plates for bulkheads are in store ... Two fuselages in [work]shops are equipped with bulkheads. 30 sheets of 10 gauge Duralumin are completed, and an output of 30 sheets per week is to be achieved in one month's time.

Immediate delivery of 30 bullet-proof windscreens per week will be made.

The firm have agreed to place 100 sets of armour plates at D of E's disposal for retrospective action in service, and a weekly supply of 15 10-gauge Duralumin skins and bullet-proof windscreens for the same purpose commencing in one month's time.

A complete modification is to be introduced in the production line on the 310th aircraft." (150)

July 1939 was also a month in which there were even more firing trials at Orfordness against the Blenheim. Held on 27th July, the trials were primarily aimed at continuing to assess the merits of self-sealing petrol and oil tanks. The inner wing petrol tanks, self-sealing with SEMAPE material, were filled with petrol. The standard outer wing petrol tank in one wing was full of water and protected by a 10swg Dural deflector plate on the under surface of the wing. The outer petrol tank in the other wing was also full of water and was protected by a 4mm armour back plate.

The oil tanks, full of oil, were to be self-sealing: SEMAPE in one wing and Henderson in the other.

Single shots of 20mm French Hispano HE ammunition at 200 yards, fired from 10° below astern, showed that a single hit caused serious damage eight times out of ten: the self-sealing tanks, filled with petrol, failed to self-seal and the fuel caught fire each time. (152) For those concerned about the protection of bombers, the results were hardly encouraging.

Squadron Leader D S Brookes, Overseer at Vickers-Armstrongs Ltd in Southampton, advised his Chief Overseer at the Air Ministry on 29th July that for Spitfires in production:

> "[Armour plate would be] Introduced into production line on N.2023 (309th) and subsequent aircraft, due for delivery about 15.8.39." (150)

Regarding retrospective action on Spitfires already delivered, armour would be fitted as follows:

> "(i.) 15 sets per week from 10/8/39 by three firm's working parties.
>
> (ii.) Three parties of two men each will be capable, with Service assistance, of dealing with 15 aircraft per week.
>
> (iii.) Time required to complete 180 aircraft in service, including 80 delivered complete ..., about two months." (150)

He also mentioned that considerable difficulties and delays had been experienced with the manufacture of the windscreen casing.

August 1939

A meeting with Hawkers to discuss the matter of rear armour was arranged for 28th August. At this time, it was understood that the only fighters in the FFF would be the Hurricanes of Squadrons Nos 1, 73, 85 and 87. No action was therefore being taken regarding rear armour plate protection for the Spitfire!

Earlier, 18th August saw Saundby writing to the ACAS with an update on the armouring position which, so far as the Hurricane and Spitfire were concerned, can be assumed to have referred to front armour only:

> "1. I have been keeping a careful eye on the retrospective fitting of armour plate in existing types and the present position is, broadly speaking, as follows:
>
> 2. Hurricane
>
> Armour is being fitted on all production aircraft from the first week in [August 1939] onwards. If the aircraft already delivered 210 have been fitted and the remainder are being done by the firm's working parties at the rate of 10 a week.
>
> 3. Spitfire
>
> Armour will be fitted on all production aircraft delivered from this week onwards. By that time 309 aircraft will have been delivered and these are now

being fitted at the rate of 15 sets per week by three working parties supplied by the firm. These parties are due to begin work on 10th August.

4. Blenheim

All aircraft delivered from Bristol after 1st September will be fitted with armour. 20 sets are being sent ... for delivery to the Service and will be fitted by the Service with the assistance of the firm's working parties. They hope to have soon 20 sets a week (above those required for production aircraft) for issue to the Service.

5. Battle

All production Battles are now coming out fitted with armour and there will be a surplus for issue to the Service for fitting to aircraft already delivered." (153)

Saundby also provided updates for the Whitley, Wellington and Hampden bombers and, on 28th August, he reported again to Douglas that:

"– DArmD had been requested on 17th July 1939, on the highest priority, to proceed with the design of detachable rear armour for the Hurricane.

– As only Hurricanes (Squadrons Nos I, 73, 85 and 87) were to be employed with the Field Force, no action had been taken on rear armour plate protection for the Spitfire.

– The thickness of armour plate used in the existing schemes (4mm) would generally be proof against .303 bullets and splinters from explosive 20mm cannon shell, but the weight of armour required to give protection against solid 20mm shot would be prohibitive. In certain cases, where there was not much structure behind the armour plate, a thickness of 9mm was employed, but the plate weighed 15lb per square foot and had to be used very sparingly. It had been proved that 20mm shot could easily penetrate the plate and it had been estimated that even 15mm plate would be penetrated." (151)

On 29th August 1939, Rowley sent to Saundby a report of a visit the previous day that he had made with a Mr Hanson (a Scientific Officer with the Directorate of Research and Development) to the Hawker factory at Kingston to discuss rear armour protection for the Field Force Hurricanes. He reported that he had found:

"...the firm most helpful and promptly sent over a draughtsman to Brooklands with us. Before tea we had cardboard templates cut out and a very reasonable scheme approved." (141)

The scheme devised at the meeting comprised:

"Head Protection

3.   Behind the pilot's head is a small cupboard in the top fuselage fairing. We decided to cover the cupboard door with 9mm plate secured with detachable screws. Thus the pilot will still be able to use the cupboard, although at some slight inconvenience, by removing the top plate.

Body Protection

4.   Just below the head plate is a slot through which goes the harness strap. It was decided to leave this slot unprotected in the interest of simplicity of design. It is a very small slot.

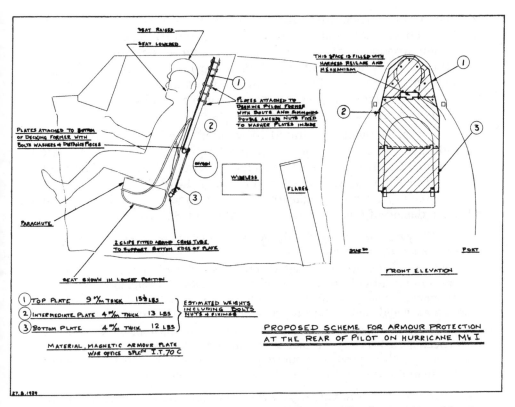

Hurricane three-piece rear/back armour scheme, The "unprotected in the interests of simplicity" slot in the head plate, through which the Sutton harness passed, is the one that let through the bullet fragments that Billy Drake received in his neck! (Public Record Office, AIR 2/5103)

5.   The back of the pilot will be protected by a 4mm plate fixed to the wooded panel behind the seat. This plate will form a continuation of the head piece and gives protection down to the small of the pilot's back.

6.   The pilot's thighs and legs will be protected by a panel of 4mm plate placed against tubular struts which form a rectangle just below and behind the seat. This rectangle is braced with wires and it may be necessary to fix the armour to this bracing in order to avoid removing the seat. (141)

It was not expected that Service Units would have any difficulty in fitting the armour: it was very simple and there were no curves or complicated shapes – just flat plates. The total weight of the plates, with fittings, was reckoned to be 46lb and would move the centre of gravity towards the tail by 0.28 inch. On Hurricanes with wooden propellers, this would place the centre of gravity aft of the accepted limit and would have to be compensated for by removing either the wireless (not an acceptable option) or the flare shute. With variable pitch or constant speed propellers fitted, the Hurricanes would be able to take all the armour and ancillary equipment without compensation. The conclusion, therefore, was that the Field Force Hurricanes of Nos 1, 73, 85 and 87 Squadrons should have their wooden propellers replaced as soon as possible in order to save their flare shutes. It remained for the firm to proceed as quickly as possible with a trial installation using ply-wood in the first instance and then mild steel plate to represent the armour. The Mild steel plates would then serve as templates for the armour plates.

Nevertheless, Douglas continued to wonder whether the Spitfire, too, should have the back armour – though he preferred not. (155) But on 31st August Group Captain D F Stevenson, Deputy Director of Operations (Home) (DDOH), with Air Vice-Marshal R H Peck OBE (Director of Operations) agreeing, advised Douglas that "no time should be lost in proceeding with the design of rear armour (detachable) for Spitfires" since:

"(a) They may be employed with the Field Force in France even in the early stages of a war as a reinforcement.

(b) H D Fighters are now faced with the possibility of encountering enemy fighters over [Britain] – as for example the Me 110 with a maximum range (at economical cruising speed) of 1350 miles. ... a German advance into the low countries would enable short range fighters to operate over England.

It seems that we should accept therefore (as we have in the case of the Hurricane) the loss in performance and incorporate this protection (detachable) as quickly as possible in future production Spitfires and arrangements made to fit it (detachable) to aircraft already in Squadrons." (156)

The feared German advance into the Low Countries was to be another nine months away but later on 31st August, at 8 o'clock in the evening, an incident was staged by Germany's Waffen SS (Armed Schutzstaffel, or protection group) at the German radio station at Gliewitz (Gliwice) on the German–Poland border that provided the excuse for what followed. At 04.45hrs the next morning, 1st September 1939, the Germans invaded Poland and as the mists gradually cleared over their airfields during the morning units of the German Air Service – the Luftwaffe – once again took to the air at war.

1 Fahey, James C, *U.S. Army Aircraft (Heavier than Air) 1908–1946*, pp 14–16, Ships and Aircraft, Virginia, 1946 (reissued 1964).
2 Bowers, Peter M, *Forgotten Fighters and Experimental Aircraft. US Army 1918–1941*, Arco Publishing Company, 1971, p 28.
3 Bowers, Peter M, ibid, pp 40–41.
4 Bruchiss, Louis, Aircraft Armament, p 17, Aerosphere, Inc., New York, 1945.
5 Duval, G R, *U.S. Pursuit Aircraft 1918–1936*, D Bradford Barton Ltd, Cornwall, England, 1975.
6 Christie, Gp Capt Malcolme G, General trends of air developments within the U.S. Air Service 22nd April 1924, AIR 2/266, piece 1A.
7 Public Record Office, AIR 10/1325, Air Intelligence Report No 11 – Notes on Aviation in the USA, 1925, Air Ministry Publication April 1926, pp 48–49.
8 Public Record Office, AIR 2/266, minute 4.
9 Smythies, S/Ldr B E, DFC, A selection of lectures and essays from the work of Officers attending the first course at the Royal Air Force Staff College 1922–23, pp 80–81, 86. V Experiences during the War, 1914–1918. Air Publication 956, December 1923, British Library reference B.S.2.p/1.
10 Park, S/Ldr K R, MC DFC, ibid, p 113. VI Experiences in the War, 1914 -1918.
11 Public Record Office, AIR 2/266, file S.23357, piece 1A.
12 Public Record Office, AIR 2/266, piece 8A.
13 Public Record Office, AIR 2/266, file S.23577, piece 10A.
14 Baker, S/Ldr G B A, MC, A selection of lectures and essays from the work of Officers attending the fifth course at the Royal Air Force Staff College 1926–27, I Service Experiences, p 15. Air Publication 1308, April 1928, British Library reference B.S.2.p/1.
15 Gibbs, Flt-Lt G E, MC, ibid, p 61 *et sec.*
16 Public Record Office, AIR 2/266, piece 13A.
17 Public Record Office, AIR 2/349, piece 93A.
18 Public Record Office, AIR 2/349, piece 97B.
19 Public Record Office, AIR 2/349, Minute 92.
20 Public Record Office, AIR 2/349, Minute 94.
21 Public Record Office, AIR 2/349, piece 95A.
22 The Columbia Electronic Encyclopedia.
23 "Comando Supremo: Italy at War", www.comandosupremo.com.
24 Douhet, Giulio, *The Command of the Air,* translated by Dino Ferrari, Coward-McCann Inc, New York, 1942.
25 Douhet, op cit, Part I (1921), Chapter II. The independent air force – Unit of combat, p 45.
26 Douhet, op cit, Part II, 2nd edition (added in 1927), section 5, Means of combat, p 114.
27 Douhet, ibid, p 114.
28 Douhet, ibid, p 116.
29 Douhet, ibid, p 118.
30 Douhet, ibid, p 105.
31 Nowarra, Heinz J and Duval, G R, *Russian civil and military aircraft 1884–1969*, pp 97–100, Fountain Press, London, 1971.
32 Brown, Commander Sheldon W, USN, Armour of Japanese Airplanes, p 1, British Intelligence Objectives Sub-Committee, RAF Museum File Reference R 018744.
33 Nowarra, and Duval, op cit, p 102.
34 Nowarra, and Duval, op cit, p 107.
35 Nowarra and Duval, op cit, p 111.
36 Slessor, Marshal of the Royal Air Force Sir John, Air power and the future of war, Lecture to the Royal United Service Institute, April 1954, published in *"The Great Deterrent"* by Cassell & Company Ltd, 1957.
37 Slessor, ibid, p138.
38 Golovine, Lt-Gen N N, *Air Strategy*, p 6, Gale and Polden Ltd, 1936.
39 Golovine, Lt-Gen N N, *Views on Air Defence*, Gale and Polden Ltd, 1938.
40 Public Record Office, AIR 2/1645, piece 1A, minute 5.
41 Public Record Office, AIR 2/1645, piece 9A, minute 7.
42 Public Record Office, AIR 2/1645, piece 9A, minute 48.

43 Public Record Office, AIR 2/1645, piece 9A, minute 49.
44 Public Record Office, AIR 2/1645, piece 9A, minute 50.
45 Public Record Office, AIR 16/43, piece 1E (AFC Report No 21). Also AIR 2/1648, piece 17b.
46 Public Record Office, AIR 16/43, piece 1C (AFC Report No 19).
47 Public Record Office, AIR 2/1648, piece 17b (AFC Report No 20, para 6).
48 Public Record Office, AIR 16/43, piece 1D (AFC Report No 20).
49 Public Record Office, AIR 2/1645, piece 41A, minute 10.
50 Public Record Office, AIR 2/1645, piece 41A, minute 33.
51 Public Record Office, AIR 2/1645, piece 41A, minute 42.
52 Public Record Office, AIR 2/1645, piece 41A, minute 47.
53 Public Record Office, AIR 20/12 (extract from file ref. S.38111, Enclosure 36B).
54 Public Record Office, AIR 2/1645, piece 54B.
55 Record Office, AIR 2/1648, piece 65A. Extract from a report from an experienced pilot in the service of the Spanish Republican Army (AFC Report No 31).
56 Public Record Office, AIR 16/259, piece 2B.
57 Public Record Office, AIR 2/1645, piece 41A, minutes 44 and 45 .
58 Public Record Office, AIR 8/214, piece 2A.
59 Public Record Office, AIR 16/259, piece 5A.
60 Public Record Office, AIR 8/214, piece 7A.
61 Public Record Office, AIR 2/1648, piece 81A (AFC Report No 35).
62 Public Record Office, AIR 2/1645, piece 91A.
63 Public Record Office, AIR 2/1645, piece 91A, minutes 2 and 3.
64 Public Record Office, AIR 2/1645, piece 112A, minute 10.
65 Public Record Office, AIR 2/1646, piece 1A, minute 28.
66 Public Record Office, AIR 2/2010. Instruction to proceed No 685824/37, Fitting of armour plating etc to Hart fuselage.
67 Public Record Office, AIR 2/3233, piece 1B.
68 Public Record Office, AIR 2/3233, piece 1A, minute 3.
69 Public Record Office, AIR 2/3233, piece 1A, minute 4.
70 Public Record Office, AIR 2/3233, piece 4A.
71 Public Record Office, AIR 2/3233, piece 3A.
72 Public Record Office, AIR 2/2010, piece 79A, A&AEE Report No M/Arm/522/1.
73 Public Record Office, AIR 2/2010, piece 56C.
74 Public Record Office, AIR 2/2010, piece 56B.
75 Public Record Office, AIR 2/2010, piece 69A.
76 Public Record Office, AIR 14/433, piece 11A.
77 Public Record Office, AIR 14/433, piece 12A.
78 Public Record Office, AVIA 18/524, A&AEE Report No M/Arm/519/1.
79 Public Record Office, AIR 2/3246, piece 25A, A&AEE Report No M/Arm/522/2.
80 Public Record Office, AIR 2/3246, piece 23A.
81 Public Record Office, AIR 2/2010, minute 82.
82 Public Record Office, AIR 20/12.
83 Public Record Office, AIR 2/3246, piece 37A; AIR 2/1649, piece 5B (AFC Report No 52).
84 Public Record Office, AIR 2/3246, piece 37B.
85 Public Record Office, AIR 2/1649, piece 5A (AFC 51). Air Staff Notes on the Application of Armour Plate to Military Aircraft.
86 Public Record Office, AIR 20/35.
87 Public Record Office, AIR 2/1646, piece 36A.
88 Public Record Office, AIR 2/1646, piece 36A, minute 16.
89 Public Record Office, AIR 2/1646, piece 36A, minute 5.
90 Public Record Office, AIR 2/1646, piece 36A, minute 6.
91 Public Record Office, AIR 2/1646, piece 36A, minute 15.
92 Public Record Office, AIR 2/1646, piece 36A, minute 22.
93 Public Record Office, AIR 2/1646, piece 36A, minute 47.
94 Public Record Office, AIR 2/1646, piece 36A, minute 48.
95 Public Record Office, AIR 2/1646, piece 36A, minute 52.
96 Public Record Office, AIR 2/1646, piece 36A, minute 53.
97 Public Record Office, AIR 2/3341, piece 2a.
98 Public Record Office, AIR 2/1646, piece 40B.
99 Public Record Office, AIR 2/3341, minute 4.

100 Public Record Office, AIR 14/72, piece 22c.
101 Public Record Office, AIR 20/12, Minute sheet (piece A20).
102 Public Record Office, AIR 14/433, piece 87A.
103 Public Record Office, AIR 14/433, piece 90C.
104 Public Record Office, AIR 14/433, piece 90A.
105 Public Record Office, AIR 2/3353, piece 3A.
106 Public Record Office, AIR 2/3353, piece 9A.
107 Public Record Office, AIR 14/433, piece 90B.
108 Public Record Office, AIR 2/3353, piece 21A. Also AIR/14/433, pieces 90A and B.
109 Public Record Office, AIR 2/3353, piece 31B.
110 Public Record Office, AIR 2/3353, piece 36A.
111 Public Record Office, AIR 2/3353, piece 37A.
112 Public Record Office, AIR 2/3353, piece 28A.
113 Public Record Office, AIR 2/3353, piece 30A.
114 Public Record Office, AIR 2/3476, piece 1A.
115 Public Record Office, AIR 2/3476, piece 6A.
116 Public Record Office, AIR 2/3476.
117 Public Record Office, AIR 2/3476, minute 13.
118 Public Record Office, AIR 2/3476, piece 12B.
119 Public Record Office, AIR 2/3476, piece 66A.
120 Monday, David (compiler), *The Hamlyn Concise Guide to British Aircraft of
     World War II*, Hamlyn/Aerospace, London, 1982.
121 Public Record Office, AIR 2/3456, piece 1A.
122 Public Record Office, AIR 2/3456, piece 5C.
123 Public Record Office, AIR 2/3456, piece 7A.
124 Public Record Office, AVIA 18/561, A&AEE Report No M/Arm/557/1.
125 Public Record Office, AIR 2/1646, piece 52K, minute 15.
126 Public Record Office, AIR 2/1646, piece 52K, minute 16.
127 Public Record Office, AIR 2/1646, piece 52K, minutes 17, 19.
128 Public Record Office, AIR 2/1646, piece 52K, minutes 39, 40.
129 Public Record Office, AIR 2/1646, piece 52K, minute 33.
130 Public Record Office, AIR 2/1646, piece 52K, minute 72.
131 Public Record Office, AIR 2/1646, piece 52K, minutes 73,75, 76.
132 Public Record Office, AIR 2/1649, piece 18C.
133 Larrázabal, Jesus Salar, *Air war over Spain*, translated by Margaret A Kelley,
     Ian Allan Ltd, 1974 (English edition), p265.
134 Public Record Office, AIR 2/1646, piece 93A, minute 35.
135 Homze, Edward L, *Arming the Luftwaffe. The Reich Air Ministry and the German
     Aircraft Industry 1919–39*, University of Nebraska Press, 1976, pp 125–126.
136 Hooton, E R, *Phoenix Triumphant, The Rise and Rise of the Luftwaffe*,
     Arms &Armour Press, London, 1994, pp 107–108.
137 Hooton, E R, ibid, p144.
138 Public Record Office, AVIA 15/739/17A.
139 Gunston, Bill, *The Illustrated Directory of Fighting Aircraft of World War II*,
     Salamander Books Ltd, 1988.
140 Nowarra & Duval, op cit, pp111–113.
141 Public Record Office, AIR 2/3233.
142 Public Record Office, AIR 14/433, piece 106A and minute 107.
143 Public Record Office, AIR 9/46, folio 5.
144 Public Record Office, AIR 2/1646, piece 93A.
145 Public Record Office, AIR 2/1646, piece 93A, minute 15.
146 Public Record Office, AIR 2/1646, piece 93A, minute 22.
147 Public Record Office, AIR 2/1646, piece 93A, minute 59.
148 Public Record Office, AIR 2/1646, piece 93A, minute 60.
149 Public Record Office, AIR 2/3351, piece 48B.
150 Public Record Office, AIR 2/5103, minute sheet.
151 Public Record Office, AIR 2/5103, minute 8.
152 Public Record Office, AIR 14/433, minute 128.
153 Public Record Office, AIR 2/5103, minute 4.
154 Public Record Office, AIR 2/5103.
155 Public Record Office, AIR 2/5103, minute 9.
156 Public Record Office, AIR 2/5103, minute 10.

IV – War, the early months:
September 1939–June 1940

On Sunday 3rd September 1939, at 11 o'clock in the morning, the British ultimatum to Germany expired and Britain was once again at war.

21 Fighters

Hurricane and Spitfire

A draft note dated September 1939 from Group Captain Saundby (DOR), indicated that centre of gravity (CG) concerns were still delaying the fitting of rear armour to the Hurricane:

> "It is an urgent requirement that Hurricanes allotted to the Field Force should be equipped with armour plate behind the pilot in addition to the forward armour plate protection.
>
> 2. Squadrons affected are Nos 1, 73, 85, 87 and possibly 29 Squadron also.
>
> 3. It is understood from Messers Hawkers that the rear armour will bring the CG too far aft in Hurricanes fitted with wooden airscrews unless the flare shoot be deleted; which is not advisable if it can be avoided.
>
> 4. Hurricanes with metal airscrews can be fitted with the rear armour without putting the CG outside accepted limits.
>
> 5. Please will you let me know whether it will be possible to equip the Squadrons detailed for the Field Force with metal airscrews and if so when they are likely to be [so] equipped." (1)

No 1 Squadron, equipped with Hurricanes, was of course the Squadron to which Paul Richey and Billy Drake were attached. On 5th September Air Vice-Marshal Douglas (ACAS), wrote to Air Vice-Marshal A W Tedder (DGRD):

> " ... I do consider it essential to have rear armour plate fitted to fighters which have to operate with the Field Force. We may reasonably anticipate a considerable amount of fighter versus fighter warfare in France.
>
> 2. The subject was thoroughly thrashed out at the 17th meeting of the Air Fighting Committee, and it was unanimously agreed that a scheme of rear armour plate should be investigated as soon as possible.
>
> 3. DOR and RDArm3(d), after consultation with Messers Hawkers, are of the opinion that reasonable rear protection can be given by three sheets of armour plate of simple design which can be fitted behind the pilot's seat, without any structural alteration to the Hurricane, and it is estimated that the fitting of the plates could be done quite easily by Service personnel.
>
> 4. ... as soon as the plates are manufactured we should send them to France to be fitted by Service personnel to the Field Force Hurricanes. I propose that we place a preliminary order for 200 sets.
>
> 5. DOR is at present investigating the problem of rear protection for the Spitfire, and from his preliminary report I judge that it will not be so easy

as in the case of the Hurricane. If this is so, I shall consider confining this modification to Hurricanes only. ..." (2)

Saundby reported on 7th September that the possibility of fitting rear armour to Spitfires had recently been investigated at Supermarines' Works. It was found that the components (eg pipelines) behind the pilot made the installation of armour plate much more complicated than for the Hurricane and that the head rest would have to be re-designed. Bearing in mind these complications and in order not to delay the production of Spitfires, which at that stage was only 5 per week and expected to rise to a "probable" 12 at the end of October, he proposed that the project for fitting rear armour for the Spitfire should be abandoned in order to concentrate on the Hurricane. Apparently by this date just over 300 Spitfires had been delivered, as compared with nearly 500 Hurricanes. Saundby was concerned over:

> "... the present unsatisfactory position regarding Spitfire production and also the difficulties and delays which we have experienced in getting the front armour for the Spitfire. It is only during the last week that the firm started turning out Spitfires fitted with front armour plate and they have scarcely begun to fit armour to those already delivered." (3)

Air Vice-Marshal R H Peck OBE, Assistant Chief of Air Staff (Operations and Intelligence) and Director of Operations agreed (4) with the conclusions of a suggestion from Douglas on 8th September that:

> "As regards argument (a) [armouring Spitfires for possible employment with the Field Force in France], this difficulty could surely be got over by sending only Hurricanes to France ... it would be highly desirable to have only one type of fighter overseas.
>
> As regards argument (b) [Home Defence Spitfires encountering enemy fighters over Britain], I do not find this very convincing. The top speed of the latest type of Me 110 is only 310mph, which is some 40–50mph slower than the Spitfire. There should therefore be no danger of the Spitfire being attacked from behind by the Me 110, unless the pilot is so foolish as to be completely surprised.
>
> I would therefore strongly urge that you should agree to forego the rear armour in the Spitfire. (5)

Once again the idea had surfaced that the pilot, in this case the Spitfire pilot, could only be expected to be attacked from behind as a result of his own carelessness. In the general mêlée of a dog-fight, surprise attacks from behind or merely passing shots of opportunity were more likely to be matters of luck than of carelessness – but of course, with the war hardly started, dog-fighting was still being thought of as impossible between the modern high speed fighters! Fighters in squadron strength would be jockeying into position to carry out their routine astern attacks on the bomber formations and would simply have to keep a good look-out for any escorting enemy fighters that might wish to make a nuisance of themselves by intervening. However, Douglas was evidently convinced in his views by these arguments and, writing to Air Commodore G B A Baker MC (DArmD) on 13th September 1939, Wing Commander R V M Odbert (DOR) advised that:

> "ACAS has decided that rear armour plate is not required in Spitfires at the moment. However, he wants a scheme produced and a mock up and drawings prepared so that if at a later date rear armour is thought to be worth while we will be in a position to fit it." (6)

This decision was actually confirmed the following month in a note of 13th October from J Hanson, a Senior Scientific Officer in the Directorate of Research and Development, to the DOR. (7)

In the meantime, Dowding wrote to the Under-Secretary of State for Air at the Air Ministry on 22nd September 1939:

> "... yesterday I ... inspected the mock-up arrangement of rear armour in the Hurricane.
>
> 2. I thought that possibly a little weight might be saved in the head-piece, which is 9mm. thick, and in the lower sheet, the area of which might be perhaps slightly reduced.
>
> 3. On the whole, however, I think that the layout is admirable, especially in view of the fact that the armour can be fitted or removed at short notice.
>
> 4. I feel sure that the Field Force Hurricane Squadrons ought to have this armour without a day's unnecessary delay, and I should like to have similar armour provided for Home Defence Fighters for use in the event of the enemy deciding to employ Fighter escorts with his raids on this country.
>
> 5. Removable rear armour should also be provided for Spitfires as soon as possible.
>
> 6. Rear armour for Blenheims is slightly less important, as they will mostly be used for night work and will carry a rear gunner." (8)

So Dowding, at least, was not yet prepared to abandon the rear armour for the Spitfire. Douglas, presumably taking up Dowding's points, wrote to Saundby on 25th September 1939:

> "It is important that the Hurricane squadrons of the Field Force Component should have their back armour installed as soon as possible. ...
>
> My reasons are:
>
> (a) that we may at any moment wish to send additional fighter squadrons to France or to exchange a decimated squadron from the Field Force to the UK, and vice versa. If all our Hurricanes have back armour, we shall have the necessary flexibility;
>
> (b) that it is possible that that the Germans may escort their bombers with fighters. The Hurricane is on the slow side, and may conceivably be attacked from the rear in certain circumstances." (8)

At this time, of course, it was not envisaged that Messerschmitt Bf 109 fighters would be appearing over Britain; flying from bases in Germany, they would simply not have the range.

On 1st October 1939 Squadron Leader J A H Louden in the Directorate of Operational Requirements minuted Saundby with a response to Dowding's letter of 22nd September 1939:

"...

2. The Hurricane with wooden airscrew cannot be fitted with rear armour unless the flare chute is deleted, otherwise the CG is too far aft. The Hurricane with the metal (VP) airscrew could be fitted with rear armour.

3. It was expected that the fitting of VP airscrews to Hurricanes would have commenced by the end of September, ... it would [now] appear that VP airscrews will be fitted to Hurricanes at about the same time as the rear armour plate is available. In case this is not so, I have asked ... [for] a decision from [Dowding] regarding the deletion of the flare chute if it is necessary to fit rear armour to Field Force Hurricanes with wooden airscrews.

4. [Dowding's] intention at present is not to fit rear armour to the Hurricane or the Spitfire immediately, but to accumulate stocks of the armour so that if enemy tactics, ie the use of fighter escorts, necessitates it, rear armour can be fitted to all Home Defence fighters "at a moment's notice".

5. With regard to front armour, all Hurricanes except those of No 1 Squadron are now fitted and arrangements have been made for No 1 Squadron to fly 50% of their aircraft at a time from France and exchange them for Hurricanes fitted with front armour. 50% (ie approximately 100) of the Spitfires in the Service have been fitted with front armour and it is estimated that all Spitfires will have been fitted by the end of November. ..." (9)

Louden had also appended a hand written note reference the rear armour for the Spitfire:

"... the templates are to be prepared but nothing further is to be done as Spitfire production is not good enough to risk any hold up due to the necessity for redesign of the pilot's head-rest which is involved in the fitting of rear armour."

Consequently, by 3rd October Saundby was able to minute the ACAS (Douglas) accordingly, adding that:

"... Production Hurricanes are being turned out fitted with front armour.

C-in-C Fighter Command has now asked that removable rear armour [for the Spitfire] should be provided as soon as possible.

You may recall that we have not gone further than the mock-up and preparation of drawings with Spitfire rear armour owing to the necessity for re-design of the pilot's head rest and consequent risk of interrupting production. In view of Fighter Command's request for this armour you may now wish to incorporate the re-designed head rest in production Spitfires at some date which would not cause delay. In view of the redesign of the head rest however, it would be difficult to put the armour into aircraft already delivered." (10)

Even so on 6th October, only three days later, Douglas was still emphasising that rear armour for the Spitfire was hardly a vital necessity:

> "... The important thing ..... is to get on with the rear armour for Hur-
> ricanes. The Spitfire is the fastest aircraft in the air at the moment, so that
> it should not really be attacked from the rear except when the pilot allows
> himself to be surprised. ...". (11)

On 10th October 1939, Dowding responded to Louden's minute regarding concerns over the effect of armour on the centre of gravity (CG) of the
Hurricane and requested that:

> "... an investigation may be made into the weight of armour it is proposed
> to fit and its actual moments about the CG of the aircraft.
>
> 2. When Hurricane aircraft are fitted with a 2 pitch airscrew (Modification
> 73) it is necessary to fit tail ballast of 25 lbs (modification 87). It is thought
> that instead of 25 lbs tail ballast, armour plate of the equivalent moment
> about the CG should be fitted instead and at the same time as the 2 pitch
> airscrews to unmodified aircraft." (12)

Louden responded on 14th October to Dowding's 10th October inter-
vention on the Hurricane, suggesting in a note to Saundby a reply to
Dowding that included:

> "... Unfortunately, the position and weight of this armour does not provide
> the necessary moment about the CG to permit the deletion of the lead ballast.
> It will therefore be necessary to retain the lead ballast when the rear armour
> is fitted. It is assumed, therefore, that you will not wish the rear armour to
> be fitted until such time as the enemy tactics demand it." (13)

With Louden's response in mind, Saundby wrote again to Dowding on
17th October:

> "... the armour [for the Hurricane] is very close to the CG, and the firm
> consider that it is unlikely that it would be possible to delete more than about
> half of the lead ballast. A final decision will be made when a set of the armour
> is available for installation." (14)

These cautious words had, however, been overtaken by events. It seems
that the decision had, in effect, already been made by 13th October in
discussions between Louden and Mr B Vaughn Williams MSc, a Scientific
Officer in the Air Ministry's Joint Directorate of Research and Development (RDArm3):

> "Action has been taken to equip all Hurricanes with back armour (Field
> Force and Home aircraft.)" (15)

Returning to the Spitfire, Dowding wrote again to the Under-Secretary
of State on 13th October:

> "... I have today inspected the Spitfire with a mock-up of the back armour
> fitted." (16)

He suggested some changes that he thought would "secure a net saving in weight", and in addition recommended:

> "... that armour be supplied for Spitfire Squadrons as quickly as is possible without interfering with the production flow." (16)

Apparently, Dowding's direct contacts with Hawkers and Vickers-Armstrongs had bypassed official channels through Saundby and ruffled a few feathers! However, Saundby was soon back in the action and on 15th October he wrote to Dowding that work was proceeding with the trial installation for the Spitfire rear armour, including modifications suggested by Dowding, and advised that:

> "... As soon as these have been approved, the firm will be instructed to go ahead with the proviso that the minimum interference with the production of this aircraft should be caused." (17)

Meanwhile, the decision by the ACAS back in the January of 1939, that armour protection for the Blenheim fighter should be abandoned, seems to have been reversed. While armouring of the Blenheim bomber was receiving attention, the fighter version was evidently receiving similar attention. On 6th October 1939, Saundby received a report on progress from Group Captain G G Dawson on the Engineering staff at Fighter Command:

> "Blenheim
>
> 25. I understand that everything possible has been done to get the front armour on the Blenheim which the Commander-in-Chief wants. There seems to be some doubt about the bullet proof windscreen, but I understand from you that ACAS has approved this, ..." (18)

Saundby subsequently advised the ACAS on 19th October:

> "The lower armour for the Blenheim Fighter
>
> 2. Templates have just gone to Hadfields, and production is expected to start in six weeks from now. Rate will rise to 20 sets per week after about seven weeks from now. ...
>
> The upper armour and the bullet-proof glass
>
> 3. The design for the windscreen and upper armour is now complete; it will take two–three weeks before the first installation is ready for trial and a further three or four weeks before production can start after that.
>
> 4. To summarise, armour for the Blenheim fighter will begin to arrive in about seven weeks from now." (2)

It is in the context of the ongoing debate about rear armour at this time that the letter of 23rd October 1939 (cf chapter 1) finds its place – a letter that reflected the frustrations of the pilots of No 1 Squadron, already in France as Part of the then Advanced Air Striking Force (AASF) and still waiting for rear armour to be fitted to their Hurricanes. Some of them, it would seem, were still waiting for their front armour as well! The delays in fitting armour to Hurricanes already fighting in France were mainly the results of technical and supply difficulties, but it is possible that there was also a perceived lack of any need for haste at the highest levels of command. Dowding himself, in a report of 25th October 1939 on the "Lessons from the First Air Combats" wrote:

> "....
>
> 7. Pilots in eight-gun Fighters are, of course, exceptionally well protected and my pleasure in the fact that there have so far been no casualties is not diminished by the fact that I had always expected that our casualties would be insignificant compared with those of the enemy.
>
> 8. What has surprised me is the very small number of bullets which have struck our Fighter aircraft at all. I believe that four is the maximum number of hits that any Fighter has received. This is probably due to the fact that the enemy gunner is often incapacitated directly the Fighter opens fire. ..." (19)

In these very early weeks of the war, combats were sporadic and against small numbers of intruders, as the Luftwaffe felt its way tentatively into a new offensive against France and Britain during what has been called the "Phoney War". Indeed, No 1 Squadron's first victory in France did not come until 30th October. However, Dowding's view that his Hurricanes and Spitfires were at that time "exceptionally well protected" does not fit in with the facts and suggests, doubtless with many other things on his mind, that he was not fully cognisant of progress in the armouring his fighters. Even so, the "lessons" that he was prepared to draw from such early engagements with the enemy seem to have been surprisingly – for such a guarded man – premature. Within barely more than a month, as "Pussy" Palmer was able to attest, there was still no full armour for the Hurricanes of No 1 Squadron and the enemy's bullets were beginning to arrive thick and fast.

It was with the 23rd October letter from the AASF evidently in mind that Air Vice-Marshall Playfair, in command of the AASF, wrote from his headquarters in France to the Under Secretary of State on 1st November 1939:

> "... I am in entire agreement with the suggestion put forward in the AASF letter, and have the honour to request that rear armouring of the type suggested should also be provided for the Hurricanes of Nos 85 and 87 Squadrons." (20)

However, the fixed pitch wooden propellers continued to present a problem and Louden wrote on 15th November:

> "As there is no alternative the flare chutes will have to be deleted if it is ever necessary to fit armour to wooden airscrewed Hurricanes. The parts of the VP airscrew modification are now becoming available and I understand that sufficient parts and rear armour will be available by January 1940 to equip all Hurricanes in the Service. Arrangements have been made to ensure that the first supplies of the VP airscrew parts go to Units in France. A certain

amount of rear armour has already been despatched to the Field Force and each plate has with it a leaflet pointing out the necessity for the deletion of the flares if the plate is to be fitted to a Hurricane with a wooden airscrew." (2)

But it was not only the Hurricanes that were a cause for concern and on 22nd November 1939, Louden wrote to RDArm3(d):

" There are now two Gladiator Squadrons in France and the ACAS has asked that armour protection should be provided for the pilot on the highest priority. I do not think we have ever considered armour protection for the Gladiator. ... Past history suggests that you should investigate rear armour as well as front armour. ...

2. A bullet-proof windscreen was developed for the Gladiator and six were made up. As these were not required they were offered to the Admiralty. One was recently delivered to them for a trial installation in a Gladiator at Lee-on-Solent. The other five are ... awaiting disposal." (2)

By 22nd November the problems with at least the front armour for No 1 Squadron began to be sorted out and in response to a Minute from the ACAS, Saundby was informed:

"... [it was] understood from Fighter Command ... that arrangements had been made for [No 1 Squadron] to fly its [Hurricanes] home 50% at a time for exchange with armoured Hurricanes from Fighter Command Squadrons. For some reason this policy was changed and the Hurricanes have, in fact, been flown home in dribbles for the installation of front armour by the firm's working party at Tangmere. Up till approximately the 12th November six armoured Hurricanes had been received by No 1 Squadron and six more were waiting at Tangmere for pilots to come and collect them. ... arrangements had been made to ensure that pilots would come and collect these aircraft as soon as possible and that there would then be only four Hurricanes without armour in the Squadron. ... these would be replaced without delay." (2)

At last, on 25th November, Saundby was able to report to Dowding that:

"... deliveries of rear armour for Hurricanes have already commenced. The first sets are being delivered to the Air Component of the Field Force. As soon as the Field Force has been equipped, sets will be available for aircraft of Fighter Command. It is estimated that sufficient sets will have been produced by January 1940 to equip all Hurricane aircraft.

2. The delivery of parts for the VP airscrew modification has also begun and priority has been given to Hurricanes of the Field Force in order that the CG difficulties involved in fitting rear armour to Hurricanes with wooden airscrews may be avoided. Sufficient sets of parts for the VP airscrew modification to equip all Hurricanes will be available by January 1940.

3. With regard to the Spitfire, 100 sets of the rear armour have been ordered, but it is not yet possible to give any date of delivery." (21)

The first 32 sets of Hurricane rear armour had indeed been despatched to France on 21st November but, as Louden was to inform the AASF on 14th December, they were delivered to the wrong Air Stores Park and lay there undetected for some time! They were eventually discovered and delivered to the Hurricane squadrons. (2)

In the meantime, on the subject of the Gladiator, Loudon had proposed to the DOR on 30th November in response to a query from the ACAS:

"2. It appears to be impossible to fit any front bulkhead, but ... the engine plus 10 gauge cowling and a bullet-proof windscreen would be satisfactory, and, of course, would take less time to incorporate. With regard to the rear armour, as you know, after the trial installation has been cleared it takes at least a further five weeks before any plate is available. ... an attempt should be made to adapt some existing armour plate for the two Squadrons of Gladiators in France. ..." (2)

On 1st December 1939 Saundby was informed that:

" ... ACAS left the question of rear armour for the Spitfire open pending report on trial installation. As you know, this trial installation was rather taken out of our hands by Fighter Command and no proper report was ever received. At the tenth DGRD/ACAS liaison meeting, however, ACAS agreed that 'although it was not proposed to fit back armour to the Spitfire immediately and production of the aircraft was on no account to be delayed, arrangements should be made for the installation to be tooled up and that it would be safe to order 100 sets forthwith'.

... In view of the very marked appetite of the Commands for armour protection, I suggest that although the Spitfire should not be attacked from behind, we should order rear armour for all Spitfires in the Service." (2)

This latter point was brought up again at the 19th meeting of the AFC on 12th February 1940, when Dowding continued to emphasise that:

"... the primary job of fighters was to shoot down bombers, not to fight other fighters, and if manoeuvrability had been sacrificed for performance [ie speed to catch the bomber] it was stupid to give that up." (22)

Even as late as March 1940, problems with the availability of rear armour for all Hurricanes, whether based at home or soon to be posted to France, and home-based Spitfires that were soon to be busy over the Channel and the coastal regions of France were not resolved. On 17th March, Air Vice-Marshal H R Michell of Fighter Command had reason to write to the Under-Secretary of State:

" ... parts are [supposed to be] available at appropriate Maintenance Units for fitting rear armour to Hurricanes.

2. A signal from France on [8th March] ... casts some doubt upon this in connection with the provision of rear armour for Nos 46, 501, 3, 79 and 242 Squadrons.

3. Instructions from this HQ have been sent to these Squadrons to demand rear armour from the appropriate Maintenance Unit.

4. I am required, however, by the AOC-in-C [Dowding] to ask the Air Ministry to reaffirm the policy that rear armour will be provided for all Hurricane and Spitfire Squadrons at Home, though it will not be fitted until needed. ..." (23)

Rowley confirmed the policy directly to Dowding on 9th April. Before that, on 1st April, Douglas had asked Saundby for an update on the situation regarding the rear armour for the Spitfire. Rowley, for Saundby, responded to Douglas on 9th April:

"1. At the 10th DGRD/ACAS Liaison meeting you decided that 'Although it was not proposed to fit back armour to the Spitfire immediately, and production of the aircraft was on no account to be delayed, arrangements should be made for the installation to be tooled up, and that it would be safe to order 100 sets forthwith'.

2. The 100 sets of plate are complete except for one small item. The necessary aircraft fittings to take the armour are being incorporated in production aircraft and are being supplied to the Service for retrospective fitting.

3. In view of the fact that we may have to send Spitfire squadrons to France and as an insurance against the use of escort fighters over this country, I recommend that we should now order sufficient armour plate to fit all Spitfires with rear armour if required." (24)

Douglas passed on the information to the ACAS on 12th April and added:

"... The point now to be decided is whether or not we shall order sufficient sets to fit all Spitfires with rear armour if required. I suggest that it would be wise to do so ... " (25)

Peck and Group Captain D F Stevenson DSO OBE MC (Director of Operations, Home) were in agreement, the latter emphasising:

"... we should press on in great haste ... no time should be lost." (26)

The underlining was in Stevenson's own hand. Douglas instructed Saundby on 14th April to see that rear armour sets were ordered for all Spitfires straight away. (27)

In the meantime also, the AFC had held its 21st meeting on 5th April 1940. It included the following Minute:

"DArmD (Air Commodore J O Andrews, DSO, MC) then referred to the statement in paragraph 11 of AFC 82, which read:

'There is no doubt that the fixed gun fighter can provide itself with sufficient armour to give itself reasonable protection from .303 inch fire coming from ahead.'

... the C-in-C Bomber Command (Air Marshal C F A Portal, CB, DSO, MC) suggested that it should not be assumed that if the enemy fighter was fully armoured they would only shoot him down by shooting through the armour. ... the C-in-C Fighter Command enquired what were the possibilities of armouring the radiator, as this was really the most vulnerable point of a fighter at present ... This led to further discussion on the armouring of fighters. ... [He] had been thinking a good deal about the problem of armouring the fighter in conditions where it was likely to engage other fighters. In these conditions they would require rear armour for the pilot, and armour for the crew of a twin engined fighter. The engines would also be very vulnerable and would require rear armour, and if the tanks were not self-sealing they would also require protection. At the present time they were going for an armoured windscreen and deflection plating. They had not in any sense armoured the engine, which at present was a form of protection in itself, but a heavy concentration of fire from four[-]gun turrets would probably put engines out of action from the front. He remarked, incidentally, that by the time they had armoured the fighter all round it would probably not be very much of a fighter[!]." (28)

However, the Chairman (Douglas) noted that:

"Efforts were being made to improve the protection of future fighters." (29)

On 2nd May the Air Ministry instructed Fighter Command to fit rear armour to all Hurricanes and Spitfires in the Command. (30)

By 10th May, the Hurricane Squadrons to which Michell had referred on 17th March were all fitted with the rear armour, but there were another two (Nos 151 and 504) that were due to be fitted within another 36 hours. (31) Which turned out to be just as well, because all of these Squadrons would soon be in action in France – or elsewhere. Nos 3 and 79 joined the Air Component in France on 10th May; No 501 (AAF) joined the AASF on 10th May; No 504, originally intended for the AASF, was diverted to the Air Component on 11th May; No 46 joined the Norwegian campaign and took part in the battle for Narvik from 26th May; No 242 (and No 17) joined the AASF on or about 5th June; No 151 was essentially Home-based, but during the Battle of France flew daily to French airfields and returned home at night. However, no Spitfires had received rear armour by 10th May, although Wing Commander T N McEvoy in the Directorate of Operations (Home) informed his Director (Stevenson) that:

" ... Fighter Command have all the drawings and instructions ready and will incorporate the armour as soon as they receive the parts. They expect the modification to take about 30 man hours per aircraft at first and later 15 man hours per aircraft when personnel have had experience in fitting. The Squadrons would probably modify about three aircraft at a time." (31)

On 19th May Group Captain R B Mansell OBE, by then DOR, wrote to Stevenson:

" Since [10 May 1940] all outstanding requirements of armour to complete the retrospective fitting of Hurricanes have been delivered. All new production Hurricanes delivered since 22.2.40 have been fitted with the rear armour and the original Squadrons with the BAFF have had this protection for some time.

2. As regards the Spitfire, ... the order of priority of fitting the armour ... is requested." (32)

McEvoy replied (33) on 21st May, pointing out that owing to the movements of Squadrons from one airfield to another – to meet operational demands for the resting and replacement of Squadrons – the order of priority for the respective fitting of armour to Spitfires would best be given in terms of airfields, rather than Squadrons, as follows:

11 Group	12 Group	13 Group
Manston	Debden	Church Fenton
Kenley	Duxford	Catterick
Biggin Hill	Wittering	Usworth
Hornchurch	Digby	Turnhouse
North Weald		Wick
Northolt		
Tangmere		

The priorities were clearly decided on the basis that the airfields closest to the military activity in France (ie those in Fighter Command Group 11, under the command of Air Vice-Marshal Sir Keith Park) were to receive earliest attention, while those farthest away (like Turnhouse and Wick in Scotland) would be the last.

On 10th June, Mansell requested from Dowding his views on suggestions that armour protection should be provided for the oil tank and pipes on the Hurricane and more generally on all fighter aircraft. (34) Dowding's views were given in a reply from Air Vice-Marshall H R Nicholl, Air Officer i/c Administration at Fighter Command, on 16th June:

"... [Dowding is] not in favour of armour protection for the oil tank and pipes in Hurricane aircraft.

2. In general, he is against the armouring of any part of Fighter aircraft except for the protection of personnel.

3. At the same time, the C-in-C favours protection of petrol, oil and glycol tanks by self-sealing material.

4. It is requested that nothing may be done, therefore, with regard to increasing armour protection of any Fighter type without first consulting the C-in-C." (35)

On the same date Mansell, informed Dowding that:

"Arrangements have been made to provide protection for the glycol [engine coolant] tanks for Spitfire and Hurricane aircraft as follows:

(a) Armour plate ... behind the upper top part of the airscrew spinner, and

(b) A 10 gauge dural skin cover, side and top of the glycol tank. This work is now in hand on the highest priority." (36)

Perhaps the two communications crossed in transit but, whatever the circumstances, Dowding vetoed the proposed modification for the Hurricane on 23rd June; (37) he was more accommodating for the Spitfire, preferring self-sealing tanks if possible in accordance with his earlier position but otherwise accepting front armour for the glycol coolant tanks. In view of these proposals and later approved modifications, it is interesting to note a report from the Air Tactics Branch back in the January of 1940, issued to the Air Fighting Committee as Report No 78 (38), in which the results of examinations of 18 German aircraft shot down showed that the majority had been brought down as a result of damage to their engines:

Cause of aircraft loss	Number of aircraft brought down	Aircraft type(s)
Damage to engine(s)	12	He 111 bomber (5), Do 18 flyingboat (2), He 115 seaplane (2), Bf 109 fighter (1), Ju 88 bomber (1), "Float plane" (1).
Damage to engine(s) and injuries to crew	2	He 111, Ju 88, bombers.
Wounding of crew	1	Do 18 flyingboat.
Anti-aircraft fire	1	Ju 88 bomber.
Damage to controls	1	Do 17 bomber.
Cause unknown	1	He 115 seaplane.

The evidence from these examinations, though limited in terms of the number of aircraft involved, ought not to have been too surprising: the engines and their functionality were particular sources of vulnerability – as firing trials against engines, in the run up to the war and even going back as far as 1913, before the previous war, had consistently demonstrated fairly conclusively. There was an "illuminating" additional comment in the Report:

> "5. A further point of interest is that, although it is known that German aircraft are equipped with very efficient self-sealing tanks. No less than 5 of the 14 aircraft which sustained damage to engines by machine gun fire caught fire in the air in addition to one which was set on fire by AA.
> ..."

So functionality of engines, their ability to continue running after sustaining damage, was not the only source of vulnerability. The technology of self-sealing fuel tanks was by no means new at the beginning of the war but, of course, it was not just the tanks that carried fuel – the fuel lines to the engine and engine components were all, given penetration by incendiary bullets or the ignition of leakages by incendiaries or sparks , likely to be set ablaze. Aeroplanes were decidedly inflammable machines in the wrong circumstances!

For the Hurricane, the bullet-proof windscreen (Mod/44) and the rear armour (Mod/128) were later included as official modifications. (39) In the case of the Spitfire, relevant official modifications up to mid-1940 were:

- Mod/119 (28.8.39), a revision of Mod 36 to facilitate production of armour plate,
- Mod/140 (10.11.39), for rear armour (fixed),
- Mod/146 (10.11.39), for rear armour (removable);
- Mod/247 (6.6.40), armour protection for the Glycol (coolant) header tank.
- Mod/248 (6.6.40), armour protection for the fuel header tank.

A process of review, leading to progressive developments in armour protection and concentrating increasingly as time went by on engine functionality, was therefore already in hand by the middle of 1940. Other modifications were to follow – additional armour for the fuel pump, additional deflection panels for the pilot's seat and detachable plate for the coolant pipes below the header tank. These later additions undoubtedly reflected the increasing involvement of the Spitfire in the general mêlée of the air fighting over South-East England and the progressive extension of incursive operations into France once the Battle of Britain had been won.

Boulton Paul Defiant

The armour protection situation for the Defiant appears to have become rather confused by the beginning of 1940. On 8th January, notwithstanding the scheme developed in February/March 1939, Louden minuted RD Arm:

> "In view of the tactics likely to be employed by Defiant pilots it is impossible to provide an adequate protection scheme for the pilot. No attempt is being made to do so and the ruling of the Armour Committee that a bullet-proof windscreen is not required still holds." (40)

Louden's minute no doubt reflected the view that in practice the Defiant, with its ability by rotating the gun turret to attack enemy bombers from any position, not necessarily from behind or in the "no allowance" position, would be subject to enemy fire from any direction and all-round armour protection was simply impracticable. However, this was evidently not the official position and, on 25th January 1940, it was minuted by Hanson (RD/Arm 3(d)) that the following scheme was being fitted to the Defiant in production:

"1. The armour carried on the Defiant is:

Pilot   4mm armour back and head plate

Gunner   9mm armour face plate.

2. This was derived as follows:

(a) It was considered at first that the Defiant would be used for [no allowance] firing and the scheme suggested by RD/Arm and agreed upon by DOR was a bullet-proof windscreen and front armour ... .

237

(b) When the Armouring Committee considered the Defiant ... it was decided that the front armour should be deleted (view endorsed by the C-in-C Fighter Command ... and recently confirmed ...) and rear protection provided as in the above scheme 1.

3. No consideration was given by the Armouring Committee to fuel protection which has recently been raised in connection with the general policy of providing 100% self sealing tanks.

It is not very convenient to apply a self sealing cover to the Defiant fuel tanks and so it has been decided, for the time being, not to proceed with the protection of fuel tanks ...

4. This latter decision appears to give rise to the impression that no armour is carried on the aircraft whereas the scheme at 1 is fitted to all Defiants" (41)

It may have taken a little time, but Rowley confirmed in a minute to McEvoy on 7th May the position stated by Hanson:

"The position in respect of rear armour for the Defiant is as follows:

2. Existing protection incorporated in production consists of a bulk-head 4mm plate behind the pilot's head, also a measure of protection is given to the pilot by the structure of the turret. The rear gunner is protected to a degree by the structure of the turret, in addition to a small piece of armour plate between the guns.

3. It is not considered that any further protection to the pilot is practicable. Protection to the rear gunner, however, could be improved by incorporating two pieces of 6mm plate on the outside of the two lower ammunition containers. This would serve a dual purpose in that it would protect both thighs of the rear gunner and also the ammunition containers, but only when the turret is turned towards the direction from which the attack is delivered. ..." (42)

There was no reference to protection for any of the oil/fuel/coolant tanks, but this was in line with Hanson's minute. However, the matter of the Defiant's armour was not quite settled and as late as 9th June 1940 Mansell wrote to Dowding, indicating his (Mansell's) decision to investigate the addition of rear armour:

"4. It is not proposed to introduce this rear armour protection to the Defiant aircraft, retrospectively or in production line at present, but it is considered very desirable to have an accepted scheme ready if required. ..." (43)

Dowding eventually gave his assent to the preparation of a scheme for rear armour protection on 17th July 1940, (44) though it is not recorded that such protection was in the event ever actually "required".

Gloster Gladiator

On 30th November 1939 Louden drafted a note to the ACAS from the DOR:

"(i) Action has been taken to provide armour protection for the Gladiator. In the past the only protection which had been developed was the bullet-proof wind-screen for the pilot. Gloucesters have been asked to put this on a production basis. It is not possible to fit the front armour bulk head to the Gladiator but a considerable degree of protection is provided by the engine, in conjunction with strengthened cowling.

(ii) A scheme for rear protection for the pilot has been drawn up but as the armour plate takes some time to manufacture I have asked DArmD to investigate immediately the possibility of adapting existing plate. ..." (2)

The records do not show when these modifications were completed, but the presumption must be that they were. The Malta Operational Intelligence Summary for the period 11th October 1940 to 10th February 1941 reported that all Gladiators had been fitted with the variable-pitch airscrew. (45) Sea Gladiators, four of them in fact, had been the sole air defence of Malta when the Italian Regia Aeronautica began their attacks on 11th June 1940, though by the end of the month the remaining three were bolstered by the presence of four Hurricanes.

The Summary also mentioned that some Short Sunderlands had been "armour plated" to give adequate protection to the rear gunner, but a shortage of armour plate had temporarily delayed the completion of this modification to the aircraft of the Squadrons involved.

Westland Whirlwind

The Westland Whirlwind appears to have been the first of the RAF's "modern fighters" to feature armour from an early stage in its development – from, in fact, the second prototype (L6845). L6845 was delivered to No 25 Squadron for service trials on 30th May 1940 and featured a bullet-proof windscreen, armour plate behind the pilot's aluminium seat and a two-part bullet-proof bulkhead in the nose through which the barrels of the four 20mm canon passed (46).

However, even for the Whirlwind, the installation of rear armour was not automatic. Rowley noted on 24th March 1940:

"... Rear armour plate is now also a requirement for the twenty fast reconnaissance Whirlwinds. Although this is not so urgent as the fitting of armour into the Spitfires, it should be incorporated with the least possible delay. ..." (47)

Yet, by 1st June 1940 Dowding was forced to write to the Under-Secretary of State:

" ... the first [Whirlwinds] have been received and allocated to No 25 Squadron.

2. No provision has been made for rear armour, and it is stressed that this is most important. ..." (48)

Dowding evidently got his way for, on 28th June, Air Commodore R B Mansell (Director of Operational Requirements) wrote to Dowding:

Whirlwind front armour in the form of bullet-proof nose bulkheads. (Courtesy Philip Jarrett).

... arrangements have been made for all Whirlwind aircraft to be fitted with rear armour.

2. The armour was not available in time to enable the first few aircraft to be fitted before delivery and the makers have been instructed to arrange for its installation in these aircraft at the Unit to which they are allotted as soon as possible." (49)

Bristol Beaufighter

At the 20th meeting of the AFC on 12 March 1940, with Douglas still in the Chair, the Chairman himself noted that:

"At the moment the Beaufighter had no rear armament at all. Was it possible that this could be dispensed with altogether? ... Could the Beaufighters be made fast enough to adopt evasive tactics if they met with superior forces of enemy fighters? (50)

As to the necessity for increasing the speed to the maximum possible, even at the expense of extra armament, the question of armour was more relevant:

"..., the Chairman remarking that as much [armour] as possible would be needed in the rear of the aircraft. The C-in-C Fighter Command suggested that provision should be made for armour. But that it should not actually be fitted ... [it] would not be required for normal trade defence work, but in the event of fighters being sent into the Heligoland Bight it would be needed very badly." (51)

However:

"The DGRD [Tedder] advised caution in this respect. He said there had been cases where the armour had been made detachable and it had resulted in many complications during the building of the aircraft. That being the case, he thought it might be better to accept the extra weight for all time ... " (52)

Tedder's wise council evidently prevailed, because the Committee went on to agree that "... rear armour is undoubtedly necessary and should be incorporated". (53) The Committee's wishes were undoubtedly fulfilled and, at the end of 1941, a survey (54) of armour protection provisions among fighter aircraft submitted to Fighter Command's headquarters by Air Vice-Marshal Trafford Leigh-Mallory included the following:

"6. The [following] BEAUFIGHTER armour is considered to be a satisfactory minimum and no alterations are recommended. ...

	Detail	Projection	Weight
1.	Front fusleage	Forward of Pilot	144.3lb
2.	Rear Fuselage	Astern of Crew	87.2lb
3.	Centre Section Rear Spar	Fuel Tank And Structure And Pilot Astern	71.1lb
	Total Weight		302.6lb"

241

22 Bombers and reconnaissance aircraft

As with the fighters under Dowding's command, so it was with the aircraft of Bomber Command. The outbreak of actual fighting, with high loss rates being suffered by the Hampdens, Blenheims and Wellingtons during daylight shipping raids during only the first month, brought forth an almost immediate enthusiasm for the protection that armour could provide. Air Commodore N H Bottomly CIE DSO AFC, a Senior Staff Officer at the Uxbridge headquarters of Bomber Command, reported to Air Chief Marshal E R Ludlow-Hewitt, the C-in-C of Bomber Command, on 21st September 1939, barely three weeks into the conflict, on the current state of armouring bombers:

"Armour

... the following is the position regarding the fitting of armour to aircraft at present in service:

Blenheim IE

Pilot – Back and seat.

Navigation – Back.

Gunner – Aft of turret.

Battle

Pilot and Observer – Dural Plate on floor.

Pilot – Back of seat.

Air gunner – Aft of cockpit.

Hampden

Pilot – Seat.

Upper and lower mid turrets.

Wing inner fuel tanks." (55)

Details of armour fitted to the Wellington Mk I were also included, but after the passage of over sixty years they do not seem to be very meaningful – even supposing that they might have been to those back in 1939.

Air Vice-Marshall Playfair, Officer Commanding the AASF (essentially No 1 Group, Bomber Command), wrote from his headquarters in France on 13th October 1939 to the Under-Secretary of State on the subject of defences for the Blenheim and the Lysander:

"... during a recent visit of an Armament Commission ..., the question was raised as to the adequacy of single Lewis guns as a rear armament in Blenheim and Lysander aircraft, in particular having in view the fact that these reconnaissance aircraft rely more particularly on rear defence against attack, and not to any great extent on their front guns." (56)

Requesting at least a doubling of their rear armament, he also suggested that:

"... the question of providing armour in both Blenheim and Lysander air-craft should immediately be considered. It is understood that both Hurricane and Battle aircraft are either already provided with armour or shortly will be, and it is further understood from Intelligence Reports that the armour on some of the Battles has already had an actual test and has proved its value. It is hoped, therefore, that armour will quickly be provided for Blenheim and Lysander aircraft." (56)

What these two apparently straightforward communications primarily indicate is that even at this early stage in the War there were some mixed messages. Bottomly's report to the C-in-C Bomber Command that armour had already been fitted to Blenheim aircraft could be taken to imply that this included the Blenheims in France, whereas Playfair's letter suggested that the Blenheims in France had not yet been armoured. Playfair's AASF Squadrons did not at the outset include any Blenheims, only Battles and Hurricanes, although two Blenheim Squadrons joined the AASF in mid-September; the Air Component under the command of Air Vice-Marshal C H B Blount CB OBE MC included both Blenheim and Lysander Squadrons. Perhaps, therefore, Bottomly's earlier report did indeed refer only to bombers at the disposal of Bomber Command at home. Nevertheless, some aircraft must by October have been fitted with armour protection and nothing could better demonstrate the enthusiasm with which the necessity for it had so quickly become appreciated than a letter of 26th October 1939 from Ludlow-Hewitt himself, to the Under-Secretary of State at the Air Ministry, emphasising that:

"   ... the need for strengthening up the defensive armour of bombers in every way possible has been confirmed by our war experience. Where this cannot be done it will be necessary to consider some special means of strengthening bomber formations, probably in the form of heavily armed bombers in the rear of the formation.

2.   The armour plating provided for bombers has proved most satisfactory, and the extension of this armour to provide protection for the wing tanks is especially required. At the present this is being done by the introduction of a flat plate, which is uneconomical in weight and provides no protection for the tanks from below. I recommend that a better method would be to strengthen up the metal of the wing over that part which covers the tanks. This strengthened part would be confined mainly to the rear portion of the wing behind the tanks, but could be carried on underneath the tanks for protection against fire from below.

3.   Consideration should also be given to the possibility of increasing the defensive strength of bombers of all types at the sacrifice of bomb load, the idea being to make possible, if it proves necessary, the special strengthening of a limited number of bombers of every type with a view to using them as a rearguard to the formations. ..." (57)

Doubtless without even realising it, what Ludlow-Hewitt was advocating was "Douhet-ism" in its full force!

But the presence of armour protection was by no means universal, certainly not in France. On 13th November, Saundby wrote to the Air Officer Commanding (AOC) the Air Component at his headquarters in France indicating that extra rear guns for the Blenheim and the Lysander were indeed being considered by the Aeroplane and Armament Experimental Establishment (A&AEE). 20 sets of Blenheim armour were also on their way to the Air Component in France and a further 22 sets were due in a few days. For the Lysander, the rear gunner's armour plate would be available in three weeks and first deliveries would go to the Air Component. (58)

On 24th November, Saundby advised the AOC HQ Air Component in France:

"... investigations are proceeding on the highest priority into the possibility of fitting double ... guns to both Blenheim and Lysander aircraft. In the case of the Blenheim it will involve some redesign of the turret ... The fitting of double ...guns to the Lysander is being investigated by the A&AEE. If these installations prove satisfactory efforts will be made to equip aircraft of the Air Component as soon as possible.

2. Arrangements have been made for the despatch of Blenheim armour to the Air Component ... Armour plate for the rear gunner of the Lysander will be available in three weeks and arrangements have been made to send the first deliveries to the Air Component." (58)

Meanwhile, 6th November had seen at Shoeburyness the last of the Blenheim firing trials of 1939. On this occasion, 13.2mm Belgian Browning copper-cupped solid ammunition was to be fired in single shots against an armoured Blenheim with self-sealing tanks from directly astern at a range of 200 yards. The pilot and observer/navigator were to be protected in the usual way: 4mm armour head and back plates for the former and 4mm armour head plate for the latter. However, on this occasion the gunner was to be protected by a 4mm armour chest plate and 4mm armour body plates in the form of a V-form bulkhead with the plates at 60° to the direction of fire. In the port wing, the petrol tank (full of water) was to be protected by a 4mm armour back plate, while the oil tank (also full of water) was to be left unprotected. In a separate Starboard wing, the petrol tank (full of petrol) was to be protected by self-sealing material (½ inch SEMAPE), as was the oil tank (full of oil).

On 1st December, a note from Louden advised that the Royal Aircraft Establishment's design of face plate for the Blenheim's rear gunner had been ordered over a month previously and that supplies were expected shortly. The Blenheim Squadrons of the Air Component in France had actually requested the ACAS, apparently "unofficially", to ensure the provision of the face plates. (2)

On 5th December Saundby, presumably replying to Ludlow-Hewitt's earlier letter to the Under-Secretary of State and probably reflecting the results of the November and earlier firing trials, reported that:

" ... the importance of methods of defence for bombers is constantly under review.

2. It is agreed that the existing armour for wing tanks provides no more than a limited protection. It has, however, now been decided that all bomber aircraft are to be fitted with 100% self-sealing tanks. By this means we hope to provide protection against both fire and loss of fuel. Retrospective action will be taken to apply self-sealing tanks as soon as possible to all existing types. It is difficult to use the self-sealing principle in integral tanks, but investigations are proceeding into the use of possible alternatives to the present method of self-sealing. It will, however, probably be necessary in such cases to rely on armour and on strengthening up the metal of the wing to act as a deflector.

3. Efforts are being made to increase the fire power and armour protection of both present and future types of bomber aircraft. ..." (59)

But the War was not going to wait and in the light of continuing losses Ludlow-Hewitt felt constrained to write once again to the Under-Secretary of State on 16th December, this time to express his concern over the vulnerability of the Wellington Bomber to attack:

"   ... in the recent air battle in which three Wellingtons were shot down by enemy fighters, it has been reported that fire appeared to originate from the port side fuel tanks which are unarmoured, while the starboard tanks are armoured.

2. It is understood that the port tanks are unarmoured owing to weight limitations. The weight of armour for the port side tanks is 110lb and can be partly offset by removing the Zwickey refuelling gear. ...

3. ... It is understood that when self-sealing tanks are eventually fitted, the increase in weight will be considerably in excess of what is now proposed." (60)

Louden replied to Ludlow-Hewitt on 25th December:

"2. Stocks of plates for starboard wing tanks are being used for this purpose, and Messers Vickers have undertaken to fit one Wellington per day at Weybridge commencing on 19th December. The firm have been instructed to communicate direct with Bomber Command in order to arrange for the aircraft to be flown over to Weybridge.

3. Vickers have also taken immediate action to fit this additional protection in production aircraft until such time as self-sealing tanks are available. ..." (61)

There was similar correspondence, with similar results, on the subject of the Hampden on 19th December and 4th January 1940. The RAF establishment was clearly responding to the experiences of the fighting squadrons, albeit slowly.

Fairey Battle

Some at least of the Fairey Battles were fitted with armour by the October of 1939 – as Paul Richey's account (cf Part I) bears witness. During 22nd and 23rd September 1939 there was an examination of the remains of two Battles shot down by Bf 109s in France on 19th September, close to the border with Germany. Both pieces of armour plating from the air gunner's position of one Battle, shot down at Hazembourg were examined; the armour from the pilot's seat and from the floor of the observer's cockpit could not be identified. From the other Battle, shot down at Juvelize, both pieces of armour from the air gunner's position and that from the pilot's seat were available; the armour from the observer's cockpit was embedded in the wreckage and it had been hoped that it would be recovered for examination later. The investigation report stated:

> "20. The only bullet marks on the pieces examined was one mark on each of those lower plates covering the air gunner's leg. In each case the bullet had struck the plate sideways and had not penetrated. In both cases however, the plate was indented and sufficiently cracked to let light through. It is considered therefore, that these plates have already shown their worth." (62)

The report concluded:

> "(i) There was considerable evidence of bullets being deflected by the aircraft structure. The bullets did not in any case penetrate the armour plating. Though in two instances the plate was badly dented by bullets which had struck after being deflected. Despite this one gunner was shot in the head and one observer in the leg." (62)

So there can be no doubt that armour had been fitted to Battles by the onset of the war, but in the cases instanced it had not saved the aircraft from being shot down. By the latter part of 1939, concern was already being expressed about the Battle's armour protection as a result of experience in the firing line:

> "It seems probable that the Battle will be used for low flying. The armour which they have got at present has doubtless saved some people's lives, but the petrol tanks in the wings seem to be the most vulnerable part of the aeroplane. Is it practicable to armour them against fire from below or possibly fit some form of self-sealing tank." (63)

There had been a visit on 27th October to Faireys' by Air Ministry staff, accompanied by personnel from No 150 Squadron of the Advance Air Striking Force (AASF), to review the situation regarding armour for the Battle. The problem was that:

> "Fighting in France has revealed that the armour provided is proving quite satisfactory except that there are certain gaps where bullets are getting through." (64)

For example, the wireless set originally thought to give added protection to the upper gunner did not do so in practice. Since the Battles operating in France at that time were without the fuselage fuel tank, it was suggested that the 300lb made available should be used to provide added crew armour of 100lb, added wing tank protection of 100lb and a further gun with ammunition amounting to 40lb. Proposals were discussed and modified at a further meeting on 20th December. Indeed, Douglas (ACAS) minuted Saundby on 27th October:

> "... the Battle squadrons are very anxious to get the step leading down from the gunner's position into the observer's cockpit fitted with armour ..." (65)

Saundby was, unfortunately, only able to advise on 8th November that:

> "It was found possible to adapt the armour plates of the existing Battle installation to fill up all the gaps, except at the point mentioned in your minute. ..." (65)

Official instructions for the fitting of armour did appear in March 1940 (66), Modification B70 190/40 of 15 March 1940 described the fitting of additional shield plates to frame 12 and the rear end of the fuel tank. Modification 925909/39 of 23 March gave similar details and drawings for:

- a back shield for the pilot,
- a shield plate for the bomb-aimer's floor,
- an air-gunner's shield at frame 12 and
- an air-gunner's shield fitted to the support bracket of the rotatable gun mounting.

These Modifications were presumably issued in consolidation of decisions made back in 1939.

Bristol Blenheim Bomber

In the case of the Blenheim in its primary rôle as a bomber, it has already been seen that the main concern throughout 1939 and early 1940 was how to increase the defensive armament by adding more guns and or gun turrets. Such armament was required to overcome what was described in a letter of 17th April 1940 to Saundby (by then an Air Commodore, Acting Air Vice-Marshal, and Assistant Chief of Air Staff, Operations Requirements and Tactics) as the "... appalling lack of defences from which the Blenheim suffers" (67). Rather despairingly, perhaps, Saundby replied on 19th April:

> "... the additional weight which we have recently put into it in the form of self-sealing tanks, armour, and additional guns has just about obliterated the bomb load." (68)

Nevertheless, the two-gun armament (.303 inch machine gun in the port wing and Vickers 'K' gun in a dorsal turret) of the Mark I Blenheims was progressively replaced in the Mark IV and V bomber versions by a five gun fitting, comprising two .303 inch guns in the dorsal turret and two more in a remotely controlled under-nose blister firing aft in addition to the original post wing gun.

But bombing and fighter work were not the only rôles envisaged for the Blenheim. Chaz Bowyer (69) has recorded that:

> "Bristol Co proposed in January 1940 a specialised derivation of the Blenheim [IV] for [close tactical support of the army] duties, though with alternative duties as a 'low-level fighter' ..."

The proposed new version, reminiscent of the Trench Fighters of the earlier War with Germany, was to be called the "Bisley". Bowyer goes on to describe that:

> "An improved design of windscreen was fitted, while in view of its intended 'deck level' roles the Bisley's whole cockpit was externally protected by some 600lb weight of detachable armour plate. Further armour-plating was thoughtfully provided for the dorsal air gunner's cockpit-cum-turret."

Vickers–Armstrongs Wellington

Until the arrival in service towards the end of 1940 and early in 1941 of the first of the four-engined "heavies", the Handley Page Halifax and the Short Stirling heavy bombers, the twin-engined Wellington was the foremost British bomber. From late 1940 onwards, a typical installation of armour protection comprised armour plates on rubber mountings for the protection of the crew against gun fire from the rear, as follows:

(i) Behind the wireless operator, between the central post and the port side of the fuselage in the upper half of the cabin; this partly protected the Pilot and the Wireless Operator.

(ii) A plate, in two parts, under the navigator's table and fixed to the geodetic bracing; this completed the protection of the Pilot and the Wireless Operator.

(iii) A pair of plates hinged to a central post aft of the sextant dome for protection when use was being made of the latter; when not being used, the plates could be folded back out of the way. (70)

Some armour plating was apparently also provided within the gun turrets. (71)

Handley Page Halifax

The Halifax built to Air Ministry Specification P.13/36, which was actually the second of the RAF's four-engined heavy bombers, entered service at the end of November 1940; the first prototype flew a year earlier, at the end of October 1939. By the November of 1939 the scheme for armour protection for the Halifax was already under review and on 21st November

Louden advised the DOR (Odbert) that:

"... The original scheme was to provide the usual armour in the turrets and to armour the back of the pilot's seat. In view, however, of the increased use likely to be made of the second pilot's seat and of the sextant position aft of the first pilot's seat when being attacked, it was felt that the armouring scheme should provide protection for these two points. It was decided that the simplest way to give adequate protection to both the pilots' positions and the sextant position would be to put an armoured bulkhead right across the fuselage behind the engine instrument panel; the bulkhead would incorporate a door of suitable width to allow easy passage for the crew. The bulkhead would be of 6mm magnetic armour and would permit of the deletion of the armour plate in rear of the pilots' seat. In addition to the bulkhead it is pro-posed to fit bullet-proof glass in rear of both the pilots' heads in lieu of the existing engine instrument board inspection windows. It was decided that a 4mm plate should be fitted to the forward bulkhead of the bomb cell. This bulkhead would provide protection for the wireless operator, the navigator and the pilot's landing flares; all being situated in the nose of the aircraft below the level of the fuselage bulkhead. The total weight of the installation will be between 350 and 400lb. It will be necessary to compensate for this either by a reduction in fuel or bomb load, but in view of the value of the protection provided I think we should accept this. Possibly [a]Sub–committee may be able to balance this increase without loss of fuel or bombs. ..." (2)

Subject to Odbert's agreement with the revised scheme, Louden was prepared to take the necessary action. Unfortunately, the records do not include Odbert's response.

23 German Aircraft

In the meantime, the RAF was trying to improve its knowledge of the extent to which enemy and especially German aircraft were armoured. A Heinkel He 111 was brought down on 28th October 1939 at Haddington, on the northern edge of the Lammermuir Hills, Scotland, by Spitfires of Nos 602 and 603 Squadrons (Auxiliary Air Force, AAF). The rear gunner and the W/T operator were both killed, but the navigator/bombaimer/ photographer was uninjured and interned in the Tower of London. The pilot was seriously wounded but survived the crash; it was reported by Squadron Leader A E Dark of the Air Tactics Branch in AFC Report No 76 that:

> "... The aircraft was riddled by so many bullets [aproximately 200 motly in the fuselage] it was impossible to count them in the time available. ... The pilot's stomach wounds were caused by 3 bullets which had entered the roof, passed through a bulkhead and several thin metal pieces of equipment and the metal back of his seat. ...
>
> I made a thorough examination and could find no sign of any armour. "
> (72)

The Aeroplane, on 9th November 1939 carried an article on an He 111K shot down by AAF Spitfires on the Lammermoor Hills in Scotland on 28th October in which the pilot was seriously wounded. (73) The article included a photograph showing the "bullet-pierced pilot's seat" referred to by Dark. Evidently, the metal plating behind the pilot was not capable of resisting the bullets from the .303 inch machine guns with which the Spitfires would then have been armed – suggesting that, indeed, it was not armour plate.

A Messerschmitt Bf 109 brought down by the French Air Force was examined on 25th and 26th September 1939 by Wing Commander C P Brown of the Air Tactics Branch; he reported in AFC Report No 72 as follows:

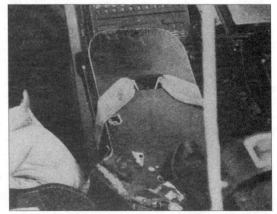

Heinkel 111 shot down in the UK in October 1939, showing bullet penetrations in the metal-backed pilot's seat. (The Aeroplane, 9th November 1939)

(Reproduced by permission of Aeroplane Magazine / www.aeroplanemonthly. com.)

"Armour. No armour was fitted and the [fuel] tank did not appear to be of the self-sealing type.

Pilot's cockpit. No armour plate was fitted." (74)

In the later months of 1939 and the early months of 1940, information continued to be scarce, as the following extracts from Fighter Command daily Intelligence Summaries (75) illustrate:

- 6 December 1939, He 115 seaplane wrecked near Sheringham – no armour mentioned;
- 9/12 February 1940, Bf 109 captured in France – no armour mentioned, but self-sealing tanks noted;
- 31 March/2 April 1940, crashed Bf 109 – no armour mentioned;
- 29 April/2 May 1940, He 111 crashed at Clacton-at-Sea – mention of armour for the first time;
- 5/7 June 1940, Ju 88 shot down in France – armour definitely reported, giving complete protection from the back to the pilot's body and head;
- 18 June 1940, Ju 88Z – now protected by armour;
- 19 June 1940, He 111 shot down over Chelmsford – armour definitely used to protect the pilot and the top/rear gunner, its value shown by the marks of what appeared to be 10–15 bullet strikes;
- 24/29 June, Ju 88 – as for 19 June;
- 5/9 August 1940, Ju 87 brought down near Ventnor – 8mm thick armour protection for the pilot's head and rear gunner, with similar armour along the gunner's floor;
- 9/13 August 1940, He 111, Do 17Z and Ju 88 – all found with *increased* armour plating.

Quite separately, an intelligence report from a Bomber Command crew dated as early as 5th January 1940 suggested that:

"... the Me 110 is armoured on front and on leading edge as bullets were smothering them at ranges of 150 yards and under with apparently effect." (76)

A French report of 6th February 1940 on an He 111H brought down in French lines clearly stated that the aircraft had no armour plating. (77) A further Air Intelligence Report dated 26th August 1940 on an Me 110 that crashed at Great Bentley near Colchester described details of three pieces of armour plate that were salvaged from the crater. (78)

What seems evident from these few reports is that armour was a rare commodity in the early months of the War. However, once the Luftwaffe began to come up against serious opposition from British fighters in the Battle of France – fighters that were more than equal to the German bombers and could compete on reasonable terms, especially given the temporary "home advantage" of operating from French airfields, with their bombers' Bf 109 and 110 escorts – defensive armour was quickly found to be not just an attractive proposition but an operational necessity. The Messerschmitt Bf 109 single-seater fighter is a case in point. The Bf 109E, a development from the Bf 109B version that served effectively in Spain, appeared in time for the invasion of Poland in September 1939 and was the mainstay of the German fighter force during the Battles of France and Britain during 1940. The early versions of the Bf 109E – the E-1 saw service in Poland and the E-3 in France and the earlier phases of the Battle of Britain – were not generally armoured, but a series of modifications resulted in the 109E-4 version comprising, according to Bickers (78): a bullet-proof windscreen, 8mm of seat armour weighing 53lb and a curved plate attached to the hinged canopy weighing a further 28.6lb. The E-4, used increasingly during the later phases of the Battle of Britain, appears to have been the first variant on which the entire production batch was fitted with the flat-topped cockpit hood with its associated armour plate behind the pilot's head; although this was retrospectively introduced on earlier models, many apparently flew throughout the Battle of Britain without this modification.(79) A few sites of crashed Me 109s, excavated in South-East England over recent years, have revealed that at least some of the fighters were fitted with a complete armour plate bulkhead behind the pilot. The bulkhead was split vertically into two halves, suggesting that it was fitted in service rather than during initial construction of the fuselage.

The Junkers Ju 87 dive bomber also served first in Spain, then in Poland and the Battle of France; though it saw some service in its B and R (long range) versions in the early phases of the Battle of Britain, it proved to be far too vulnerable to British fighters to remain in the Battle and was soon withdrawn. The Ju 87 B/R, being designed specifically to attack ground targets in tactical support of the advancing German Army, was equipped with a minimum of armour for protection. The arrival of the

Table 23.1. Comparison of Ju 87 B/R and D variants

Armour	Ju 87 B/R	Ju 87 D
Frontal:		8mm
Windshield:		2 inch b.p. glass
Pilot's seat:	8mm	Head, 10mm
		Back, 4-8mm
Dorsal:	8mm; occ 2 inch b.p. glass	5mm (in roof)
Lateral:		6mm (cockpit sides)
Ventral:		5mm (floor plates)
Bulkhead:	9mm	8mm (for gunner)
Engine	Coolant flaps, 4mm	Radiators, 3.5mm

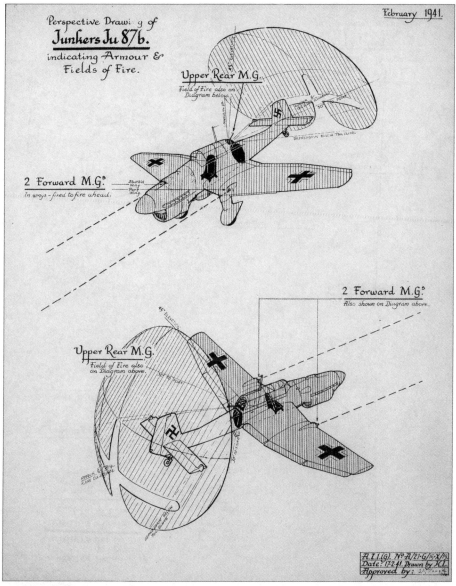

(Public Record Office, AIR 20/64)

D-series, in the run up to Germany's Operation Barbarossa (invasion of Russia) in June 1941, led to a number of extensively armoured versions that were used increasingly on the Russian Front in the tank-busting rôle. A comparison of the armour fitted to the B/R and D variants is summarised, from an American intelligence source document (80), in Table 23.1.

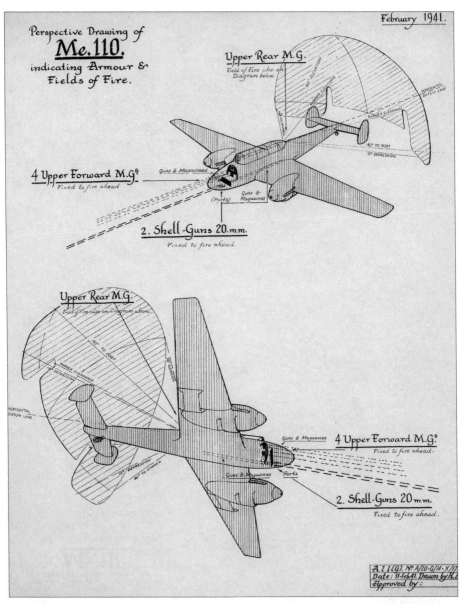

(Public Record Office, AIR 20/43)

From the start of hostilities, the RAF gathered what information it could about the armour protection of German aircraft on a continuing basis. In February 1941 the Air Intelligence Branch actually provided drawings showing the armour fitted to various German aircraft.(81) (82)) If these drawings were truly representative of the protection schemes fitted by the beginning of 1941, they were evidently still fairly basic and minimal.

1 Public Record Office, AIR 2/3353.
2 Public Record Office, AIR 20/12.
3 Public Record Office, AIR 2/5103, Minute 13.
4 Public Record Office, AIR 2/5103, Minute 15.
5 Public Record Office, AIR 2/5103, Minute 14.
6 Public Record Office, AIR 2/5103, piece 17A
7 Public Record Office, AIR 2/5103, piece 21A.
8 Public Record Office, AIR 2/5103, piece 18A
9 Public Record Office, AIR 2/5103, piece/minute sheet 18B.
10 Public Record Office, AIR 2/5103, Minute 19.
11 Public Record Office, AIR 2/5103, Minute 20.
12 Public Record Office, AIR 2/5103, piece 22A.
13 Public Record Office, AIR 2/5103.
14 Public Record Office, AIR 2/5103, piece 25A.
15 Public Record Office, AIR 2/3353, piece 51C.
16 Public Record Office, AIR 2/5103, piece 23A.
17 Public Record Office, AIR 2/5103, piece 24A.
18 Public Record Office, AIR 20/167, document FC/S.17786/Tech/D.O.
19 Public Record Office, AIR 16/299, piece 1A.
20 Public Record Office, AIR 2/5103, piece 28A.
21 Public Record Office, AIR 2/5103, piece 33A.
22 Public Record Office, AIR 2/1646, piece 113A, minute 52.
23 Public Record Office, AIR 2/5103, piece 43A.
24 Public Record Office, AIR 2/5103, minute 47.
25 Public Record Office, AIR 2/5103, minute 49.
26 Public Record Office, AIR 2/5103, minute 51.
27 Public Record Office, AIR 2/5103, minute 52.
28 Public Record Office, AIR 2/1647, piece 14C, minutes 30–33.
29 Public Record Office, AIR 2/1647, piece 14C, minute 34.
30 Public Record Office, AIR 2/1647, piece 14C, minute 58.
31 Public Record Office, AIR 2/5103, piece 61A, minute 1.
32 Public Record Office, AIR 2/5103, piece 61A, minute 5.
33 Public Record Office, AIR 2/5103, piece 61A, minute 6.
34 Public Record Office, AIR 2/5103, piece 67A.
35 Public Record Office, AIR 2/5103, piece 70A.
36 Public Record Office, AIR 2/5103, piece 69A.
37 Public Record Office, AIR 2/5103, piece 71A.
38 Public Record Office, AIR 2/1650, piece 9A.
39 Schedule of Specified Parts, Air Publication AP 1564A, Vol III, Part 1, July 1940. RAF Museum.
40 Public Record Office, AIR 2/3476, minute 10.
41 Public Record Office, AIR 2/3476, minute 13.
42 Public Record Office, AIR 2/5103, minute 59.
43 Public Record Office, AIR 2/5103, piece 66A.
44 Public Record Office, AIR 2/5103, piece 73A.
45 Public Record Office, AIR 20/70, Malta Operational Summary 11th October 1940–10th February 1941, Appendix C.
46 Robertson B, Westland Whirlwind, Kookaburra Technical Publications, Series 1, No 4, 1965.
47 Public Record Office, AIR 2/5103.
48 Public Record Office, AIR 2/5103, piece 64A.
49 Public Record Office, AIR 2/5103, piece 72A.
50 Public Record Office, AIR 2/1647, piece 1A, minute 29.
51 Public Record Office, AIR 2/1647, piece 1A, minute 35.
52 Public Record Office, AIR 2/1647, piece 1A, minute 36.
53 Public Record Office, AIR 2/1647, piece 1A, minute 37.
54 Public Record Office, AIR 2/5103.
55 Public Record Office, AIR 14/433, piece 134B.
56 Public Record Office, AIR 2/5103, piece 27A.
57 Public Record Office, AIR 2/5103, piece 41A.
58 Public Record Office, AIR 2/5103, piece 31A.

59 Public Record Office, AIR 2/5103, piece 42A.
60 Public Record Office, AIR 2/5103, piece 36A.
61 Public Record Office, AIR 2/5103, piece 37A.
62 Public Record Office, AIR 2/1650, piece 11A.
63 Public Record Office, AIR 2/3456, piece 14A.
64 Public Record Office, AIR 2/3456, piece 5A.
65 Public Record Office, AIR 2/2620, piece 71A.
66 Battle I – Armour Protection for the Crew, Air Publication AP 1527A/J.10–W, 23.3.40. RAF Museum.
67 Public Record Office, AIR 2/4185, piece 25A.
68 Public Record Office, AIR 2/4185, piece 26A.
69 Bowyer Chaz, *Bristol Blenheim*, Ian Allan Ltd, 1984, page 29.
70 Air Publication AP 1578B, Vol I, Section II, December 1941. RAF Museum.
71 Air Publication AP 1578B, Vol I, Section I, November 1940. RAF Museum.
72 Public Record Office, AIR 2/1650, piece 30A, Appendix "A".
73 *The Aeroplane*, November 9 1939, p2.
74 Public Record Office, AIR 2/1650, piece 13A.
75 Public Record Office, AIR 16/234, Fighter Command Intelligence Summaries, Nos 1–216, September 1939–December 1940.
76 Public Record Office, AIR 20/64.
77 Public Record Office, AIR 2/8653, piece 13, AFC Report No 84, Appendix A.
78 Bickers, Richard Townshend, *The Battle of Britain*, Salamander Books Ltd, 1990, 1997, 2000.
79 *Aerodata International No 4*, Visual Arts Publications, 1978.
80 German Aircraft and Armament, US Informational Intelligence Summary No 44–32, October 1944, Brassey's, Washington DC, 2000. RAF Museum.
81 Public Record Office, AIR 20/64.
82 Public Record Office, AIR 20/43.

V Postscript
24 Armour protection for all!

By the end of 1940, when the Battle of Britain had been won and thoughts were focussing on prosecuting the air war in enemy-held territory by day as well as by night, armour protection had become firmly established as a defensive requirement for fighting aircraft of pretty well all types. The doubts and uncertainties about the extent of and even the need for protection that had bedevilled progress in the fitting of armour in British aircraft – and, seemingly, in German aircraft also – evaporated in the face of hard and bitter experience once the actual air fighting began. Dowding's natural preoccupation with shooting down the enemy bombers had been proved to be possible only to the extent that his Spitfires and Hurricanes could evade or fight their way through the hoards of escorting Messerschmitt Bf 109 and Bf 110 fighters. The scout-v-scout combats of the First War, thought for so long not to be possible between the "modern high speed fighters", were no longer a thing of the past but the unavoidable present.

As the War progressed into 1941, Fighter Command turned to the offensive through massed sweeps ("Rhubarbs") into the skies of France aimed at bringing the Luftwaffe to battle and achieving an air superiority in which Bomber Command could work more effectively by day as well as by night. When the Rhubarbs failed to achieve the objective and suffered disproportionate losses at the hands of the German fighters that were then fighting over (in effect) their own territory, the RAF turned to "Circuses" – daylight bombing raids in which small numbers of bombers were escorted by masses of fighters. The bombers were effectively the bait used to draw up the German fighters. Although the bombers did useful work and the Bf 109Fs and later the Focke-Wulf FW 190s were indeed drawn up, the territorial advantage to the Germans and the superiority of their aircraft at that stage over the Spitfire Mk Is, IIs and Vs meant that the disproportionate RAF losses continued.

The Spitfire Mk V came into service in 1941 and actually continued in service well into 1944. The armour fitted to the Mk VC, exemplifies the extents to which schemes for protection evolved for fighter aircraft as they took the war into the skies over Europe and, increasingly, turned to the ground attack rôle as fighter-bombers. From about 1942 onwards, requirements for "protection" in the form of steel armour plate to stop bullets and shell fragments as well as light metal plating to deflect them even began to appear in the detailed Air Ministry specifications for new aircraft and marks. The specification of 9th May 1942 for the Spitfire Mk XX, originally designed as the Mk IV with a single-stage supercharged Rolls-Royce Griffon engine in a redesigned Mk II/III airframe, illustrates the way in which the requirements for protection were being formulated:

SPITFIRE Mk Vc
ARRANGEMENT
OF ARMOUR
13TH JULY 1942

4MM STEEL ARMOUR
BACK PILOT'S HEAD
BACK PILOT'S KNEE
FRONT HEADER TANK
FRONT AMMO BOXES

4MM STEEL ARMOUR
FRONT FUEL TANK
BASE WINDSCREEN
BACK SEAT

'X' Double removable front armour

Proposed new armour plate

10MM ALCLAD DEFLECTOR | TOP + SIDES FUEL TANK
TOP AMMO BOXES
BOTTOM AMMO BOXES

8SWG DURAL DEFLECTOR | BOTTOM SEAT

1⅞ THICK B.P. GLASS | WINDSCREEN

The armour fitted to the Spitfire Mk VC, reproduced from a drawing dated 13th July 1942. The "X" on the drawing denotes removable armour. (1)

259

<u>"Pilot</u>

"Protection is required against .303 AP ammunition from in front and from the rear, at a range of 100 yards and from 20° on all sides of the thrust-line of the aircraft, when flying at a height of 15,000 feet. A 1½ inch bullet-proof glass windscreen is acceptable on this aeroplane.

<u>Fuel and oil</u>

All fuel and oil tankage, including auxiliary tankage, must be self-sealing if possible against 20mm ammunition. The pipe lines should be positioned so as to receive as much protection as possible from the aircraft structure and be covered with a self-sealing material.

<u>Engines</u>

Protection should be provided for the engines under the same conditions as that for the pilot.

<u>Ammunition</u>

Armour plate protection is to be provided for the 20mm ammunition under the same conditions as that for the pilot." (2)

Although the details specified for protection from this time forward varied from one aircraft type to another, it is clear from the proposed Spitfire Mk XX that the lessons of earlier years had at last been fully incorporated into design thinking. As events were to turn out, the Mk XX never got beyond a mock-up of the Mk IV; it was cancelled in June 1942, the RAF's needs then being met by the Merlin 61-engined Mk IX. (4)

The use of armour protection was not confined to the day fighters; the Beaufighter and Mosquito nightfighters were also fitted with bullet-proof windscreens and armour. The Beaufighter had front armour variously reported as 6mm or 9mm thick and armour in the fuselage behind the crew, while the Mosquito was fitted with 9mm front armour and 6mm rear armour. (4)

Almost from the outset of the First World War it had been appreciated that in a single-engined tractor aircraft the pilot was, in principle at least, protected against fire from ahead by the engine in front of him. Oddly, the principle did not at that time seem to apply in reverse – a pusher aircraft, with the engine behind the pilot and/or crew, was considered to be indefensible against attack from behind because the gunner (with his manually aimed gun) could not fire backwards through the arc of the propeller at an attacker from astern. During the Second World War, there was actually a return to the principle. The American-built Bell P-39 Airacobra, with its engine installed behind the pilot's cockpit, began to appear in Britain in the June of 1941 and briefly equipped No 601 Squadron RAF. The Airacobra was a genuine "tractor" machine, not a "pusher": the propeller was at the front and was driven by a shaft from the engine that passed forward, beneath the pilot's seat and legs. The

Airacobra was protected from ahead by a (by then) conventional bullet proof windscreen and by armour plate at the forward side of the pilot's instrument panel in front of him (5). An Air Ministry conference was held on 5th November 1941 to consider future armouring requirements for a range of fighter aircraft; the conference was chaired by Air Vice-Marshal R S Sorely OBE DSC DFC, Assistant Chief of Air Staff (Technical). So far as protection against attack from behind was concerned – according to a series of recommendations that were circulated on 4th November by Wing Commander W R Brotherhood, for the Directorate of Operational Requirements, and considered at the conference – the pilot of the Airacobra had to be content with:

"... bullet-proof glass behind his head. Protection to his back is provided by the engine. No extra protection [is] recommended." (6)

This particular recommendation was accepted at the conference, (7) though the RAF quickly lost interest in the aircraft type; it was, however, used in great numbers and with success by both the United States Army Air Force (USAAF) and by the Soviet Union.

Somewhat later, in the May of 1943, Air Vice-Marshal Harry Broadhurst in command of the RAF in the Western Desert submitted a report to the Advanced Air Headquarters Middle East on: "Employment of Hurricane IID Aircraft During the period 9th March – 30th April 1943". The report touched on the matter of armour protection as protection against ground fire:

"Damage to aircraft and design of armour

26. A survey of damage to aircraft hit by A.A. has been made and although it has not been possible to examine all aircraft fully as some are total wrecks and some are in mined areas, sufficient evidence has been obtained to justify recommendations for the armouring of certain vulnerable parts of the aircraft. A detailed list of damage to aircraft ... shows that of 32 aircraft hit by AA fire only 4 could be repaired by the Unit without robbing other aircraft for spares.

27. Most of the serious damage to aircraft has occurred in belly landings after being hit by flak, and although aircraft with holes in the wings and fuselage caused by direct hits with large calibre explosive shells have flown back to base, only one hit with a small calibre bullet on more vulnerable parts of the aircraft has been sufficient to cause a belly landing. The most damaging hits were those on the engine and coolant and fuel systems.

28. It is probably impossible to provide sufficient armour to prevent damage from large calibre shells, but protection to the oil and fuel systems from .303 inch calibre bullets fired from in front, below or to the side of the aircraft is absolutely essential if heavy casualties to aircraft are to be avoided." (8)

In an appendix to his report, dated 12th May 1943, Broadhurst was more expansive on the protection of his Hurricanes against ground fire:

"...

2. Hurricane aircraft have always proved to have been able to stand severe structural damage in fuselage and mainplanes. This has been upheld in the operations undertaken by the Hurricane IID.

3. All Marks of Hurricanes have been modified with armour plate to provide protection for the pilot, the coolant header tank and the engine from enemy aircraft fire from behind and above. This armour plate modification has been very successful.

4. Hurricane IID aircraft flying low over ground troops, will, in theory, expose a very large and unprotected vulnerable area to ground fire. The lower half of the engine, the oil system with its many oil pipes, including the tank in the leading edge of the port centre section, the cooler central and well underslung and the filter in the starboard centre section, the coolant radiator and the large diameter pipes both to and from it, are all equally vulnerable.

5. The vulnerability of the whole area has been proved in practice by the many instances where even one or two small arms ball rounds entering any one section of it has proved to be sufficient to bring the aircraft down.

6. It is submitted that to make the aircraft as equally immune from damage from concentrated small arms ground fire as from air to air fire the whole of the lower engine bay and the area of the centre section which includes the oil tank, oil and coolant pipes and radiators should be shielded by armour plate.

7. Unfortunately the introduction of this armour plate would increase the weight of the aircraft considerably and the majority of such weight would be added well forward of the centre of gravity.

8. It is therefore suggested that if this type of aircraft is envisaged as a future weapon the most practical way of protecting such aircraft would be to design one in which engine coolant and oil system were all enclosed by armour plate, the armour plate itself forming the main structure. The radiators should if possible be placed on the top side of the aircraft and if this is not practical they should be protected fore and aft by two long horizontal armour plate louvers. Such protection would not restrict the air flow through the radiator and is considered to be the most practical manner of prevention small arms fire and shrapnel from either directly entering or ricocheting into the radiator." (9)

It is evident from these extracts from Broadhurst's report that by 1943 the RAF in the Western Desert had finally come full circle in arriving at a position that paralleled remarkable closely a position that the RFC and the German Air Service had arrived at on the Western Front at the end of 1917 – and, in principle at least, similar solutions were being offered. Broadhurst's suggestion, that vulnerable parts of the aircraft should be encased in armour plate that formed the main structure, was exactly the solution that the Germans put into practical effect in the battlefield as the Junker J I/J 4. The British did not go that far in 1918, Weir's proposal having been summarily rejected and the Sopwith Salamander being little more than a token step in that direction, nor does it seem that the RAF went so far in 1943 as fully to adopt Broadhurst's suggestions. Nevertheless, improvements to the armour protection schemes for fighting aircraft – especially for those types assigned to ground attack/close air support work – continued to be made as the war progressed.

On the bomber front armour protection was just as much a subject of on-going review as it was for the fighter types, as the Minutes of the Air Fighting Committee continued to show, and reached something of a crisis point in dissent at the highest command levels in 1942. At the 22nd meeting of the Committee on 28th August 1941 a subject for discussion was: "improved protection for bombers against enemy fighter attacks by night". Among those present at the meeting were Air Vice-Marshal N H Bottomley (DCAS), Air Vice-Marshal R S Soreley (ACAS(T)), Group Captain R V M Odbert (DDOR II), Air Vice-Marshal R H M S Saundby (Senior Air Staff Officer, Bomber Command), Air Commodore J Whitworth Jones (DF Ops) and Group Captain G D Harvey (Fighter Command), as well as Lord Cherwell for the Cabinet Offices. The discussion considered two specific issues concerning armour protection:

– increased armour at the expense of bomb loads and

– increased armour for rear turrets.

On the first issue:

"... Saundby said it was impracticable to extend indefinitely the fitting of armour to aircraft; and it always happened that there was an "Achilles heel" somewhere. He did not think, on the whole, that this progressive addition of armour made the aircraft proportionately less vulnerable. With several tons of armour it was still possible to bring an aircraft down. Perhaps the most important thing, if more armour were contemplated, was to armour the back of engines.

... Sorely agreed. He said there was approximately 1,000lb of armour on heavy bombers at the moment, and a trial installation was being made on the Lancaster (primarily with a view to day operations) which would add a further 2,000lb of armour to the detriment of bomb load. This included armouring the engines. He considered that the limit had just about been reached.

... Whitworth Jones mentioned that in considering armour it would be wise to think of it in terms of the 20mm cannon, which was now the principle armament of all modern night fighters.

... Saundby said that it was necessary to put on enough armour to force the enemy to retain his cannons and not revert to machine guns, and mentioned that apart from its protective properties against direct hits by gunfire, it undoubtedly afforded protection against splinters of flak and fragments of explosive canon shell.

The Chairman enquired whether Bomber Command's opinion was that the present amount of armour was satisfactory. ... Saundby said that he would like to see the results of the experiment on the Lancaster, but he felt rather sceptical about the decrease in vulnerability accruing from a further increase in armour. Moreover, there was no great demand from the crews for any increases. With regard to protection against flak, he felt that more could probably be done by tactics than by armour.

... Saundby [also pointed out that] <u>increasing the armour on turrets had tended to reduce the air gunner's field of view</u>, which already needed improvement. A moveable sheet of armour might prove to be a partial solution, and this was being tried out on the FN 20 [Fraser Nash turret]." (10)

(Author's Note: the underlining in the above extracts is in the original Minutes.)

It is possible to see in these remarks a continuation of the sort of "ivory tower"-ism that had characterised much of the debate before the war. The suggestion that it was necessary to "put on enough armour to force the enemy to retain his cannons and not revert to machine guns" was certainly an odd position to take up – the view of Sq Ldr Brodie after witnessing the effects of solid 20mm cannon fire in the Blenheim trials back in the November of 1938 was that he would "far prefer to be up against a fighter armed with ... 8 Browning guns"! According to Brodie that long ago, before the war started, the debate on air gunnery was already moving in favour of the adoption of cannon guns as the most effective weapon for bringing down aircraft in aerial combat. The blast effect of even the few cannon shells likely to strike during fleeting aerial encounters was reckoned to be much more damaging to all-metal aircraft structures, especially the wings and tail-plane structures of the large and robust heavy bombers, than the more penetrating ball and armour-piercing machine-gun rounds – as even the firing trials back in the January of 1938 had amply demonstrated. Consequently the Germans, who had employed a mix of cannon and machine-guns from the outset of the conflict, were in any case unlikely to revert to machine-guns as the main armament for their fighters – the trend was quite the opposite. There was no doubt that explosive ammunition like cannon shells would defeat the thicknesses of armour plate that were currently in use but, with their contact fuses, were likely to explode at the outer surfaces of the targets so that in practice the armour would only have to protect against splinters and fragments from the shells or knocked off the structure – which it was well capable of doing. But there was little comfort to be had in crew protection if the aircraft was blown apart around them! Of course, there was little comfort to be had in any of these arguments for the unfortunate tail gunners!

The comment about there being "no great demand from the crews" for any increases in armour protection belies the probability that they were not exactly encouraged to make such demands. The views of the bomber crews on such matters as the tools and aids that they used, the tactics that they operated and even creature comforts like draught exclusion were undoubtedly sought and responded to, but the basic machine in which they flew appears largely to have been a "given", the armour being just part of the fabric – hardly, if at all, noticed. It is perhaps as well that they were largely ignorant of the quite literally bloody-minded discussions about armour protection that were being pursued on their behalf.

If the deliberations in the Committee seem today to have been a little unworldly, it is important to realise that they were being held against a background of the developments in the air war at that time. The onset of "Rhubarb" and "Circus" operations thrust the older and lighter bombers – the Whitleys, Hampdens, Blenheims, Wellingtons and even the unsuccessful RAF-operated early (Boeing B-17) Fortresses (Mk I) – into the daylight over German-held territory; protected by fighter escorts. They still suffered losses but, with their already limited bomb-carrying capacities (except for the B-17s), they had little scope for any increases in their barest minimum of armour protection. Night operations deeper into Europe were beginning to build up, especially by the heavy bombers like the Stirling (August 1940), the Halifax (November 1940) and in due course the Lancaster (December 1941). The heavies also suffered mounting losses as the German night-fighters and ground defences began to respond with increasing effect; but they had at least a little more room for increases in armour at the expense of bomb load. Meanwhile the Germans had opened their campaign against Russia in the June of 1941 (Operation Barbarossa) and there was political pressure on Britain to increase activity in Western Europe in order to ease the pressure on the Russians in the East – hence the possibility of daytime operations with the Lancaster, the bomber with the greatest load-carrying capacity and therefore the greatest capacity for increasing the weight of armour. Indeed, hardly had the Lancaster entered service when on 17th April 1942 twelve aircraft from No 44 and No 97 Squadrons were ordered to bomb – in daylight – the submarine diesel engine works at Augsburg near Munich, deep in the South-East of Germany. Seven of the Lancasters were lost in the operation, four to fighters over France on the outward leg and the remainder to flak over the target, but even the five surviving aircraft were damaged. (11)

Although the Augsburg raid was held to be a demonstration that unescorted daylight operations by heavy bombers deep into enemy territory were extremely hazardous and undesirable, Air Chief Marshal Sir Arthur Harris KCB OBE AFC, who had been appointed Commander-in-Chief of Bomber Command on 22nd February 1942, was not implacably opposed to daylight operations when necessary – though preferably escorted. The employment of his Command's light and medium bombers in "Circus"-type operations, typically on comparatively short-range coastal and close-inland targets, was ample proof of this and there was no suggestion that these should not continue. But, given the concerns over the accuracy of night bombing at that time, the operational necessity for longer range heavy bombing raids in daylight – or at least at dusk, when the bombers could escape under the cover of darkness – could not be avoided.

It was in the July of 1941 that a series of discussions began, between Air Ministry technical staff, the A&AEE and the aircraft constructors (A

V Roe), with the object of "providing a high degree of [armour] protection for the crew and vital parts of Lancaster aircraft for use in daylight operations to be undertaken in the spring of 1942". (12) It is instructive to note that Bomber Command did not appear to have been involved these discussions. The notes of a meeting held on 9th July 1941, appended as Appendix C, gave a comprehensive assessment of the need for protection – at least where the pilot and the engines were concerned. There was a further meeting at Woodford Aerodrome on 9th August 1939, at which details for all aspects of the proposed armouring scheme were set out as the basis for the preparation of a mock-up. As well as the pilot and the engines, the navigator, the W/T operator, the bomb-aimer and the various gunner stations were all to be provided with some armour, in addition to existing provisions where necessary. Where practicable, the additional armour was to be "easily detachable. (12) The notes of these meetings demonstrate the extent to which the debate on armour protection had moved on from the "whether or not " idealism to the "what is to be protected" and "how much can be got away with" practicalities.

The exclusion of Bomber Command from the decision to add extra armour to Lancasters for daylight operations was to have very rude consequences. With such operations in prospect and as a result of the technical discussions, Air Chief Marshal Sir Wilfrid Freeman, Vice-Chief of Air Staff at the Air Ministry, took it upon himself not merely to suggest but actually to arrange for the production of a number (initially twelve) of specially armoured Lancasters. There is no reason to doubt that he had the best of intentions – the improved survivability of bombers and their crews against attacks during daylight that seemed shortly to be inevitable. But, in suggesting that the first batch of the aircraft should be used on what amounted to an "experimental" basis and in apparently failing to appreciate the operational consequences of what he intended, he ran headlong into conflict with Harris. If Harris was implacably opposed to anything, it was the risking of his precious Lancasters (of which he already had too few at the time) and of his even more precious crews in what he considered to be poorly thought out and quite unrealistic "experiments". Consequently, Harris objected to Freeman's interference and a series of uncompromising exchanges between the two officers ensued. Freeman wrote to Harris on 26th May 1942:

> "... In spite of your objections, we have decided to go on with the specially armoured Lancaster for daylight operations. The first twelve aircraft are now almost ready for delivery ... for final fitting. They should begin to come through to you ... at the rate of one aircraft every three days beginning about 6th June.
>
> An additional order for a further 100 of these specially armoured Lancasters has already been placed and delivery should begin about September of this year. You will thus have about four months this Summer in which to form

an opinion of their value in daylight operations.

... As the primary object of the special armour is protection against fighter attack, I should like you to use the Lancasters in the first instance over occupied territory either against objectives selected from the current "Circus" lists, or against some of the industrial targets referred to in [other correspondence]. Although these operations should not be limited to raids with direct fighter cover, it will clearly be necessary to consult Douglas [Air Marshal Sholto Douglas, Commander-in-Chief, Fighter Command from November 1940] so that he can provide cover for the Lancasters on their way to and from the targets, and give indirect protection by means of diversionary sweeps.

I know you do not like the specially armoured Lancasters, but I want you to give them a really thorough trial. The lessons which we hope to learn from them about daylight attack may be of enormous value and affect the whole range of tactical doctrine." (13)

The finally approved protection scheme for the specially armoured Lancasters is described in Appendix D; regrettably, the related drawing(s) appear to have been lost. It can be contrasted with the "standard" armour protection, as fitted to the Lancaster Mks I and III, which comprised:

- armour plate on the back of the pilot's seat and above the seat behind his head;
- an armoured bulkhead, consisting of a frame and two doors, at former 7 in the centre section of the fuselage aft of the radio operator's station and the astro-dome;
- armour plate for the outboard engines, at the bottom of the fireproof bulkhead and at the bottom of the front end of the rear fairing (the inboard engines were deemed to be sufficiently protected by the undercarriage assembly); and
- self-sealing protective coverings cemented over the whole surfaces of the fuel and oil tanks. (14)

Harris responded scathingly to Freeman on 1st June:

"... The object of putting these special aircraft on to day bombing is apparently to attempt assessment of their vulnerability as compared to the ordinary Lancaster by exposing them to the attacks of the enemy fighters and recording the result.

... I do not understand why this information could not be obtained without losing valuable aircraft and still more valuable trained crews by firing at one specially armoured aircraft with various types of German ammunition, on a range such as that at Orfordness, and assessing the results as was done when the original armour schemes were introduced. I expect this has already been done." (15)

Setting out what he regarded as the disadvantages, Harris continued:

"... A disproportionate price would be paid for this information in the loss of extremely valuable aircraft and crews and in avoidable depression of morale. This price might be very high indeed, since if the formation were intercepted by an overwhelming number of fighters there is no doubt that very few, whether armoured or unarmoured, would survive. Their fate would depend therefore, on chance – not armour." (15)

Finally, Harris recommended that one of the initial twelve special Lancasters should indeed be subjected to firing trials. For the rest, his recommendations left little doubt as to his intentions:

"... As much as possible of this additional armour should be made easily and quickly detachable.

... the remaining 11 special Lancasters [of the first batch] should be delivered with all the armour in position. The additional armour will then be detached, held in Unit stores and fitted only when some special operation which makes it desirable to do so is ordered.

... the 100 additional special Lancasters should either be cancelled or delivered with all the armour in position, the detachable portion of which will be removed and held in Unit stores.

...the [Bombing Development Unit should] develop tactics. If the Squadron tries to do it by day the crews will not survive long enough to develop anything." (15)

Nothing could be clearer: Harris intended to store the detachable armour and forget it!

Freeman's reply on 3rd June 1942 was correspondingly terse, being addressed "STRICTLY PERSONAL, to be opened by addressee only":

"... I thought that over a period of 1½ years I had got accustomed to your truculent style, loose expression and flamboyant hyperbole, but I am not used to being told – for such is the implication of ... your letter – that I am deliberately proposing to risk human lives in order to test out an idea of my own, which in your opinion is wrong.

When it was first decided to add additional armour to the Lancaster, it was considered that a return to daylight raiding would be necessary and that every effort should be made to reduce casualties to a minimum. It was recognised that a reduction in bomb load would be necessary; but why not, if the weight of bombs reaching the target is greater than it would otherwise have been? It is possible, for example, that our casualties on the Augsburg raid might have been 50% less if the additional armour had been carried by our aircraft.

Instructions have been given for the armour to be made as far as possible detachable and I should now be glad if you would carry out the orders given to you in the letter dated 26th May." (16)

The final chapter in this tale of dispute seems to have been Harris's letter of 6th June 1942 to Freeman, in which he countered Freeman's arguments and explained, rather oddly but doubtless honestly, that all but the last section had been written by his staff and therefore represented the views within his Command, not merely his own. However, he concluded bluntly:

> "... If, therefore, this armoured Lancaster proposal is to stand I must ask for an official directive to which I can register an official protest." (17)

Some months later, Freeman went back to the Ministry of Aircraft Production to which he had formerly been attached and there the argument rested. The twelve Lancasters at issue were duly delivered to No 207 Squadron at Bottesford; what happened to the others is unknown but, presumably, the "special" armour was abandoned and they went into service without it. Saundby nevertheless gave instructions on 1st September 1942 for the employment by day and by night of (again presumably) the initial batch of specially armoured aircraft, the armour and the under-turret to be installed for daylight operations and removed for night operations (18). Nothing has been found in the records to show that they were ever used on operations with the special armour installed, although No 207 Squadron certainly took part in daylight raids. According to operational data provided by John Hamlin (19), the Squadron flew 53 daylight or part-daylight (as distinct from overnight) operations from 24th February 1941 until 31st August 1942, mostly in the earlier months of the period; between 1st September 1942 and 31st July 1944 the Squadron flew only 8 daylight/part-daylight operations, each involving some 5-15 Lancasters, so there was little opportunity to use the special armour – had anyone been inclined to do so. After July 1944, the Squadron's daylight operations became much more frequent until the end of the war – though, by that time, it is to be suspected that the special armour had gathered much dust in some forgotten corner of an airfield somewhere in England.

Notwithstanding his dispute with Freeman, Harris fully recognised that at least high level operations by day – too high for the German flak and high enough to bring the German fighters up where the bombers' escorts could get at them – would continue to be necessary in appropriate circumstances. (20) There can be no doubt that many such operations were flown by Bomber Command's squadrons throughout the course of the war, without the benefit of any "special" armour protection.

As German aircraft continued to intrude over British territory the evidence of January 1940 and Broadhurst's report from the Western Desert, highlighting engine damage as the major source of aircraft loss, were supported by useful extensive evidence from a quite different source. A report in 1943/44 on the "Causes of Crashes of Enemy Aircraft in this Country [Britain]" (21) showed that of the German aircraft brought down by fighter action over 50% of some types and a third or more of others were the result of hits to the engine and/or cooling system:

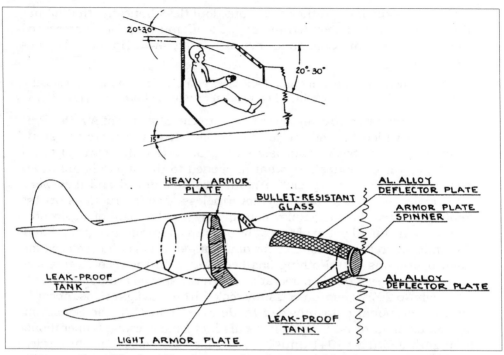

Apparently a Hawker Hurricane, showing a scheme for armour protection. (After Alter, "Passive Defence")

Me 109	57% (out of 233 aircraft)
Me 110	59% (out of 73 aircraft)
Ju 88 (Bomber)	43% (out of 105 aircraft)
Do 17	53% (out of 47 aircraft)
Do 217	36% (out of 26 aircraft)
He 111	65% (out of 119 aircraft)
Fw 190	0% (out of 5 aircraft).

Of course these were not British aircraft and the data provided no direct information about the effectiveness of British armour protection, but the German wrecks were at least available. British wrecks were, in the main, inaccessibly scattered over enemy-held territory in Europe and rendered accessible in the Western Desert only by the ebb and flow of the battle lines, yet there was no reason to suppose that British engines were any less susceptible to gunfire than their German counterparts. What the German evidence suggested – if, indeed, further corroboration was by then necessary – was that, while little could realistically be done to protect the functionality of the engine as a whole, extending the early protection schemes in aircraft like the Spitfire and Hurricane to encompass vulnerable parts like the oil and coolant systems was likely to do some good.

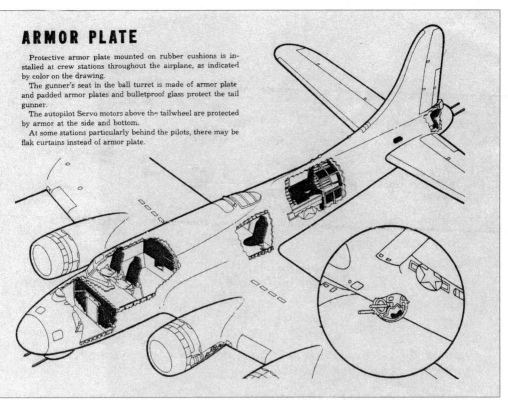

ARMOR PLATE

Protective armor plate mounted on rubber cushions is installed at crew stations throughout the airplane, as indicated by color on the drawing.

The gunner's seat in the ball turret is made of armor plate and padded armor plates and bulletproof glass protect the tail gunner.

The autopilot Servo motors above the tailwheel are protected by armor at the side and bottom.

At some stations particularly behind the pilots, there may be flak curtains instead of armor plate.

Boeing B-17 Flying Fortress, showing a scheme for armour protection.
(USAAF Official)

Table 24.1. Armour protection of German fighting aircraft

Aircraft Type	Armour
Bombers	
Do 217E	Pilot's seat, back and head; dorsal; ventral.
Ju 88A4	Pilot's seat, back and head; dorsal; ventral.
Ju 88S	Pilot's seat, back and head; oil coolers.
He 111H	Pilot's seat; dorsal; lateral; ventral; fuselage bulkhead; engine.
He 177	Comprehensive armour protection.
Ju 87D	Frontal; windscreen; Pilot's head and back; dorsal; ventral; bulkhead; radiators.
Ju 188	Pilot's seat, back and head; dorsal; ventral.
Me 410	Frontal; windscreen; dorsal; rear bulkhead.
Fighters – Single Engine	
Me 109G	Windscreen; Pilot's seat, head and back; bulkhead.
FW 190A	Front cowling; windscreen; Pilot's seat and back.
Fighters – Twin Engine	
Do 217J	Windscreen; pilot's seat; dorsal; lateral; ventral; front and rear bulkheads.
Me 110	Frontal; windscreen; Pilot's head and back; ventral; bulkhead.
Ju 88C	Frontal bulkhead; windscreen; Pilot's seat; dorsal; ventral.
Me 410	Frontal; Pilot's head, seat and back; dorsal; bulkhead; engine.

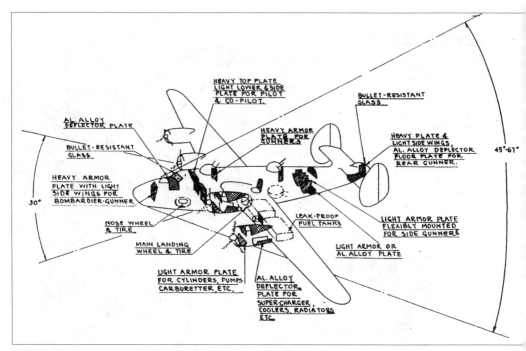

Apparently a Consolidated B-24 Liberator, showing a scheme for armour protection. (After Alter, "Passive Defence")

Moreover, the concerns that arose in the late 1930s about the possibility of the Germans adopting more widespread use of heavy calibre cannon guns were fully realised as the war progressed and could not continue to be disregarded. Consequently, from late 1940 onwards, the provisions for armour protection for fighting aircraft were subject to continuous review, type by type, and – subject inevitably to the constraints imposed by the need to maintain, for any individual type, its combat handling capability and operational performance – some quite extensive schemes were put into place that were intended to give improved protection, particularly to engine ancillaries, against splinters and shrapnel from both canon shells and anti–aircraft fire.

So commonplace did the armouring of fighting aircraft eventually become that by 1943 the concept of "passive protection", or "passive defence", had become almost a technology in its own right, at least in America. Horace J Alter, a consulting Engineer, presented an analysis of passive defence at the Airplane Design Session, Eleventh Annual Meeting, of the International Aeronautics Society of New York in January 1943. The analysis was subsequently published in *Aeronautical Engineering Review* (22), the journal of the American Institute of Aeronautical Sciences, and included two drawings of the distribution of armour that showed just how far armour protection had come by the middle period of the War in fighters like (apparently) the Hawker Hurricane and bombers like the American

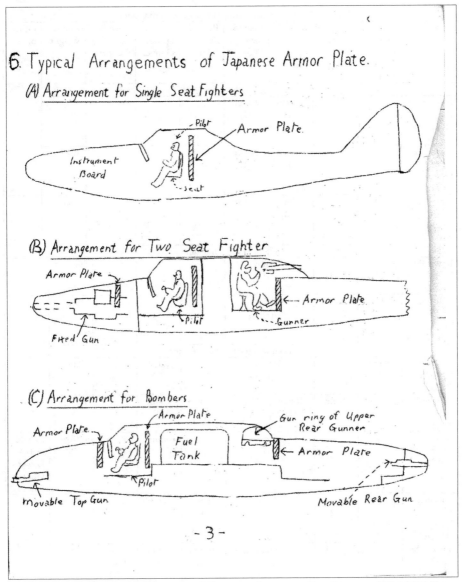

6. Typical Arrangements of Japanese Armor Plate.

(A) Arrangement for Single Seat Fighters

(B) Arrangement for Two Seat Fighter

(C) Arrangement for Bombers

- 3 -

(Royal Air Force Museum Library, document reference RO18744)

Table 24.2. Armour protection of Japanese fighting aircraft

Type	Behind Fixed M.G magazine	Front of instrument board	Behind main Pilot–Head	Behind main Pilot	Behind Sub-Pilot	Behind upward Gunner	Chamber of Tail Gunner	Approx Weight	Other parts
Fighters-Single engine									
Nakajima Ki-43 Hayabusa "Oscar"			16mm (1)	16mm (1)				40kg	
Nakajima Ki-44 Shoki "Tojo"			16mm (1)	16mm (1)				40kg	
Nakajima Ki-84 Hayate "Frank"			8mm (2)	16mm (1)				40kg	
Fighters – Twin engine									
Kawasaki Ki-102a "Randy"			16mm (1)					50kg	
Kawasaki Ki-45 Toryu "Nick"			16mm (1)					50kg	
Bomber attack – Twin engine									
Kawasaki Ki-102b "Randy"	8mm (1)		16mm (1)			12mm (1)		80kg	
Mitsubishi Ki-21 "Sally"		8mm (1)	16mm (1)	16mm (1)	16mm (1)	16mm (1)		120kg	
Kawasaki Ki-48 "Lily"			16mm (1)			16mm (1)		100kg	Behind & below Lower Gunner 8mm (1)
Nakajima Ki-49 Donryu "Helen"		8mm (1)	16mm (1)	16mm (1)	16mm (1)			120kg	
Mitsubishi Ki-67 Hiryu "Peggy"			16mm (1)	16mm (1)	16mm (1)	Floor 16mm (1)		120kg	

Consolidated Vultee B-24 Liberator. The Boeing B-17 Flying Fortress too, at least in its later variants, was also fitted with an extensive scheme of armour protection which included flak curtains. The twenty B-17Cs that unsuccessfully entered into active service in high altitude daylight raids over Europe with No 90 Squadron RAF in 1941 were apparently both lightly armed and lightly armoured. The extensive re-designing through the D and E variants that resulted from the early combat experience included more armour protection. (23), (24) By 1945, Louis Bruchiss had included a whole chapter on armour protection in his book on Aircraft Armament, (25) which made due reference to Alter's paper and reproduced his "Hurricane" and "Liberator" drawings. The British four-engined heavy bombers, mainly operating by night and reaching a peak of achievement with the Avro Lancaster, were not – with the exception of the specially armoured Lancasters intended for daylight raids – armoured to anything like the same extent as their daylight American counterparts.

Throughout the war, the RAF continued to build up data on foreign aircraft, especially German. In 1944, the Air Defence of Great Britain (ADGB) headquarters issued an extensive summary of the performances, armour and armament of the current range of German fighters and bombers. (26) An extract from the ADGB summary is given in Table 24.1. Evidently, the provision of armour protection for the Luftwaffe's aircraft had become not so much a special event but a routine requirement.

Once America had been drawn into the War by Japan's attack on Pearl Harbour, the Japanese Air Service too began to take note of the need for armour protection. An interview in October 1945 of Major Koinumaru, a Japanese Army research Metallurgist, by Commander Brown USN revealed the extent to which armour protection had been adopted. Table 24.2 extracted from Commander Brown's Report (27) gives the details of armour protection for many of the later Japanese aircraft, in the form of sketches and a table. The figures in brackets after the armour thicknesses in the table refer to the number of sheets/plates fitted. According to Commander Brown's Report, the Japanese investigated the use of composite armour sheets – with "double or triple layers of steel arranged at distances from each other (the optimum distance between 2 sheets of armour was stated to be two bullet lengths)". The entry for the Ki-84 pilot's head protection appears to be an example of a two-sheet composite. They did not, apparently, make use of Duralumin deflector plates, or flak curtains such as were used in American bombers like the later B-17s. Arrangement "(B)" might well be a representation of the Ki-45 or 102a, though "(A)" bears no resemblance to any of the single-engine fighters listed in the table – all of which had radial engines. Arrangement "(C)" could well have typified the Ki-49 or Ki-67. However, it would be unreasonable to rely upon the sketches as being anything other than what they appear to be – crude depictions of general schemes of protection.

25 Engine power – The final solution

The story of armour protection for fighting aircraft has followed the views expressed by men like Trenchard, Dowding and their respective counterparts, views shaped inevitably by the prevailing wisdoms of their times, and the ways in which those views changed as the result of many trials and tests that began in 1911 and reached their culmination during the late-1930s and early 1940. The issue of armour protection was undoubtedly something of a side-show, compared with the overall developments of the air weapon and of radar-guided defensive operations by day and night; it was nevertheless part of a much wider debate about the weight of fighting aircraft versus their operational performance. The debate dogged the design and development of fighting aircraft from their beginning until the arrival of powerful piston engines like the Rolls-Royce Merlin/Griffon and later the even more powerful jet engines – engines that over time developed so much extra power that they could lift virtually anything and rendered the debate largely irrelevant. The Spitfire, which in one form or another served throughout the whole war and in all theatres, typifies the point. Spitfire test pilot Jeffrey Quill (28) illustrated the extremes:

	Spitfire Mk I	Seafire 47
Weight, normal	5,820lb	10,300lb
Maximum engine horsepower	1,050	2,350
Power plant weight	2,020lb	3,650lb
Maximum speed	362mph	452mph
Maximum rate of climb	2,500ft/min	4,800ft/min
Rate of roll at 400 mph	14deg/sec	68deg/sec
Weight of fire	4lb/sec	12lb/sec
Fuel capacity	85gal	154gal
Maximum range	575 miles	1,475 miles

The progressive developments in engine power, allied to the many design changes that enabled the power to be used to maximum effect, evidently had remarkable results. For all its near doubling in weight, the Seafire 47 far outstripped the Spitfire Mk I in terms of performance; it was 25% faster on the level, had twice the rate of climb, had nearly five times the rate of roll, over twice the range and still delivered three times the weight of projectiles. Given the scale of improvements in performance like these – what price, then, a few pounds of armour?

1 Public Record Office, AIR 2/5103.
2 Public Record Office, AVIA 10/359.
3 Quill, Jeffrey , *Spitfire*, Arrow Books Ltd, pp 215–222.
4 Public Record Office, AIR 2/5103.
5 Bruchiss, Louis, *Aircraft Armament*, Aerosphere Inc, New York, 1945, pp 130–135.
6 Public Record Office, AIR 2/5103, piece 133D, Notes on improved armour protection for fighters.
7 Public Record Office, AIR 2/5103, piece 133B.
8 Public Record Office, AIR 2/5103, piece 78A, p 6.
9 Ibid, Appendix C, pp 5–6.
10 Public Record Office, AIR 2/8653, piece 26, minutes 40–45.
11 Terraine, John, *The Right of the Line*, Hodder & Stoughton Ltd (Scepter edition), 1988, pp 492–493.
12 Public Record Office, AVIA 15/1251, piece 17B.
13 Public Record Office, AIR 20/5842, piece 10A .
14 Air Publication 2062A, Avro Lancaster manuals.
15 Public Record Office, AIR 20/5842.
16 Public Record Office, AIR 20/5842, piece 11A.
17 The papers of Sir Arthur Harris, File H16, piece 40, Royal Air Force Museum, Hendon.
18 Public Record Office, AIR 14/2176, piece 3A.
19 Hamlin, John, *Always Prepared. The story of 207 Squadron Royal Air Force*, Appendix IV, Air–Britain (Historians) Ltd, 1999.
20 The papers of Sir Arthur Harris, File H59, piece 75, Royal Air Force Museum, Hendon.
21 Public Record Office, AIR 2/5103, piece 212B.
22 Alter, Horace J, Passive Defense – The Protective Armouring of Military Aircraft, *Aeronautical Engineering Review*, April 1943, Vol 2, No 4, pp 45–53.
23 Birdsall, Steve, *The B-17 Flying Fortress*, Morgan Aviation Books, Box 20754, Dallas, Texas, 75220, 1965.
24 Gunston, Bill, *The Illustrated Directory of Fighting Aircraft of World War II*, Salamander Books Ltd, London, 1988.
25 Bruchiss, Louis, op cit.
26 Aircraft of the German Air Force – Performances, Armour and Armament, H/Q Air Defence of Great Britain, Neg No 1495, March 1944. (Royal Air Force Museum Library, document reference L 76.)
27 Armour of Japanese Airplanes, reported by Commander Sheldon W Brown USN (October 1945), British Intelligence Objectives Sub-Committee Report No B.I.O.S./J.A.P./P.R./894. (Royal Air Force Museum Library, document reference R018744.)
28 Quill, Jeffrey , op cit, p 304.

APPENDIX A

AIR MINISTRY SECRET SCIENTIFIC AND TECHNICAL
MEMORANDA No S.1/39

ADVISORY NOTE ON HOW ARMOURING MAY AFFECT DESIGN*

1. It is the present policy to provide a limited amount of protection against the fire of .303 calibre guns for the crew, tanks and engines of operational types of aircraft. Broadly, the aim is to protect these vulnerable parts of bombers and [General Reconnaissance] aircraft, flying boats and Army Co-operation aircraft from fire directed from astern and from angles up to 30° to the flight path line. A similar protection is to be provided for fighters against fire directed from ahead.

2. It may not be possible to comply fully with these desiderata on all types but the protection of crew is of first importance, the tanks second and the engine third.

3. In order to achieve the best protection with the least weight, it is clear that the essential armour may be used with advantage to protect other important and vulnerable working parts, and items of equipment. Also, the layout may be arranged to allow full advantage to be taken of the protection afforded by the aeroplane structure. As points of detail, non-essential equipment may be sometimes arranged to shield the essential equipment; push pull controls of fairly large diameter tubes or rods which are unlikely to be severed by a single bullet or fragment of shell are superior to controls incorporating tie rods, cables and chains.

4. Ammunition of .303 calibre does not require protection and could be used to supplement the protection given by the aircraft structure and by the armour. Ammunition of 20mm calibre must be stowed in a protected place or, if this is not possible, special protection must be arranged. Bombs do not require protection. Consideration should be given to stowing pyrotechnics in a protected place but this is relatively unimportant. Oxygen bottles should be placed as far away from fuel circuits as possible. It is necessary to provide for very rapid replacement of the bullet–proof glass used in armoured windscreens.

5. If the above points are kept in mind when laying out the design of a new aeroplane, much weigh may be saved. Detailed information regarding types and weights of armour plate and deflector plate are available at the Air Min+istry and will be supplied to designers on request.

(March 1939)

*Source: Public Record Office, AIR20/12.

APPENDIX B

THE RÔLE OF THE FIELD FORCE FIGHTER – EXTRACTS FROM THE AIR FIGHTING COMMITTEE REPORT NO 59*

The special Field Force Fighter

13. ...

The fixed gun fighter possesses speed and the ability to destroy a bomber which is denied any great freedom of manoeuvre. Its utility against a manoeuvring aircraft is at least doubtful. Its unsuitability for operation under conditions where it is liable to attack from astern and its inability to fight any form of rearguard action, or to break off combat at will far from its base, place it at a great disadvantage.

In the present state of air gunnery, the problem of shooting at angles involving large deflections is far from being solved.

The turret fighter must therefore close in to very short range in order to ensure obtaining a reasonable number of hits, except when attacking from below and behind. Although such tactics would be feasible against a formation of high speed bombers under home defence conditions, particularly at night, it is doubtful to what extent they would be successful against a reconnaissance aircraft free to manoeuvre. Perhaps the most that can be said is that the turret fighter would have more opportunities to bring its guns to bear in these circumstances than would a fixed gun fighter. A further drawback of the turret fighter is that it is itself vulnerable from astern and below.

14. From the foregoing, it appears that neither the fixed gun nor the turret fighter, as they exist today, is entirely suitable for employment as a field force fighter. It is difficult to lay down definitely the requirements for a field force fighter until ... trials ... have been carried out, but it appears that the following qualities are desirable:

(i) A sufficiently high speed to intercept enemy bomber and reconnaissance aircraft. (It would obviously be impracticable to have a speed sufficient to enable it to intercept enemy fixed gun fighters).

(ii) A reasonable degree of manoeuvrability.

(iii) Powerful offensive and defensive armament. It is desirable that the defensive armament should be so arranged as to be capable, when required, of supplementing the offensive armament.

15. It may still be necessary to provide some squadrons for the special purpose of attacking enemy bombers and distant reconnaissance aircraft which have penetrated our forward defensive zone. For this duty speed and climb will be paramount, and it may therefore be necessary to include some squadrons of high performance fixed gun fighters, particularly in view of the possible overlap of Home Defence and Field Force zones ... .

The secondary Rôle of the Fighter

16. The close support function of the Field Force Fighter is defined ... as follows:

"Two–seater fighter squadrons selected to form part of 'the Air Contingent of the Field Force will also be required to carry out low flying attacks with bombs or machine gun fire'."

17. Since the departure of the [Hawker] Demon this training requirement has been impossible to meet. Pending the production of the Defiant the Field Force fighter squadrons have been equipped with the Blenheim fighter. The Defiant ... cannot use its guns below the horizontal. The Blenheim carries four fixed forward-firing machine guns in the bomb stowage position. The Blenheim therefore can only carry out low flying bomb attacks if its "fighter" guns are removed, and the Defiant can bomb but cannot carry out effective machine gum attack.

18. It is generally accepted that the use of fighters in this rôle is one to be resorted to only in special circumstances. The reasons for this view are, briefly, that a low flying fighter is vulnerable to fire both from the air and from the ground. The necessity of offsetting this vulnerability by maintaining high speed militates against precision in the attack. The type of target involved, on the other hand, is generally small and probably dispersed. It therefore requires precision if it is to be successfully dealt with. The casualties which will almost certainly be sustained, will, except under the special circumstances referred to, be out of all proportion to the results achieved. The special circumstances in which this use of aircraft is justified are to maintain momentum in the pursuit of a beaten and disorganised enemy and to delay the enemy's attack when our defence is in danger of ceasing to be a retreat and is becoming a rout.

19. It may be advanced in contravention of this view that aircraft have been successfully used in this rôle in Spain, where in fact, they have been used in the forward area as mobile artillery. This is true, but it must be remembered that they were so used in the face of negligible opposing air force, and that reports have clearly indicated that the effects achieved have been in inverse ratio to the discipline and morale of the enemy troops. The material effects of low flying attack against troops are bound to be small. The moral[e] effects, against well trained and disciplined troops, will amount to no more than a temporary nuisance.

20. It may also be said that, although the modern high speed fixed gun fighter was not expected to be of much value as a weapon for attacking troops on the ground, recent trials of Hurricanes showed that considerable effect was obtainable. It must nevertheless be remembered that these trials amounted to no more than firing practice against a ground target. The slope of the ground was such that the target area was tilted toward the approaching fighter. The target itself was clearly and conspicuously marked and, for the safety of the spectators, white strips led the aircraft inevitably to the target. No tactical conditions were introduced and the vulnerability of the attacking aircraft to fire from the air and from the ground was not taken into account.

21. The high speed which the Field Force fighter must necessarily have militates against accurate fire against a ground target. The need for concentrating his fire power in the directions most suited to destruction of enemy aircraft conflicts with the ability to direct it downwards, as also does the need for the low flying fighter to protect himself from attack from above. Finally, ... the low flying pilot must know thoroughly the ground over which he is to

operate, a condition which will not exist if fighter pilots are normally employed in their primary rôle.

22. One is therefore driven to the conclusion that the modern type of fighter is not suited to the "close support" rôle which has been assigned to it. It seems that the limitations of machine gun fire at modern speeds are such that the bomb is the proper weapon for close support. The best aircraft and the most efficient crew for the attack on ground targets with bombs will be found in the bomber squadrons. It is therefore concluded that low flying attack should be the duty of the Field Force bomber. Whether the present type of bomber is suited to carrying out that duty is another question ... .

23. It is therefore suggested that the Field Force fighter must be designed for its primary rôle and that its efficiency in that rôle should not be lessened by the conflicting demands of a secondary duty for which it is ill suited and which can better be carried out by a bomber.

A.T.*

25.4.39.

* Author's note. The A.T. was presumably (then) Air-Vice Marshal Arthur W Tedder, who was at the time Director-General of Research and Development.

*Source: Public Record Office, AIR20/1649, Piece 34A.

APPENDIX C

ADDITIONAL ARMOUR PROTECTION FOR THE LANCASTER[a]

A preliminary investigation to provide the Lancaster with the highest possible degree of armour protection for daylight operations was made by OR6
and RDArm3(d) at A&AEE on the 9th July 1941. An attempt has been made to
make the Pilot and engines invulnerable to .303AP fire coming from within 40°
all round dead astern. Limited protection is also provided against AA fire.

Pilot

The Pilot is already protected by 4mm armour plate attached to the seat
back with a 9mm hinged plate protecting the Pilot's head. The main armour
bulkhead in the fuselage is some 15ft aft of the Pilot, who is very well protected against fire from directly astern, and from within cone of about 15°
all round astern. He is, however, vulnerable to fire from above, below and
to either side. Additional protection could be provided by means of 4mm or
6mm plates attached to the sides of the seat back and inclined forward at
about 60°. A better method, however, if practicable from an installation point
of view, would be to provide 4mm armour side pieces which could be slid
forward on runners to protect the Pilot's sides when required. This would give
very good protection against both fighter attacks and AA fire. The weight of
both the above schemes would be about 35lb[b].

The bottom of the Pilot's seat should be fitted with 4mm armour plate for
a weight of 10lb. To protect the Pilot's legs against fighter attacks from below
astern and to afford him adequate protection against AA bursts immediately
below the aircraft, parts of the cockpit floor should be covered with 4mm
armour plate. This would require about 6 square feet with a weight of 40lb.

The total weight for the Pilot's extra protection will be about 90lb including fittings.

It is recommended that a standard Pilot's seat should be designed to incorporate as much armour protection in its construction as possible. Such
a seat could be fitted to several types of aircraft.

Engines

The armour protection scheme already recommended for the engines weighs
about 260lb for the whole aircraft. This scheme has been retained except for
the protection for the top of the engines. Instead of the present 10swg Dural
plate a similar plate of 4mm armour, about 6½ square feet, should be fitted
across the top of each engine to protect the glycol [coolant] header tank, coolant pipes and vulnerable components between the cylinder blocks.

In addition a curved 4mm armour plate should be attached to special fittings on the engine bearers and engine bulkhead to protect the space between
the back of the engine and the bulkhead. The top of the supercharger and
other components attached to the back of the engine are vulnerable in this
area to fighter attacks from above astern. This scheme will provide a very high
degree of protection to the top of the engine and the vulnerable components
in rear if it. The weight will be about 80lb.

[a] Source: Public Record Office, AVIA 15/1251, Piece 17B, APPENDIX A.
[b] The underlining of the weights in the text is in the original document.

The inboard engines are set slightly forward from the leading edge [of the wing] than the outboard engines, and a small segment of 8mm armour plate attached to the bulkhead at the top would complete the protection of the former. Weight 10lb.

The supercharger and other vulnerable components at the back of the inboard engines are well protected against fire from directly astern by the retracted under carriage and wheel, but the only protection afforded to these components on the outboard engines is by a self sealing oil tank located at the bottom of the engine nacelles immediately in rear of the bulkhead. It will be necessary to protect the space between the wing spar and the top of the oil tank by means of a 6mm armour plate mounted on the tubular members in the nacelle above the rear of the oil tank. Weight 35lb.

To protect the sides of the engines and vulnerable components in rear of them against fire coming from the quarter, a 4mm armour plate of about 9 square feet area on each side could be attached to the engine and engine bearers inside the cowling. This protection would be required on both sides of the outboard engines, but only on the outboard side of the inboard engines as the inboard side of these engines is screened by the fuselage. The weight would be 120lb for each of the outboard engines and 60lb for each of the inboard engines.

For the protection of the radiators it is recommended that the existing scheme should be retained, as it is impossible to provide extra protection for these units without making the whole cowling in a heavier gauge material. It would be possible, however, to provide some protection against anti aircraft fire to the sides and bottom of the radiators by wrapping 6mm armour plate around them. This would also give protection to the sides of the radiator against fighter fire from the quarter. Weight 30lb.

Total Weights

The total weight of the above scheme would be 90lb for the Pilot, and about 900lb for the engines.

APPENDIX D

CS.1495

NOTE ON SPECIAL ARMOUR SCHEME FOR LANCASTER*

In July 1941, a preliminary investigation was made into the possibility of improving the armour protection of one of the new heavy bomber types for use on special daylight operations.

The basic assumptions being:

(i)   A sacrifice of not more than 2,000lb of the bomb load would be acceptable. Complete protection against AA splinters for all members of the crew and vital parts of the aircraft would be totally impracticable on weight considerations, as protection would be required from all directions.

(ii) Against aircraft capable of a top speed in the neighbourhood of 300 miles an hour, fighter attacks would have to be made within a fairly narrow angle from astern. Any attacks on the beam or between beam and quarter would be of a fleeting nature at long range and few hits from these angles would be obtained.

(iii) Protection was required primarily against fixed gun fighter attacks coming from within 40° of the line of flight from astern with some additional protection against AA splinters for the first pilot [and] on the engines. Full protection against 7.92mm AP ammunition at 200 yards range was practicable. Against heavier calibre partial protection only could be expected.

2.   From available information, it appeared that losses on operations had been fairly equally divided between anti-aircraft fire and fighters. It was assumed that the percentage of losses from fighter attack would increase as deeper penetrations into defended territory were made in daylight. Improved tactics appeared to offer the best hope of reducing casualties from AA fire.

3.   It was considered, therefore, that casualties on daylight operations could be considerably reduced if a high degree of immunity to fighter attacks could be achieved. Investigation showed that by the application of a suitable protection scheme, vulnerability of a heavy bomber to fighter attacks could be much reduced as the direction from which these attacks would come was known and the damaging effect from the fighters' ammunition had been assessed from firing trials.

4.   The Me 109F was fitted with one 15mm plus two 7.92mm machine guns. Adequate protection against the 7.92 calibre was practicable within the limits of weight, but to give a similar degree of protection against 15mm was impracticable. Firing trials, however, have shown that a substantial measure of protection against this calibre would be afforded by the 7.92 protection. The enemy use a large proportion of HE and HE incendiary in their 15 and 20 mm guns. These shells have a direct action fuse which detonates on contact with the aircraft skin. The 7.92 protection would stop the splinters from this HE and HE incendiary ammunition. In addition, a fair degree of protection would be given against 15mm solid projectiles which were unstabilised by passage through structure, oil tanks, etc, before striking armour.

---

* Source: Public Record Office, AVIA 15/1251, Piece 17B, APPENDIX A.

5. The crew forward of the main armour bulkhead would be immune to a high proportion of 15mm strikes, as firing trials have shown that even the 15mm AP bullet is broken up and deflected by the fuselage structure and equipment.

6. From the above, it will be seen that the effectiveness of the enemy fighters' armament would be seriously reduced, while the fighter itself remained vulnerable to the considerable volume of .303 fire from the bombers' turrets.

7. A most important advantage of the armour scheme lies in the reduced likelihood of the bomber being shot down from long range astern by the fighter. To gain decisive results, the fighter would have to come into close range where the chances of being shot down by the bomber's defensive armament would be greatly increased.

8. The 7.92 protection would also give protection against AA splinters over the same angles, and firing trials have shown that protection against 7.92 AP is sufficient to stop all types of Oerlikon 20 mm ammunition, except AP. The Me 110 is fitted with the latter weapons.

9. A protection scheme has been completed for the Lancaster I (Merlin XX) which meets the requirements of paragraph 1(iii) above for crew, engines and fuel system except in the case of the tail and mid-upper turrets where armour protection must be limited so as not to interfere with the gunners' view. The weight falls within the limit of 2,000lbs. Details of the protection afforded are as follows:

(Protection is against 7.92mm AP at 200 yards except where otherwise stated.)

CREW

(i) First Pilot

80° cone astern. Armour on the bottom of the seat, on the floor below the seat and side wings of the seat protect against AA splinters from below and on either side. Protection also effective against 15mm solid ammunition up to 10° on the port side and up to approximately 20° on the starboard side.

(ii) Second Pilot (Fire Controller)

At astro hatch 35° all round astern except for his head which is protected up to 30° on either side by bullet proof glass. Existing protection probably adequate to stop 15mm AP up to 10° from astern.

(iii) Navigator

80° cone astern except for a small area on the port side of the aircraft above his head. Armoured seat bottom gives some protection against AA splinters. Probable protection against 15mm AP similar to fire controller.

(iv) Bomb Aimer

No additional protection against fire from astern considered necessary. Armour on the floor of the bomb aimer's station will protect against AA splinters from below when in the prone position.

(v) Wireless Operator

Station immediately forward of the existing armoured bulkhead. Is protected up to 60° on the starboard side and up to 30° on the port side. Protection against 15mm, similar to fire controller. Some protection from AA splinters by armoured seat bottom.

(vi) Mid-Upper and Tail Gunners

Extra protection has been added to the sides of these turrets to protect against attacks from 60° on either side of astern. This will give protection to the gunners against simultaneous combined attacks. The tail gunner and the upper part of the mid-upper gunner's body remain vulnerable to 15 mm AP, as thicker armour is impracticable from weight considerations. Existing protection is adequate against 15 mm HE and HE incendiary.

(vii) Mid-Under Gunner

Approximately 70° astern.

ENGINES

Outboard

(viii) A very high degree of protection against 7.92 AP fire is provided for the engines for an 80° cone astern. Almost complete protection is provided against attacks from dead astern. On the outboard engines an armoured bulkhead is placed on the nacelle behind the oil tank which protects the oil tank and pipes, fuel pipes and other vulnerable engine components forward of the fire-proof bulkhead. 15mm projectiles which pass through the armour bulkhead and the oil tank would probably not penetrate forward of the fire-proof bulkhead. An armour plate is fitted between the front spar webs to protect the upper part of the engine against attacks from above astern. Small armour plates are inserted vertically on either side of the oil tank to protect against shots missing outside the rear bulkhead behind the oil tank. The top of the engine is protected by an 8swg-Dural plate which will deflect 7.92mm AP, up to 20°. The space between the rear edge of theis Dural plate and the fire-proof bulkhead is protected by a curved 4mm armoured plate. This protects vulnerable components at the back of the engine and the supercharger against attacks from astern and above. Both sides of the outboard engines are protected by 4mm plates which will deflect 7.92mm AP up to 45°. They also protect sides of the engines to a great extent from AA splinters. The coolant and oil radiators are protected from the side and below against 7.92mm AP and AA splinters by a girdle of 4 mm armoured plate.

(ix) Inboard

Firing trials have shown that the retracted undercarriage mechanism and wheel afford adequate protection to the back of the inboard engines. An armoured plate of 9 inch width is located in a vertical plane just aft of the fire-proof bulkhead to protect against shots missing the undercarriage mechanism on the outboard side. The top of the engine, the outboard side and the coolant and oil radiators are protected in a similar manner to the outboard engines.

(x) Fuel System

A thicker self sealing cover has been fitted to the fuel tanks which provides almost complete immunity to leaks from 7.92 AP thus minimising the risk of fires caused by fuel leaking into the wing. Firing trials have shown that these fires are the most destructive. Fires caused inside the tank usually go out of their own accord. Better protection is also given against 15mm solid by these covers. A loose canvas bag is to be placed around the fuel tanks in their nacelles to be inflated with ... gas from a bottle as an additional protection against fire. The fuel pipes which are already well protected against fire from astern by being positioned forward of the front spar are to be of the flexible self sealing type which gives substantially better protection against fuel loss.

FUTURE DEVELOPMENT

10. The Lancaster II (Hercules VI) is considered to be a more suitable aircraft than the Lancaster I for daylight operations. It has a higher speed and the radial sleeve valve engines are much less vulnerable to fighter attack and AA splinters. Firing trials against running sleeve valve engines with 7.92 AP have shown that cylinders may be perforated without stopping the engine. The ancillary equipment at the back of the radial engines is less vulnerable than similar equipment at the back of the Merlin. Protection should therefore only be required against fire from astern and it would be possible to provide armour of sufficient thickness to protect against 15 and 20mm AP ammunition for the same or less weight than is at present required to protect the Merlin engines against 7.92 ammunition only. With such protection it is considered that fighters would find it extremely difficult to stop the bomber's engines.

11. An entirely new type of fuel tank is under development and designs are almost complete for the Lancaster. This tank consists of a number of internal cells and firing trials have shown that it is practically immune to 20mm solid and AA splinters. It also gives better protection against incendiary ammunition. The RAE are developing a promising system for separating inert gases from the engine exhaust for circulating in fuel tanks. The new type of tank, by virtue of its design is eminently suitable for the application of this anti-incendiary device. Immunity to fire should, therefore, be of a high order.

21/4/42

Bibliography

Primary sources

Official RFC/RAF papers stored in the files of the National Archives of the Public Record Office at Kew, principally under AIR and AVIA references, full details of which are given in the reference lists following each Part of the book.

The papers of Sir Arthur Harris, File H59, Royal Air Force Museum, Hendon.

Armour of Japanese Airplanes, report by Commander Sheldon W Brown USN (October 1945). Royal Air Force Museum Library, document reference R018744.

German Aircraft and Armament, Informational Intelligence Summary No 44-32, October 1944, Brassey's, Washington DC.

Official Histories and publications

Jones, H A, *The War in the Air – Being the Story of the Part Played in the Great War by the Royal Air Force*, Volumes 2–6, Clarendon Press.

Air Publication AP 1578B, Vol I, *Vickers Wellington.*

Air Publication AP 1527A/J.10-W, *Battle I – Armour Protection for the Crew*, 1940.

Air Publication 2062A, *Avro Lancaster.*

Secondary sources

Aerodata International No 4, Messerschmitt 109E, Visual Arts Publications, 1978.

Andrews, C F and Morgan, E B, *Vickers Aircraft since 1908*, Putnam, 1988.

Andrews, C F, *Vickers Aircraft since 1908*, Putnam, London, 1969.

Bickers, Richard Townshend, *The Battle of Britain*, Salamander Books Ltd, 1990, 1997, 2000.

Bowers, Peter M, *Forgotten Fighters and Experimental Aircraft. US Army 1918-1941*, Arco Publishing Company, 1971.

Birdsall, Steve, *The B-17 Flying Fortress*, Morgan Aviation Books, Box 20754, Dallas, Texas, 75220, 1965.

Bowyer Chaz, *Bristol Blenheim*, Ian Allan Ltd, 1984.

Bruce, J M, *The Sopwith Fighters*, Arms & Armour Press, 1986.

Bruce, J M, *British Aeroplanes 1914–18*, Putnam, 1957.

Bruchiss, Louis, *Aircraft Armament*, Aerosphere Inc, New York, 1945.

Brindley, John F, *French Fighters of World War Two*, Volume 1, Hylton Lancy Publishers Ltd, England, 1971.

Casari, R B, *Encyclopedia of US Aircraft, Part 1, 1908 to April 6, 1917*, Robert B Casari (Publisher), 1970, Volume 2.

Christienne, Charles & Lissarague, Pierre, *A History of French Military Aviation*, Smithsonian Institutional Press, Washington DC, 1986.

Columbia Electronic Encyclopedia (The).

Comando Supremo: Italy at War, www.comandosupremo.com.

Corum, James S, *The roots of Blitzkrieg, Hans von Seeckt and the German military reform*, University Press of Kansas, 1992.

Douhet, Guilio, *The Command of the Air*, translated by Dino Ferrari, Coward-McCann Inc, New York, 1942.

Drake, Billy (with Shores, Christopher), *Billy Drake, Fighter Leader*, Grub Street, London, 2002.

Duval, G R, *U.S. Pursuit Aircraft 1918–1936*, D Bradford Barton Ltd, Cornwall, England, 1975.

Fahey, James C, *U.S. Army Aircraft (Heavier than Air) 1908-1946*, Ships and Aircraft, Virginia, 1946 (reissued 1964).

Golovine, Lt-Gen N N, *Air Strategy*, Gale and Polden Ltd, 1936.

Golovine, Lt-Gen N N, *Views on Air Defence*, Gale and Polden Ltd, 1938.

Gray, Peter & Thetford, Owen, *German aircraft of the First World War*, Putnam, 1962.

Gunston, Bill, *The Illustrated Directory of Fighting Aircraft of World War II*, Salamander Books Ltd, London, 1988.

Henshaw, Trevor, *The Sky their Battlefield*, Grub Street, 1995.

Hooton, E R, *Phoenix Triumphant, The Rise and Rise of the Luftwaffe*, Arms &Armour Press, London, 1994.

Homze, Edward L, *Arming the Luftwaffe. The Reich Air Ministry and the German Aircraft Industry 1919-39*, University of Nebraska Press, 1976

Lanchester, F W, *Aircraft in Warfare – The Dawn of the Fourth Arm*, Constable, London, 1916.

Larrázabal, Jesus Salar, *Air war over Spain*, translated by Margaret A Kelley, Ian Allan Ltd, 1974 (English edition).

Monday, David (compiler), *The Hamlyn Concise Guide to British Aircraft of World War II*, Hamlyn/Aerospace, London, 1982.

Morrow, John H Jr, *The Great War in the Air – Military Aviation from 1909 to 1921*, Airlife Publishing Ltd, England, 1993.

Neumann, Maj Georg Paul, *The German Air Force in the Great War*, (translated by J E Gurdon), Hodder and Stoughton Ltd, London, 1920.

Nowarra, Heinz J & Duval, G R, *Russian civil and military aircraft 1884-1969*, Fountain Press London, 1971.

Richey, Paul, *Fighter Pilot*, (ed Diana Richey), Cassell & Co, London, 2001. (First published by B T Batsford Ltd, 1941.)

Robertson, Bruce, *Sopwith – The man and his aircraft*, Air Review Ltd, 1970.

Robertson B, *Westland Whirlwind*, Kookaburra Technical Publications, Series 1, No 4, 1965.

Sagar, Arthur, *Line Shoot. Diary of a Fighter Pilot*, Vanwell Publishing Limited, Ontario, 2002.

Slessor, Marshal of the Royal Air Force Sir John, *The Great Deterrent*, Cassell & Company Ltd, 1957.

Terraine, John, *White Heat – the new warfare 1914–1918*, Guild Publishing, 1982.

Terraine, John, *The Right of the Line*, Hodder & Stoughton Ltd *(Scepter edition)*, 1988.

Van Haute, André, *Pictorial History of the French Air Force, Volume 1, 1909–1940*, Ian Allen Ltd, London, 1974

Journals

Alter, Horace J, *Passive Defense – The Protective Armouring of Military Aircraft*, Aeronautical Engineering Review, April 1943, Vol 2, No 4.

Lanchester, F W, *Aircraft in Warfare*, Engineering, September 18th, September 25th and October 23rd 1914 issues.

Various issues of the journals *Flight, The Aero* and *The Aeroplane*.

Index

(Note: Page numbers in **bold** refer to illustrations.)

Hawker Hurricane: no rear armour, vii-viii, 16-19, **21**, 122; cutaway, **23**; dog fighting not possible, 129; flying trials, 171, 174, 183; front armour, 159, 164; defences against, 174; action being taken, 178; firing trials, 183-189, **188**, **189**; ground attack rôle, 201; modifications, 236; Mk IID, 261-262; front armour, 215, 217, **219**; back/rear armour, viii, 213-214, 218-**219**, 224, 226, 231; armouring, **270**; CG/propeller problem, 219-220, 224, 227-228, 230-231.
Hawker Tempest V: 201.
Hawker Typhoon: 178; 201.
Heinkel He 59: cannon guns in Spain, 210.
Heinkel He 111: 171; shot down in Scotland, **250**, 251; shot down in Western Desert, 270.
Heinkel He 115: shot down (1939), 251
Henri Farman military armoured hydro-biplane: 27.
Henschel Hs 123: 201.
Henschel Hs 129: **200-202**.
Higgins, AV-M (later AM) Sir John F A: maintains policy against armour for Wapiti, 113-115; agrees to investigate armoured seats for Wapiti, 117.
Hill, Capt (RNAS) F W: first Secretary to the Air Fighting Committee, 128; criticisms of agent's armouring schemes (1937), 144; no requirement for protecting tanks (Hart trials), 152; Blenheim firing trials, 175; Hurricane firing trials, 183, 185-186; armour protection for Defiant, 190-191.
Hill, Lt (later ACM Sir) Roderic M: armoured SE 5 seat, 65; 97.
Hoare, Sir Samuel: armour protection for aircraft in the Middle East, 112-113.
Home Defence Fighter/Fighter (HDF): to shoot down bombers, 200; rear armour not required, 211-213.

Illyushin IL-2 Sturmovik: 203-**204**.
Illyushin TsKB-55/BSh-2/TSKB-57: 204.
Ilya Muramets: "Flying Fortress", 69.
Insall, Observer Officer A J: armoured SE 5, 97.

Jahnow, Obst R, first German air fatality of WW I: 24.
Japanese fighting aircraft: 273-275, **273**.
Jones, A H: armour protection not required for Defiant, 191.
Jones, Air Cdr J Whitworth: improved armour for bombers, 263.

Junker J I/J 4: armoured machines, 56, 60, 62, 261; "alert", 70-5; **71**, **72**, **73**; in service (1918), 80; downward firing guns abandoned, 87.
Junker Ju 87 Stuka: 201; armour protection, 251-**253**.
Junker Ju 88: protection by speed, 195.
Junker-Fokker CL I: all metal construction, 55, 60.

Kawasaki aircraft: Ki-45 "Nick", 274, 275; Ki-48 "Lily", 274; Ki-102a/b "Randy", 274-275.
Koinumaru, Maj: armour protection for Japanese aircraft, 123, 275.

Lanchester, Dr Frederick W: (**39**); 41-7, 51.
Larrázabal, Jesus Salar: rear armour for I-16 ("Mosca"), 197.
Lecointe, Sadi: wounded by ground fire (Aug 1914), 24, 42.
Le Hamel, Battle of, 1918: ground attacks by British aeroplanes, 57.
Leigh-Mallory, AV-M (later ACM Sir) Trafford: Beaufighter armour, 241.
Longcroft, Brig Gen (later AV-M Sir) Charles A H: ground attack orders, 3rd Ypres, 54.
Louden, Sq Ldr J A H: Hurricane rear armour/CG problem, 227-228, 231-232; Defiant armour, 238; Gladiator armour, 238-239; Blenheim rear gunner's face plate, 244; vulnerability of Wellington, 245; Halifax, 249.
Lowe, W Cdr J C M: armour in German aircraft (Jan 1939), 205-206.
Ludlow-Hewitt, ACM Sir Edgar Rainey: **169**; Hart Firing trials & tank protection, 152; armour for bombers, 168; first appearance at AFC, 169; what ammunition to be used against fighters, 172; escorts for bombers, 212; current state of armour (Sept 1939), 242; strengthening bomber armour & formations, 243; vulnerability of Wellington, 245.
LVG aeroplanes: unarmoured, 50, 59; "battle planes", 52; armoured, 65; B I/II, 59.

MacLean, Gp Capt (later A Cdre) Lachlan L: vision through bullet-proof glass, 134.
Malta: Gladiators & armoured Sunderlands, 239.
Mann, Sq Ldr (later A Cdre) William E G: original member of AFC, 128.
Mansell, L T G: front armour for Hurricanes & Spitfires, 215.

Potez 54: possible armouring to reduce vulnerabiliry, 138.

Quill, Jeffrey: Spitfire-Seafire 47 comparison, 276.

Rabatel, M: patented Hispano-Suiza armour scheme, 143.
Ranford, Wq Cdr V B: production/retrospective fitting of armour to Blenheim, 214-215.
Richey, F/O (later Wg Cdr) Paul H M: x; 18; 246.
Republic P-47 Thunderbolt: escort rôle, 121; ground attack rôle, 201.
"Rhubarbs": 258; 265.
Rothermere, Lord (Harmsworth, Harold Sydney): armoured German aeroplanes, 70; Trenchard's response, 78; Aircraft Development Committee, 85.
Rougeron, C: armoured spinner, 143.
Rowley, W Cdr (later A Cdre) Herbert V: comments on Paris agent's views, 145; Hart firing trials, 156-157; Blenheim firing trials, 175; Hurricane firing trials, 185; Defiant armouring, 210; detachable rear armour for Field Force Fighters, 213-214; armour for bombers, 214; rear armour schedule for Hurricane, 218-219; Defiant rear armour, 238; Whirlwind armour, 239.
Royal Aircraft Factory/Establishment: firing trials against engines (1913), 31-32; examination of AEG J I, 66-67.
Royal Aircraft Factory AE 3 "Farnborough Ram" armoured pusher, 82-83, 85, 87, 89-91, **93**-94.
Royal Aircraft Factory BE 2c tractor biplane: armoured seats, 39-**40**, 47, 61; "transparent", **41**, 42-43; trench fighters, 49; armour plated, 62-64, **63**;
Royal Aircraft Factory Farman Experimental FE 2b biplane: unarmoured, 61; ground attack trials with AE 3 gun mounting, 88-90.
Royal Aircraft Factory NE 1 night fighter: 72; 93.
Royal Aircraft Factory RE 8: armour plating, 63.
Royal Aircraft Factory SE 5A: experimental armour seat, 65; rear armour for, 97-98; front protection, 136.
Royal Air Force: creation, 33.
Russian aircraft: SPB(D) armoured fast dive bomber, 124; VIT-2 Airborne Tank Fighter, 124.
Ruthenia: ceded to Hungary (1938), 198.

Sagar Fl Lt (later Squadron Commander) Arthur: saved by Spitfire rear armour, xi, **15-16**.
Salmond, Maj Gen (later MRAF Sir) John M: Salamander prototype, 91.
Salmond, AV-M (later CAN) Sir W Geoffrey H: ground strafing, 107.
Salmson Type 2 Army Corps two-seater: French armoured machine design, 77-78.
Saundby, W Cdr (later AM Sir) Robert H M S: **207**; original AFC member, 128; Hart firing trials, 156-161; defensibility of bombers against fighters, 172-174; Blenheim firing trials, 174-176, 178; progress report on other aircraft, 184; Hurricane firing trials, 184-185; protecting tail gunners, 196; armour for bombers, 207-208, 263; Hurricane rear armour, 214; armour for Field Force Hurricanes, 224; rear armour for Spitfires, 225; armour for Hurricanes & Spitfires, 227; Blenheim/Lysander defences, 244; protection of bombers, 244-245; response to requests for further Battle armour, 247; bomb load obliterated by Blenheim defences, 247.
School of Musketry, Hythe: 28.
Serby, J E, RAE: chairman, Modifications Committee, 208, 210.
Shoeburyness Experimental Establishment: effects of shell detonations on balloons, 25; firing trials against suspended targets & kites, 28-31; Blenheim firing trials, 214, 244.
Short, 2nd Lt C W: ground attacks near High Wood (WW I), 50.
Short Stirling: armour protection for, 165, 166, 168, 178; removable tank protection, 206-207.
Short Sunderland, Malta: armour plated, 239.
Short tractor biplane: firing trials against, 29-**30**.
Sikorski aeroplanes: destroyed by ground fire (Aug 1914), 47; Type Ye2 "Flying Fortress", 69, 105.
Slessor, MRAF Sir John: quote, (iii), x; ignorance of Douhet, 124.
Smith, W Sydney: AE 3 armour, 88.
Smythies, Sq Ldr Bernard E: low flying/ground attacks, 108.
Somme, Battle of the, 1916: trench fighters/ground attacks, 49-50; German "Storm Fliers", 59.
Sopwith Buffalo: armoured two-seat tractor, **96**, 98.